BIRDS OF THE BLUE RIDGE MOUNTAINS

A GUIDE FOR THE

BLUE RIDGE PARKWAY,

GREAT SMOKY MOUNTAINS,

SHENANDOAH NATIONAL PARK,

AND NEIGHBORING AREAS

BY MARCUS B. SIMPSON, JR.

ILLUSTRATIONS BY H. DOUGLAS PRATT

THE UNIVERSITY OF NORTH CAROLINA PRESS

CHAPEL HILL & LONDON

BIRDS

of *the* BLUE RIDGE

MOUNTAINS

The paper in this book meets the guidelines for permanence and durability of
the Committee on Production Guidelines for Book Longevity of the Council on
Library Resources.

Manufactured in the United States of America

96 95 94 93 92   5 4 3 2 1

Library of Congress Cataloging-in-Publication Data

Simpson, Marcus B.

  Birds of the Blue Ridge Mountains : a guide for the Blue Ridge Parkway,
Great Smoky Mountains, Shenandoah National Park, and Neighboring Areas /
by Marcus B. Simpson, Jr. ; illustrations by H. Douglas Pratt.

      p.   cm.

  Includes bibliographical references and index.

  ISBN 0-8078-2018-0 (alk. paper). — ISBN 0-8078-4363-6 (alk. paper : pbk.)

  1. Birds—Blue Ridge Mountains Region—Identification.   2. Natural history
—Blue Ridge Mountains Region.   I. Pratt, H. Douglas (Harold Douglas),
1944– .   II. Title.

QL683.B57S56   1992

598.29755—dc20   91-24620

                                                                      CIP

To Lois T. Goforth,

whose teaching has inspired

so many in the field of biology

and natural sciences

CONTENTS

PREFACE

I didn't realize it at the time, but I began the research for this book on a bright June day in the early 1950s, when my father showed me a Black-throated Blue Warbler, singing among a profusion of purple blooms in the rhododendron thickets high on Craggy Pinnacle. That experience seems like only yesterday, and the enthusiasm it sparked has grown stronger through my years of exploring the Blue Ridge. In the 1960s I spent summers as a nature and hiking counselor at a boys' camp in the mountains, followed by more structured fieldwork in the region through research grant support. By the early 1970s, I was determined to write a book on the birds of the Blue Ridge Mountains, but it was not until the spring of 1988 that I actually sat down and began putting all the pieces together. It was soon apparent to me that the broad scope of the project would require a lot of telephone calls, visits, and correspondence with old colleagues and with many new contacts.

The final product, *Birds of the Blue Ridge Mountains*, is intended to be an introduction and practical guide to the bird life of this beautiful and diverse area. The book is not a tedious tabulation of every bird sighting in the region! Instead, I have attempted to paint a broad picture of the geography, climate, forests, and birds, accompanied by detailed instructions on how to visit and explore the best spots for bird-watching. I hope the book will enhance your enjoyment and understanding of the Blue Ridge Mountains and, perhaps, spark in you a determination to preserve the region's natural resources and beauty.

Many people contributed their time, energy, and ideas to this book. I would like to express my deep appreciation to the following individuals, without whose generosity and help the project would not have been possible. Particular thanks go to Harry E. LeGrand, Jr., Eloise F. Potter, Norwood Middleton, and Alan Smith for their exhaustive critiques of the manuscript.

Others reviewed portions of the manuscript or provided suggestions or field data on sites and species. For such assistance, my thanks go to John Alderman for information on hawk migration and Mahogany Rock; to

Fred J. Alsop III for data on the Great Smokies, Roan Mountain, and Ferguson Fields; to Stan Bentley for data on the New River; to Dan Brauning for information on South Mountain; to Don Cofer for information on the Foothills Trail; to James H. Coman III for records from Alleghany County, N.C.; to Thelma Dalmas for data and many suggestions on the Parkway in Virginia; to Tom DeBusk for data on the Rocky Knob area; to Allen de Hart for information on hiking trails and topography throughout the Blue Ridge; to Michael Donahue for records from the Roanoke Sewage Treatment Plant; to Jane Earle for data from South Mountain; to Glen Eller for data from Roan Mountain; to George Ellison for records and information on Ferguson Fields; to Maxilla Evans for information on Lake Junaluska and Chimney Rock Park; to Ken Gabler for records at Caledonia State Park; to Thomas M. Haggerty for data from Price and Cone parks; to David Holt for data on hawk migration; to Deuane Hoffman for records and information on South Mountain; to Randy Johnson for trail information at Grandfather Mountain; to Clyde Kessler for data from the Rocky Knob area; to Barry Kinzie for Parkway information in the Roanoke area; to Rick Knight for data and information at Roan Mountain; to Travis Knowles for suggestions on many Parkway sites; to YuLee Larner for many suggestions and data on Virginia sites; to Norwood Middleton for extensive suggestions on sites in Virginia; to Steve Miller for trail information at Grandfather Mountain; to Myriam Moore for data on hawk migration; to Charles P. Nicholson for data and suggestions for the Great Smokies, Unicoi Mountains, and Roan Mountain; to Jim and Owen J. McConnell for data on the Unicoi Mountains and portions of the Little Tennessee River valley; to Richard H. Peake for data and suggestions at many sites in North Carolina and Virginia; to J. Dan Pittillo for information on plant communities along the Parkway and other sites; to Irvin Pitts for data and information on Caesar's Head State Park and Mountain Bridge Wilderness; to Mike Purdy for records at the Roanoke Sewage Treatment Plant; to Rick Pyeritz for data on Ferguson Fields and at numerous sites on the Parkway in North Carolina; to Steve Santner for records from South Mountain; to Pam Scarborough for data from Grandfather Mountain; to Frederick R. Scott for numerous suggestions on birding sites in Virginia; to Philip C. Shelton for records from the Mount Rogers area; to William and Norma Siebenheller for suggestions and records on the Parkway and adjacent areas from Asheville to the Smokies; to Alan Smith for extensive suggestions on the North Carolina portion of the Parkway and adjacent areas; to George Stubbs for records from Rocky Knob; to Simon Thompson for all the information and records from Chimney Rock Park; to David Wallace for records from Gambrill State Park; and to Jerry and Ruth Young for records at Lake Julian and along the French Broad River. Special thanks also go to Dotty Parton for permission to include Ferguson Fields in the book.

U.S. Department of the Interior and U.S. Forest Service personnel who provided information, maps, and assistance include Arthur C. Allen, Janet N. Bachman, Dorothy Cook, Don DeFoe, H. Frank Findley, Terry Lindsay, Bernard Miller, Martin T. Morris, Nora Murdock, Philip T. Noblitt, Dan Roddy, Bambi Teague, and Gary Willison. North Carolina state government staff who contributed to the project include Allen Boynton, who provided virtually all the data on Peregrine Falcon nesting sites; John Gerwin and David Lee, who helped with data from Grandfather Mountain, the Unicoi Mountains, and a number of Parkway sites; Harry E. LeGrand, Jr., who provided data on the Hiwassee River basin, Fontana area, Alleghany County, Rocky Bottom, and numerous Parkway sites; and Dwayne Stutzman, who provided information on the Mountains-to-Sea Trail. In Pennsylvania, Genny Volgstadt helped with information on the Kings Gap area at South Mountain.

Additional thanks go to Suzanne Bell, Sandra Eisdorfer, David Perry, and Heidi Perov of the University of North Carolina Press. And finally to my wife, Sallie, for her interest and patience.

ABBREVIATIONS

AT	Appalachian Trail
BRP	Blue Ridge Parkway
FSR	U.S. Forest Service road
ft.	feet
GA	Georgia route
GSMNP	Great Smoky Mountains National Park
M	milepoint
MD	Maryland route
MP	milepost marker
MTS Trail	Mountains-to-Sea Trail
NC	North Carolina route
NC SR	North Carolina state road (some are unpaved)
OL	overlook
PA	Pennsylvania route
PA SR	Pennsylvania state road (some are unpaved)
RCGNRT	Rock Castle Gorge National Recreation Trail
SC	South Carolina route
TN	Tennessee route
US	U.S. route
USFS	U.S. Forest Service
USGS	U.S. Geological Survey
VA	Virginia route
VA SR	Virginia state road (some are unpaved)

BIRDS OF THE BLUE RIDGE MOUNTAINS

INTRODUCTION

The Blue Ridge Mountains have attracted naturalists since the earliest days of exploration and settlement. Drawn by a rich abundance of flora and fauna, both amateur and professional biologists have poured over these ancient mountains in search of adventure and scientific discovery. The region's bird life is among the most diversified and interesting in eastern North America, due to the wide range of elevations and the great variety of plant communities. The highest mountains harbor plants and birds typical of the northern United States and Canada—relict and often disjunct populations that were forced south during the harsh climates of the last ice age. In contrast, the valleys and lowlands are home to species typical of the Piedmont and Coastal Plain of the southeastern United States. In many areas, therefore, a drive of less than one hour is ornithologically similar to a trip from the Georgia piedmont to New England.

Despite considerable development, much of the region has been set aside for preservation and protection as state and national parks, national forests, wilderness areas, and scenic motor routes such as the Blue Ridge Parkway and Skyline Drive. Numerous overlooks, easy highway access, attractive recreation areas, and an extensive network of trails make the Blue Ridge Mountains one of the best areas for bird-watching in the East.

Birds of the Blue Ridge Mountains provides an introduction to the bird life of the Blue Ridge Mountain Province from southern Pennsylvania to the hills of north Georgia. It primarily focuses on birds found along the Blue Ridge Parkway—the motor road that links Shenandoah National Park and Great Smoky Mountains National Park. The best birding trails, overlooks, and roadside sites are described in detail for each major locality along the Parkway and in many adjacent or nearby "hot spots." Following the locality descriptions, a checklist gives a brief account of each species' occurrence, habitats, elevation range, and relative abundance. For the most sought-after birds, the species account also includes a list of spots described in the book where the bird is most likely to be found.

This book is specifically designed to help different people accomplish different goals. Serious bird listers can use the finding guide and cross-referenced species accounts to identify places that could be visited to see a desired bird. People who want to know which species are present at some favorite trail or recreation area will find a discussion of bird life and plant communities for most major sites in the region. The guide not only accommodates this spectrum of interests but also includes information concerning different types of physical activity required to explore each site. For handicapped access, roadside birding, or strenuous backcountry climbing, the guide can be used to select the right spot for each birder's needs.

Bird-watching in the Blue Ridge provides a pleasant combination of impressive scenery, beautiful forests and wildflowers, good exercise, and an opportunity to escape the artificiality and pressures of day-to-day life. So get your binoculars and field guide and come sample the natural delights of the high country!

How to Use This Book

Designed for use with an illustrated field guide, *Birds of the Blue Ridge Mountains* consists of six major sections. The first provides an overview of the geomorphology, climate, vegetation, and bird life of the region. Section 2 includes basic practical information on bird-watching methods, hiking skills, trails, sites that are suitable for the handicapped, a list of "hot spots," tips on watching the autumn hawk migration, and notes on owl study.

Sections 3 through 5, the major portions of the book, are devoted to bird finding in the Blue Ridge. Sections 3 and 4 give detailed information on birds, habitats, trails, and facilities found at major recreation areas along the Blue Ridge Parkway and at nearby spots, including Shenandoah National Park, Great Smoky Mountains National Park, Mount Mitchell State Park, various wilderness tracts, state parks, and many national forest areas. (Section 3 is a guide to areas in Virginia; Section 4 to those in North Carolina.) Section 5 describes major areas located more than 15 miles from the Parkway. The access routes to these sites are generally described beginning from the nearest or most convenient exit on the Parkway.

The sixth section is a checklist of birds of the Blue Ridge Mountain Province. Relative abundance, habitat preference, elevation range, and dates of occurrence are given for each species. For certain rare or "special-interest" birds, the species account also contains a list of spots described in the book where the bird is most likely to be found. Black-capped Chickadees, for example, are shown in the checklist as occurring on Alum Cave Bluffs Trail. The reader can then consult the index for the trail name and look up its description in the site-guide material in Section 4. This cross referencing is not provided for widely distributed birds or for birds found in areas not covered in the site guide.

Finally, at the end of the book, readers will find suggested reading and information on resources available to assist outdoors enthusiasts.

The decision to include or omit a particular site was often difficult, and many birding localities had to be excluded. Some good spots are on private property, and permission cannot be obtained for public access. Even when trespass is not an issue, private holdings are subject to development or alteration that could quickly make them unsuitable for birding. Other interesting bird-watching sites involve places where it is difficult, dangerous, or impossible to park a car. In some instances, good birding areas are very remote or require elaborately detailed instructions for access. The route into certain backcountry spots cannot be accurately described. In other cases, state or federal officials have requested that a site be excluded because of the presence of endangered species or for other environmental considerations. Most included sites, therefore, are found in public lands that have been designated in perpetuity as natural recreation areas, where trails, overlooks, and other facilities ensure a productive and pleasant visit.

I have hiked every trail included in this book and have written the descriptions and bird lists of each route mostly from my own notes, which were gathered from 1957 to 1991. Data on some areas were kindly provided by individuals listed in the Preface. Additional records are derived from *American Birds, Chat, Migrant, Raven, Oriole, Wilson Bulletin*, and other sources listed in References and Suggested Reading. Trail mileages are taken mainly from published figures by the U.S. Park Service, U.S. Forest Service, state parks, trail conferences, and hiking guidebooks. When highway mileages are stated using decimals (e.g., "7.0 miles"), the data are based on my own odometer readings; when stated without decimals (e.g., "7 miles"), the data are taken from published highway maps. Elevations and place names are based mostly on U.S. Geological Survey topographic maps.

Bird Finding in the Blue Ridge Mountains

Sections 3 through 5, describing selected bird-watching sites in the Blue Ridge Mountain Province, form the bulk of the book. Principle emphasis is on the Blue Ridge Parkway, the 469-mile motor route that links Shenandoah National Park and Great Smoky Mountains National Park, both of which are also included. Information is provided for many state and local parks, wilderness tracts, and U.S. Forest Service recreation areas. Each locality description is divided into six key elements: highlights, season, access, maps, facilities, and the site guide.

"Highlights" sections briefly list the most interesting or important bird species found in a particular site. "Season" indicates which time of year is best for visiting the spot. The "Access" section describes briefly how to reach the particular area using the Parkway, Skyline Drive, or major U.S. and state highways.

When describing mileages on the Parkway and Skyline Drive, the conventional method is to refer to milepost markers placed along the roadways. MP 0 is located at the northernmost point of the Parkway at Rockfish Gap, Va., and MP 469 is near the Oconaluftee River at the Parkway's southern end near Cherokee, N.C. Running from north to south, marker mileage is a convenient way to locate a spot to within a tenth of a mile. For example, Wild Turkeys are sometimes noted on the Parkway at a point 0.9 miles south of MP 216; thus the site guide would indicate the exact milepoint, M 216.9, as the spot to check. Using the car's odometer in combination with a particular milepost will allow you to find sites quickly and reliably. When a particular spot is actually at the marker post itself, like Mahogany Rock Overlook at mile 235, then the site is designated as MP 235.

References to the "right" and "left" sides of the Parkway and Skyline Drive conventionally assume you are heading southward. Bear in mind that "north" and "south" are also being used in a conventional designation rather than in a strictly geographic sense when mentioned in the context of the Skyline Drive and Blue Ridge Parkway. In some areas, such as from Beech Gap (M 423.2) to the Oconaluftee River (MP 469), the Parkway is actually heading geographically to the northwest, but for convention and consistency, the route is still described as southbound.

Some descriptions on the Blue Ridge Parkway have additional material designated as "Note," which appears under "Access." This material calls attention to any peripheral sites more than 15 miles from the Parkway that are most easily accessed from the particular Parkway area being described. For instance, if you are birding in Doughton Park, check the Doughton description to find a note about Mount Rogers, an important site almost 40 miles from the Parkway. You will find it is most easily reached by turning off the Parkway at US 21, just north of Doughton Park. Then read the section on Mount Rogers and decide whether to visit the area.

The "Maps" section lists topographic and trail maps of the area that are available from the U.S. Geological Survey, U.S. Forest Service, and other sources. These maps are especially valuable to serious hikers or birders who wish to determine elevations and precise locations of any important records or observations. Highway maps are also included in many sections to orient visiting birders. The "Facilities" material includes the nearby campsites, accommodations, gasoline, food, and visitor centers. Detailed information, phone numbers, and mailing addresses are listed in some instances, although most of this material is included in the appendix on resources.

The site guide provides a general introduction to the geomorphology, vegetation, and history of the area, followed by a detailed account of major birding sites, such as trails, overlooks, or roadways. Trail information includes mileage, hiking difficulty, route description, vegetation, elevation changes, and a list of the most common or important birds that might be encountered. Whenever appropriate, special note is made if a spot is suitable for handicapped use, either from cars or wheelchairs. Maps are included for major sites, but these are not intended to substitute for the detailed topographic and trail maps listed in the section entitled "Maps."

The species lists appearing in the site guide apply mostly to late spring and summer months. Don't expect to see everything on the list, and don't be surprised to find some birds that are not mentioned. Be sure to get into the field at the right time of day, or you may find very few species.

THE
BLUE
RIDGE
MOUNTAIN
PROVINCE

AN OVERVIEW

I

Geomorphology and Climate

Forming the geologic backbone of eastern North America, the Appalachian Highlands extend some two thousand miles from Canada's Gaspe Peninsula to the hills of northern Georgia. Through much of the region, the cold, moist climate in the high elevations creates an ecological refuge for animals and plants whose evolutionary history links them to the biota of Canada and the northern United States. At the region's southern end, the mountains increase dramatically in mass and elevation, with the Blue Ridge Mountain Province of Georgia, the Carolinas, Tennessee, and Virginia forming a biological archipelago of northern species surrounded by, and intermingled with, the flora and fauna of the Southeast.

The current distribution of plant and bird life in the southern Appalachians reflects the influence of the last glacial period, some 10,000 to 12,000 years ago. At that time, the polar ice cap extended as far south as Ohio and Long Island Sound, and the accompanying cold climate pushed the northern flora and fauna deep into the southeastern United States. As the glaciers retreated during the close of the Pleistocene, slowly warming temperatures forced the spruce, fir, and northern hardwood forests back to the north and up the slopes of the southern mountains, where they survived into modern times as disjunct communities in the cool climates of the highest peaks and ridges. Dozens of bird species in the Blue Ridge Province are closely associated with relict northern forests and mixed mesophytic woodlands of the region. As a result, many northern birds reach their southernmost breeding limit in the Blue Ridge Mountains.

Geologically, the Blue Ridge Province is composed of some of the world's oldest and most durable rocks. In contrast to surrounding provinces, the Blue Ridge consists largely of Precambrian formations that were laid down prior to the appearance of vertebrate life. Most rocks are igneous and metamorphic structures that date back more than one billion years. Repeated periods of uplift and erosion created the present landscape, and some geologists suggest that portions of the range may once have towered above the present height of the Himalayas.

The Blue Ridge Mountain physiographic province begins southwest of Harrisburg, Pa., as a series of low ridges, seldom exceeding 2,000 feet in elevation, that gradually increase in size as they sweep through Maryland and northern Virginia. South of Front Royal, Va., the ridge lines become a well-defined range, generally around 3,000 feet in elevation and five to fifteen miles wide. Scattered outliers and parallel ridges extend onto the Piedmont Province to the east and onto the Ridge and Valley Province along the western flank. The Allegheny Mountains, which comprise the remaining portion of the southern Appalachians, rise to the west along the edge of the Great Valley opposite the Blue Ridge.

From Front Royal, Va., to the vicinity of the Roanoke River gap, the Blue Ridge continues mostly as a steep mountain ridge, rising decisively from the surrounding lowlands. The Shenandoah, James, and Roanoke rivers form in the Great Valley on the range's western slopes. The Shenandoah flows north to join the Potomac River at Harpers Ferry. The Potomac, James, and Roanoke rivers pass through deep gaps in the range as they flow eastward onto the Piedmont. The east slopes of the range are drained by the Rappahannock River and branches of the James River.

Most of the terrain is covered by medium to mature second-growth oak and pine forests, with cove hardwoods and hemlock on moist slopes and ravines. Major peaks in the ridge portion of the province include Hawksbill (4,049 ft.), Stony Man Mountain (4,010 ft.), The Priest (4,056 ft.), Apple Orchard Mountain (4,225 ft.), and Flat Top (4,004 ft.).

South of the Roanoke River gap, the character of the topography changes considerably. No longer a high ridge, the province widens into the broad, undulating Blue Ridge Plateau, covered with scattered knobs, ridges, and low mountains at elevations typically between 1,200 to 3,000 feet. This irregular tableland slopes gently toward the north and west, with the northwestward-flowing New River draining much of its southern portion and the Roanoke River system forming the watershed for the province's

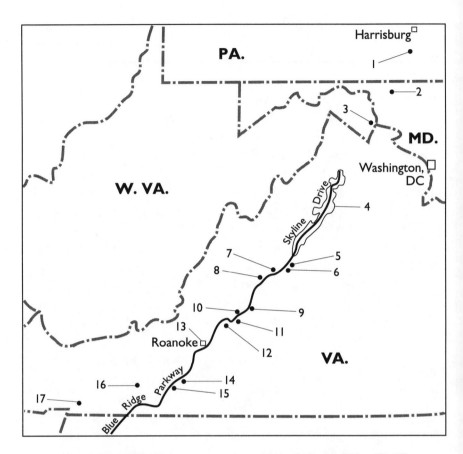

1. South Mtn. (210–18)
2. Northern Blue Ridge (208–10)
3. Harpers Ferry (205–8)
4. Shenandoah National Park (50–59)
5. Rockfish Gap (59–61)
6. Humpback Rocks (61–62)
7. Big Levels (62–66)
8. Whetstone Ridge (66–67)
9. James River and Otter Creek (67–70)

10. Apple Orchard Mtn. (70–75)
11. Peaks of Otter (75–81)
12. Harvey's Knob (81–82)
13. Roanoke Mtn. (82–85)
14. Smart View (85–86)
15. Rocky Knob (86–91)
16. New River (105–6)
17. Mt. Rogers (219–28)

Locations of Major Bird-watching Sites in the Blue Ridge Mountain Province, Northern Half

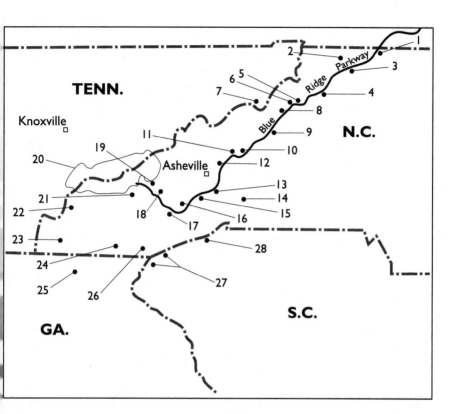

1. Cumberland Knob (92–94)
2. New River (101–5)
3. Doughton Park (94–101)
4. E. B. Jeffress Park (106–7)
5. Moses Cone Park (107–12)
6. Julian Price Park (112–16)
7. Roan Mtn. (228–36)
8. Grandfather Mtn. (116–26)
9. Linville Gorge (127–33)
10. South Toe High Country (134–40)
11. Mt. Mitchell and Black Mtns. (140–47)
12. Great Craggy Mtns. (148–53)
13. French Broad River Valley (153–55)
14. Chimney Rock Park (236–39)
15. Mt. Pisgah Area (156–67)

16. Shining Rock (168–74)
17. Southern Great Balsam Mtns. (174–81)
18. Plott Balsam Mtns. (181–84)
19. Northern Great Balsam Mtns. (184–90)
20. Great Smoky Mtns. National Park (194–203)
21. Little Tennessee River Valley (190–93)
22. Unicoi Mtns. (239–48)
23. Hiwassee River Basin (255–56)
24. Nantahala Mtns. (248–55)
25. North Georgia Highlands (272–75)
26. Highlands Plateau (256–60)
27. Southeastern Blue Ridge
    Escarpment Gorges (260–69)
28. South Carolina High Country (269–72)

Locations of Major Bird-watching Sites in the Blue Ridge Mountain Province, Southern Half northern half. Along the plateau's eastern edge, however, the terrain is dramatically different, often forming a spectacular gradient that drops off precipitously some one to two thousand feet to the Piedmont Province below. Viewed from the Piedmont, the irregular escarpment of the Blue Ridge Plateau appears as an almost continuous wall of abruptly rising mountains.

Steeply descending streams plunge down the escarpment's eastern rim, carving the plateau edge into a jumble of beautiful ravines and ridges. Fairly mature second-growth oak and pine forests cloak these ridges, while adjacent ravines contain lush cove hardwood stands. Both the Blue Ridge Plateau and the subjacent Piedmont have been extensively cleared for farming and settlement; so the rugged escarpment itself generally contains the region's largest tracts of continuous woodland. The plateau elevation increases gradually from north to south. Thus the plant and bird life generally become more typically "northern" in the southern end of the province around Julian Price and Moses Cone parks, while in the Roanoke Mountain area the environment is more piedmont than montane.

Near the Virginia–North Carolina line, the New River valley marks the transition from the Blue Ridge Plateau to a region of high mountain ranges stretching south to Georgia. South of Virginia, the Blue Ridge Province consists of two major mountain ranges that enclose a vast interior tableland, averaging 2,000 to 2,500 feet in elevation, which is subdivided by other high ranges. As suggested by Bill Sharpe, editor of the *State* magazine, the structure can be simplistically compared to a stepladder, in which the two major ranges, the Blue Ridge Mountains on the east and the Unaka chain on the west, run approximately parallel to each other in a southwesterly direction from the North Carolina–Virginia border to northern Georgia. The irregular cross steps or rungs of the ladder consist of the so-called transverse mountain ranges, such as the Blacks, Great Craggies, Newfounds, Great Balsams, and Nantahalas. At the province's southern end, the Blue Ridge and the Unaka chains merge almost imperceptibly in the Georgia highlands.

The two ranges thus form a mountain rim around western North Carolina, encompassing about eight thousand square miles of interior valleys and a jumble of transverse ranges. The distance between the crests of the Blue Ridge and the Unakas varies considerably. Near the Virginia border they are fifteen to twenty miles apart, but from Saluda Gap near Tryon it is almost 140 miles to the Unaka crest. The Unaka chain forms most of the state boundary between Tennessee and North Carolina and includes a number of named ranges, such as the Iron, the Great Smoky, and the Unicoi mountains. The eastern range is called the Blue Ridge Mountains throughout its entire length.

A curious feature of the region is that the western Unaka chain is generally higher than the eastern Blue Ridge chain, yet all the major rivers, including the Hiwassee, Little Tennessee, Pigeon, French Broad, Watauga, and Toe, escape the interior valleys through gorges carved across the western rim. Geologists have suggested that the Unaka chain is younger than the Blue Ridge, so that the rivers have been able to maintain their westward gradients into the Mississippi basin by carving through the Unakas more rapidly than the Unakas rose during periods of uplift. As a result, the continental divide follows the Blue Ridge crest, despite an average elevation around 1,000 feet lower than the Unakas.

The striking difference in topography on opposite sides of the New River valley is apparent when one recalls that only a handful of Blue Ridge peaks exceed 4,000 feet from the New River to Pennsylvania, but south of the New River, there are 225 mountains over 5,000 feet and 49 that rise above 6,000 feet in elevation. These lofty ranges south of the New River are covered in part by forests similar to those in the northern portion of the Blue Ridge, such as cove hardwoods and oaks; but the higher terrain also contains the province's most extensive tracts of spruce-fir forests, northern hardwoods, and heath thickets.

The transition from the Blue Ridge Plateau to the high southern ranges is accompanied by major changes in climate as well as in vegetation. As a general rule throughout the mountains, with increasing elevation there is a decrease in temperature and an increase in precipitation. For each 1,000 feet gained in elevation, the mean temperature decreases about two to three degrees F, roughly equivalent to a change of 200 to 250 miles in latitude. Thus, average July temperatures are about 75° at Gatlinburg, Tenn. (1,460 ft.), 70° at Highlands, N.C. (3,850 ft.), 62° on Grandfather Mountain (5,280 ft.), and 59° on Mount Mitchell (6,684 ft.). Farther north, the July average in the Shenandoah Valley (900 ft.) is around 70°, but at nearby Big Meadows (3,510 ft.) in Shenandoah National Park, the average is 66°. The harsh winter conditions in the higher elevations are reflected in January averages—28° at Mount Mitchell and 24° at Big Meadows.

Although the inverse relation between elevation and temperature is fairly consistent in the southern Appalachians, the relationship between precipitation and elevation is considerably more complex, owing to differences in local topography and variations in the direction and moisture content of prevailing winds. Air cools while rising to pass over a mountain range, and cold air can hold less moisture than warm air. Therefore, condensation occurs on the upper slopes in the form of fog, clouds, rain, or snow, making the summits considerably wetter than the valleys.

However, the "rain shadow" phenomenon occurs when these moisture-laden winds are cooled and lose much of their water content in crossing a mountain range, resulting in heavy precipitation on the windward side but relatively low rainfall on leeward slopes and in downwind valleys. In addition, the average water content of prevailing winds is greater in the southern portion of the Blue Ridge Province than in the northern and central sections. The mountains of Tennessee and the Carolinas are affected by warm, often saturated air masses from the Gulf of Mexico and southern Coastal Plain, whereas weather in the Virginia mountains is dominated by the comparatively drier weather systems that move across the center of the continent.

The heaviest rainfall in the Blue Ridge Province probably occurs in the gorges of the southeastern escarpment, where the Savannah River headwaters form in the Toxaway, Horsepasture, Chattooga, Thompson, and Whitewater rivers. Here moist Gulf Coast air masses first encounter mountainous terrain, resulting in annual rainfalls as high as 100 to 120 inches in some spots. Heavy precipitation also occurs in the Great Smoky Mountains, which form an abrupt barrier to weather systems from the Southwest and from the Gulf Coast. On Clingman's Dome (6,642 ft.) in the Smokies, the average annual precipitation is 85 inches, but downwind to the east, Asheville (2,100 ft.) receives only about 40 inches and Mount Mitchell (6,684 ft.) about 70 inches, in large part because of the rain shadow created by the Smokies and by other mountain ranges. The drier climate in the northern portion of the Blue Ridge is apparent by comparing the 80 inches annual rainfall at Highlands, N.C. (3,850 ft.), near the North Carolina–Georgia line, with the 50 inches at Big Meadows (3,510 ft.) in Shenandoah National Park, the latter site probably also affected by a rain shadow created in the Allegheny Mountains of West Virginia.

As a result of these various factors, the climate in the high country is characterized by wet, cool summers and cold, harsh winters. The first snows usually fall well before Thanksgiving, and ice and snow regularly persist through March on the highest peaks. Strong winds, sometimes exceeding a hundred miles per hour, are not uncommon on the most exposed mountains, and dense fog and freezing precipitation can occur in almost any month of the year. Such conditions create an environment in which the bird and plant life contrasts sharply with that of the surrounding Piedmont and Coastal Plain of the southeastern United States.

Vegetation and Bird Life

Coniferous forests dominated by Fraser fir and red spruce occur on the highest mountains of the Blue Ridge Province. Prior to the 1970s, spruce was the predominant tree up to around 6,000 feet; above that elevation it was gradually replaced by fir, which often formed a solid canopy on the highest peaks. With the extensive die-off of Fraser fir in the 1970s and 1980s, the red spruce is now the more abundant species through most of the region. Other major trees include mountain ash, fire cherry, mountain maple, striped maple, yellow birch, and, occasionally, beech, buckeye, and serviceberry. These spruce-fir forests once occupied much of the terrain above 4,500 feet at Mount Rogers, Grandfather Mountain, and Roan Mountain; in parts of the high Blue Ridge; in the Black Mountains and immediately contiguous Great Craggies, Pisgah Ridge, and the Plott Balsam and Great Balsam mountains; on Shining Rock Ledge; and in the Great Smokies. Scattered stands of red spruce are more widespread, including well-known tracts at Long Hope Creek and in the Cowee Mountains. In the past hundred years, however, more than 90 percent of the spruce-fir forests in the southern Appalachians have been destroyed by logging, wildfires, balsam woolly adelgids, and what are believed to be the effects of airborne pollutants.

Birds typically associated with spruce-fir forests from late spring through summer include Northern Saw-whet Owl, Hairy Woodpecker, Common Raven, Black-capped Chickadee, Red-breasted Nuthatch, Brown Creeper, Winter Wren, Golden-crowned Kinglet, Veery, American Robin, Cedar Waxwing, Black-throated Green Warbler, Blackburnian Warbler, Canada Warbler, and Dark-eyed Junco. Some of the most elusive and localized birds of the southern Blue Ridge, such as Red Crossbill and Pine Siskin, seem to have a predilection for spruce-fir forests, especially in years with heavy seed crops. Hermit Thrushes occur at Mount Rogers, at Grandfather, in the Black Mountains, and occasionally at Roan Mountain and in the Smokies. A small population of Swainson's Thrush is present at Mount Rogers; Purple Finches are regular at Mount Rogers and occasional at Grandfather. Magnolia Warblers occur in spruce-hardwood and spruce-heath transitions at Mount Rogers, at Long Hope Creek, at Grandfather, and in the Black Mountains. Most modern summer records of the Olive-sided Flycatcher, rarest of the Blue Ridge breeders, are confined to spruce-fir forests in the Smokies. The few summer records of Yellow-bellied Fly-catchers have been closely associated with these conifers at Mount Rogers, Grandfather Mountain, and Mount Mitchell.

Northern hardwoods occur along the lower border of spruce-fir forests at elevations mostly above 4,300 feet and usually infiltrate the adjacent conifers in an irregular transition zone. Northern hardwood communities often appear as a successional stage following disruption of spruce-fir forests, and stands dominated by beech or buckeye may occupy some high mountain gaps. Dominant trees are beech and yellow birch, along with sugar maple, red maple, northern red oak, fire cherry, and serviceberry. On rocky north-facing slopes and at elevations above 3,800 feet in Shenandoah National Park, isolated stands of northern hardwood may also be found, with sweet birch and yellow birch as dominant trees.

When northern hardwood forests occur in close proximity to sizable spruce-fir tracts, many bird species noted in the coniferous woods will be present in the northern hardwoods as well. Other birds observed in late spring and summer include Ruffed Grouse, Black-billed Cuckoo, Barred Owl, Yellow-bellied Sapsucker, Downy Woodpecker, Blue Jay, Solitary Vireo, Chestnut-sided Warbler, Black-throated Blue Warbler, and Rose-breasted Grosbeak.

Communities dominated by various species of oak form the most extensive forests of the southern Blue Ridge Mountains. Prior to the arrival of chestnut blight, these forests were called oak-chestnut communities, but with removal of American chestnut as a canopy species, botanists now classify them as mixed oak or occasionally oak-hickory forests. Dominant species include white oak, scarlet oak, chestnut oak, black oak, and northern and southern red oaks, along with red maple, a variety of hickories, sourwood, white pine, pitch pine, Table Mountain pine, serviceberry, and black locust. Generally reaching their upper limits around 4,500 feet, oak forests differ notably in response to local conditions of soil, slope, moisture, and exposure. In the high elevations, some tracts of stunted northern red oaks grow with such an open canopy as to be dubbed "oak orchards" because of their resemblance to cultivated fruit orchards.

Birds of oak forests vary considerably, depending on elevation, maturity, and tree species growing in the particular area. Species associated with the forest type in late spring and summer include Sharp-shinned Hawk, Cooper's Hawk, Broad-winged Hawk, Red-tailed Hawk, Ruffed Grouse, Wild Turkey, Black-billed Cuckoo, Yellow-billed Cuckoo, Eastern Screech-Owl, Great Horned Owl, Barred Owl, Whip-poor-will, Downy Woodpecker, Hairy Woodpecker, Northern Flicker, Pileated Woodpecker, Eastern Wood-Pewee, Acadian Flycatcher, Least Flycatcher, Eastern Phoebe, Great Crested Flycatcher, Blue Jay, American Crow, Carolina Chickadee, Tufted Titmouse, White-breasted Nuthatch, Carolina Wren, Wood Thrush, American Robin, Gray Catbird, Solitary Vireo, Red-eyed Vireo, Scarlet Tanager, Rose-breasted Grosbeak, and Chipping Sparrow. Warblers are particularly well represented, including Chestnut-sided, Black-throated Blue, Black-throated Green, Black-and-white, American Redstart, Worm-eating, Ovenbird, Louisiana Waterthrush, Hooded, and Canada. Some of the more mesic oak forests may have Cerulean Warbler and Kentucky Warbler as well, particularly in the Virginia portion of the Blue Ridge.

Oak forests often contain a variety of conifers, but in some areas, pines achieve a dominant status in the forest composition. Found mostly at low to middle elevations in the Blue Ridge, pine-dominated woodlands typically occur in shallow, rocky, or poor soils; on dry ridges; and on steep, exposed slopes. Forest composition and the associated bird life vary greatly, depending on the age and species of the pines, the nature of the understory or shrub layer, and the elevation, slope, and orientation of the topography. Widespread species include pitch pine, Virginia pine, short-leaf pine, Table Mountain pine, and white pine. Bird life is often rather sparse in pine forests, particularly if a single tree species dominates. Birds are usually most abundant when the pine forest has a rich and diversified understory.

Birds found in pine-dominated forests during late spring and summer include Sharp-shinned Hawk, Cooper's Hawk, Eastern Screech-Owl, Ruby-throated Hummingbird, Downy Woodpecker, Hairy Woodpecker, Eastern Phoebe, Blue Jay, Carolina Chickadee, Tufted Titmouse, Wood Thrush, American Robin, Yellow-throated Vireo, Red-eyed Vireo, Yellow-throated Warbler, Black-and-white Warbler, Northern Cardinal, and Rufous-sided

Towhee. Some species that are associated with the Coastal Plain or Piedmont are found in the Blue Ridge Province mostly, or entirely, as small, localized populations in pine woodlands, mainly at low elevations. Principal examples are Red-cockaded Woodpeckers, Brown-headed Nuthatches, and Pine Warblers. Red Crossbills and Pine Siskins may occur in pine forests, along with other winter finches during major invasion years. As in many parts of their range, Long-eared Owls seem to prefer pine forests in the Blue Ridge Province, where their only confirmed nesting records have been in white pine groves. During winter months, Long-eared and Northern Saw-whet Owls also use dense pine and cedar stands for roosting sites.

Cove hardwood, or mixed mesophytic, forests are present in moist coves, ravines, and valleys at low and middle elevations, rarely up to 4,500 feet. Richest and most diversified of Appalachian forest types, cove hardwoods typically involve eight to twelve species of trees, including tuliptree, sugar maple, yellow buckeye, yellow birch, red oak, red maple, white oak, basswood, white ash, beech, and black cherry. In areas of heavy rainfall, such as the Smokies, these forests achieve their optimal development, and many trees of world-record size are found. In drier parts of the Blue Ridge Province, such as central Virginia, cove hardwood forests are generally less diverse than in the Carolinas and Tennessee.

The avifauna of cove hardwoods is quite rich and includes virtually all species noted previously for oak forests, although many birds do not occur at all elevations. Additional residents during late spring and summer are Blue-gray Gnatcatcher, Northern Parula, Northern Cardinal, and Summer Tanager. In steep areas along the Blue Ridge escarpment where mature tuliptrees dominate at the upper end of open coves, Cerulean Warblers often occur in localized mini-colonies. Where rosebay rhododendron forms a thick streamside understory in cove forests, Swainson's Warblers are sometimes found, generally in areas below 3,000 feet in elevation.

Although Canada hemlock is a widespread tree in the southern Blue Ridge, there are sites where it achieves status as one of the dominant species. These hemlock forests occur as low as 1,000 feet and rarely up to 5,500 feet, mostly in cool, moist sites such as sheltered coves and north-facing ravines. Late spring and summer birds include many species typical of deciduous woodlands, in addition to certain birds that are also found in spruce-fir forests, often at considerably higher elevations, such as Red-breasted Nuthatch, Brown Creeper, Winter Wren, Golden-crowned

Kinglet, Veery, and Blackburnian Warbler. Curiously, not every apparently suitable stand of hemlock has these high-country birds: all are present at Trout Lake (3,760 ft.) and Sim's Creek (3,600 ft.) in North Carolina, but the nuthatch, creeper, and kinglet are absent from the Limberlost (3,350 ft.) in Shenandoah National Park, some 240 miles to the northeast. Other characteristic species include Northern Parula, Black-throated Green Warbler, Canada Warbler, Rose-breasted Grosbeak, and Dark-eyed Junco. Red Crossbills and Pine Siskins are not infrequently associated with hemlocks. Some of these species are present occasionally in monotonous stands of white pine that are found at low to middle elevations.

Rosebay rhododendron and mountain laurel are widespread constituents of the shrub understory of most forest communities, but Catawba rhododendron often occurs in dense heath balds or "slicks" on steep and exposed slopes and cleared areas in the high elevations. Renowned for their spectacular profusion of blooms in June, these balds are home to Winter Wren, Gray Catbird, Chestnut-sided Warbler, Black-throated Blue Warbler, Canada Warbler, Dark-eyed Junco, and an occasional Song Sparrow.

The other major type of high-elevation opening is the grass bald. In many cases these high meadows are known to be a result of logging and fires, as at Shining Rock Ledge and on Pine Mountain and Wilburn Ridge near Mount Rogers. In other instances, as on the Roan massif, their origin remains a mystery. Few birds inhabit grass balds, but American Woodcock, Horned Lark, Vesper Sparrow, Song Sparrow, and Dark-eyed Junco may be present in late spring and summer. Northern Harriers and a rare Golden Eagle may occur in winter, and the very rare and elusive Snow Bunting shows up erratically at such spots as Round Bald or Big Meadows. Other species are associated with the edge or margin of the balds, such as Northern Bobwhite, House Wren, and Indigo Bunting.

A floodplain forest may be present along the large rivers, where dominant trees are tuliptree and sycamore, often with catalpa, willows, alders, river birch, and other species in disturbed areas. These riparian forests occur in stretches along the Potomac, Shenandoah, James, Roanoke, New, and French Broad rivers. Similar forests are also present in spots on the Little Tennessee, Hiwassee, and Watauga rivers. Although localized in distribution, some breeding-season birds typically associated with these forests include White-eyed Vireo, Yellow-throated Vireo, Warbling

Vireo, Yellow Warbler, Yellow-throated Warbler, Prothonotary Warbler, and Northern Oriole. Other river birds are Green-backed Heron, Wood Duck, Spotted Sandpiper, and Belted Kingfisher. Various swallows and flycatchers are often found along river banks.

Disturbed areas, including old fields, disclimax communities, and a complex array of secondary successional communities, occur at all elevations in the Blue Ridge Province where the original forests have been removed or the canopy has been disrupted or damaged. A variety of birds may occur in summer, depending on the extent of deforestation, the elevation, and the type of secondary vegetation present. Species typically associated with such habitats are Turkey Vulture, Northern Bobwhite, American Woodcock, Mourning Dove, Ruby-throated Hummingbird, Alder Flycatcher, Willow Flycatcher, Eastern Kingbird, Tree Swallow, Northern Rough-winged Swallow, Barn Swallow, House Wren, Eastern Bluebird, Gray Catbird, Northern Mockingbird, Brown Thrasher, Blue-winged Warbler, Golden-winged Warbler, Chestnut-sided Warbler, Prairie Warbler, Common Yellowthroat, Yellow-breasted Chat, Northern Cardinal, Indigo Bunting, Field Sparrow, Song Sparrow, Eastern Meadowlark, Brown-headed Cowbird, and American Goldfinch.

The current distribution of bird life in the Blue Ridge Mountains reflects dramatic changes in the ecology of the region over the past century. Although visitors typically experience pleasant feelings of permanence and stability when contemplating a beautiful mountain scene, the environment here is actually quite fragile and has been anything but constant since the arrival of European settlers. Studies by John S. Cairns (1863–95), William Brewster (1851–1919), and other nineteenth-century naturalists provide data that show how much things have changed in the southern mountains.

Although lowland farms and high pasture clearings dotted the landscape long before the Civil War, environmental alterations began on a major scale with the arrival of the logging industry in the final decades of the nineteenth century. Lumbering practices of the day gave little or no consideration to the future, and much of the southern Blue Ridge was stripped clean and left to burn and erode. Some of the worst damage involved spruce-fir forests, in part because conditions in the Blue Ridge favor the invasion of deciduous shrubs and hardwoods once these conifers have been removed. More than 90 percent of the original spruce and fir in the southern Appalachians was destroyed by logging and wildfires, and the few tracts that were preserved from the ax have subsequently fallen victim to other problems.

Balsam woolly adelgids were accidentally introduced in the United States around 1900, and by 1957 they had spread to the Mount Mitchell area and begun a devastating attack on Fraser firs. Control measures have proven largely ineffective, and extensive damage is now present in almost all fir stands in the southern Blue Ridge. Additional trouble for coniferous forests emerged in the 1970s with the decline of red spruce, which are not infested by adelgids. Environmental problems associated with airborne pollutants, such as heavy metals and acid rain, are suspected as major causative factors. Although no birds seem to be totally dependent on spruce-fir forests, the decimation of these conifers has undoubtedly resulted in significant declines in the populations of many birds that are highly associated with the community.

Other plant pathogens and insect pests have profoundly altered the composition and appearance of mountain forests during the twentieth century. Accidentally imported from Asia, chestnut blight appeared in New York in the early 1900s and by 1918 had spread as far south as Peaks of Otter. By 1930 some 90 percent of American chestnut trees in the North Carolina mountains were infected, and seemingly overnight the chestnut disappeared as the dominant tree in the Blue Ridge, where it had formerly made up nearly 40 percent of the deciduous forest. In addition to creating large openings in the canopy, the loss of chestnut trees greatly reduced the nut crop and adversely affected many animals, including the Wild Turkey.

Gypsy moths were intentionally brought to America for silkworm-breeding experiments, but some escaped in Boston in the late 1860s and began their spread. The often massive defoliation that occurs in high-infestation areas can result in tree death, particularly if outbreaks occur in consecutive years. Hickories, maples, and especially oaks are favored targets of the scourge, which may cause mortalities as high as 50 percent in some oak forests. By 1983 gypsy moths had arrived in Shenandoah National Park, and by 1989 they had spread to the northern end of the Blue Ridge Parkway. Because control measures have as yet proven inadequate, the long-term impact of these pests on forest composition and bird life of the Blue Ridge are potentially serious.

Understory plants have also become a concern in the 1990s. Flowering dogwoods are being attacked and killed by a fungus, and rosebay rhododendrons have been dying in some areas, possibly due to drought.

Perhaps the changes that bode worst for Blue Ridge birds are occurring far away from the area. Tropical deforestation in South and Central America continues unabated, removing critical winter habitat for many birds that breed in North America. Some scientists consider more than fifty species to be at risk, including many flycatchers, thrushes, vireos, tanagers, and warblers that pass through or nest in the Blue Ridge Mountains. Assessing the problem is difficult, because much of the data gathered over the past century is fragmentary, sketchy, and subjective. For a readable and well-referenced introduction to the problem, see Terborgh's *Where Have All the Birds Gone?*. The issue remains controversial, but if the worst scenarios prove to be accurate, the name "Warbler Road" may assume implications equivalent to the name "Pigeon Gap"—an ironic and unintended commentary on the way things used to be.

From the studies of resident and visiting naturalists, a tantalizing yet incomplete picture emerges of Blue Ridge bird life in the last decades of the nineteenth century. Golden Eagles were regularly noted year-round in the high mountains, and Bald Eagles nested locally on the French Broad River. American Bitterns were probable breeders along the French Broad, and Black Rails nested in its marshy borders. Olive-sided Flycatchers summered on the Highlands Plateau and the upper Black Mountains, where Black-capped Chickadees were resident and large numbers of post-breeding American Swallow-tailed Kites were often seen in late summer. Huge flocks of Passenger Pigeons wintered in the Blue Ridge and even nested south of Charlottesville in 1874, but by the 1890s a single bird was a big event. Northern Orioles seem to have been considerably more widespread than at present, but the Wild Turkey had been hunted to the point of extreme rarity. Peregrine Falcons nested on numerous high cliffs and bluffs. Red-headed Woodpeckers were far more common and widespread.

The decline or extirpation of many of these species over the ensuing years can often be attributed to fairly specific causes, but in other instances the events are hard to understand. One of the most dramatic changes in Blue Ridge birds involves the disappearance of Bewick's Wren as a nesting species. In the 1880s and 1890s, the Bewick's was described as abundant, widespread, conspicuous, breeding from the lowest valleys to the highest peaks, and noted "everywhere." By the 1930s the bird had become "rather scarce," and by the 1970s the Bewick's was virtually absent from the region. The causes of this seemingly inexorable disappearance are uncertain, but speculation focuses on competition with House Wrens, House Sparrows, and European Starlings.

Although certain species have declined or disappeared from the Blue Ridge, others have expanded their ranges and pushed southward down the Appalachian high country. Disruption and removal of original forests and the advent of farms and towns created extensive tracts of diverse habitat, but it is not always apparent why one species has exploited these changes while other species have failed to do so.

House Sparrows, then known as English Sparrows, colonized the southern Blue Ridge as early as 1884, and Song Sparrows rapidly extended their summer territories into the North Carolina mountains in the 1890s. Chestnut-sided Warblers are more common and widely distributed now than before the advent of logging and the chestnut blight. American Woodcock have used the numerous openings created by deforestation as sites for their aerial courtship displays. Barn Swallows appear far more common and widespread than at the beginning of the twentieth century. European Starlings arrived in the mountains during the 1920s, after becoming established in the surrounding Piedmont, and Brown-headed Cowbirds have steadily increased throughout the region, as have House Wrens, following their influx in the 1930s. Prior to clearing of forests in the East, Horned Larks bred only on the prairies and tundra of western and central North America, but by the 1930s, the species had become established as a nester in pasturelands of the Blue Ridge.

From the 1960s to the late 1980s, many "northern" birds were noted as summer residents in areas where they had not been detected previously. Swainson's Thrushes became established at Mount Rogers and were subsequently joined by Hermit Thrushes, which also expanded their summer range to Roan, Grandfather, the Blacks, and the Great Smokies. Yellow-bellied Flycatchers nested at Mount Rogers in the 1970s and early 1980s, during which time Alder and Willow Flycatchers were found in increasing numbers and at new localities through much of the southern mountains. Tree Swallows have recently moved south, using natural cavities as well as bluebird boxes for nesting sites. Peregrine Falcons have been reintroduced, and Golden Eagles are again noted occasionally in winter. Purple Finches have become well established at Mount Rogers and are sometimes found at Grandfather and Roan in summer. House Finches have been nesting in the Blue Ridge since the 1970s and seem almost certain to invade settled areas throughout the region. Wild Turkeys have increased conspicuously in recent years, and attempts to reintroduce the Peregrine Falcon as a nesting species have shown encouraging results.

Continued change seems inevitable. Alterations over the past hundred years may seem mild in comparison with what could take place between now and the end of the twenty-first century.

BIRD-WATCHING IN
THE BLUE RIDGE

Bird-watching Basics

The rapidly growing popularity of bird study is not surprising. Increased environmental awareness and a renewed interest in physical fitness have prompted many to widen their range of outdoor activities. Birding can be enjoyed by the entire family, and you don't have to spend a small fortune on equipment to participate. An excellent introduction to basic bird-watching skills and equipment is provided by Connor's *The Complete Birder*.

Binoculars are a good investment, but the bewildering array of models and prices can be confusing. For birding in the mountains, light-gathering capacity is generally more important than magnification, because much of your time will be spent gazing into dense vegetation at relatively close range along wooded trails. Thus 40- or 50-mm objective lenses are generally preferable to 35-mm lenses. Magnifications of 7-, 8-, and 10-power are typically available in combination with these different objectives.

Select only models with a single center-focus knob and with one separately adjustable ocular to allow you to adjust for your own visual idiosyncrasies. Test the center focus knob to see how quickly it responds; if the knob action is stiff and sluggish, the bird may be gone before you get the binoculars in focus! And compare carefully for weight—some models begin to feel like the proverbial millstone after a day's hiking in the backcountry.

If you are concentrating on autumn hawk migration, you may prefer to emphasize magnification over light gathering, in which case 10-power binoculars could be the best choice. In addition, you might consider a 20-power spotting scope, mounted on a gunstock, shoulder brace, or fast-action tripod for stability. Regardless of your choice of optics, wearing a cap or hat with a brim will help reduce the glare between your eyes and the ocular lens. The brim will also help keep rain and mist off your glasses.

A good field guide is a must. Roger Tory Peterson's *A Field Guide to the Birds*, for eastern and central North America, is among the most popular and also is the easiest to fit into a small pack or even your jacket pocket. *A Guide to Field Identification of Birds of North America*, by Robbins, Brunn, and Zim, is also popular. The National Geographic Society's *Field Guide to the Birds of North America* and the Audubon Society's three-volume *Master Guide to Birding* are also excellent. Many birders prefer to own more than one guide, as the books often supplement each other with different text and color plates. With a group hike, it is easy to bring along a veritable library of field guides by having each participant carry a different book.

Perhaps of equal importance for Blue Ridge birding is a guide to bird songs. Again, many tape and record sets are available, including those designed to accompany the Peterson field-guide series—*A Field Guide to Bird Songs of Eastern and Central North America*—and the National Geographic Society's *Guide to Bird Sounds*. Specialty tapes of warblers, owls, and other bird groups are also marketed by various publishers and organizations.

If you are unfamiliar with the songs of birds that you wish to see, then spend some time reading song descriptions in guidebooks and listening carefully to recordings of particular species before you head into the field. Owing to the often dense vegetation and steep terrain in the mountains, considerable effort is required to get a good look at many birds. Most veteran birders rely on song recognition for at least 90 percent of their identifications when surveying breeding birds in a mountain forest. Unless you can recognize species by their sounds, you will spend a lot of time and energy trying to see what turns out to be the "wrong" bird, while something you need for your life list goes unnoticed.

To lure birds out of thickets and canopies, some birders carry along a tape recorder with cassettes of the songs and call notes from species of particular interest. Playing the bird's song, especially near its territory during the breeding season, may cause the bird to come in quite close to the observer. On other occasions, it may provoke a silent and unseen bird into an outburst of song and activity, thereby making its detection and identification easier.

There are problems with recorders, however. Many biologists are opposed to the indiscriminate use of tape players in the field, especially around rare species or birds that are near the extreme limits of their distribution.

Heavy use of recorders can disrupt the nesting cycle: the disappearance of Yellow-bellied Flycatchers at Mount Rogers and of Swainson's Warblers at several spots on the Maryland coastal plain has been attributed to birders' excessive use of tapes. Because many birds are already under considerable environmental pressure, the ecologically sensitive choice would be to leave tape players at home. In some parks and public lands, moreover, their use is regarded as a form of wildlife harassment and is strictly prohibited. Probably their most legitimate use is in surveying for common owls, but even here the activity should be conducted with awareness of each species' nesting cycle so as to minimize risks to the young. And as a practical matter, it may be cumbersome and tiring to carry a recorder and tapes on a hike.

A much easier and apparently less destructive approach to bird luring is the use of "squeaking" or "pishing." Many songbirds will come in quite close to see what the fuss is all about. Try making high-pitched squeaks and long kissing sounds by vigorously sucking the back side of your hand. Some people can simply purse their lips and kiss the air to achieve the same effect. "Pishing" is a hissing noise made by exhaling over tightly clenched teeth while rapidly opening and closing your lips—the sound is rather like the scolding notes of a wren. Some birds, such as Carolina Wren, Canada Warbler, and Ovenbird, are unable to resist this racket and may get so close that you can't use your binoculars. Other birds, such as chickadees, Tufted Titmouse, Black-throated Blue Warbler, and Chestnut-sided Warbler, will often come in long enough for you to get a good look. Inexplicably, some species, such as Black-and-white, Hooded, and Black-throated Green Warblers, seem just as likely to ignore the noise or even to stop singing and move farther back into the woods.

For best results, bird-watching must be adjusted to birds' behavior. During the nesting season of late spring and summer, songbirds and most other forest species are at their peak activity in the first three hours immediately after sunrise and then again for about two hours just before sunset. Some species are more likely than others to remain active all day—Red-eyed Vireos and Indigo Buntings never seem to run out of energy—but most birds are relatively quiet during the heat of the day. Birds also may become active for a brief spell just after a rain shower has passed. Bird activity at other seasons tends to be a bit more uniformly spread over the course of the day, although the peak still usually occurs before 10 A.M.

The annual cycle for most species begins with the return of the first spring migrants, usually in the last two weeks of March, when such birds as Winter Wren, American Robin, Gray Catbird, Solitary Vireo, and Black-and-white Warbler wander back to the high country from their winter ranges in the valleys, Piedmont, and Coastal Plain of the southeastern United States. Permanent-resident birds are usually active by then as well, with Carolina Chickadees, Tufted Titmice, Northern Cardinals, Rufous-sided Towhees, and Song Sparrows all in a stir.

The bulk of spring migration occurs from around early April through early June, as birds that overwinter in the tropics and in the southeastern United States arrive in the Blue Ridge to nest or pass through on their way to more northern regions. The greatest number of species and individual birds is usually found in the mountains from late April through late May. Most spring migrants tend to stay in the valleys and along low- to middle-elevation ridges, probably because of the relative scarcity of food and lack of foliage at higher elevations. In general, the largest concentrations occur just after a northward-moving warm air mass collides with a southward-pushing cold front.

The peak intensity of territorial and nesting activity occurs from mid-May through early July. This is the time when most birders like to visit the mountains, as birds are generally easiest to see and are found in habitats and localities where they are "supposed to be." This is also a good time for laurel, azaleas, and rhododendrons, as well as many wildflowers—making a visit to the mountains particularly satisfying. Information in this book on bird finding (Sections 3 through 5) focuses primarily on the nesting season from late May through early summer.

By mid-July, singing activity for most species has declined notably, and many birds are suddenly hard to find. With completion of nesting activities, some birds begin to disperse and wander into habitats and elevations well beyond those selected for breeding territory. In the lowlands, a few wading birds also arrive by late July, having dispersed inland from their coastal nesting grounds.

August is probably the dullest birding month of the year in the mountains, but September and October bring a surge of migrants heading south for winter. The heaviest concentrations of migrating songbirds usually occur in the higher elevations for a couple of days after the passage of a cold front. The concentrated movement of Broad-winged Hawks in mid-September is followed by a more dispersed flow of other raptors that continues into early December. Most nonresident songbirds have abandoned the high country long before Thanksgiving, and the first snows usually find only permanent and winter residents.

The austere beauty of the mountain winter provides a backdrop for viewing not only hardy resident birds but also many northern species, including Golden Eagles, Northern Harriers, and winter finches such as Red Crossbills, Evening Grosbeaks, and Snow Buntings. Great Horned Owls may begin their nesting cycle even before the New Year. While March snows still linger in the high country, Northern Saw-whet Owls and American Woodcocks proclaim the coming spring long before the first delicate green leaves herald the returning migrants.

Hiking and Backcountry Bird-watching

Many visitors to the high country want to get into the woods for a better look at the bird and plant life. Not only will a backcountry hike enhance your appreciation of the mountains, but it may also be the quickest, or only, way to find certain species. Compared with most birding trails on the coast or Piedmont, however, hiking routes in the mountains are generally more of a physical challenge and require more attention to planning and proper equipment. Even if you are only going for a short walk, there are some basics to consider. Because the primary goal is enjoying the birds, remember to keep things simple and the equipment light. The following suggestions are based on many years' experience in leading hikes with birders who didn't come prepared, thereby spoiling the outing not only for themselves but also for their companions as well.

Proper footgear is a crucial but highly individual matter. A huge selection of boots and hiking shoes is available. There are only a few rules to remember: know what kind of hiking you plan to do and concentrate on what feels comfortable. Most birding walks involve easy to moderate half-day hikes, in which case something lightweight may be fine. For wilderness camping, steep climbing, all-day hikes, or rough terrain, heavier shoes or even boots may be needed. When fitting the shoe, wear the same socks that will be worn on the hike. If you are wearing flimsy nylon socks or stockings when choosing footgear, you may discover that what felt pleasantly snug at the store has been transformed into a torture device when worn with thick socks. If the shoes need a breaking-in period, do it before the first hike. Many of the new materials require little or no break-in, but give your feet at least some time to adjust. And don't plan to wear dress shoes or tennis shoes for anything longer than a ten-minute stroll!

Socks are also a matter of individual preference. Some hikers choose thick wool socks. Many prefer the new thick polypropylene socks, which not only help keep the feet dry by wicking away the perspiration but also are thick and soft enough to protect against the friction and impact trauma that contribute to blisters. Others like the "double-sock" technique, using a thin liner sock, made of cotton or polypropylene, and an outer sock, usually wool.

If the trail guide or map suggests that you may have to ford a wide or deep stream, then put at least one light bath towel in the pack, along with a two-foot-square piece of thick plastic sheeting or a plastic garbage bag. Then you can take your shoes and socks off, wade through the water, put the plastic down on the opposite bank to keep your pants from getting muddy when you sit down, and dry off your feet before putting them back into those nice dry socks and shoes!

Keeping your feet dry is one of the most important things to do to avoid blisters. Socks are very light and take little space in a pack, so consider taking along one or even two extra pairs, carefully sealed in waterproof plastic sandwich bags. If your feet get soaked from rain, sweat, dew, streams, or standing water, you can change socks and try to wipe most of the excess water out of the inside of the boots or shoes before resuming the hike.

In selecting clothing for a hike, the obvious considerations involve temperature and precipitation. For comfort and safety, the single most important rule in hiking the southern Appalachians is that you should always take adequate rain gear. Getting drenched is not just unpleasant; it can be fatal in the high country. Even in midsummer, hypothermia, or "exposure," remains among the most common causes of death for hikers in the mountains. Getting soaked to the skin in a cold, windy rainstorm may be more than your metabolism can fight. Never mind that the sky is clear when you start—always carry a poncho or some other protection.

The new ripstop nylon and Gore-Tex materials are lightweight and breathable. Many ponchos can be folded almost as small as a wallet, so you can stick one in your hip pocket even if you aren't using a pack. Some hikers prefer fitted rain gear, which is not as likely to flap around in the wind or snag on twigs and briars. Avoid impermeable materials, however, as you may get as wet from your own trapped perspiration as from the rain. There is one final benefit from rain gear: because you can stay dry, you won't be as tempted to sit under a tree to avoid getting wet in a storm, thereby making yourself a potential victim of lightning.

The rest of your wardrobe should be based on the layer principle. Instead of wearing one light shirt and one heavy jacket, get a cotton T-shirt, a wool or synthetic long-sleeved shirt, a sweater, and a jacket or windbreaker. That way you can dress up or down in response to changes in temperature, wind, and precipitation. In summer, consider taking both shorts and long pants, starting with whichever is more comfortable and changing with the weather. In winter, you may want to include insulated underwear and even more layers, as well as ski gloves and a wool or synthetic ski mask or balaclava. A light hat or cap with a brim can help reduce glare when looking through binoculars and may even help keep a heavy drizzle off your glasses.

The choice of a pack will depend on how much paraphernalia you plan to haul. Most day hikes are well served with one of the various sizes of fanny packs, some of which are quite roomy. Large versions have padding to protect your back and can accommodate clothes, food, camera, maps, water bottle, field guides, and first-aid items. Some hikers use a regular shoulder-strap backpack, which unfortunately causes significant shoulder fatigue for many people and has a tendency to snag branches and limbs in areas of thick vegetation. Fanny packs have an additional advantage for birders of being very easy to remove for quick access to field guides, maps, and notebooks. In fact, many birders wear the fanny pack on their stomachs, so they can get at what they need without even breaking their stride!

Selection of food depends mostly on your personal tastes and the duration of the jaunt. For a day hike, it is smart to include items that provide sugar, fat, and protein. Beef jerky sticks, slices of cheddar cheese, nuts, fruits, and hard candy are good. Avoid anything greasy, and bring some antacid tablets just in case! A popular and well-balanced hiking menu can include "GORP," short for "Good Old Raisins and Peanuts." You can custom design your own version. One recommended mixture is 8 to 12 ounces of unsalted dry-roasted peanuts with 8 to 12 ounces each of raisins, semisweet or milk chocolate chips, and peanut butter chips. Divide the final product into plastic zip-sealing bags, which can be refrigerated until ready for use. For an all-day hike, GORP provides fat, protein, and plenty of carbohydrates. Soft fruits, sandwiches, potato chips, and some crackers tend to get smashed unless placed in the top of a regular backpack; and milk chocolate bars often melt down in summer, so you may prefer to avoid such fare.

Not many years ago, there were still safe and delicious freshwater springs in the mountains. Most are now unfit, even with "purification" tablets, and the water must be boiled first. Carry plenty of tap water, therefore, and don't wait until you feel thirsty to drink. Canteens and plastic water bottles come in all shapes and sizes, but you might prefer a "wine-skin" version, which is soft, pliable, and collapsible. These are a lot more comfortable than having the corner of a canteen kicking you in the back with every step.

Other items to consider include a compass and local topographic and trail maps, particularly if you are hiking an area that is remote or that has lots of trails. Detailed trail guidebooks are available for many areas. Notebooks, field guides, and pen or pencil can be well protected from rain and perspiration by carrying them in a plastic zip-sealing bag.

A small first-aid kit is all right, but don't overdo it. For management of blisters, bring some pieces of moleskin and a pair of small scissors to cut it into the right shape to protect damaged areas. Bring a needle and tweezers for extracting splinters, small thorns, and ticks. Throw in a few shapes and sizes of adhesive bandages or maybe even a sterile pad and small roll of tape. A small vial of iodine may be helpful to clean off cuts or abrasions. Insect repellent is seldom needed in the southern Appalachians, but a small bottle of sunscreen may be helpful.

If you are allergic to insect stings, get a "kit" from your doctor or pharmacy and read the instructions before heading into the woods. Carrying a "snakebite kit" is not generally recommended, but some people feel compelled to do so. A small to medium flashlight with recently tested batteries is a good idea, particularly if you hike alone and might need to attract attention at night because of an injury. An elastic bandage may help stabilize a sprained or twisted ankle or knee joint.

And don't forget to bring along some common sense. Know your physical limitations, and don't push yourself. If you haven't had much exercise recently, at least try walking a mile or two around your neighborhood on several days preceding the hike.

The above suggestions will get you through an average day hike for birding. If you plan overnight hiking or extensive backpacking and camping, then refer to one of the many useful books on the subject. Check the mail-order catalogs or visit a sporting-goods store or an outfitter to examine a selection of books and equipment.

In addition to the problem of hypothermia, there are some other health and safety issues. Most birders prefer to hike with friends, but if you insist on going alone, be sure to let a responsible adult know exactly where you are and what time you plan to check in with him or her upon returning. Don't put a note with this information in the window of your car, unless you want to collect insurance for vandalism or theft. Don't laugh—this happens more often than you might believe!

Many hikers worry about venomous snakes, and it is smart to be alert and avoid risky spots, such as rocky outcroppings, dense underbrush, wood piles, downed trees, and any place that you cannot see where you are stepping or placing your hand. Read up on care for snakebites if you want to, but in forty years and thousands of miles hiking the Blue Ridge, I have found poisonous snakes on a trail on only two occasions. Many seasoned hikers have never seen or heard even one.

You may occasionally encounter a black bear on one of your hikes. Unless cornered or injured, the males are usually frightened by people and will run away as fast as possible. A female with cubs is another story. If you come up on a bear, freeze immediately and calmly look around to see if there is any evidence of cubs nearby. If so, try to move quietly and quickly away from them, taking particular care not to get between the cubs and the adult or to make any sudden movements or loud noises. Any adult that sees you and does not turn and run should be considered hostile and dangerous—probably a mom with cubs. Unless you are a very stealthy walker, however, most bears will detect you in time to disappear without your being aware they were watching.

Rabies continues to be a problem in the eastern United States. Skunks and raccoons are among the most common victims. Around campgrounds and picnic areas, healthy animals may be rather tame; but along a backcountry trail, most wild animals are normally shy and retiring. If any animal behaves erratically or aggressively, assume the worst and get away as fast as possible. Then report the details to a ranger.

When you come in from a day hike, it is advisable to check yourself or have someone help check you for ticks. The big, easy-to-see kinds may carry Rocky Mountain spotted fever. Lyme disease, a chronic and often debilitating illness, is usually spread by a very small tick, which looks like a tiny freckle or mole. Use fine tweezers to remove the pests, taking care not to crush them or to leave the head buried in your skin. If in doubt, put the tick in a vial of alcohol and take it in for identification. Rash, fever, headache, fatigue, joint and muscle aches, neurological problems, mental changes, or general malaise should prompt an immediate visit to your physician.

Several precautions are recommended to minimize the risk of being bitten by ticks when hiking in grassy, brushy, or woodland areas. Tuck your pant legs into your socks and keep your shirt tucked into your pants; this will keep ticks on the outside, where they can be more easily spotted and removed. Wear light-colored clothes, which makes it easier to see the dark ticks, and inspect your clothing frequently. Use tick repellents, applied according to the label instructions on shoes, socks, cuffs, and pant legs.

There are more trails in the Appalachians than most people could cover in a lifetime of walking. In the Blue Ridge Province, many of the best routes for birding are also among the most scenic and botanically diversi-fied trails in the region. This happy combination enhances the satisfaction you may find in hiking trails along the Parkway and in nearby state and national parks and national forests.

The following list indicates some of the best trails for easy to mod-erate birding hikes, ranging from an hour up to half a day in duration. Most of these routes are suitable even if you are not in very good physical condition, as long as you use common sense and don't try to rush. Each trail varies in length, strenuousness, and habitat. Refer to the appropriate site guides for specific information. Many of these trails are described in detail by Adkins in *Walking the Blue Ridge*, by de Hart in *Hiking the Old Dominion* and *North Carolina Hiking Trails*, or in other trail guides listed in References and Suggested Reading.

In Shenandoah National Park, Laurel Prong Trail and Limberlost Trail are highly recommended for spring and summer birds of oak and hem-lock forests, respectively. Elk Run Trail and Johnson Farm Trail at Peaks of Otter are good for woodland and field species. South of Roanoke, the Smart View Loop Trail and the Rocky Knob Picnic Ground Loop Trail are excellent for woodland summer residents. At Doughton Park, the Fodder Stack Trail is popular, and Cedar Ridge Trail and Grassy Gap Fire Road are only moderately strenuous if hiked downhill, passing through oak and cove hardwoods, respectively. Trout Lake Trail at Cone Park and Sim's Creek at nearby Price Park are nestled in beautiful hemlock-cove forests;

Cone's Bass Lake Trail and Price Park's Price Lake loop trail are easy and popular routes for a variety of habitats and birds.

At Grandfather Mountain, the Tanawha Trail climbs through an extensive heath bald across Rough Ridge, and the Black Rock Trail runs through spruce and northern hardwoods. Nearby Linville Gorge can be sampled from Erwin's View Trail or from the first mile of Babel Tower Trail. Farther south, the old Perley Toll Road and adjacent parkway shoulder from Bald Knob Ridge trailhead are easy routes for spruce-fir and northern hardwood birds. At nearby Mount Mitchell State Park, the Commissary Shelter Road from Stepps Gap is a delightful and fairly easy walk through spruce woods and heath thickets. Although steep in spots, the Mountains-to-Sea Trail south from Balsam Gap into the Craggies provides both scenic views and good access to spruce and northern hardwood birds. Craggy Gardens Trail is renowned for the spectacular Catawba rhododendron display and birds typical of heath and hardwood communities.

Around the Mount Pisgah area, excellent birding in northern hardwoods, oak orchard forests, rhododendron balds, and some hemlock stands can be found at Laurel Mountain Trail, Buck Spring Gap Loop Trail, and Fryingpan Gap Trail. Farther south, Graveyard Fields Trail and Ivestor Gap Trail to Shining Rock provide a diversity of habitats seldom encountered elsewhere along the Parkway. Devil's Courthouse Trail is steep, but the views from the summit are good for autumn hawks and the route is among the best in the area for spruce-fir residents. The Mountains-to-Sea Trail from Buckeye Gap to Bearpen Gap is excellent for many elusive spruce-fir and northern hardwood species.

In the Northern Great Balsams, the Balsam Mountain Nature Trail and the shoulder of the Heintooga Spur Road north of the campground are excellent for spruce-fir birds. Low- and middle-elevation forest birds can be sampled along Laurel Falls Trail in the Great Smoky Mountains National Park, where Alum Cave Bluffs Trail is strenuous in parts but worth the effort for spruce-fir birds and scenery.

At the northern extremity of the Blue Ridge Province, easy hiking trails at Kings Gap Environmental Education and Training Center traverse a variety of habitats, including the only site in the province where Long-eared Owls have been known to nest.

Near Mount Rogers, the Rhododendron Gap Trail from Grayson Highlands State Park traverses grass balds on its way to a rhododendron-spruce bog, with connections along the Appalachian Trail to the summit of Mount Rogers. At Roan Mountain, the Balsam Road provides solitude, an easy walk, and good views of spruce-fir birds. Moderately strenuous in spots, the Appalachian Trail north from Carver's Gap to Grassy Ridge Bald is interesting in summer and winter for residents of high-elevation grass balds. At Chimney Rock Park, the Forest Stroll Self-guided Nature Trail is a short but diversified bird walk. Raven Cliff Falls Trail at Mountain Bridge Wilderness and Recreation Area is well known for spring migration and oak-forest nesting birds. To see Swainson's Warblers and many other summer breeders, try the trail along the Chattooga River and East Fork Chattooga between the Walhalla National Fish Hatchery and Burrell's Ford, as well as sections of the Foothills Trail near the Toxaway River. In the Nantahala Mountains, good hikes include Pickens Nose Trail and sections of the Appalachian Trail north and south of Deep Gap and Mooney Gap. In north Georgia, the Arkaquah National Recreation Trail from the summit of Brasstown Bald is good for middle- and high-elevation summer species.

Birding for the Handicapped and Physically Impaired

Everyone has special interests, needs, and limitations when it comes to physical activity. Fortunately, many sites on the Parkway and in the adjacent public recreation areas offer enjoyable bird-watching for persons with significant physical impairments, as well as for those who lack the time or inclination for hiking mountain trails. In fact, with planning, patience, and a little bit of luck, you can hear or see just about every species from a car or wheelchair that could be found by hiking into the backcountry.

Many places are suitable for wheelchair use or for birding from a parked car. The numerous roadside overlooks are good spots, especially when surrounded by woods on a steep slope, which permits an easy angle for looking directly into the canopy below the site. Most overlooks are paved, wide, flat, and fairly level. Some are bordered by a curbed sidewalk that is also suitable for wheelchairs. Paved loop roads through many picnic areas and campgrounds provide some excellent birding sites from a wheelchair or parked car. When using a wheelchair, however, be especially alert for careless drivers in overlook parking lots and on the loop roads, and stay off the main roadways. With the availability of wheelchairs designed for trail use, even previously inaccessible routes are now a possibility, so check out spots whose descriptions sound promising even if they are not specifically recommended in this book.

Roadside birding is an alternative, but safety often becomes an issue. In general, the best routes are U.S. Forest Service gravel or dirt side roads that ramble through the backcountry woodlands. There are a number of spots on the Parkway where you can get completely off the pavement onto the shoulder, but the Park Service generally discourages this practice because of the hazard of passing traffic, the chance of getting stuck, and the damage done by tires. Regardless of which routes you choose, do not try to bird-watch from a moving vehicle. Always get completely out of the roadway, come to a full stop, put the car in park, and engage the hand brake.

The following is a list of places and routes that are good bird-watching sites for persons with physical limitations and handicaps, as well as for people who are not interested in hiking. Because the suitability and ease of access vary considerably, you should read the site descriptions in Sections 3 through 5 of the book before planning a visit.

Among the best overlooks in Shenandoah National Park are Hemlock Springs OL for spring and summer forest birds and Point OL, Stony Man Mountain OL, and Calf Mountain OL for autumn hawk migration. Most campgrounds and picnic areas at the Shenandoah park are also good for car or wheelchair birding.

At the Blue Ridge Parkway's north end, Rockfish Gap is the primary spot for autumn hawks, and nearby VA 610 is good for roadside birding for spring migration and summer warblers. Wheelchair access to the Pioneer Farm near Humpback Rocks sometimes provides views of American Woodcock and Wild Turkey, and Humpback Rocks parking lot and picnic grounds permit access to spring and summer oak forest birds from wheelchair or car. Bald Mountain at Big Levels is not bad for views from the car, and Otter Creek campground and overlooks along Otter Creek are suitable for watching from wheelchair or auto. At James River Visitor Center, the paved path to the footbridge is steep but wheelchair accessible for looks at many birds seldom found elsewhere along the Parkway.

Farther south, Warbler Road is perhaps the best roadside birding in the southern mountains during spring migration and summer, and you can watch for Wild Turkey from the car at Floyd Fields. At nearby Peaks of Otter picnic ground and Flat Top Trail parking lot, wheelchair and auto access are good for spring and summer birds of middle-elevation forests, whereas Harvey's Knob OL is a prime site for autumn hawk migration. To see shorebirds, waterfowl, and gulls, take the side excursion off the Parkway to the Roanoke Sewage Treatment Plant.

Between Roanoke and the North Carolina line, Smart View picnic grounds is good for wheelchair- or car-based looks at oak-forest summer residents, and VA 860 is an interesting route for roadside viewing of cove hardwood species. The Rocky Knob picnic grounds and Rocky Knob campground are also suitable for birding from wheelchair or car.

In North Carolina, Mahogany Rock OL is a favored place to watch the autumn hawk migration from your car. Prime spots to listen for owls include most Parkway overlooks at Doughton Park. Many uncommon and local summer residents, such as Warbling Vireo and Northern Oriole, can be viewed from your car along NC SR 1549 as it follows the South Fork of the New River. South of Lewis Fork OL, roadside birding can yield Cerulean Warblers in summer. At Julian Price Park, Boone Fork Trail from the picnic grounds is sometimes dry enough for wheelchair access to the wetlands for Alder Flycatcher. A portion of the Tanawha Trail north from the Linn Cove Visitor Center is accessible by wheelchair and a beautiful spot for summer residents of spruce and northern hardwoods.

Farther south on the Parkway, the Linville Falls Visitor Center parking lot, picnic grounds, and campground yield a large variety of summer birds from either the car or wheelchair, as does Crabtree Meadows campground. The elusive Swainson's Warbler is among the interesting species that may be heard from your car along Curtis Creek Road; FSR 2074 and FSR 472 on the opposite side of the ridge provide good roadside birding down to Black Mountain Recreation Area and campground.

High-elevation spruce-fir forest birds are found at Stepps Gap parking area and in the parking lots at the restaurant and summit in Mount Mitchell State Park. In the Great Craggy Mountains, Craggy Dome parking lot and Craggy Gardens parking lot are suitable for wheelchair or car views of rhododendron and northern hardwood species. Nearby Bull Creek OL is a prime spot for Cerulean Warblers.

In the French Broad River valley, Lake Julian Park yields some low-country species and water birds from your car. Nearby Bent Creek Recreation Area and Sandy Bottom Recreation Area are good spots for birds associated with the floodplain forest along the French Broad River. When not too muddy, the area may be suitable for wheelchairs.

At the Pisgah area, the Mount Pisgah parking lot and the Pisgah Inn parking lot are good spots for wheelchairs and birding from the car to see summer residents of middle- to high-elevation hardwood forests. The Mount Pisgah campground is an outstanding site for wheelchair birding in rhododendron thickets and mixtures of spruce and northern hardwoods. Leaving the Parkway toward Brevard on US 276 south, the Headwaters Road leads to a spot for viewing a Peregrine Falcon nesting site, and the nearby Davidson River campground and Sycamore Flats picnic area provide a network of flat loop roads for birding in woodlands along the Davidson River.

Farther south on the Parkway, Graveyard Fields OL yields a good look from cars or wheelchairs into the top of rhododendron and hardwood thickets, and FSR 816 at Black Balsam Knob has many of the same birds found at Graveyard Fields, as well as nesting Alder Flycatchers and wintering raptors. Nearby Devil's Courthouse OL, Courthouse Valley OL, Richland Balsam OL, and Lone Bald OL are prime spots to hear Northern Saw-whet Owls and other spruce-fir and northern hardwood birds. At Roy Taylor OL you can take a wheelchair out onto a wooden platform in the canopy of a spruce-hardwood stand.

In the Plott Balsam Mountains and Northern Great Balsam Mountains, birding from the car is good at most overlooks, including Waterrock Knob parking lot, which is suitable for wheelchairs and good for spruce-fir species. Black-capped Chickadees are among the birds noted on the Heintooga Spur Road at the Heintooga picnic area parking lot and Balsam Mountain campground, which are suitable for wheelchairs. Also on the spur road, Wolf Laurel Gap is good from the car and Black Camp Gap has a wheelchair-accessible trail that leads to Least Flycatchers in summer. The Round Bottom Road begins at the end of Heintooga Spur Road and provides outstanding birding from the car as it descends to the Oconaluftee River valley.

In the Great Smoky Mountains National Park, paved trails around Oconaluftee Visitor Center are good for wheelchair access to riverside and field birds. Spruce-fir species can be seen from wheelchair or car at Newfound Gap. Birding from the car is possible on Clingman's Dome Road, Roaring Fork Motor Nature Road, and Cades Cove Loop Road, with wheelchair birding possible in some spots at the last site. Another place with good access is Sugarlands Nature Trail at park headquarters at Gatlinburg.

At the extreme north end of the Blue Ridge Province, Ridge Road in Pennsylvania's Michaux State Forest provides roadside birding through a unique region of pine-oak scrub barrens. At nearby Kings Gap Environmental Education and Training Center, paved trails are specifically designed for wheelchairs, including the Whispering Pines Trail, which provides a potential spot to see Long-eared Owl. In northern Maryland, the Cunningham Falls Trail at Catoctin Mountain Park is wheelchair accessible.

In the Mount Rogers area, a prime spot is FSR 89 on Whitetop Mountain, where you can drive into a spruce-fir forest that may have Northern Saw-whet Owls and other coniferous species. Grindstone campground is great for birding from cars or wheelchairs; listen especially for Least Flycatcher. The parking lot at the summit visitor center and loop roads at the picnic area and campgrounds at nearby Grayson Highlands State Park are excellent for both wheelchair and car birding. Magnolia Warblers and Black-capped Chickadees are possible at the summit lot.

Some roadside birding is possible from Carver's Gap parking lot and from parking lots and the loop road at Roan Mountain, but the best spot is Roan Mountain Gardens Loop Trail, a paved route specifically designed for wheelchair use through a beautiful heath-spruce garden.

In the southern end of the Blue Ridge Province, excellent roadside birding from the car is possible on FSR 67, FSR 69, and FSR 711 in the Nantahala Mountains. At Cliffside Lake Recreation Area on the Highlands Plateau, portions of the roadway are good for birding from the car, particularly around the camping area. Swainson's Warblers can be heard and sometimes seen from the car on Bull Pen Road, along the road to Walhalla National Fish Hatchery, and near Eastatoe Creek in the southeastern Blue Ridge escarpment gorges. Blue-winged Warblers can sometimes be heard and seen from the car along NC SRS 1150 and 1556 near Murphy, N.C. The autumn hawk migration may be viewed from a wheelchair at the overlook adjacent to Chimney Rock Park. In the Unicoi Mountains, the Maple Springs Observation Area has a paved, wheelchair-accessible trail for excellent looks at middle-elevation forest birds; and the combination of FSR 81 and Tellico Plains–Robbinsville Scenic Highway provides roadside birding through a spectrum of mountain habitats. In northern Georgia, good roadside birding is possible from FSR 4 and also from wheelchairs in the parking lot and summit at Brasstown Bald.

The Park Service and Forest Service are working to make their facilities more accessible for persons with physical handicaps. Contact the various headquarters offices listed in Resources for current updates on areas you want to visit.

Hot Spots and Highlights

The "hot spot" has become a sacred notion in birding. Everyone seems interested in finding the greatest variety and largest number of birds with the least amount of effort or travel. Along the coast, large concentrations of birds may accumulate at localized feeding or resting spots, nesting colonies, or migration "funnels," so that a visit can be planned to a particular place with anticipation of great results.

This tactic does not work very well in the Blue Ridge. Except for the autumn hawk migration and an occasional spring "warbler wave," big flocks are seldom encountered in the mountains. Songbirds and forest species tend to be more widely and uniformly dispersed than coastal species during the nesting season, in migration, and in winter. Many of the less-common species are limited to widely separated localities, and the region's geography and highways do not lend themselves to the frantic "big day" mentality.

Nevertheless, a select number of birding spots in the Blue Ridge possess some outstanding feature worthy of special notice. Some areas have an unusually large variety of birds; others are good sites for certain rare or localized species. A particular site may be the best example of a given habitat, such as spruce-fir forest or rhododendron bald. Best of all are those places with that magic blend of beautiful scenery, interesting botany, a rich and diverse bird population, easy access, and just enough solitude so that all thoughts and feelings vanish except for the joy of the present moment.

Although the choices are admittedly subjective, the following list enumerates those sites that I believe can be considered the quintessential birding spots in the area covered by this book. For the particular details, refer to the site guides in Sections 3 through 5.

In Shenandoah National Park, South River Falls Trail is renowned for spring songbird migration and summer birds of middle-elevation forests. At the Parkway's north end, Rockfish Gap provides one of the best spots in the eastern United States to watch the autumn hawk migration. Along the

James River, the Canal Locks Trail offers three species of nesting swallows, low-country woodland and field birds, and riparian species, plus a variety of transients during much of the year. Many consider Warbler Road to be the best roadside birding in the Blue Ridge Province, not only for spring migration but also for the diversity of summer birds, the latter resulting from the cross-sectional range of elevations and habitats sampled. Farther south, Rock Castle Gorge National Recreation Trail combines backcountry hiking with good looks at spring and summer birds of oak and cove hardwood forests.

Northern Oriole and Warbling Vireo are among the interesting summer species found by roadside birding on NC SR 1549, which parallels the scenic South Fork of the New River in North Carolina. Trout Lake Trail at Cone Park and nearby Sim's Creek at Price Park pass through some of the best examples of old-growth hemlock cove forest in the Blue Ridge Mountains—prime habitat for many birds typical of middle and high elevations. The Parkway's Tanawha Trail combines scenery, botany, and birding on a superbly engineered route on Grandfather Mountain, loftiest peak on the Blue Ridge front.

In the Black Mountains, Commissary Shelter Road is a fairly easy stroll along a scenic route that is excellent for summer residents of rhododendron thickets, spruce-fir, and northern hardwoods. Many of the same birds can be found along the Mountains-to-Sea Trail between Balsam Gap and Stepps Gap, although the route is considerably more rugged and the vegetation more mature. Fine scenery, distinctive plant communities, and good birding are possible on segments of the Mountains-to-Sea Trail south from Balsam Gap through the Great Craggy Mountains to Beetree Gap.

Near Mount Pisgah, Buck Spring Gap Loop Trail and adjacent hikes offer a diversified summer avifauna associated with northern hardwood forests, heath thickets, and hemlock stands. A quick side trip to Headwaters Road from March through late summer provides a chance to see nesting Peregrine Falcons at Looking Glass Rock. Farther south on the Parkway, Ivestor Gap Trail to Shining Rock is an easy hike through a complex mosaic of high-elevation plant communities that resulted from logging and wildfire destruction of the original spruce-fir forests. At nearby Devil's Courthouse, the conifers escaped the fire, leaving a good spot for spruce-fir birds, particularly the Northern Saw-whet Owl. In the Great Balsam Mountains, the stretch of Mountains-to-Sea Trail between Buckeye Gap and Bearpen Gap traverses grass balds, spruce-fir woods, and northern hardwoods for many elusive high-elevation summer residents, such as Black-billed Cuckoo.

In the Great Smoky Mountains, Alum Cave Bluffs Trail to Mount LeConte is a botanic and scenic delight, as well as the best spot in the southern mountains for Olive-sided Flycatchers. The drive along Clingman's Dome Road provides easy access to spruce-fir and northern hardwood birds such as Northern Saw-whet Owl and Black-capped Chickadee.

Many excellent sites require trips more than 15 miles from the Parkway. At the extreme north end of the Blue Ridge, Pennsylvania's South Mountain area contains unique pine-oak scrub barrens along Ridge Road—the only spot in the province where Nashville Warblers nest. On the northwest edge of South Mountain, Kings Gap Environmental Education and Training Center is the only confirmed breeding site for Long-eared Owl in the Blue Ridge, and nearby Huntsdale Fish Hatchery is the only spot for summering Virginia Rail, Black-crowned Night-Heron, and Swamp Sparrow.

Near Harpers Ferry, W.Va., the Chesapeake and Ohio Canal provides a beautiful and easy hike along the Blue Ridge gap of the Potomac River, where spring songbird migration can be outstanding and birds such as Warbling Vireo, Prothonotary Warbler, and Northern Oriole are regular in summer. A visit to the summit of Mount Rogers remains the best bet during the breeding season for some of the region's most localized northern species, such as Swainson's Thrush, Hermit Thrush, Magnolia Warbler, and Purple Finch. The Appalachian Trail from Roan High Knob across Carver's Gap north to Grassy Ridge Bald is known for spruce-fir birds in summer and for elusive Snow Buntings in winter. Peregrine Falcons, Swainson's Warblers, and spectacular geology are present at Chimney Rock Park.

In the Nantahala Mountains, the combination of FSRs 69 and 711 provides one of the best roadside birding routes in the province. Another excellent roadside circuit combines FSR 81 and Tellico Plains–Robbinsville Scenic Highway in the Unicoi Mountains. Swainson's Warblers are the prime attraction along the Chattooga River, which is accessible on Bull Pen Road and on trails and roads between the Walhalla Fish Hatchery and Burrell's Ford. In the Little Tennessee River valley, Ferguson Fields is among the best spots in the province for spring migration, particularly for shorebirds. To see many high-country birds near the extreme southern limit of their breeding ranges, try exploring the summit of Georgia's Brasstown Bald.

One hesitates to draw the line, because so many other spots could easily be included in the most highly recommended category. After all, to paraphrase a common bumper sticker, "The worst day birding in the Blue Ridge is better than the best day at work."

Autumn Wings: The Fall Hawk Migration

The autumn hawk migration provides some of the most exciting and pleasant birding experiences possible in eastern North America. This great translocation follows a fairly predictable pattern each season, though day-to-day movements may vary considerably. Some individuals begin to wander south in August, but heavy action starts in September and continues through November, with a few stragglers lingering into December. Although weather systems, seasonal change, and local geography are key elements governing the hawks' movements, each species has its own particular time frame and behavior patterns in the annual sojourn.

September is probably the most popular time for hawk watching, because the often spectacular migration of Broad-winged Hawks is concentrated around the middle of the month, when the weather is usually still mild and comfortable. Peak daily flights of several thousand Broadwings are not unusual, and record days have exceeded ten thousand birds at major sites. The biggest flights are usually during the second or third week of September, but some peak days may occur in the last week of the month. Ospreys also pass through from mid- to late September, generally as solitary birds. Other migrants noted most often in September include American Kestrel and Bald Eagle, the latter a decidedly infrequent transient.

As crisp October heralds the arrival of crimson and gold foliage, Sharp-shinned Hawks become the predominant migrant, while the less-common Cooper's Hawk reaches its maximum numbers. Toward the end of the month, Red-tailed Hawks become increasingly conspicuous, usually as solitary birds that rely heavily on deflected updrafts of prevailing winds along the high ridge lines. The Red-tailed migration continues into November, accompanied by Red-shouldered Hawks and Northern Harriers. Although rarely noted, Northern Goshawk and Golden Eagle are most likely to appear in November, when the high forests are devoid of leaves.

Even though broad generalizations can be made about the timing of each species' migration, the actual movement of individual birds is strongly affected by daily weather patterns. Usually the best time to see a large flight of hawks is one or two days after a cold front has passed across the mountains, particularly when a low-pressure area is centered at the same time over New York, New England, or southeast Canada. Cold air seems to stir the birds into moving south, and strong westerly or northwesterly winds associated with such weather patterns provide excellent updrafts along the Blue Ridge crest line.

Hawks exploit two major types of local atmospheric phenomena to maximize the efficiency of their southward migration: thermals and deflective updrafts. Thermals form as huge bubbles or columns of warm air, rising from fields and cleared areas on the ground that become heated by the sun's rays. As a warm air mass ascends higher into the cool atmosphere, the dew point may eventually be reached, at which point moisture condenses to form a cumulus cloud. Hawks may use such thermals by soaring in a tight spiral within the bubble, as rising air carries them higher and higher. When the thermal approaches its maximum altitude, hawks break out and glide in a long linear descent, searching for another free ride. This strategy, incidentally, was long ago recognized and copied by practitioners of the sport of glider soaring.

Although all North American raptors use thermals to help in migration, Broad-winged Hawks are particularly dependent on this flight style. When large numbers of Broad-wings collect in a rising thermal, the swirling flock is dubbed a "kettle," one of the most aesthetically pleasing sights in bird-watching. Of course, thermal soaring can also enable the hawks to attain such a high altitude that they are no longer visible from the ground.

The second major way that hawks enhance their efficiency is by gliding near the crest line of mountain ridges, where surface winds are deflected sharply upward as they cross the range. When westerly or northwesterly winds strike the slopes of the Blue Ridge Mountains, air currents are forced up and across the crest, providing strong uplift for birds following the ridge southward. Red-tailed Hawks, eagles, and Sharp-shinned Hawks rely heavily on this method, which is much less frequently used by Broad-wings. The optimal deflective uplift often occurs close to the ridge summit, so that openings, rocky outcroppings, and cliffs near the top of the ridge provide an excellent vantage point for watching hawks as they move past.

The daily flights of migrating hawks occasionally start between 7:00 and 8:00 A.M., but the more common pattern is for the first movements to begin between 9:00 and 10:00 A.M. and continue until about 3:00 or 4:00 in the afternoon. This pattern is certainly convenient for those birders who like a leisurely breakfast, and many hawk watchers plan to be set up at their posts by 9:00 A.M.

A particularly interesting phenomenon is the midday or noon lull that takes place in some hawk flights, especially those involving Sharp-shinned, Broad-winged, and Red-tailed Hawks. This interruption or decline in the number of passing hawks may occur for one to two hours around noon. One explanation for lulls is that by midday the use of thermal soaring has allowed hawks to achieve an altitude where they cannot be seen by ground observers.

Enjoying the autumn hawk watch requires the right equipment. Many observers use Parkway overlooks, making it easy to bring along in your car almost everything you might need. When the weather is mild, a folding lawn chair can be set up next to the car. With cold or windy conditions, many watchers retreat to the warmth of their vehicles and watch through the windows. Sweaters, jackets, windbreakers, and lap blankets allow flexibility in adapting to changing weather in the course of the day or weekend. A wide-brimmed hat or cap is extremely helpful in reducing glare, and some observers use sunglasses as well. A good sunscreen lotion helps if you plan to sit out all day. Don't forget a thermos of your favorite soup or hot drink and a cooler with whatever food appeals to you. And finally, be sure to bring along plenty of patience, because not every day has a big flight.

The most popular binoculars for hawk watching are center-focus models with 10X magnification, allowing good long-distance detection of birds and optimal visualization for field marks as they come into closer range. Twenty-power spotting scopes mounted on a gunstock, a shoulder brace, or a fast-action tripod can also be useful if you want a better view of individual birds. A number of books and field guides on hawk migration are available. For record keeping, a clipboard helps hold things down in the often gusty wind, regardless of whether you use a notebook or large data sheets. Some observers buy an owl decoy from a sporting goods shop or farm store and place it on a pole nearby. Hawks will occasionally swoop by the impostor, providing a close but fleeting view of the bird.

Perhaps the best spot for hawk watching is one that you discover on your own. If you are just getting started, however, it is better to visit one of the many well-established lookouts scattered along the Parkway, most of which are listed below and described in detail in the site guides of Sections 3 through 5. Fortunately, there are many options in choosing a vantage point, and most of the best sites are at overlooks and parking lots, where flat paved lots are suitable for persons with physical limitations. Some birders choose a hike to more rugged and isolated settings.

The premier sites are in the ridge province, where the mountain range often consists of a single ridge line rising sharply one to two thousand feet above the surrounding valley and Piedmont. The prime hot spot for autumn hawks on the Parkway is at Rockfish Gap (M 0), where the northern end of the Parkway joins the Skyline Drive's southern terminus. Afton OL (M 0.2) and Raven's Roost OL (M 10.7), both just south of Rockfish, provide other vantage points, albeit with less privacy. Nearby Shenandoah National Park has a number of good places, including Hawksbill, Stony Man, and Mary's Rock, all of which require a bit of hiking, and Calf Mountain OL, where you can watch from the car. Farther south on the Parkway are Irish Creek OL (M 42.4) and Buena Vista OL (M 45.6). Many excellent sites are found near Peaks of Otter, including a major station at Harvey's Knob OL (M 95.3) as well as Mills Gap (M 91.9), Purgatory Mountain (M 92.2), Sharp Top (M 92.4), Montvale (M 95.9), and Great Valley (M 99.6) overlooks. Some hikers like to head up the Flat Top Trail (M 83.6) at Peaks of Otter and take the spur to Cross Rocks and the Pinnacle for a remote vantage point.

Five widely scattered spots along the plateau province provide good hawk watching between Roanoke and Boone. At Rocky Knob Recreation Area, check the Saddle Parking OL (MP 168) and the vicinity of Rocky Knob Visitor Center (MP 169). Near Cumberland Knob, try parking at MP 219. Just north of Doughton Park, Mahogany Rock OL (MP 235) and nearby Scott Ridge are excellent sites. Thunderhill Parking OL (M 290.5) near Boone is also popular.

In the high country between Boone and Asheville, try the hike to Grandfather Mountain's Ship Rock from Rough Ridge parking lot at M 302.8

or a side trip to Table Rock Mountain at Linville Gorge. Other potential sites include overlooks farther south at Three Knobs (M 338.8), Black Mountains (M 342.2), Licklog Ridge (M 349.2), and Mount Mitchell view (M 349.9). The fire tower on Green Knob (M 350.4) provides a spectacular 360-degree view. A side trip to the summit parking lot at Mount Mitchell State Park (M 355.4) is often productive. In the nearby Great Craggy Mountains, Craggy Pinnacle OL (M 364.1) and the hike to the summit are popular, along with the view east at Craggy Gardens Visitor Center (M 364.6). South of Asheville, good flights have been reported at Mill's Valley OL (M 404.5) and at Devil's Courthouse (M 422.4).

Good spots away from the Parkway include Caesar's Head State Park in South Carolina and Chimney Rock Park in North Carolina. At the northern end of the province, try Wildcat Rocks on Pennsylvania's South Mountain, as well as Washington Monument State Park and Blue Ridge Summit Vista and Hog Rock at Catoctin Mountain Park in Maryland.

For additional information and reading, see Heintzelman's *The Migration of Hawks* and *A Guide to Northeastern Hawk Watching*, as well as Clark and Wheeler's *A Field Guide to Hawks*.

Owl Quest

The extensive tracts of unbroken woodland in the southern Appalachians provide ideal habitat for owls. Six species are resident in the region, and two others, the Short-eared Owl and the Snowy Owl, are rare and erratic winter visitors from the north. Owl study is a popular activity in the southern mountains, and the Parkway and adjacent public parks and recreation areas are ideal spots to hear and see these intriguing birds.

A few general tips may be helpful in finding owls. Although you can sometimes hear them or get one to answer during the daylight hours, best results are obviously obtained at night. Many owls are most active in the few hours immediately following sundown, which is convenient if you want to get to bed at a reasonable hour!

Choose heavily wooded areas, particularly those around ravines and slopes, where you have a good angle for hearing calls from a lot of terrain. Many of the Parkway's overlooks are good spots, and even the campgrounds and picnic areas can be worth trying for Great Horned Owl, Barred Owl, and Eastern Screech-Owl. Northern Saw-whet Owls are quite localized and should be sought in spruce-fir and adjacent northern hard-wood forests.

A floodlight is obviously essential. Try to get one with an adjustable or a fairly wide beam to increase your odds of initially finding the bird. Some owlers carry two lights: a broad beam for scanning the trees and a narrow beam for intense light on the bird once it is located.

A good-quality tape recorder is popular with some birders as a way to get the owls calling and to lure them closer. You can use the calls from field-guide records and tape sets or tape your own one- to five-minute seg-ments of calls for each species. Some birders learn to give a pretty good imitation of many owl calls, and almost anyone can whistle an imitation of the Saw-whet's notes.

Be patient when working with owls. After stopping at a potential spot, wait and listen a while before whistling or trying the recorder. Whistle or play the tape for about ten to fifteen seconds, enough time for a couple of repetitions of the call. Then listen quietly for at least a minute before repeating the performance. Try cupping your hands behind your ears to enhance the sensitivity of hearing. And don't forget that owls will prey on each other, so start with the smallest species first, such as the Northern Saw-whet Owl or Eastern Screech-Owl, and progress to the larger species in sequence. If you begin with the Great Horned tape, the other owls will probably stay very, very quiet. Also, remember that successful luring can result in your getting a solid whack on the head by an agitated owl; consider wearing a cap that you don't mind loosing.

Long-eared Owls are the rarest and most elusive of the owls reported from the Blue Ridge. Their status, numbers, and distribution remain very poorly defined in the region. Except for one sight record at the Nature Con-servancy's Bluff Mountain, all recent reports in the southern portion of the Blue Ridge have been based on calling, as at Grandfather Mountain and at Beartree campground near Mount Rogers. Owls have quite a repertoire of noises, including many sounds that are not found on the commercially available tape and record guides to bird song. Caution should be exercised when reporting Long-eared Owls based solely on their calls. Try using a tape recorder to lure the bird into range for spotlighting. Long-eared Owls typically prefer dense coniferous trees and forests, such as white pine, hemlock, or spruce-fir, but mixed woodlands are also a possibility.

At the northern end of the Blue Ridge Province, Long-eared Owls are resident and nesters in white pine woodlands of Pennsylvania's South

Mountain. Confirmed breeding records have been obtained along Whispering Pines Trail at Kings Gap Environmental Education and Training Center.

Barn Owls are also very rarely reported in the southern mountains, and almost all records are from the vicinity of farm buildings, churches, and old abandoned houses. The few sightings in the region are at spots far removed from the Parkway and from the other recreation sites described in this book.

Probably the most sought-after owl in the region is the Northern Saw-whet. These tiny raptors are found mostly in spruce-fir and adjacent northern hardwood forests at Mount Rogers and Whitetop, at Grandfather Mountain, at Roan Mountain, in the Black Mountains, in the Great Craggy Mountains, on Pisgah Ridge, in the Plott Balsam and Great Balsam mountains, on Shining Rock Ledge, and in the Great Smoky Mountains. The birds are most active just after sunset and just before sunrise, although they often call all night when the weather is mild. The peak of the calling season occurs in April and May, but they may be heard from mid-March through June or mid-July and erratically into August. Their typical song consists of a series of resonant, bell-like whistles or cooing notes repeated at a rate of one to two notes per second. Calling often lasts with only rare interruption for over an hour.

Northern Saw-whet Owls seem to remain active longer on moonlit nights, and they are easiest to hear on calm nights when the wind is not howling through the trees. Contrary to popular opinion, Saw-whets are usually active on foggy, rainy, and windy nights, but such conditions make it much harder for you to hear them, not to mention the discomfort and driving hazards. Cupping your hands behind your ears will often enhance detection when listening conditions are marginal. Always listen carefully for a few minutes to see if any owls are hooting before whistling an imitation of their song, which sometimes causes the birds to stop calling! By varying the pitch and speed of whistling, you may get better results at luring the birds or getting them to call loudly enough to locate their position. Remember to bring winter clothing, especially in April, when subfreezing temperatures are common at night in the remote, high areas where these owls occur.

The other three resident owls are fairly easy to find at many wooded overlooks, campgrounds, and picnic areas. Barred Owls are probably the most conspicuous of the owls in the Blue Ridge. They are heard calling most often in spring and summer, and they are more likely than the other owls to be active during daylight hours. Barred Owls are also the most common owl in the region's high elevations, although they are more often encountered in cove hardwood forests and mature oak forests at low to middle elevations.

Great Horned Owls do most of their calling from December through February and are least noisy at the time when Barred Owls are most actively hooting. Great Horned Owls tend to avoid the high elevations, and they are rarely heard during the daytime. At night, however, they frequently perch in exposed locations, such as dead or bare trees adjacent to pastures and fields, where they may be seen around dawn or dusk with a bit of careful scanning.

Eastern Screech-Owls also tend to be most common in low and middle elevations. Often heard calling in March, they remain quiet from April through June and resume their hooting in late summer. Their noisiest months are September and October. Like the Great Horned Owl, they are seldom active during daylight hours. However, they will sometimes respond during the day to a tape recording or whistled imitation of their calls.

Don't forget an energy snack and a thermos of coffee or tea for the late drive back to your accommodations. For some interesting reading, get a copy of Johnsgard's *North American Owls*.

THE BLUE RIDGE PARKWAY AND ADJACENT SITES

VIRGINIA

Please refer to "Bird Finding in the Blue Ridge Mountains" in the Introduction, which explains how the bird-finding sections are organized.

Shenandoah National Park and Skyline Drive

Highlights: Middle-elevation woodland nesting species, spring songbird migration, autumn hawk migration.

Season: Year-round, but best in spring through fall.

Access: The park's north entrance is at Front Royal, Va., on US 340 south of I-66, some 60 miles west of the Washington, D.C., beltway and a few miles east of I-81. Thornton Gap (M 31.5) is on US 211 9 miles east of Luray, Va., and 21 miles east of exit 67 on I-81. Swift Run Gap (M 65.7) is 6 miles east of Elkton, Va., and 22 miles east of Harrisonburg, Va., on US 33. Rockfish Gap (M 105.4) is at US 250 and I-64, 91 miles west of Richmond, Va., 18 miles west of Charlottesville, Va., and 12 miles east of Staunton, Va.

Maps: USGS "Big Meadows," "Elkton East," "Fletcher," "Old Rag Mountain."

Facilities: Accommodations in the park at Skyland Lodge (M 41.7), Big Meadows Lodge (M 51.2), and Lewis Mountain Cabins (M 57.5). Camping with tent and trailer sites: 186 sites at Matthews Arm (M 22.2), 244 sites at Big Meadows (M 51.2), 32 sites at Lewis Mountain (M 57.5), and 231 sites at Loft Mountain (M 79.5). Gasoline at Elkwallow Wayside, Big Meadows Wayside, and Loft Mountain Wayside. Food at Big Meadows, Skyland, Elkwallow, Panorama, and Loft Mountain; groceries and snacks at the store at each campground. Books, maps, and information at Dicky Ridge Visitor Center (M 4.6) and Harry F. Byrd Sr. Visitor Center at Big Meadows

(M 51.0). For information, contact Shenandoah National Park, Luray, VA 22835 (703-999-2266 or 703-999-2282).

Barely an hour's drive west from the Washington beltway, Shenandoah National Park provides a wilderness retreat in the Blue Ridge Mountains and a prime area for observing the bird life of Virginia's highlands. The park encompasses some 194,600 acres of mountainous terrain along a 75-mile segment of the Blue Ridge Province between Front Royal and Rockfish Gap. Elevations range from 530 feet in the park's northeast corner to 4,049 feet on the summit of Hawksbill, but most of the narrow ridge line averages around 3,000 feet. Hawksbill and Stony Man Mountain (4,010 ft.) are the first peaks south of the Catskills to rise above 4,000 feet. This portion of the Blue Ridge is only about five miles wide, with numerous outlier ridges extending onto the Piedmont Plateau to the east and into the Shenandoah River valley to the west. The plant and bird life in the park is characteristic of the upper Piedmont and middle elevations of the south-central Appalachians.

The history of Shenandoah Park is closely tied to that of the Blue Ridge Parkway and the Great Smoky Mountains National Park. Following years of discussion, Congress in 1926 authorized the establishment of Shenandoah and Great Smoky Mountains national parks, and plans were approved in 1933 to link the two parks by a scenic motor road through the Blue Ridge. Shenandoah National Park was dedicated in 1936, and in 1976 some 40 percent of the area was designated for Wilderness status. With its proximity to major metropolitan centers of the East Coast, the park receives heavy public use, averaging nearly two million visitors annually.

The predominant vegetation is second-growth oak forests, many of which cover land that had been severely damaged prior to the park's establishment. Cove forests occur at lower elevations and scattered stands of hemlock are present in many areas. Small tracts of northern hardwoods and isolated spruce and fir trees are found on the highest peaks, but a true spruce-fir community is absent.

Bird life in most of the park is typical of middle-elevation deciduous and coniferous forests. A few fields, meadows, and human settlements support a different avifauna. Some 205 species of birds have been recorded.

The most popular spots for bird study are in the central third of the park, where the greater range of elevation supports more species than can be found in the northern and southern portions. Birding opportunities are

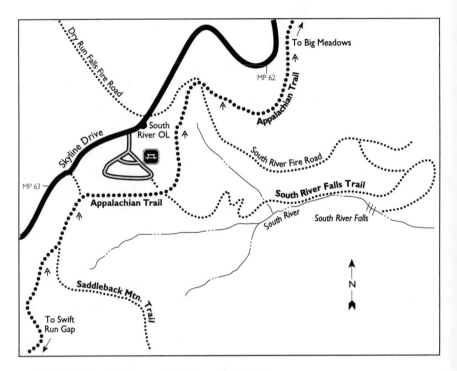

South River Falls Trail, Shenandoah National Park, Va.

diverse. There are more than 500 miles of hiking trails, including some 95 miles of the Appalachian Trail. Less strenuous bird-watching, often suitable for the physically impaired, is available at seventy-five overlooks along the Skyline Drive, at four major campgrounds, and in many picnic areas. Bridle trails and cross-country skiing provide additional options. The major access to the park is from the Skyline Drive, which meanders along the crest for 105 miles south to Rockfish Gap, where the Blue Ridge Parkway begins. Although most of the hiking routes in the park are suitable for birding, six trails have become special favorites.

The **South River Falls Trail** deserves its reputation as the park's premier hike for breeding birds and spring migrants. The steep trail and hillside contour provide a good perspective for looking into the forest canopy, and bird density and variety are notable during spring and summer months. Although this moderately strenuous trail can be done as an in-and-out trek totaling 2.6 miles, the best birding results are obtained when combined with the South River Fire Road and AT as a loop route of 3.3 miles. Get a copy of the South River Falls Trail map from one of the visitor centers or study the large mapboard at the trailhead before starting out. The trail originates at the parking area in the east end of South River picnic area, about 0.2 miles from the entrance at M 62.8 on the Skyline Drive.

Beginning at 2,940 feet near the trailhead, the route descends for 1.3 miles to its lowest point at 2,120 feet near the falls. This first portion of the trail passes through mixed, second-growth, oak and pine forests before entering lush cove hardwoods and hemlock stands along South River. Beyond the falls overlook, the trail ascends about 250 yards to a junction with an old road; turn left on this road and continue about 0.4 miles to the junction with South River Fire Road. Turn left on the fire road and proceed through mature oak woods about 1 mile to the AT; turn left on the AT and go about 0.4 miles to the South River Falls Trail; turn right onto the trail and go 0.1 miles back to the parking lot.

During late spring and summer months, species to be expected along the South River Falls Trail, Fire Road, and AT include Yellow-billed Cuckoo, Ruby-throated Hummingbird, Downy Woodpecker, Pileated Woodpecker, Eastern Wood-Pewee, Acadian Flycatcher, Blue Jay, Carolina Chickadee, Tufted Titmouse, White-breasted Nuthatch, Carolina Wren, Winter Wren (along South River), Blue-gray Gnatcatcher, Veery, Wood Thrush, American Robin, Gray Catbird, Solitary Vireo, Yellow-throated Vireo, Red-eyed Vireo, Scarlet Tanager, Rose-breasted Grosbeak, Rufous-sided Towhee, and American Goldfinch. This hike is particularly renowned for its summer warbler population, which regularly includes Northern Parula, Chestnut-sided Warbler, Black-throated Blue Warbler, Black-throated Green Warbler, Blackburnian Warbler, Cerulean Warbler, Black-and-white Warbler, American Redstart, Worm-eating Warbler, Ovenbird, Louisiana Waterthrush (along South River), Kentucky Warbler, and Hooded Warbler.

Another excellent birding hike is the upper portion of **Laurel Prong Trail** between the AT and Laurel Gap. Turn at M 55.1 into the paved parking lot on the left at Booten's Gap (3,235 ft.) and take the AT north from the lot for 0.5 miles to the junction (3,460 ft.) with Laurel Prong Trail on the right. Proceed down Laurel Prong Trail 1.0 mile to Laurel Gap (3,220 ft.), where you may wish to turn around and retrace your route back to the parking area or explore the several trails that lead beyond the gap. This moderate-to-easy trail passes through an open forest of oak, maple, birch, and mountain laurel on the south slope of Hazeltop, third-highest peak in the park.

In late spring and summer, this scenic trek will likely yield Ruffed

Grouse, Downy Woodpecker, Pileated Woodpecker, Eastern Wood-Pewee, Acadian Flycatcher, Blue Jay, White-breasted Nuthatch, Veery, Wood Thrush, American Robin, Solitary Vireo, Red-eyed Vireo, Chestnut-sided Warbler, Black-throated Blue Warbler, Black-and-white Warbler, American Redstart, Canada Warbler, Scarlet Tanager, Rose-breasted Grosbeak, Indigo Bunting, Rufous-sided Towhee, Dark-eyed Junco, and American Goldfinch. If you want a longer hike, get a copy of the Camp Hoover Trail map from a visitor center and study the possibilities of an 8-mile loop route involving Laurel Prong, Mill Prong, and the AT.

Three trails lead to the 4,049-foot summit of **Hawksbill**, the highest point in Shenandoah National Park. The 300-degree view from the peak provides one of the park's best spots for watching the autumn hawk migration in September and October. In winter, the mountain may yield Red Crossbill, Pine Siskin, and Evening Grosbeak, along with more common winter residents and permanent residents. During spring and summer, the trails are excellent sites to observe birds associated with a fairly mature forest of oak, maple, and birch. A copy of the Hawksbill Trail map will help you choose your route.

The easiest hike is from the upper Hawksbill parking lot on the right at M 46.7 (3,635 ft.). Proceed on this trail about 0.7 miles to a dirt road, turn right onto the road, and then go about 0.4 miles to the top, for a round-trip of 2.1 miles. Although more rigorous, the trail from Hawksbill Gap parking lot (3,365 ft.) on the right at M 45.6 often has a greater variety of birds than found on the other two routes. From the trailhead in the middle of the lot, this strenuous, rocky path ascends steeply up the mountain's northeast side; retrace your steps for a round-trip of 1.7 miles. A third alternative is to take the AT south from Hawksbill Gap about 1.2 miles to a trail on the left, which runs 0.9 miles to the summit; return to the parking lot by going down the steep northeast trail to the gap.

Species at Hawksbill in late spring and summer include Ruffed Grouse, Downy Woodpecker, Eastern Wood-Pewee, Great Crested Flycatcher, Blue Jay, Common Raven, Veery, Wood Thrush, Gray Catbird, Solitary Vireo, Chestnut-sided Warbler, Black-throated Blue Warbler, Black-and-white Warbler, Ovenbird, Canada Warbler, Rose-breasted Grosbeak, Rufous-sided Towhee, Dark-eyed Junco, and American Goldfinch. Watch also for Black Vulture, Turkey Vulture, Broad-winged Hawk, and Red-tailed Hawk. Peregrine Falcons have recently been reintroduced.

For a stroll to the top of Shenandoah Park's second highest peak, **Stony**

PRATT
1991

Canada Warbler

Man Nature Trail is an easy 1.6-mile round-trip hike through a forest of oaks, yellow birch, maples, eastern hemlock, and scattered red spruce and balsam fir. Beginning at the Stony Man parking lot near the north entrance to Skyland at M 41.7, the trail climbs from 3,680 feet to the summit at 4,010 feet, where open cliffs provide a delightful spot for autumn hawk watching and a clear view of the Shenandoah Valley below. During the nesting season, the trail is a good spot for Downy Woodpecker, Eastern Wood-Pewee, Common Raven, Blue Jay, Carolina Chickadee, Tufted Titmouse, Veery, Wood Thrush, American Robin, Solitary Vireo, Chestnut-sided Warbler, Black-throated Blue Warbler, American Redstart, Ovenbird, Canada Warbler, Scarlet Tanager, Rose-breasted Grosbeak, Indigo Bunting, Rufous-sided Towhee, Dark-eyed Junco, and American Goldfinch. To enhance your appreciation of the hike, get a copy of the "Stony Man Nature Trail" booklet to read along the way and start early to avoid the crowds.

The Big Meadows area contains two tracts of high-elevation wetlands that are of special interest to botanists and birders alike. Unique within the

park, the Big Meadows Swamp and Big Meadows consist of shallow wetlands, both drained by Hogcamp Branch, perched on a gently sloping tableland at an elevation of about 3,500 feet. The **Story-of-the-Forest Nature
Trail** is an easy 1.8-mile, self-guiding hike that begins along the north
entrance road (MP 51) to the Harry F. Byrd Sr. Visitor Center and passes
through woods and close by the **Big Meadows Swamp** before arriving at
the campground, where a return trail heads back to the visitor center. Late
spring and summer species include many typical middle-elevation birds,
such as Downy Woodpecker, Hairy Woodpecker, Pileated Woodpecker,
Northern Flicker, Blue Jay, Carolina Chickadee, Tufted Titmouse, White-
breasted Nuthatch, Wood Thrush, American Robin, Gray Catbird, Cedar
Waxwing, Solitary Vireo, Chestnut-sided Warbler, Black-throated Blue
Warbler, Black-and-white Warbler, American Redstart, Scarlet Tanager,
Rose-breasted Grosbeak, Indigo Bunting, Rufous-sided Towhee, Chipping
Sparrow, and Dark-eyed Junco.

The **Big Meadows** itself, site of the park dedication ceremonies by Presi-
dent Roosevelt in 1936, is at MP 51 across the Skyline Drive from Byrd
Visitor Center, where you can park and carefully walk across the roadway
to explore the open expanse of boggy wetland. The area was cleared in
precolonial times, probably by Indians or wildfires, and by the 1900s more
than 1,000 acres were barren, largely from overgrazing by cattle. With the
establishment of the park, however, the open tract has been considerably
reduced in size by reforestation and encroachment of pioneering plants, a
process that is somewhat delayed by the poorly drained soils and cold environment. Currently only a few hundred acres remain as meadow, which is
artificially maintained by the Park Service. Some 270 vascular plant species
have been reported here, including many wildflowers and ferns. No official
trails exist in the meadow, although numerous footpaths and animal runs
are easily visible. The central area can be quite wet and muddy, however,
so come with appropriate footwear.

Special birding attractions at the meadows include American Woodcock aerial displays at twilight and early evening from mid-March to late
April. Ruffed Grouse and Wild Turkey may occasionally be seen along the
woody margins at any time of year. Common Snipe are sometimes found
in the wet central area during spring and fall migration, and Northern
Harriers and rare Snow Buntings may be present from late fall through
winter. During the spring and summer nesting season, possible species
include Turkey Vulture, Northern Bobwhite, Northern Flicker, Barn Swal-

low, Common Raven, Eastern Bluebird, Gray Catbird, Brown Thrasher, Cedar Waxwing, European Starling, Chestnut-sided Warbler, Common Yellowthroat, Indigo Bunting, Rufous-sided Towhee, Chipping Sparrow, Field Sparrow, Song Sparrow, Eastern Meadowlark, Brown-headed Cowbird, and American Goldfinch. Although uncommon to rare, five species may be found at the meadows in late spring and summer that are rather infrequently encountered elsewhere along the Skyline Drive or Blue Ridge Parkway. Be alert for Willow Flycatcher, Least Flycatcher, Tree Swallow, Blue Grosbeak, and Vesper Sparrow in appropriate spots.

Another popular site that combines botany with birding is the **Limberlost Trail**, an easy 1.2-mile loop that wanders through a spectacular grove of giant hemlocks, many from 300 to 400 years old, admixed with ancient red spruce and white oaks that may exceed five hundred years in age. According to legend, George F. Pollock, founder of nearby Skyland resort, paid lumbermen $10 per tree to leave this old growth uncut. Trail access is from a gravel fire road that turns left off the Skyline Drive just south of MP 43 and quickly leads to a small parking area (3,350 ft.), where the trailhead is clearly marked. To avoid confusion, get a copy of the "Whiteoak Canyon & Skyland Maps" from a visitor center to show the route and interconnections with the heavily used trails to the canyon waterfalls.

Pine Siskin and other winter finches may remain here late into spring, Barred Owl and Winter Wren are permanent residents, and Veery and Blackburnian Warbler are special attractions during the breeding season. Other species found in spring and summer in the Limberlost include Downy Woodpecker, Eastern Wood-Pewee, Acadian Flycatcher, Blue Jay, Common Raven, Carolina Chickadee, Tufted Titmouse, Wood Thrush, American Robin, Gray Catbird, Cedar Waxwing, Solitary Vireo, Red-eyed Vireo, Chestnut-sided Warbler, Black-and-white Warbler, American Redstart, Scarlet Tanager, Indigo Bunting, Rufous-sided Towhee, Dark-eyed Junco, and Brown-headed Cowbird.

Many of the seventy-five overlooks along the Skyline Drive are good birding spots, especially for the physically impaired or for those who wish to sample the park's bird life without hiking. **Mary's Rock Tunnel Overlook** (2,550 ft.) at M 32.4 often provides Pileated Woodpecker, Eastern Phoebe, Common Raven, Winter Wren, and Chestnut-sided Warbler. **Hazel Mountain Overlook** (2,775 ft.) at MP 33 may yield Eastern Wood-Pewee, Acadian Flycatcher, Veery, Wood Thrush, American Robin, Gray Catbird, Yellow-throated Vireo, Red-eyed Vireo, Chestnut-sided Warbler, Black-and-white Warbler, Ovenbird, Scarlet Tanager, and Dark-eyed Junco. The same species are usually found at nearby **Meadow Spring parking area** (2,850 ft.) at M 33.5, where two popular routes, the **Buck Hollow Trail** and **Hazel Mountain Trail**, are also noted for Great Horned and Barred Owls, as well as for middle-elevation deciduous and mixed woodland breeding species. Park at **Hemlock Springs Overlook** (3,380 ft.) at M 39.7 and carefully walk the shoulder south, checking the hemlocks and hardwoods in late spring and summer for Eastern Wood-Pewee, Eastern Phoebe, Tufted Titmouse, Winter Wren, Veery, Wood Thrush, Gray Catbird, Solitary Vireo, Chestnut-sided Warbler, Black-throated Blue Warbler, Black-throated Green Warbler, Blackburnian Warbler, American Redstart, Rufous-sided Towhee, and Dark-eyed Junco. In winter, the hemlocks are worth scanning for finches, such as Pine Siskins and crossbills.

Although Shenandoah Park has been somewhat overshadowed by nearby Rockfish Gap for the study of autumn hawk migration, there are a number of excellent sites in the park where southbound raptors can be observed. Three locales require a hike, but several overlooks allow hawk watching from the car. The best spot is the summit of **Hawksbill**, where the 300-degree view is unexcelled. The summit of **Mary's Rock** is popular, although the 1.8-mile hike from the Panorama at M 31.6 near Thornton Gap is rather strenuous. **Stony Man** summit is good for west winds and has the advantage of being a rather easy hike from the Skyland area. Among the better overlooks in the central section of the park are **Point Overlook** at M 55.6 (3,235 ft.), where one can watch from the car or descend to the trail below the overlook, turn left on the trail, and walk to a ledge for an open view and more privacy than provided at the overlook itself. **Stony Man Mountain Overlook** at M 38.6 (3,097 ft.) and **Hughes River Gap parking lot** (3,090 ft.) just north of Stony Man Mountain OL at M 37.9 have clear views west into the valley. Near the south end of the park, **Calf Mountain Overlook** at M 98.9 (2,480 ft.) has a fine perspective to the northwest into the Shenandoah Valley, while in the northern third of the park, **Hogback Overlook** at MP 21 is often worthwhile. For general information on the fall hawk migration, see "Autumn Wings" in Section 2.

Many of the park's campgrounds and picnic areas are excellent for spring and summer birds, and the generally level, paved circuit roads are usually suitable for the physically impaired, including those who wish to bird from a wheelchair. In particular, the oak woods, trails, entrance road, and field margins around **Matthews Arm campground** (2,750 ft.) at M 22.2 are perhaps the best bet in the park for Wild Turkey.

Rockfish Gap

Highlights: Autumn hawk migration, spring songbird migration, summer warblers.

Season: Spring through fall.

Access: Rockfish Gap is located at MP 0 on the BRP or M 105.4 at the Skyline Drive terminus, with connectors to I-64. On I-64 it is 13 miles west to exit 56 on I-81 near Staunton, Va., and 18 miles east to Charlottesville, Va.

Maps: USGS "Waynesboro East," "Waynesboro West," "Sherando."

Facilities: Gasoline, food, and accommodations are available at the gap, at nearby Waynesboro, and at Staunton and Charlottesville.

Located at the beginning of the Blue Ridge Parkway at MP 0, Rockfish Gap is widely considered the premier site to watch the autumn hawk migration in the Blue Ridge Mountains. An additional attraction is VA 610, a nearby dirt road that is excellent for spring songbird migration and summer warblers.

Rockfish Gap (1,909 ft.) is a classic wind gap, formed when the Shenandoah River captured and diverted the headwaters of Rockfish River, whose drainage once extended west of the Blue Ridge but now lies east of the gap. The site has a rich history, serving as a migration route for buffalo, hunters, traders, settlers, and Stonewall Jackson's troops. The otherwise handsome scenery is now marred by the Gordian knot of highway sprawl in the gap, although the resultant easy accessibility by car contributes to the spot's popularity.

From early September through November, avid hawk watchers are usually "on duty" here each day to record the spectacle. The Holiday Inn and its adjacent parking lot serve as the action center, with observers setting up lawn chairs on the patio under the shelter of the restaurant overhang. Others choose to watch from vehicles at the parking-lot edge. The spot is ideal for the physically impaired, with wheelchair access through the inn or from the flat, paved parking lot.

From the patio, the view east over the Piedmont and north along the Blue Ridge provides a clear line of sight for the usual migration pattern, with the hawks often appearing near the relay towers to the northeast and coming toward the southwest, sometimes across the gap and sometimes over the Piedmont, where kettles may form on warm days. Another perspective is from the northwest corner of the parking lot, which gives a good angle into the valley for hawks moving down the Shenandoah or passing through the gap. Peak daily counts at Rockfish are sometimes quite high. Record days here have included 11,783 Broad-winged Hawks, 509 Sharp-shinned Hawks, 751 Red-tailed Hawks, 72 American Kestrels, 5 Bald Eagles, 13 Cooper's Hawks, and 3 Merlins. Golden Eagles, Peregrine Falcons, and Northern Goshawks are reported each year but usually only on a few occasions. For details on fall hawk migration, see "Autumn Wings" in Section 2.

Lots of other migrants pass through as well, including Black and Turkey Vultures, Great Blue Herons, waterfowl, woodpeckers, and numerous songbirds. Following the passage of an autumn weather front, migrating songbirds often die after crashing into the Holiday Inn windows. Spring migration is occasionally interesting here, evidenced by a peak one-day count of 90 Ospreys. Although seldom visited during summer, the Parkway shoulder at Rockfish Gap is a good spot for Yellow-breasted Chat and other typical Piedmont birds.

The other main attraction at Rockfish is VA 610, which parallels the Parkway south of the gap through an oak forest with a thick mountain laurel understory. Head south on the Parkway to M 2.1, where a short connector on the right leads to VA 610. Turn left onto VA 610 and stop frequently during the next 4 miles to look and listen from the car or to get out and stroll along the flat gravel road. Although the road is lightly used, be sure to allow plenty of room for cars to pass by.

Late spring and summer birds here are typical of middle-elevation deciduous forests of the central Blue Ridge. This is a particularly good spot for warblers, including the Black-throated Blue, Pine, Cerulean, Black-and-white, Worm-eating, Kentucky, and Hooded, along with American Redstart and Ovenbird. Other expected species are the Pileated Woodpecker, Downy Woodpecker, Eastern Wood-Pewee, Acadian Flycatcher, Eastern Phoebe, Blue Jay, American Crow, Carolina Chickadee, Tufted Titmouse, White-breasted Nuthatch, Wood Thrush, Gray Catbird, Solitary

Vireo, Red-eyed Vireo, Scarlet Tanager, Rufous-sided Towhee, Chipping Sparrow, and Indigo Bunting.

Humpback Rocks

Highlights: Woodcock courtship, oak-forest nesting birds; Wild Turkey.

Season: Spring and summer.

Access: The Humpback Rocks area is between M 5.8 and 8.4, just south of Rockfish Gap at MP 0; from Rockfish Gap, I-81 is 13 miles to the west, and Charlottesville, Va., is 18 miles to the east on I-64.

Map: USGS "Sherando."

Facilities: Rest rooms and information at the Pioneer Farm Exhibit.

Noted for its spectacular outcroppings of Catoctin greenstone, **Humpback Rocks** looms above the Parkway 6 miles south of Rockfish Gap. To catch the spring songbird migration or to see the summer residents of middle-elevation oak forests, turn left at MP 6.0 into the Humpback Gap parking lot. The steep and strenuous summit trail begins at the south end of the lot at an elevation of 2,360 feet and goes 0.8 miles to the AT. Turn left onto the AT and proceed 800 feet to the "big rocks" (3,210 ft.), or turn right and proceed south on the AT across the summit (3,650 ft.). For a longer hike, follow the AT south to Humpback Rocks picnic area, which is accessed via a 0.3-mile connector trail that turns right off the AT 3.7 miles from Humpback Gap parking lot. These trails pass through old oak forests with many large trees, a thick laurel understory, and excellent spring wildflowers.

Typical birds in late spring and summer include Downy Woodpecker, Pileated Woodpecker, Carolina Chickadee, Tufted Titmouse, White-breasted Nuthatch, Carolina Wren, Veery, Wood Thrush, Solitary Vireo, Red-eyed Vireo, Chestnut-sided Warbler, Black-throated Blue Warbler, Cerulean Warbler, Black-and-white Warbler, Ovenbird, Scarlet Tanager, Rufous-sided Towhee, Chipping Sparrow, Dark-eyed Junco, and American Goldfinch. For the physically impaired or those not wishing to hike, the level parking lot provides good birding, including most species found along the trail.

Another good spot, particularly for the physically impaired, is **Humpback Rocks picnic area** (3,080 ft.), located on a paved side road to the left at M 8.4. Two paved loops with numerous pull offs circle through an open, medium-age oak forest. These loop roads are generally suitable for wheelchairs or easy strolling, as long as you stay alert for cars. For those who wish to get back into the woods, the Catoctin Trail is a moderate 0.2-mile hike beginning at a pull off 0.3 miles from the Parkway on the outer loop. The connector trail from the picnic area also leads to the AT, which can be hiked 3.7 miles north to Humpback Rocks and the Humpback Gap parking lot. Late spring and summer bird species here are essentially the same as those observed on the Humpback Rocks Trail, although Veeries and juncos are less often seen at the picnic grounds.

The **Pioneer Farm Exhibit** (2,320 ft.) is noted as a site to observe the aerial courtship display of American Woodcock during twilight and early evening in late March and early April. Park at the visitor center on the right at M 5.8 and proceed down the easy trail at the south end of the lot to the restored farm exhibit. Just inside the first gate is the garden area, where woodcock are often noted. The trail is paved and suitable for wheelchair use for much of the route. Continue through the exhibit to the second fence, which opens into a broad field, where Wild Turkey may sometimes be seen along the woodland edge in early morning or late afternoon.

Other spring and summer species around this site are typical of cleared farmlands, fields, and adjacent open woodlands: Turkey Vulture, Ruffed Grouse, Ruby-throated Hummingbird, Downy Woodpecker, Northern Flicker, Eastern Wood-Pewee, Eastern Phoebe, Great Crested Flycatcher, Eastern Bluebird, American Robin, Yellow-throated Vireo, Red-eyed Vireo, Cerulean Warbler, Black-and-white Warbler, American Redstart, Kentucky Warbler, Common Yellowthroat, Indigo Bunting, Rufous-sided Towhee, Chipping Sparrow, Field Sparrow, Grasshopper Sparrow, Eastern Meadowlark, and American Goldfinch.

Big Levels Area

Highlights: Summer residents of middle- to low-elevation oak forests.
Season: Spring and summer.

Access: From I-64 at Rockfish Gap (MP 0), the area is 22 miles south on
   the BRP.
Maps: USGS "Big Levels," "Sherando."
Facilities: At Sherando Lake there are boat rentals, picnic sites, concession
   stands, and sixty-five campsites.

Big Levels is among the least-explored birding areas along the
Parkway, even though the diversity of habitat and a network of backcountry trails enhance its attractiveness for those desiring a wilderness
experience. Big Levels is a high, broad crest that meanders northward into
the Great Valley from its junction with the Blue Ridge at Bald Mountain.
This mountain ridge separates the James River basin from the Shenandoah River system, with the Saint Mary's River and Wilderness on the
west slope and the South River and Sherando Lake Recreation Area on
the east side. The extensive unbroken tracts of fairly mature oak forests
support a sizable population of owls and typical low- to middle-elevation
nesting birds.

The **Bald Mountain area** is worth exploring. At M 22.1 on the Parkway, next to Bald Mountain parking lot (3,252 ft.), turn right onto FSR
162, which heads out quite a distance along the upper ridge of Big Levels.
You can park at the lot and walk along the road or drive and stop at
intervals to look and listen for Ruffed Grouse, Wild Turkey, Downy and
Pileated Woodpeckers, Eastern Wood-Pewee, Veery, Gray Catbird, Solitary
Vireo, Chestnut-sided Warbler, Black-throated Blue Warbler, Black-and-
white Warbler, Hooded Warbler, Scarlet Tanager, Rose-breasted Grosbeak, Rufous-sided Towhee, and Dark-eyed Junco. At 1.0 mile from the
Parkway, a spur road turns right for a 0.3-mile run to the summit of Bald
Mountain (3,566 ft.). Red-breasted Nuthatches were reported during the
nesting season in pine stands farther along FSR 162 in years past—the only
such records along the Parkway north of Cone Park some two hundred
miles to the south.

Many trails in **St. Mary's Wilderness** are accessed from FSR 162 along
the crest of Big Levels. To ensure a safe hike, study the route descriptions in
de Hart's *Hiking the Old Dominion*, obtain detailed topographic and trail
maps, and check with the Forest Service rangers before venturing into this
remote and often rugged area. One fairly easy route is the Bald Mountain
Trail, a moderate 2.2-mile trek that begins on the left of FSR 162, about
0.7 miles from the Parkway, and comes out on the Parkway opposite Fork

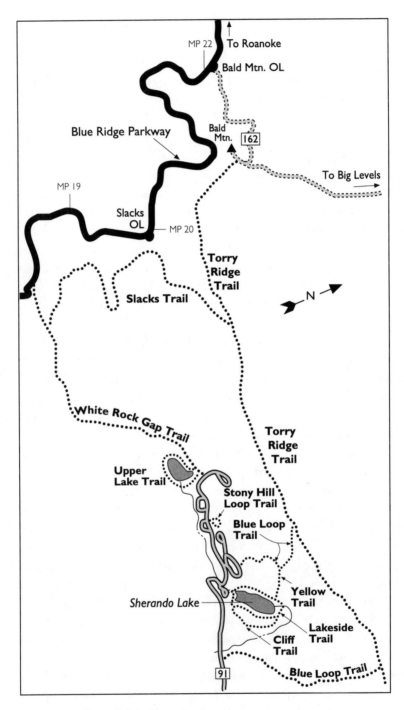

Big Levels and Sherando Lake Recreation Area, Va.

Mountain Overlook at MP 23. Bird life along the trail is identical to that noted above for Bald Mountain.

On the opposite slope of Big Levels, **Sherando Lake Recreation Area** contains a series of interconnecting trails that run between the Parkway, Big Levels ridge, and Sherando Lake, a 24-acre impoundment nestled in the valley of Back Creek, a tributary of the Shenandoah. From the Parkway, turn right onto VA 814 at M 16.1 and proceed 4.3 miles to the sign for a left turn at the entrance to Sherando Lake. The lower lake (1,839 ft.) and adjacent campgrounds are popular and busy during the summer months, and Upper Lake, Lakeside, and Cliff trails may be too crowded for undisturbed bird-watching except in the early morning. Good birding and solitude may be found on the White Rock Gap Trail, which runs 2.5 miles from Upper Lake (1,910 ft.) to White Rock Gap (2,547 ft.) on the Parkway, and the interconnecting Slacks Trail, which runs 2.6 miles to Torrey Ridge Trail. The Torrey Ridge Trail is a 3.15-mile route between Torrey Furnace and FSR 162 near Bald Mountain, with connectors to Sherando Lake via Blue Loop Trail. These moderately strenuous trails are described in detail by Adkins and by de Hart.

Bird life in the Sherando Lake region is quite diversified. Great Blue Heron, Green-backed Heron, and Belted Kingfisher may be seen at the lake; and Eastern Screech-Owl, Great Horned Owl, and Barred Owl are reported throughout the woodlands. The network of forest trails is excellent in spring migration and offers typical species in summer such as Downy Woodpecker, Pileated Woodpecker, Eastern Wood-Pewee, Acadian Flycatcher, Eastern Phoebe, Blue Jay, Carolina Chickadee, Tufted Titmouse, White-breasted Nuthatch, Carolina Wren, Veery, Wood Thrush, American Robin, Gray Catbird, Cedar Waxwing, Solitary Vireo, Red-eyed Vireo, Scarlet Tanager, Northern Cardinal, Indigo Bunting, Rufous-sided Towhee, Song Sparrow, and American Goldfinch. The area is also good for summer warblers: Northern Parula, Chestnut-sided Warbler, Black-throated Blue Warbler, Black-throated Green Warbler, Black-and-white Warbler, American Redstart, Worm-eating Warbler, Ovenbird, Louisiana Waterthrush, Kentucky Warbler, Common Yellowthroat, and Hooded Warbler.

Two nearby Parkway overlooks are worth a quick stop for birders with an interest in history. **Three Ridges Overlook** at M 13.1 and **The Priest Overlook** at M 17.6 provide views of the only documented nesting sites of the Passenger Pigeon in the Blue Ridge Mountains. In the spring of 1874,

Ruffed Grouse

Paul B. Barringer, later medical professor at the University of Virginia, visited the hatchery on Three Ridges Mountain, where "primitive nests and young covered every inch of available space on the trees," while "a neighboring peak, the Priest, also had miles and miles of area devoted to these same hatcheries." Barringer observed flocks of "hundreds of thousands, a mile long and half a mile deep," whose "passing overhead concealed the whole heavens."

Whetstone Ridge Area

Highlights: Summer birds of hemlock ravines and high meadows.
Season: Spring and summer.

Access: From VA 56 at M 27.2. On VA 56 it is approximately 7 miles to
Steeles Tavern near exit 54 on I-81.

Map: USGS "Montebello."

Facilities: Gasoline, gifts, and meals at Whetstone Ridge (M 29.7).

Two interesting and distinctly contrasting bird sites are found near
the Whetstone Ridge Recreation Area (M 29.7). Stop at **Big Spy Mountain
Overlook** (3,200 ft.) on the right at M 26.3 and check the close-cropped,
rocky, open field by walking north and south along the Parkway shoulder
or up the short trail to the crest. Species here in late spring and summer
may include Horned Lark, Vesper Sparrow, and Grasshopper Sparrow,
although more frequently encountered birds are Turkey Vulture, Eastern
Bluebird, American Robin, Barn Swallow, Gray Catbird, Indigo Bunting,
Rufous-sided Towhee, Chipping Sparrow, Field Sparrow, Song Sparrow,
and American Goldfinch. House Wrens and Northern Cardinals may be
present in farmlands northeast of the overlook.

A particularly lovely birding spot is the deep northwest-facing ravine
known as **Stillhouse Hollow** on the slope of Painter Mountain, where a
canopy dominated by Canadian hemlock, yellow birch, maples, and oaks
extends on either side of Stillhouse Hollow parking area (3,000 ft.) at
M 31.6. Stop and walk along the Parkway shoulder for 0.2 miles south
and 0.4 miles north of the overlook to watch and listen for Black-billed
Cuckoo, Eastern Wood-Pewee, Acadian Flycatcher, Barn Swallow, American Crow, Wood Thrush, Cedar Waxwing, Solitary and Red-eyed Vireos,
Northern Parula, Chestnut-sided Warbler, Black-throated Green Warbler,
Black-and-white Warbler, Worm-eating Warbler, Ovenbird, Hooded Warbler, Scarlet Tanager, and Dark-eyed Junco.

James River and Otter Creek

Highlights: Swallow nests, valley and Piedmont summer birds, fall nighthawk
migration.

Season: Spring through fall.

Access: The James River Visitor Center (M 63.6) and Otter Creek campground (M 60.7) are just north of the BRP junction with US 501 at M 63.7.

From the BRP on US 50I it is I5 miles to Lynchburg, Va., and 9 miles to
Glasgow, Va.

Map: USGS "Big Island."

Facilities: Rest rooms, books, and information at the visitor center; meals at
Otter Creek Restaurant near the campground; forty-two tent sites and
twenty-five trailer sites at the campground.

The lowest elevation along the Parkway occurs where the James
River carves its way through the Blue Ridge and emerges from the Great
Valley to flow east across the Piedmont. Here the tumbling waters of Otter
Creek descend to enter the James opposite the site of an old canal lock,
a remnant of years when the waterway was a major commercial link between the interior valley and eastern Virginia. The vegetation and bird life
are more typical of the Piedmont and Coastal Plain than of the mountains;
thus a number of species here are seldom found elsewhere along the Parkway. Birding activities center around the James River Visitor Center and
along the Otter Creek Trail.

The **James River Visitor Center** (668 ft.) at M 63.6 has information on
the region's ecology and history, and the adjacent picnic grounds and two
interpretative trails provide easy access to the bird life of the river valley. The picnic area and visitor center often have Downy Woodpecker,
Eastern Wood-Pewee, Carolina Wren, Northern Mockingbird, Carolina
Chickadee, Red-eyed Vireo, Song Sparrow, and American Goldfinch. The
sycamore trees at the river edge in the picnic grounds sometimes have
Yellow-throated Vireo and Yellow-throated Warbler. Proceed from the
visitor center down the paved path to the river, where two trails begin near
the base of the bridge.

The easy 0.2-mile **Canal Locks Trail** crosses a suspension footbridge
over the James and leads to a restored James River and Kanawha Canal
lock along the river's south bank, which is lined by sycamores and cultivated fields. In summer, the bridge is home to dozens of Barn Swallows
and Cliff Swallows, while Tree Swallows sometimes nest in bluebird boxes
in the neighboring fields. From the center of the bridge you can scan the
river and its sand spits for shorebirds, especially in spring and fall. Post-
breeding coastal waders may wander through in August and September,
and waterfowl are occasionally seen in migration or during winter. For a
particularly interesting spectacle, come here around sunset during the last
week of August, when large flocks of migrating nighthawks, often number-

ing over 700 to 800 birds, may be seen flying down the river. Broad-winged Hawk migration can also be interesting here in mid-September, and Belted Kingfishers may be seen year-round.

Continue across the bridge to the south bank canal area and check the fields in late spring and summer for Eastern Kingbird and Yellow-breasted Chat and the sycamores and woody borders for Yellow-throated Vireo, Yellow Warbler, Yellow-throated Warbler, and Prothonotary Warbler, species rarely found elsewhere along the Parkway. Other birds here in late spring and summer include Northern Bobwhite, Mourning Dove, Eastern Wood-Pewee, Eastern Phoebe, American Crow, Carolina Wren, Blue-gray Gnatcatcher, Eastern Bluebird, American Robin, Gray Catbird, Brown Thrasher, Cedar Waxwing, Red-eyed Vireo, American Redstart, Common Yellowthroat, Northern Cardinal, Indigo Bunting, Song Sparrow, Common Grackle, and American Goldfinch.

Return to the north side of the bridge and take the 0.4-mile **Trail of Trees** hike, a sometimes moderately steep, self-interpretative loop trail through a wooded ravine along the river edge. This is a good spot at night for Barred Owl, and during spring and summer months one may encounter Downy Woodpecker, Wood Thrush, American Robin, Carolina Chickadee, Tufted Titmouse, White-breasted Nuthatch, Yellow-throated Vireo, Warbling Vireo, American Redstart, Ovenbird, and other deciduous woodland species.

For a more extended hike, try **Otter Creek Trail**, which runs from Otter Creek campground and restaurant at M 60.7 (777 ft.) for 3.8 miles down to the James River Visitor Center, a change of only 110 feet in elevation. The easy stroll follows close by the banks of Otter Creek, through a medium to mature forest of oak, maple, tuliptree, pines, hemlock, and scattered rhododendron and laurel. Although sometimes noisy from the tumbling waters of the creek, the trail often provides a good look at Belted Kingfisher, Downy Woodpecker, Northern Flicker, Eastern Wood-Pewee, Acadian Flycatcher, Eastern Phoebe, American Crow, Carolina Chickadee, Tufted Titmouse, Carolina Wren, Wood Thrush, American Robin, Cedar Waxwing, Solitary and Red-eyed Vireos, Northern Parula, Pine Warbler, Black-and-white Warbler, Louisiana Waterthrush, Indigo Bunting, and Song Sparrow. The trail connects to many Parkway overlooks, conveniently permitting short hikes rather than the entire route, if so desired.

Among the more interesting overlooks along the trail is **Otter Lake**, at

M 63.1 (655 ft.), where post-breeding waders sometimes show up in mid- to late summer. Great Blue Heron, Great Egret, Little Blue Heron, Tricolored Heron, Green-backed Heron, and even White Ibis have all put in an appearance here, although the lake is often empty. An easy 1-mile loop trail encircles the lake, but you can see most of the shoreline from the paved parking area. The lowest elevation anywhere on the Parkway is at 646 feet, just south of the lake.

The overlooks along Otter Creek are broad and flat, providing good birding possibilities for the physically impaired, and the James River Visitor Center is wheelchair accessible. The paved path down from the visitor center and onto the James River footbridge can be negotiated by wheelchair, but the route is steep enough that assistance is required to get safely down and back up.

Apple Orchard Mountain

Highlights: Spring songbird migration, "Warbler Road"; Wild Turkey.
Season: Spring and summer.
Access: The area is 14 to 16 miles south on the BRP from the junction with
　　US 501 at M 63.7 and 5 to 7 miles north of Peaks of Otter (M 86); from the
　　Peaks it is 10 miles to US 221 in Bedford, Va., by VA 43.
Map: USGS "Arnold Valley."
Facilities: Gasoline, food, lodging, and campground at Peaks of Otter (M 86).

The highest elevation in the Virginia portion of the Blue Ridge Parkway occurs at 3,950 feet on the shoulder of Apple Orchard Mountain, where beautiful stands of stunted northern red oak trees grow with open canopies resembling an orchard. The mountain and surrounding area provide some of the most interesting and diversified birding in Virginia's high country, with added benefits of solitude and privacy. In summer months, when birding trails at nearby Peaks of Otter are often crowded, you will likely have the Apple Orchard area virtually to yourself. Three major attractions here are the dirt road to the mountain summit, the area at Floyd Fields, and the now-legendary "Warbler Road," which provides an altitudinal cross-section of southern Appalachian nesting birds.

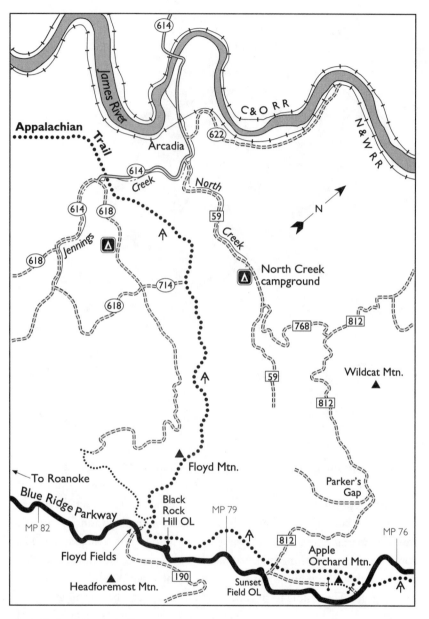

Apple Orchard Mountain, Va.

Veery

To explore the upper portions of **Apple Orchard Mountain** (4,225 ft.), park at Sunset Field OL at M 78.4, walk about 150 feet down FSR 812 at the north end of the lot, and turn right onto a dirt road that heads up toward the summit. This smooth, open road ascends gradually for 1.4 miles from 3,474 feet at the parking lot to 3,960 feet at a metal gate. The route passes through medium to mature oak woods, with some hickory, maple, yellow birch and a dense understory of rhododendron and mountain laurel. It is possible to bird this road from the car, but turning around at the gate can be tricky. The Veery chorus is particularly fine here at dawn and dusk, and Ruffed Grouse are often encountered. Other birds found in late spring and summer include Wild Turkey, Barred Owl, Downy Woodpecker, Hairy Woodpecker, Pileated Woodpecker, Eastern Wood-Pewee, Eastern Phoebe, Common Raven, Winter Wren, Wood Thrush, American Robin, Gray Catbird, Solitary Vireo, Chestnut-sided Warbler,

Black-throated Blue Warbler, Cerulean Warbler, Ovenbird, Canada Warbler, Scarlet Tanager, Rose-breasted Grosbeak, Rufous-sided Towhee, and Dark-eyed Junco. Most of these species are typical of middle- to high-elevation oak forests of the central Blue Ridge.

Another good birding site is around **Floyd Mountain**, a few miles south of Apple Orchard. Park at **Floyd Fields** (3,200 ft.), an unmarked clearing at M 80.4 where FSR 190 takes off to the left toward Headforemost Mountain. Wild Turkeys are occasionally seen at Floyd Fields or down the Forest Service road, the first part of which is an easy stroll for typical oak-forest nesting species. Turkeys are most active in early morning or late afternoon. You can get excellent views of woodland nesting birds by walking north from Floyd Fields along the Parkway shoulder toward Black Rock Hill OL, or by walking south along the Parkway toward Peaks of Otter. For about 0.7 miles south from Floyd Fields, the Parkway runs through a beautiful forest of hemlocks, oaks, and rosebay rhododendron, prime habitat for Blackburnian Warbler and many species noted previously along the dirt road on Apple Orchard Mountain.

The other attraction here is a hemlock forest in the north-facing cove along the upper reaches of Cornelius Creek. Take the fire road across the Parkway from Floyd Fields parking lot, go about 125 yards beyond the metal gate, and watch for the unmarked trailhead on the right, about 25 yards beyond the Parkway boundary signs. The trail drops off downhill about 200 yards to a shelter for the AT. Just beyond the shelter the trail passes into an old hemlock stand, one of the best spots for Blackburnian Warbler in the Virginia Blue Ridge. Other species along this easy route in spring and summer include Barred Owl, Acadian Flycatcher, Common Raven, Veery, Solitary and Red-eyed Vireos, Cerulean Warbler, Black-and-white Warbler, American Redstart, Ovenbird, and Scarlet Tanager.

Regarded by many as the best roadside birding route in the Blue Ridge, **"Warbler Road"** is actually a 13-mile-long interconnected series of USFS and county roads that descends some 2,600 feet from the Parkway to the James River. With its diversity of elevation and habitat, Warbler Road provides an outstanding all-day trip for nesting species in summer or for the spring migration from mid-April to late May. In early May, when breeders and migrants are both present, up to twenty-five warbler species may be encountered in one day. During spring migration, check for warbler waves around the catkins in the high oak canopy, which is often devoid of leaves until mid-May. Upper portions of the route are lightly used, and there are plenty of pull offs and spots where the road is wide enough for you to park, watch and listen from the car, or get out and stroll along the roadway.

Warbler Road begins as FSR 812, which starts on the right near the north end of Sunset Field OL (M 78.4) at 3,472 feet on the side of Apple Orchard Mountain. In the nesting season, stop frequently, look, and listen during the first mile for Ruffed Grouse, Wild Turkey, Downy and Pileated Woodpeckers, Eastern Wood-Pewee, American Crow, Common Raven, Tufted Titmouse, Veery, Wood Thrush, American Robin, Solitary Vireo, Chestnut-sided Warbler, Black-throated Blue Warbler, Cerulean Warbler, Black-and-white Warbler, American Redstart, Ovenbird, Canada Warbler, Scarlet Tanager, Rose-breasted Grosbeak, Indigo Bunting, Rufous-sided Towhee, and Dark-eyed Junco.

By the time you arrive at Parker's Gap (2,850 ft.), 2.8 miles from the Parkway, you may also have encountered Black-billed Cuckoo, Carolina Chickadee, White-breasted Nuthatch, Red-eyed Vireo, and Worm-eating, Kentucky, and Hooded Warblers. At 5.9 miles from the Parkway there is an area on the left where ice-storm damage and clear-cutting formerly provided habitat for Blue-winged, Golden-winged, and Brewster's Warblers; but now one is more likely to find Common Yellowthroats or Kentucky Warblers.

At 6.0 miles from the Parkway, FSR 812 forms a T-shaped intersection with FSR 768. Turn left onto FSR 768 toward North Creek campground and stop frequently along the road for Cerulean, Black-and-white, Worm-eating, and Hooded Warblers, as well as American Redstart, Ovenbird, and Indigo Bunting. FSR 768 goes 2.7 miles to its junction with FSR 59, which runs along North Creek.

Turn right from FSR 768 onto FSR 59 and pull off at intervals along the road. Between the intersection and North Creek campground are riparian deciduous tracts and stands of hemlock and white pine, which often have Eastern Phoebe, Carolina Chickadee, Tufted Titmouse, Northern Parula, Black-throated Green Warbler, Pine Warbler, Ovenbird, and Louisiana Waterthrush. Continue birding along FSR 59 until its junction in 2.8 miles with VA 614.

Turn right onto VA 614, go 0.5 miles, and turn right again onto VA 622, toward Solitude. Cross the bridge over Jennings Creek, and continue 1.6 miles to a small gravel pull off on the left, which permits parking without blocking the road. Walk back about 0.1 miles to the wooded swamp along the road and watch for nesting Wood Ducks, Prothonotary Warblers, and lots of mosquitoes. Retrace the route back to VA 614, turn right onto 614, and proceed 0.1 miles to Arcadia General Store.

Park at the store and walk very carefully along the narrow shoulder of VA 614 toward the railroad crossing and bridge over Jennings Creek, a total of 0.3 miles from the store. In wet bottomlands and sycamore flats between the railroad right-of-way and bridge, listen and look for Yellow-billed Cuckoo, Warbling Vireo, Orchard Oriole, Northern Oriole, Yellow Warbler, Prairie Warbler, and Blue Grosbeak. Return to the car and continue on VA 614 toward I-81.

At 1.1 miles beyond Arcadia General Store, VA 614 crosses the James River, elevation 800 feet. Park in the gravel lot on the left just before the bridge or drive across the bridge and park in the pull off on the left. Check the sycamores lining the river banks by watching from the bridge area or by carefully climbing down the steep embankment to cross the railroad tracks (watch out for trains!) for a closer view. The stretch of the James River half a mile above and below this bridge is good for Green-backed Heron, Yellow-billed Cuckoo, Yellow-throated Vireo, Warbling Vireo, Yellow Warbler, and Yellow-throated Warbler. From the bridge, either travel 1.2 miles on VA 614 to the junction with I-81 (exit 48, MP 169), or retrace the route back to the Parkway.

Peaks of Otter

Highlights: Middle-elevation oak-forest nesting species.

Season: Spring and summer.

Access: Peaks of Otter Visitor Center is located at M 85.9, near the junction with VA 43; on VA 43 it is 10 miles to US 221 in Bedford, Va. South on the BRP it is 20 miles to the junction with US 460 at M 105.8; on US 460 it is 9 miles to Roanoke, Va.

Maps: USGS "Peaks of Otter"; USFS "Jefferson National Forest Map Glenwood Ranger District."

Facilities: Lodge, restaurant, snack bar, and gift shop open all year; campground with eighty tent sites and sixty-two trailer sites; gasoline station open from spring through fall; visitor center with books, maps, and interpretative materials. Year-round facilities also in Bedford and Roanoke.

The 4,200-acre Peaks of Otter Recreation Area is among the most popular and heavily used sites on the Parkway. Formed of erosion-resistant igneous granites, the twin peaks of Sharp Top and Flat Top rise strongly from the Blue Ridge to dominate the surrounding topography. The northwestern portion of the area drains into the James River valley, while southeast-flowing Stoney Creek heads onto the Piedmont. The region is heavily wooded, mostly with medium to mature oak forests and cove hardwoods. These forests are excellent for spring songbird migration and for breeding-season residents characteristic of middle elevations in the Blue Ridge.

Late spring and summer birds typical of oak forests and fields may be seen around the Peaks Lodge, the picnic grounds, and the campground. Beginning in front of the lodge, **Abbot Lake Trail** (2,500 ft.) is an easy 1-mile loop walk, where a Great Blue Heron or Green-backed Heron is occasionally found in summer. Other species along the trail and in nearby **Peaks of Otter picnic grounds** and **campground** include Mourning Dove, Chimney Swift, Downy Woodpecker, Eastern Wood-Pewee, Eastern Phoebe, Great Crested Flycatcher, Blue Jay, American Crow, Carolina Chickadee, Tufted Titmouse, Eastern Bluebird, Wood Thrush, American Robin, Gray Catbird, Brown Thrasher, Ovenbird, Scarlet Tanager, Northern Cardinal, Indigo Bunting, Rufous-sided Towhee, Chipping Sparrow, Field Sparrow, Song Sparrow, and American Goldfinch. The picnic-grounds entrance is 0.7 miles down VA 43 from its junction with the Parkway at MP 86.

The flat parking lots of the picnic area provide easy strolling and wheelchair access or birding from the car. The campground woods can be a good walk in spring migration, but the road is generally too steep to be safe for wheelchairs. Although the Abbot Lake Trail is paved near the lodge and is wheelchair accessible from the parking lot, the sections that run through the woodlands, where the best birding is found, are not suitable for wheelchair use.

Another easy bird walk is along the Parkway shoulder between Fallingwater Cascades parking area at M 83.1 and **Flat Top parking lot** at M 83.5. Here the road cuts through the head of a cove hardwood forest of tulip-

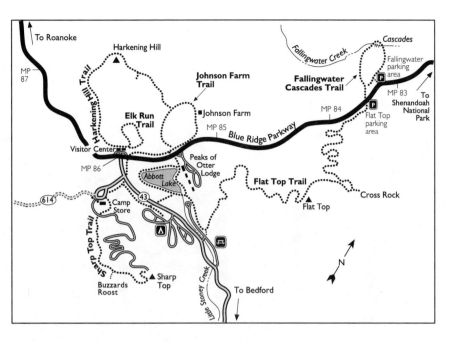

Peaks of Otter, Va.

trees, maples, and oaks at about 2,500 feet elevation near Wilkerson Gap. Park at either lot and walk carefully along the left shoulder for good looks into the canopy, which is one of the best spots on the Parkway for Cerulean Warbler. Other late spring and summer birds include Downy Woodpecker, Eastern Wood-Pewee, Solitary and Red-eyed Vireos, Black-throated Blue Warbler, Blackburnian Warbler, Black-and-white Warbler, American Redstart, Ovenbird, Kentucky Warbler, and Scarlet Tanager.

To see the greatest variety of birds at the Peaks, one can choose from five major trails that vary in length, difficulty, and habitat. These routes are all rather heavily used during the summer months. By arising early enough to catch the peak of bird activity in the first two hours after sunrise, you will usually be able to watch the birds before the crowds arrive. The following trails are listed in order of increasing difficulty. Refer to the trail guidebooks by Adkins and by de Hart for more details.

Elk Run Trail is a fairly easy 0.8-mile self-guiding loop that begins behind the visitor center (2,525 ft.) at M 85.9 and passes through a hardwood forest with some large old-growth trees. Typical late spring and summer birds include Downy Woodpecker, Eastern Wood-Pewee, Aca-

Rose-breasted Grosbeak

PRATT
1991

dian Flycatcher, Great Crested Flycatcher, Blue Jay, Wood Thrush, American Robin, Gray Catbird, Solitary and Red-eyed Vireos, Black-and-white
Warbler, Ovenbird, Kentucky Warbler, and Scarlet Tanager.

For a mixture of field and forest species, try the **Johnson Farm Loop
Trail,** a 2-mile circuit that can be accessed near the north end of the visitor
center parking lot or along the paved path that runs from the lodge under
the Parkway. This easy-to-moderate trail goes to a restored farm dating
from 1854. In addition to the species listed on the Elk Run Trail, you may
encounter Mourning Dove, Chimney Swift, Ruby-throated Hummingbird,
American Crow, Carolina Chickadee, Tufted Titmouse, Cerulean Warbler, American Redstart, Worm-eating Warbler, Northern Cardinal, Indigo
Bunting, Rufous-sided Towhee, and Chipping Sparrow.

The **Harkening Hill Loop Trail** is a moderate to occasionally steep and
strenuous 3.3-mile hike that goes from the Johnson Farm Trail back to the
visitor center by way of the summit of Harkening Hill (3,364 ft.), a high
ridge with panoramic views. The trail runs through an attractive mixed
deciduous woodland with laurel understory, where typical late-spring and
summer birds include Pileated Woodpecker, Chestnut-sided Warbler, and
Dark-eyed Junco, in addition to most of the species listed for the Elk Run
and Johnson Farm trails.

Perhaps the best birding hike at Peaks of Otter is the **Flat Top Mountain
Trail,** which ascends to the summit of Flat Top at 4,004 feet, the highest point in the area. This moderate to occasionally strenuous trail can be
hiked either from the picnic grounds near the lodge, a rather steep 1.8-mile
route, or from the Flat Top parking lot along the Parkway. The preferred
route for birding begins at Flat Top parking lot at M 83.5 (2,610 ft.) for
a 2.8-mile hike to the top (the rest of the trail descending 1.8 miles to
the picnic area). By arranging transportation or a car drop-off, you can
hike the entire 4.6 miles of trail across the mountain. The first part of the
trail passes through a cove hardwood forest where Cerulean Warblers and
American Redstarts are conspicuous in late spring and summer. The route
continues in a beautiful oak forest with an extensive understory of mountain laurel, which provides the added pleasure of a spectacular profusion
of flowers in June.

This is a good trail for Solitary and Red-eyed Vireos, as well as many
warblers, including Chestnut-sided Warbler, Black-throated Blue Warbler,
Cerulean Warbler, Black-and-white Warbler, American Redstart, Worm-

eating Warbler, Ovenbird, Hooded Warbler, and Canada Warbler. Other breeding-season species include Downy and Pileated Woodpeckers, Eastern Wood-Pewee, Acadian Flycatcher, Carolina Chickadee, Tufted Titmouse, Veery, Wood Thrush, Scarlet Tanager, Northern Cardinal, Rose-breasted Grosbeak, Dark-eyed Junco, and American Goldfinch. At 2.1 miles from the parking lot, a side trail takes off for 0.1 miles to Cross Rocks, a good spot for watching the autumn hawk migration. The main trail becomes notably steeper near the summit, where northern hardwood forests occur and Winter Wrens and Blackburnian Warblers are occasionally reported. The view of the surrounding mountains is excellent from rocky outcroppings at the top of the mountain.

The neighboring peak, **Sharp Top**, can be climbed by one of the steepest and most strenuous trails on the Parkway, or you can take the shuttle bus to the parking lot just below the summit, explore the area, and return by bus or hike down, provided you have strong knees and ankles. Unfortunately, the bus service, available only during summer months, usually starts at 10 A.M., thereby arriving on the mountaintop after the period of early-morning bird activity has passed. The trail and the bus service begin at the campground store in the parking lot across from the visitor center at M 85.9. The hike ascends 1,400 feet in only 1.6 miles to the 3,875-foot peak. Late-spring and summer species here are essentially the same as those found on Flat Top, except that Winter Wrens and Blackburnian Warblers are not expected. The view from the top is a sweeping 360-degree perspective of the mountains and of the Piedmont to the east.

Harvey's Knob Overlook

Highlights: Autumn hawk migration.

Season: Autumn.

Access: Harvey's Knob OL is at M 95.4, about 10 miles south of Peaks of Otter and 10 miles north of the BRP junction with US 460 at M 105.8. On US 460 it is 9 miles to Roanoke, Va.

Map: USGS "Montvale."

Facilities: Gasoline, food, lodging, and camping at Peaks of Otter and at Roanoke.

South of Peaks of Otter, the Blue Ridge runs in a southwesterly direction for more than ten miles as a single, narrow, straight ridge that rises sharply some 1,500 feet above the Great Valley and the Piedmont. This ideal configuration for migrating raptors is exploited by avid hawk watchers at numerous overlooks along this section of the Parkway.

The most popular and heavily used spot for autumn hawk study here is **Harvey's Knob Overlook** (2,524 ft.), on the right at M 95.4. This wide, flat parking area is often manned by birders recording detailed hawk migration data from September through November. Park, watch from the car, or set up a lawn chair facing north or northwest out into the James River valley and wait for hawks to come gliding down the ridge.

Broad-wings begin to appear in late August, usually building to peak numbers between the second and third weeks of September. Ospreys generally pass through in September, and Sharp-shinned Hawk numbers increase as Broad-winged Hawk flights begin to taper off. Red-tailed Hawks are noted mostly in November. Cooper's Hawks, Red-shouldered Hawks, Northern Harriers, American Kestrels, and Golden Eagles are reported in most years. Although the northbound migration is much lighter in the spring months, one should look for Red-tailed Hawks in March, Broad-winged Hawks in April, and Ospreys in the last two weeks of April.

Other nearby overlooks are often suitable, depending in part on wind conditions. Try **Mills Gap** (M 91.9), **Purgatory Mountain** (M 92.2), **Sharp Top** (M 92.4), **Montvale** (M 95.9), and **Great Valley** (M 99.6).

Roanoke Mountain and River Valley

Highlights: Low-elevation breeding species, migratory waterfowl, and shore-birds.

Season: Spring through fall.

Access: The River Trail (M 114.9), Roanoke Mountain Loop Road (M 120.4), and campground (M 120.5) are north of the BRP junction with US 220 at M 121.3, from which it is 4 miles north to Roanoke, Va., and 19 miles south to Rocky Mount, Va.

Maps: USGS "Garden City," "Roanoke."

Facilities: Seventy-four tent sites and thirty trailer sites at Roanoke Mountain

campground; accommodations, food, and gasoline at nearby Roanoke. For
information on the Roanoke Sewage Treatment Plant, contact the office
at 703-981-2400.

The Roanoke River gap marks the transition between the ridge
province to the north and the plateau province to the south. As in the James
River area, the relatively low elevations, ranging from 800 feet near the
river to 2,200 feet on Roanoke Mountain, are associated with plants and
birds more typical of the Piedmont than of the mountains. The woodlands
are mostly second-growth oak, with pine stands and cove hardwoods in a
few areas. In addition to the numerous bluebird nesting boxes along the
Parkway, birding attractions here include three trails for woodland species
and a side trip down to the river for migratory shorebirds and waterfowl.

Although crowded on weekends, the **Roanoke River Trail** is an easy 0.7-
mile round-trip hike through an old oak and hemlock forest along rocky
cliffs above the Roanoke River gap. Park in the lot at M 114.9 and allow time
to study the self-interpretative plaques describing trees along the route.
Late spring and summer birds include Belted Kingfisher, Downy Woodpecker, Northern Flicker, Eastern Wood-Pewee, Eastern Phoebe, Northern
Rough-winged Swallow, Blue Jay, American Crow, Carolina Chickadee,
Tufted Titmouse, Carolina Wren, Blue-gray Gnatcatcher, Wood Thrush,
Red-eyed Vireo, Black-and-white Warbler, Indigo Bunting, and Song Sparrow.

Check out the fairly mature oak forests around **Roanoke Mountain
campground** (1,420–1,500 ft.) for many of the same birds, in addition
to Summer Tanager, a typical Piedmont species that is rarely encountered
anywhere else on the Parkway in summer. Turn right onto the road at
M 120.5 and proceed 1.2 miles to the campground entrance. A good birding
trek here is the 5.4-mile **Chestnut Ridge Trail**, a moderately rigorous loop
hike that encircles the campground, with several short connector trails
providing access from the camping area or from the Chestnut Ridge OL
just before the campground entrance. For a more extended hike, or for
birding from horseback, try the **Roanoke Valley Horse Trail**, an 18.5-mile
route that connects with Chestnut Ridge Trail. Details on both routes are
provided by Adkins.

Another route for late-spring and summer birds is along **Roanoke
Mountain Loop Road** and **Roanoke Mountain Summit Trail**. Turn left
at M 120.4 for a 3.7-mile paved road toward the top of Roanoke Moun-

tain. Stop and listen at overlooks along the road. Park at the lot (2,161 ft.) 1.8 miles from the Parkway for the trailhead to the summit (2,193 ft.). The overlooks and easy-to-moderate 0.2-mile round-trip hike combine good views with typical oak-hickory summer residents, such as Downy Woodpecker, Eastern Wood-Pewee, Blue Jay, Carolina Chickadee, Tufted Titmouse, Wood Thrush, American Robin, Red-eyed Vireo, Rufous-sided Towhee, and Chipping Sparrow.

To see some of the migratory shorebirds, waterfowl, and gulls that occur in the Great Valley west of the Blue Ridge, take a side excursion to the **Roanoke Sewage Treatment Plant**. Exit onto US 220 north at M 121.3 and proceed into Roanoke toward I-581; at 5.0 miles from the Parkway take exit 6 onto Elm Avenue (VA 24) east and proceed 0.8 miles to the stoplight at 13th Street. Turn right onto 13th and drive 0.8 miles to Carlisle Avenue, the first street on the left after the Roanoke River bridge. Turn onto Carlisle, go one block, and turn left onto Kindred Street; go one block to Brownlee Avenue; turn left onto Brownlee and go 0.2 miles to the main entrance to the plant. If coming from I-81, drive 6.5 miles on I-581 to exit 6 and proceed as noted on Elm Avenue. Check in at the office in the building at the end of the road near the metal fence; drive through the gate and proceed along the river edge for 0.4 miles to the sludge ponds. Do not walk on the sludge, which is more than ten feet deep in spots. Check the impoundments, sludge ponds, processing tanks, mudflats, and river border. Bring along a spotting scope for good views of the shorebirds.

Species reported during spring shorebird migration include Black-bellied Plover, Semipalmated Plover, Greater Yellowlegs, Lesser Yellowlegs, Solitary Sandpiper, Spotted Sandpiper, Semipalmated Sandpiper, Least Sandpiper, White-rumped Sandpiper, Pectoral Sandpiper, Dunlin, Wilson's Phalarope, and Red-necked Phalarope. Various gulls and swallows are often present. In summer months, additional species include Green-backed Heron, Yellow-crowned Night-Heron, Sanderling, Western Sandpiper, Baird's Sandpiper, Stilt Sandpiper, and Short-billed Dowitcher. Many spring and summer birds pass through again in the fall months, when Lesser Golden-Plover, Buff-breasted Sandpiper, and American Pipit are more likely to occur. A visit in winter may yield Great Blue Heron, Hooded Merganser, accipiters, American Kestrel, Killdeer, Common Snipe, Ring-billed Gull, and Belted Kingfisher. Almost anything can turn up here, as evidenced by the 239 species reported at the plant. Despite this impressive species list, results are often erratic; the number of individuals and species on any given visit may be low, depending in part on the status of the impoundments.

Smart View Area

Highlights: Middle-elevation forest species; Cerulean Warblers.

Season: Spring and summer.

Access: Smart View Recreation Area (M 154.5) and VA 860 (M 159.3) are on the BRP just north of Rocky Knob Recreation Area (M 167) and VA 8 (M 165.4). From the BRP on VA 8 it is 6 miles to Floyd, Va., and 21 miles to Stuart, Va.

Map: USGS "Endicott."

Facilities: Rest rooms only. Campground and cabins are about 12 miles south on the BRP at Rocky Knob Recreation Area.

The Smart View area offers two excellent sites to observe the spring songbird migration and the breeding birds associated with oak and cove hardwood forests on the Blue Ridge escarpment.

Smart View Recreation Area (2,560 ft.) lies along the edge of the Blue Ridge Plateau and is known for its handsome stands of old-growth oak forest. Smart View's birds can be observed by exploring the picnic grounds or by hiking the moderately easy 2.6-mile loop trail that encircles the site. The picnic area is located in a medium to mature oak forest, with a paved road suitable in spots for wheelchair use. Arrive early to avoid the noisy crowds, especially on weekends.

The **Smart View Loop Trail** provides more privacy and contains more species than the picnic grounds. The route can be done in two parts. The 1.4-mile south loop begins near the parking area just before the wooden entrance gate and passes through a forest of huge white and northern red oaks, mixed with sweet birch, red maple, hickory, and dogwood, before arriving at Trail's cabin. The best birding, however, is usually on the northern 1.2-mile trail segment that extends from the cabin through cove hardwoods before entering an open field and returning to the parking lot at the entrance gate.

Cerulean Warblers are often found along the north loop of the trail.

Other regular spring and summer birds here are Red-bellied Woodpecker, Downy Woodpecker, Pileated Woodpecker, Eastern Wood-Pewee, Acadian Flycatcher, Great Crested Flycatcher, Blue Jay, American Crow, Carolina Chickadee, Tufted Titmouse, White-breasted Nuthatch, Blue-gray Gnatcatcher, Wood Thrush, Brown Thrasher, Red-eyed Vireo, Solitary Vireo, Black-and-white Warbler, American Redstart, Worm-eating Warbler, Ovenbird, Kentucky Warbler, Hooded Warbler, Scarlet Tanager, Northern Cardinal, Indigo Bunting, Rufous-sided Towhee, Chipping Sparrow, Field Sparrow, Red-winged Blackbird, Eastern Meadowlark, Brown-headed Cowbird, and American Goldfinch.

Just south of Smart View, VA 860 is a quick side excursion east of the Parkway for a close look at warblers and other spring and summer birds in cove hardwood forests of a steep ravine in the headwaters of Shooting Creek. Turn left off the Parkway at M 159.3 onto VA 860 and proceed through fields and farms until the road arrives at the plateau edge, where, at 1.8 miles from the Parkway, it enters a beautiful cove hardwood forest and begins its descent toward the Piedmont. Following close by the stream, the road has numerous pull offs where you can park and observe birds from the car or get out and stroll along the shoulder for a view into tuliptrees and rhododendrons along this tiny tributary of the Dan River. The best birding is in the first 3 miles after entering the forest at the head of the ravine. Conspicuous late-spring and summer species include Eastern Wood-Pewee, Acadian Flycatcher, Blue Jay, Tufted Titmouse, Blue-gray Gnatcatcher, Wood Thrush, American Robin, Yellow-throated Vireo, Red-eyed Vireo, Solitary Vireo, Northern Parula, Cerulean Warbler, Black-and-white Warbler, American Redstart, Louisiana Waterthrush, Kentucky Warbler, Hooded Warbler, and Scarlet Tanager.

Rocky Knob Recreation Area

Highlights: Spring songbird migration, middle-elevation nesting species, fall
hawk migration, Wild Turkey, Horned Larks.

Season: Spring through fall.

Access: The visitor center (MP 169) is south of the junction with VA 8 at BRP

M 165.4. On VA 8, it is 6 miles north to the US 221 junction in Floyd, Va., and 21 miles south to Stuart, Va., via US 58.

Map: USGS "Woolwine."

Facilities: Eighty-two tent sites and twenty-eight trailer sites at campground at M 167.1; books, maps, and information at visitor center at MP 169.

In the long stretch of Parkway between Peaks of Otter (M 85) and Doughton Park (M 240), the best birding is undoubtedly at Rocky Knob. This 4,500-acre national recreation area extends along the edge of the Blue Ridge Plateau and down into Rock Castle Gorge, named for its distinctive outcroppings of crystalline quartz that resemble the turrets of an old castle. Sheltered on the south by Brammer Spur, the gorge is a 1,500-foot-deep ravine carved into the escarpment face by the waters of Rock Castle Creek. In addition to the birding attractions, the area is renowned for beautiful oak forests on the slopes and ridges and for lush cove hardwoods along the waterways. More than twenty-five species of ferns are present, the wildflower variety provides a continual spectacle, and many salamanders occur in the wet areas. Because elevations range from 3,572 feet on Rocky Knob down to 1,700 feet near the mouth of the gorge, the bird life is a mixture of middle-elevation mountain species and those typical of the Piedmont. Many birds can be observed at overlooks, the picnic area, and the campground. The network of trails provides opportunity for hikes through fields, meadows, and forests of the backcountry.

The major trail at Rocky Knob is **Rock Castle Gorge National Recreation Trail**, a strenuous 10.8-mile loop that runs along the escarpment rim, descends into the gorge near the upper end, follows Rock Castle Creek for much of its course, and ascends back to the escarpment near the mouth of the gorge. Although some choose to do the entire route, most birders selectively hike those segments of the trail that offer the best birding. Portions of the trail along the escarpment edge closely parallel the Parkway and connect with it at the campground and at various overlooks along the way. Hikers can arrange vehicle drop-offs or retrace their steps for a variety of custom-designed routes.

A particularly good route for spring and summer birds is that segment of the trail beginning at **Saddle Overlook** (3,380 ft.) at M 167.9 and running south across the summit of Rocky Knob toward the picnic grounds and visitor center. About 100 yards from the overlook, the trail divides,

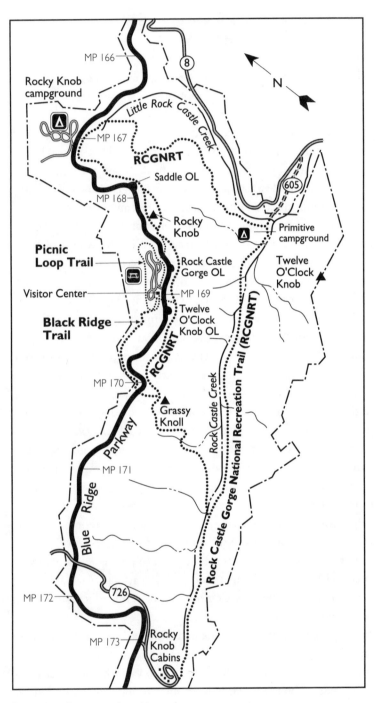

Rocky Knob Recreation Area, Va.

with the white-blazed left branch heading to a shelter and open view near the summit, and the red-blazed right fork skirting around the west slope of the knob. Both routes provide good birding, and the two trails rejoin on the opposite side of the knob, forming a moderate loop of about 1.1 miles. The forest of oak, hickory, maple, and laurel is a good place to hear and see Downy and Pileated Woodpeckers, Eastern Wood-Pewee, Eastern Phoebe, Great Crested Flycatcher, Carolina Wren, Cedar Waxwing, Solitary Vireo, Yellow-throated Vireo, Red-eyed Vireo, Scarlet Tanager, Indigo Bunting, Rufous-sided Towhee, and Chipping Sparrow. Although uncommon, Rose-breasted Grosbeaks are sometimes seen. Warblers are often conspicuous here, including Chestnut-sided, Black-throated Blue, Cerulean, Black-and-white, Kentucky, and Hooded, as well as American Redstart and Ovenbird.

Another excellent segment of the trail is the moderately strenuous 2-mile portion that descends into the gorge from Grassy Knoll (3,480 ft.) to Rock Castle Creek (2,600 ft.). Park on the shoulder at M 170.2, where the **Black Ridge Trail** crosses the Parkway, and listen carefully for Grasshopper Sparrows in the fields on the right. Cross the fence ladder on the left side of the Parkway and follow the blue-blazed Black Ridge Trail uphill through pasture lands toward the summit of Grassy Knoll. Listen for Horned Larks, which are often present in the close-cropped rocky field on the left of the trail. Near the crest, at 0.2 miles from the Parkway, the trail ends in a T-shaped intersection with the RCGNRT. For a chance at Vesper Sparrows, turn left onto the RCGNRT and explore the grassy fields to the north. Then reverse direction and head back south on the RCGNRT, continuing through a cattle guard at the fence and past the radio towers on the summit, before descending into the gorge.

Near the creek at the bottom of the gorge, the trail passes through a magnificent cove hardwood forest, where plaques and an interpretative folder, "Hardwood Cove Nature Trail," describe the major trees and shrubs. Just after crossing the creek, the trail connects with a dirt fire road that runs upstream toward the Rocky Knob Cabins or downstream toward the gorge mouth and the parking lot near VA 605. Explore up and down the road and then retrace the route back to Grassy Knoll, or have transportation arranged at either end of the dirt fire road. This hike is often outstanding in spring migration and for breeding species. The gorge is one of the few sites along the Parkway where both Black-billed and Yellow-billed Cuckoos occur. Solitary, Yellow-throated, and Red-eyed Vireos are usually present,

Scarlet Tanager

and a variety of warblers may be found, including Chestnut-sided, Black-throated Blue, Black-throated Green, Cerulean, Black-and-white, Worm-eating, Kentucky, and Hooded, along with American Redstart, Ovenbird, and Louisiana Waterthrush. Rose-breasted Grosbeaks and Scarlet Tanagers are usually noted, as well as Downy and Pileated Woodpeckers, Eastern Wood-Pewee, Acadian Flycatcher, Blue Jay, Carolina Chickadee, Tufted Titmouse, Carolina Wren, Wood Thrush, and American Robin.

As noted above, much of the trail follows a fire road between the Rocky Knob Cabins and VA 605, thereby providing two access routes to the gorge and its bird life. To get to the upper end, turn left at M 174.1 onto VA

758 (Woodberry Road) and go 0.7 miles to the intersection with VA 726; turn left onto 726 and then immediately right at the sign for Rocky Knob Cabins; go 0.1 miles down this road to the curve where the fire road begins at a metal gate on the right. If you hike in from this spot, be prepared for two slippery and sometimes dangerous stream fordings before arriving at the RCGNRT, which comes down from Grassy Knoll. To get to the bottom end of the gorge and to the dirt fire road, turn off the Parkway at M 165.2 onto VA 8 south; go 3.5 miles to the junction with VA 605; turn right onto 605 and go 0.5 miles to a small parking area near the metal gate and signs at the fire road.

Less-strenuous birding is available at **Rocky Knob picnic area** (3,150–3,200 ft.) and **Rocky Knob Picnic Ground Loop Trail**, behind the visitor center at MP 169. Portions of the picnic area are suitable for birding from the car or from a wheelchair, and the 1.3-mile loop trail is relatively easy. Both the paved road and the trail pass through a handsome forest of oak, hickory, maple, and hemlock, with an understory of rosebay rhododendron and mountain laurel. The loop trail begins just behind the visitor center building; be careful not to get onto the Black Ridge Trail, which leads off to the south. Typical late spring and summer species include Downy Woodpecker, Eastern Wood-Pewee, Acadian Flycatcher, Eastern Phoebe, American Crow, Tufted Titmouse, White-breasted Nuthatch, American Robin, Brown Thrasher, Cedar Waxwing, Solitary Vireo, Red-eyed Vireo, Chestnut-sided Warbler, Black-throated Blue Warbler, Black-and-white Warbler, Worm-eating Warbler, Ovenbird, Hooded Warbler, Scarlet Tanager, Indigo Bunting, Rufous-sided Towhee, Chipping Sparrow, and American Goldfinch.

The **Rocky Knob campground** (3,000–3,100 ft.) at M 167.1 also provides easy strolls, and the loop roads are suitable for wheelchairs. Birds are the same as those found at the picnic area, although Great Crested Flycatcher, American Redstart, and Northern Cardinal are more often noted at the campground. Both areas can be excellent during spring songbird migration.

The Rocky Knob area is also a good spot to see Wild Turkeys. The best bet is to check the edge between fields and woodlands along the Parkway from M 168.5 to 170.5 and around M 173, preferably in the early morning or late afternoon. Other activities include the autumn hawk migration, which can often be observed from the Saddle OL at M 167.9 or from the shoulder on the Parkway across from the visitor center at MP 169.

THE BLUE RIDGE PARKWAY AND ADJACENT SITES

NORTH CAROLINA

Cumberland Knob Area

Highlights: Middle-elevation forest species, autumn hawk migration; Wood
   Duck, Wild Turkey, Horned Lark.
Season: Spring through fall.
Access: Cumberland Knob Recreation Area (M 217.5) is just south of the
   BRP junction with NC 18 (M 217.3). Taking NC 18 from that junction, it is
   15 miles north to Sparta, N.C., and 22 miles south to Mount Airy, N.C.
Map: USGS "Cumberland Knob."
Facilities: Picnic grounds, rest rooms, visitor center, and gift shop with
   books, maps, and information at M 217.5.

The Cumberland Knob area offers bird species associated with a
variety of habitats typical of the Blue Ridge Plateau, such as pasturelands,
small ponds, and escarpment deciduous forests, including cove hardwoods
in headwater ravines of the Yadkin River system.

Located at M 217.5, **Cumberland Knob Recreation Area** is a 1,000-acre
tract on the plateau edge near the site where construction first began on the
Blue Ridge Parkway in 1935. Although frequently crowded during summer months, the parking area, picnic grounds, and immediately adjacent
oak forests often provide good birding opportunities for the physically
impaired. For those who wish to combine hiking with birding, two trails
begin at the visitor center, where the trailheads are clearly marked with
wooden signs. The **Cumberland Knob Trail** is an easy 0.6-mile loop climb
to the top of Cumberland Knob, from 2,740 feet at the parking lot to 2,860
feet at the summit, passing through an open oak forest with heath understory. Birds found in late spring and summer include Downy Woodpecker,
Eastern Wood-Pewee, Eastern Phoebe, Great Crested Flycatcher, Blue Jay,

White-breasted Nuthatch, Carolina Wren, American Robin, Gray Catbird, Brown Thrasher, Solitary and Red-eyed Vireos, Worm-eating Warbler, Ovenbird, Hooded Warbler, Indigo Bunting, Rufous-sided Towhee, Chipping Sparrow, and American Goldfinch.

The steep and strenuous **Gully Creek Trail** is a 2.5-mile loop that descends 780 feet into a beautiful cove hardwood forest in one of the precipitous ravines typical of the Blue Ridge Plateau escarpment. The western half of the trail passes through a mature open forest of oaks, maples, and hickories, whereas the eastern half of the trail follows close by Gully Creek through a forest of tuliptrees, maples, oaks, and rhododendron. The entire route is excellent birding, although the eastern pathway is so close to Gully Creek that the noisy cascades make it hard to hear the birds. Almost anything can turn up here in spring migration, and during late spring and summer months one may find Ruffed Grouse, Yellow-billed Cuckoo, Downy Woodpecker, Pileated Woodpecker, Eastern Wood-Pewee, Acadian Flycatcher, Great Crested Flycatcher, Blue Jay, American Crow, Carolina Chickadee, Tufted Titmouse, White-breasted Nuthatch, Carolina Wren, Blue-gray Gnatcatcher, Wood Thrush, Gray Catbird, Red-eyed and Solitary Vireos, Northern Parula, Black-throated Blue Warbler, Black-throated Green Warbler, Black-and-white Warbler, American Redstart, Worm-eating Warbler, Ovenbird, Louisiana Waterthrush, Hooded Warbler, and Scarlet Tanager. Black-billed Cuckoos are reported occasionally in summer.

Bird-watching along the **Parkway shoulder** near Cumberland Knob consists of three main attractions. To avoid serious accidents, remember to slow down, pull completely off the road, and come to a full stop before looking for birds.

One of the best areas anywhere on the Parkway for Wild Turkeys is along the wooded edges of fields and pasture between M 211 and M 224. Most active around dusk, turkeys are often reported near the state line at M 216.9 and just north of the entrance to Cumberland Knob between M 217.3 and 217.5. An excellent spot is the woodland edge of the field on the right at MP 218—one of the few good sites with room to get the car safely onto the shoulder and off the Parkway. Turkeys often cross the roadway at MP 224, where the Parkway cuts through a wooded ridge.

Close-cropped pastureland on the right side of the Parkway between M 207.5 and 207.7 is a good spot in summer for Horned Larks and other field species, such as bluebirds, meadowlarks, and Field Sparrows. Park along VA 608 at M 207.7 rather than on the Parkway shoulder, which is too narrow here for safe clearance.

Finally, a noisy but often good spot for autumn hawk migration, particularly Broad-winged Hawks in mid-September, is at MP 219. Park on the right shoulder of the Parkway, carefully cross the road, and set up a lawn chair on the grassy slope beyond the rock wall. You can get a good view here of the Piedmont and southbound hawks.

Two nearby mill ponds on the Parkway are often worth a stop. **Hare Mill Pond** (2,590 ft.) at M 225.2 may have nesting Wood Ducks in summer and migratory mergansers and other waterfowl in spring and fall, not to mention an occasional beaver. **Little Glade Mill Pond** (2,709 ft.) at M 230.1 and Little Glade Creek below the pond are good for summer warblers, such as Chestnut-sided Warbler, Louisiana Waterthrush, and Hooded Warbler.

Doughton Park

Highlights: Middle-elevation forest species, owls, autumn hawk migration; Wild Turkey, Canada Warbler.

Seasons: Year-round, but mainly spring through fall.

Access: Doughton Park is between BRP M 238 and 245, just south of the US 21 junction at BRP M 229.6. On US 21 it is 7 miles north to Sparta, N.C., and 25 miles south to Elkin, N.C. The park is north of the NC 18 junction at BRP M 248.1. On NC 18 it is 24 miles south to North Wilkesboro, N.C., and 15 miles north to Sparta.

(Note: The easiest route from the BRP to Mount Rogers, an important nearby site, is a 40-mile drive that begins by exiting at BRP M 229.7 onto US 21 north. This junction is about 9 miles north of Doughton Park on the BRP.)

Maps: USGS "Whitehead," "Glade Valley."

Facilities: Gasoline station, restaurant, picnic grounds, and Bluffs Lodge Motel with twenty-four rooms at M 241.1; campground at M 239.3 with 107 tent sites and 25 RV sites.

Known as "The Bluffs" prior to 1961, Doughton Park was named in memory of Robert Lee "Muley Bob" Doughton, a staunch advocate

Wild Turkey

of the Blue Ridge Parkway during much of his long tenure (1911–53) as Ninth District congressman from North Carolina. The 6,000-acre park encompasses a particularly attractive and rugged section of the Blue Ridge escarpment, where two beautiful deep coves are enclosed by ridges that converge downslope toward the Piedmont. Except for cleared fields along the Parkway, most of the region is cloaked in unbroken oak and cove hardwood forests. The steep eastern slopes drain into the Yadkin River system, and west-flowing streams head into the New River. Elevations range from 3,800 feet on Bluff Mountain to 1,425 feet on Basin Creek.

A network of good hiking trails offers diverse bird-watching experiences at Doughton. Two easy-to-moderate trails follow along the plateau escarpment rim, while four moderate-to-strenuous routes extend from the high country down onto the Piedmont. Although most of the trails are heavily wooded, there are a number of windfalls and large openings in the

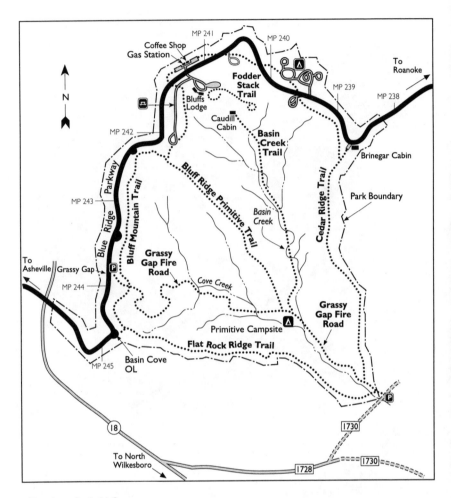

Doughton Park, N.C.

forest, for in September 1989, the eye of Hurricane Hugo passed directly across Doughton Park, wreaking considerable havoc upon many of the older and larger trees.

Perhaps the most popular hike is **Fodder Stack Trail**, a moderate 1.0-mile round-trip that runs on the plateau edge from Wildcat Rock (3,790 ft.) to Fodder Stack (3,615 ft.). Turn left at M 241.1 onto the road to Bluffs Lodge and continue past the lodge to the far end of Wildcat Rock parking lot, where the trail begins. The route is noted for its wildflowers, Table Mountain pines, Carolina hemlocks, large-toothed aspens, and views over the Piedmont and Basin Creek Cove from the rocky outcroppings along the way. Species typical of middle-elevation oak forests are present in late spring and summer, such as Cedar Waxwing, Solitary Vireo, Red-eyed Vireo, Scarlet Tanager, Rose-breasted Grosbeak, and Dark-eyed Junco. Six species of warblers are usually noted, including Chestnut-sided, Black-throated Blue, Black-throated Green, Black-and-white, Canada, and Ovenbird. Other regular birds are Black Vulture, Turkey Vulture, Eastern Wood-Pewee, American Crow, Common Raven, Carolina Chickadee, Tufted Titmouse, White-breasted Nuthatch, American Robin, Gray Catbird, Indigo Bunting, Rufous-sided Towhee, Chipping Sparrow, Field Sparrow, and Song Sparrow.

The other plateau trek is the easy-to-moderate **Bluff Mountain Trail**, a 7.5-mile hike paralleling the Parkway from Brinegar Cabin (M 238.5) to Basin Cove OL (M 244.7). This route connects with four backcountry trails, overlooks along the Parkway, the campground, the restaurant, and the picnic area, permitting a variety of custom-designed hikes to suit your needs. The trailheads and connectors are well marked at each access point. A popular birding route is the segment between Alligator Back OL (M 242.4) and Basin Cove OL (M 244.7), where mature oak and cove forests contain essentially the same species noted at Fodder Stack. Another interesting portion goes through close-cropped pastureland south of Bluffs Lodge toward the last parking lot in the picnic grounds. Horned Larks and Grasshopper Sparrows are often present in summer along this trail on the hillside south of the lodge.

Of the many recreation areas along the Parkway, Doughton is unique in having a variety of trails that can be hiked from the crest of the Blue Ridge down to the Piedmont, allowing naturalists to experience the transition in vegetation and bird life associated with changes in elevation. The steep Bluff Ridge Primitive Trail is not recommended for birding; but **Cedar Ridge Trail, Flat Rock Ridge Trail**, and **Grassy Gap Fire Road** are excellent bird routes for those willing and able to hike the backcountry. The trails are not heavily used, so birders will usually find solitude and quiet. All three routes converge near the mouth of the cove, permitting a different hike back up to the Parkway for those who do not wish to retrace their steps.

Alternatively, one can arrange for a pickup or leave a car at the small lot just beyond Basin Creek on NC SR 1730. To get there, take NC 18 south from the Parkway at M 248.1 toward North Wilkesboro; proceed 6.2 miles on NC 18 to the junction with NC SR 1728, which turns left opposite the "NC

Game Lands" sign; go 4.1 miles on NC SR 1728 to its junction with NC SR 1730; go 2.1 miles on NC SR 1730 to the bridge over Basin Creek; park in the lot just beyond the bridge, but do not leave any valuables anywhere in the car.

With a few exceptions, lists of breeding-season species are quite similar for the three trails. Birds usually found in late spring and summer on all trails include Ruffed Grouse, Downy and Pileated Woodpeckers, Eastern Wood-Pewee, Blue Jay, Carolina Chickadee, Tufted Titmouse, White-breasted Nuthatch, Wood Thrush, American Robin, Gray Catbird, Cedar Waxwing, Solitary and Red-eyed Vireos, Scarlet Tanager, Rose-breasted Grosbeak, Indigo Bunting, and Dark-eyed Junco. Ovenbirds are usually conspicuous, in addition to Chestnut-sided, Black-throated Blue, Black-throated Green, Black-and-white, and Hooded Warblers. Although infrequently encountered elsewhere on the Blue Ridge Plateau, Canada Warblers are regular along the upper end of all three routes.

Much of Grassy Gap Fire Road passes through a moist cove forest along Cove Creek: so Acadian Flycatcher, Carolina Wren, and Louisiana Waterthrush are more often seen here than on Cedar Ridge Trail or Flat Rock Ridge Trail, which follow the ridge lines through dry oak forests. The two ridge trails are more likely to have Sharp-shinned Hawk, Cooper's Hawk, and Worm-eating Warbler. Ravens are more frequent on the upper portion of Cedar Ridge Trail, but Black and Turkey Vultures are most often seen from rocky outcroppings along Flat Rock Ridge Trail. Walk along NC SR 1730 near the parking lot at the bottom and watch for Yellow Warbler, Prairie Warbler, Kentucky Warbler, Common Yellowthroat, and Yellow-breasted Chat.

For **Cedar Ridge Trail**, park at Brinegar Cabin (M 238.5) and go through the cattle guard at the end of the lot for a 0.2-mile connector trail that runs to the trailhead for both Cedar Ridge Trail and Bluff Mountain Trail. Turn left onto Cedar Ridge Trail and begin the 4.4-mile descent from 3,520 feet down to 1,425 feet at NC SR 1730. The route goes through a beautiful oak forest, with rhododendron and laurel understory, and eventually into cove forests near the bottom. Just before the first switchbacks, note the clearing to the left near large rock outcroppings; cliffs across the ravine are used as nesting sites by Turkey Vultures and Common Ravens. Forest openings along the trail give clear views of Basin Cove below and of the steep escarpment of the plateau edge.

The **Grassy Gap Fire Road** is a wide, smooth dirt road that offers hikers good views of birds in the surrounding trees. Park on the left at M 243.9 (without blocking the gate). The road runs 6.5 miles from 3,218 feet at the Parkway down to 1,425 feet at NC SR 1730. Be prepared for multiple stream crossings along the route, which descends quickly into cove hardwoods.

Flat Rock Ridge Trail goes 5.0 miles from 3,312 feet near the trailhead at Basin Cove OL (M 244.7) down to NC SR 1730. Rocky outcroppings at 1.6 and 1.7 miles give views of Bluff Mountain, Cove Creek, and soaring vultures. This is an excellent route for observing hawks in summer.

Benjamin Franklin thought the Wild Turkey should be our national bird, and it would certainly be a leading candidate for the official park bird at Doughton. Flocks of up to thirty-five turkeys are occasionally reported along the Parkway here, although smaller groups are more the rule. The best area is the stretch of **Parkway shoulder** between M 243.5 and MP 246, where the birds cross the road and split-rail fences in early morning or late afternoon. Park along the shoulder and check field edges and woodland borders. Stop at Basin Cove OL (M 244.7) and walk north along the Parkway past the cemetery at M 244.5. Cross the fence and scan the woods and fields, especially around the old farm buildings downslope. Check with the rangers for other good spots with recent sightings.

Doughton Park may well be the best all-round spot along the Parkway for raptors. As noted previously, Sharp-shinned Hawks are occasionally encountered in summer along Flat Rock Ridge Trail or Cedar Ridge Trail. The elusive Cooper's Hawk is also resident at Doughton, but it is seldom observed except as a fall transient. Red-tailed and Broad-winged Hawks are readily seen from overlooks and along the trails in summer. Turkey Vultures are a permanent fixture. The Black Vulture, generally rare and local in the southern Blue Ridge, is often noted at Mahogany Rock OL (MP 235), Wildcat Rock OL (beyond Bluffs Lodge near M 241), and Basin Cove OL (M 244.7), as well as along Flat Rock Ridge Trail.

With its large tracts of mature woodlands, the park harbors a considerable owl population, including Great Horned Owl, Barred Owl, and Eastern Screech-Owl. Stop along the Parkway, listen carefully, and play tapes of the calls, starting with the Screech and working up to the Great Horned. Try any overlook, although good bets are at **Devil's Garden** (M 235.7), **Brinegar Cabin** (M 238.5), **Alligator Back** (M 242.4), and **Basin Cove** (M 244.7).

An excellent place to catch the autumn hawk migration near Doughton is in the vicinity of **Mahogany Rock**, 4 miles north of the campground.

The southbound raptors can be observed from several vantage points, the easiest and most popular being next to the Mahogany Rock OL (3,436 ft.) on the right at MP 235. Pull off onto the broad, grassy, flat area along the Parkway just where the paved road heads down to the actual overlook. The hawks usually come in from the northeast, appearing just beyond Mahogany Rock, the broad rounded hill east of the overlook. Ideal for the physically impaired, this spot also allows you to watch from lawn chairs if the weather is mild or to sit inside your vehicle when it is cold and blustery.

For a higher angle view of the hawks and surrounding scenery, combined with more privacy, a moderate 30-minute hike leads from Mahogany Rock OL to the old cable-car facility on **Scott Ridge** (3,762 ft.). Cross the Parkway to the side opposite the MP 235 marker and walk into the woods on the barely discernible footpath; this path runs past large rock outcroppings on the left for about 150 yards until it hits a hairpin turn in the old jeep road to the summit. Proceed uphill to the right on this road, which soon follows the ridge and heads south to the remaining concrete foundations of the cable-car site. Although surrounding woods are beginning to obscure some of the view, the perspective here remains excellent for hawk watching. The hawks are usually first sighted near Bullhead Mountain to the northeast, with the flight line coming across Mahogany Rock and then over Scott Ridge.

Other interesting spots near Doughton include **Hare Mill Pond** at M 225.4, which often has nesting Wood Ducks, migratory mergansers, and an occasional beaver. **Little Glade Mill Pond** and Little Glade Branch at MP 230 are good in late spring and summer for Acadian Flycatcher, Ovenbird, Louisiana Waterthrush, Hooded Warbler, and Dark-eyed Junco. South of Doughton, **Meadow Fork Creek** parallels the Parkway between MP 246 and NC 18 at MP 248, where the open fields are a good spot for Killdeer and Tree and Barn Swallows; Belted Kingfishers are noted along the stream.

For a side excursion to find Swainson's Warblers, exit the Parkway onto US 21 at M 229.6 and proceed 10 miles south toward Elkin, N.C., to NC SR 1002. Turn right onto NC SR 1002 and go 4.3 miles to NC SR 1784. Turn right onto NC SR 1784 and go 2.5 miles to the entrance and park office for **Stone Mountain State Park**. From the park office, continue on for 2.8 miles to a road on the left that goes 0.5 miles to the small parking lot for the trailheads and a picnic area. Take the 1.2-mile Stone Mountain Falls Trail, which passes through beautiful thickets of rosebay rhododendron along tumbling mountain streams before arriving at the waterfalls. Listen along this route for the Swainson's, which are present in some years. Be sure to arrive early, especially on weekends, as this easy trail can be packed with hikers in late spring and summer. Get a copy of the park's trail map and explore other routes in the park, which has an interesting mixture of Piedmont and mountain birds.

The New River

Highlights: River-valley species; Warbling Vireo, Northern Oriole, Empidonax flycatchers.

Season: Spring and summer.

Map: USGS "Mouth of Wilson."

Facilities: Food, gasoline, accommodations, and camping at Doughton Park and in Sparta, N.C., and Laurel Springs, N.C., and in Fancy Gap, Va., and Hillsville, Va. For park information, contact the New River Trail State Park, Rt. 1, Box 81X, Austinville, VA 24312.

If you think the Magnolia Warbler was misnamed, consider the New River, which is actually the oldest river system in North America and second only to the Nile in antiquity. Originating more than 100 million years ago in the ancient Appalachians, the ancestral route of the New River extended across present-day Ohio, Indiana, and Illinois to empty into the northern arm of the Gulf of Mexico. Over the millennia, the meandering route of the river became deeply incised into the underlying rocks, as periods of mountain-building uplift occurred. The glacial ice sheets subsequently obliterated much of the ancient drainage pattern, diverting the flow into the Ohio River. In more recent times, the valley has been inhabited by American Indians and extensively cleared for agriculture and timber. Portions of the area are now protected, in part, as a national and state natural and scenic river. The headwaters of the New River drain much of the southern portion of the Blue Ridge Plateau province, and the bird life along the river includes a number of species infrequently noted elsewhere so close to the Parkway. Two sites, one in North Carolina and the other in Virginia, provide access to the river edge.

To explore the South Fork of the New River, exit the Parkway at MP

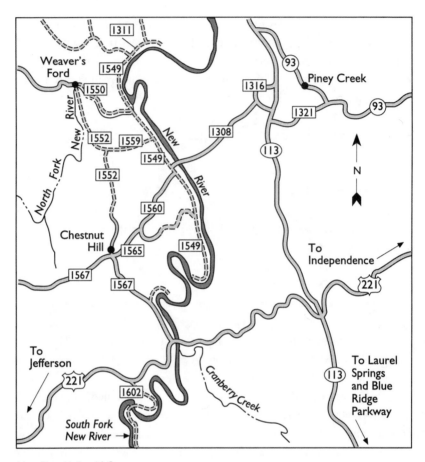

New River Valley, N.C.

248 onto NC 18 north toward Laurel Springs and Sparta. At 2.8 miles from
the Parkway on NC 18, turn left onto NC 113 north. Go 9.0 miles on NC
113 to where NC SR 1316 turns off to the left; go 0.3 miles on NC SR 1316
and then turn left onto NC SR 1308, which goes 2.2 miles to a bridge over
the New River next to Rivercamp USA. During late spring and summer,
Warbling Vireos are sometimes found in the sycamores at the entrance to
Rivercamp. Cross the bridge over the New River, turn left onto NC SR
1560, and go 0.1 miles to NC SR 1549.

Turn left onto NC SR 1549, which runs close by the river for several miles
of excellent birding. Stop frequently along here, particularly at 0.2 and 0.8

miles, where stands of sycamore and Balm-of-Gilead trees are usually home in late spring and summer to Yellow-throated Vireo, Warbling Vireo, and Northern Oriole. Check the thickets for Willow Flycatcher and Yellow-breasted Chat. Scan the river for Spotted Sandpiper, Tree Swallow, Northern Rough-winged Swallow, and Barn Swallow. Continue about 2.2 miles from the bridge, then retrace your route. When stopping, pull well over and take care not to block private driveways.

Return to NC SR 1560, turn right, and proceed past the bridge to continue north along the river edge on NC SR 1549, stopping frequently. At 0.3 to 1.0 mile north of the bridge there are willow and shrub thickets. At 1.4 miles the road crosses the North Fork New River bridge; turn right just after crossing the bridge and continue on NC SR 1549, checking for Spotted Sandpiper, Willow Flycatcher, and swallows. At 2.1 miles, NC SR 1549 enters the woods; at 2.6 miles, turn right onto NC SR 1311 and proceed to the junction with NC SR 1310 at 3.2 miles. Turn around and head back to the bridge over the North Fork, but proceed on NC SR 1550 to Weavers Ford and then south on NC SR 1552 toward Chestnut Hill, stopping at regular intervals for field and riparian birds. Then retrace the route back to the bridge at NC SR 1308 and thence to the Parkway. The elevation along this portion of the river is around 2,500 feet.

Another good spot is the 1-mile section of NC SR 1567 immediately north of New River bridge across US 221. Turn west onto US 221 at the junction with NC 113 and go 4 miles to the New River General Store, just beyond the bridge. Turn right at the store onto NC SR 1567 and check the thickets along the river for Willow Flycatcher.

Many other good birding sites are scattered along the North and South forks of the New River. To explore the region thoroughly, get detailed highway maps of Ashe and Alleghany counties and note the segments of state and county roads that parallel close by the riverside.

For a different approach to birding, try a canoe trip down the New River. Numerous outfitters service the area, and most allow custom-designed trips, letting you decide when and where to put in and take out. Birding by canoe gives a closer view and access to much of the river that cannot be reached by car or trail. However, basic canoeing skills are needed to make the trip safe and fun, and it may be hard to divide your attention between the birds and the rapids. Portions of North Carolina's **New River State Park** are designed to accommodate canoeing and riverside camp-

Northern Oriole

ing, and the bird-watching is often excellent in the park lands. Contact the park headquarters at P.O. Box 48, Jefferson, NC 28640. For listings of the canoe outfitters in the area, contact the Ashe County Chamber of Commerce, West Jefferson, NC 28694.

Whether explored by canoe or from state roads, the area demonstrates a striking diversity of bird life. During late spring and summer, the main attractions along the river, fields, and wooded hillsides include Empidonax flycatchers: Acadian, Willow, and Least; three swallows: Tree, Northern Rough-winged, and Barn; four vireos: White-eyed, Yellow-throated, Warbling, and Red-eyed; and two orioles: Orchard and Northern. Wood Duck, Spotted Sandpiper, and Belted Kingfisher are regularly present. Osprey are commonly seen during spring migration in April. Nesting warblers are richly represented, with Golden-winged, Yellow, Prairie, Black-and-white, and Hooded, along with Northern Parula, American Redstart, Ovenbird, Common Yellowthroat, and Yellow-breasted Chat.

Other late-spring and summer species include Turkey Vulture, Broad-winged and Red-tailed Hawks, American Kestrel, Wild Turkey, Northern Bobwhite, Mourning Dove, Black-billed and Yellow-billed Cuckoos, Whip-poor-will, Red-bellied Woodpecker, Downy Woodpecker, Pileated Woodpecker, Northern Flicker, Eastern Wood-Pewee, Eastern Phoebe, Great Crested Flycatcher, Eastern Kingbird, American Crow, Carolina Chickadee, Tufted Titmouse, White-breasted Nuthatch, Carolina Wren, House Wren, Blue-gray Gnatcatcher, Eastern Bluebird, Wood Thrush, American Robin, Gray Catbird, Brown Thrasher, Cedar Waxwing, Scarlet Tanager, Northern Cardinal, Blue Grosbeak, Indigo Bunting, Rufous-sided Towhee, Chipping Sparrow, Field Sparrow, Song Sparrow, Red-winged Blackbird, Eastern Meadowlark, Common Grackle, Brown-headed Cowbird, and American Goldfinch.

Farther downstream in Virginia, the **New River Trail State Park** follows the river for 57 miles between Galax, Va., and Pulaski, Va. Quick access from the Parkway is to exit at M 199.5 onto US 52 north at Fancy Gap; proceed 1.0 mile to the junction with VA 148; turn left onto VA 148; and go 0.8 miles to I-77. Turn north onto I-77 and go 15.5 miles north to exit 5; turn off onto VA 69 and go 0.3 miles into Poplar Camp. Turn left onto US 52 north toward Fort Chiswell and proceed 1.4 miles to VA SR 624; turn left onto state road 624 and go 0.1 miles to the entrance to Shot Tower State Park. Access to the New River Trail is well marked near the Shot Tower.

If the gate is locked, turn right onto VA SR 608 and proceed to its junction with US 52 near the river bridge, where you can park near the trail.

The New River Trail, located on Norfolk and Western's old railroad bed, provides easy, flat hiking along the river. Explore the trail about 1 or 2 miles upstream from the park, checking in late spring and summer for Spotted Sandpiper, Willow and Alder Flycatchers, Warbling Vireo, and Northern Oriole. The woodlands along the river are great for migrating songbirds in April and May, along with Osprey in the last half of April. Expected summer species include Eastern Wood-Pewee, Acadian Flycatcher, Carolina Wren, American Robin, White-eyed Vireo, Yellow-throated Vireo, Red-eyed Vireo, Yellow Warbler, American Redstart, Scarlet Tanager, Common Grackle, and Indigo Bunting.

E. B. Jeffress Park Area

Highlights: Middle-elevation forest species; Cerulean Warblers.

Season: Spring and summer.

Access: Cascades Trail parking lot (M 271.9) and Lewis Fork OL (M 270.2) are north on the BRP from its junction with US 421 at M 276.4 near Deep Gap. From the BRP on US 421 it is 12 miles to Boone, N.C., and 26 miles to North Wilkesboro, N.C.

Map: USGS "Maple Springs."

Facilities: Rest rooms at Cascades Trail parking lot.

The Jeffress Park area provides good spots for spring migration and breeding-season birds associated with oak and cove hardwood forests, including some of the best Parkway sites in North Carolina for Cerulean Warblers.

E. B. Jeffress Park is a 600-acre tract dedicated to the man who chaired the N.C. Highway Commission in 1934 and was an avid proponent of the Parkway. Perched at the edge of the Blue Ridge Plateau, the park is best known for the Cascades waterfalls along Falls Creek, which plunge through a steep ravine toward the Yadkin River valley of the Piedmont some 2,000 feet below.

The **Cascades Nature Trail** is a moderately strenuous 1.2-mile loop trail that descends from 3,570 feet at the trailhead to around 3,400 feet at the falls. Beginning near the rest rooms at the north end of the parking lot, this excellent birding trail passes through a fairly mature oak forest with an understory of rhododendron and laurel before entering typical cove hardwoods along the stream, with Fraser magnolia, hemlock, and birch. For the first 100 feet, the trail is paved and level, providing wheelchair access into the upper oak woods. The usual late spring and summer birds here include Downy Woodpecker, Eastern Wood-Pewee, Carolina Chickadee, Tufted Titmouse, White-breasted Nuthatch, Wood Thrush, Solitary Vireo, Black-throated Blue Warbler, Black-throated Green Warbler, Black-and-white Warbler, Ovenbird, Hooded Warbler, Canada Warbler, Scarlet Tanager, Rufous-sided Towhee, and Dark-eyed Junco. Arrive early if you come on weekends, as this popular spot gets crowded during the summer months.

Near **Lewis Fork Overlook** just north of Jeffress Park, the Parkway passes through the head of a cove hardwood forest that contains tall tulip-trees, maples, and oaks. Pull completely off onto the shoulder around M 270.5 and look and listen from the car or stroll along the roadside. Alternatively, park at Lewis Fork OL at M 270.2 (3,295 ft.) and walk south along the Parkway shoulder to the area between M 270.4 and 270.7. During the nesting season, Cerulean Warblers are usually present here, along with Pileated and Downy Woodpeckers, Black-billed Cuckoo, Eastern Wood-Pewee, Eastern Phoebe, Acadian Flycatcher, Blue Jay, White-breasted Nuthatch, Carolina Wren, Wood Thrush, Red-eyed and Solitary Vireos, Black-throated Blue Warbler, Black-throated Green Warbler, Black-and-white Warbler, American Redstart, Ovenbird, Scarlet Tanager, and Indigo Bunting. Another good bet for Cerulean Warblers is to pull off on the left shoulder opposite MP 277, just north of **Stony Fork Valley Overlook** (3,504 ft.) near Deep Gap.

Moses H. Cone Park

Highlights: Middle- and high-elevation summer residents, fall hawk migration.
Season: Year-round, but mainly spring through fall.
Access: Cone Park is south of the junction with US 321 at BRP M 291.9; from

the BRP on US 321, it is 7 miles to Boone, N.C., and 2 miles to Blowing
Rock, N.C.

Map: USGS "Boone."

Facilities: Rest rooms, books, maps, and information at Cone Manor
(M 294.1); gasoline, food, and accommodations in Blowing Rock and
Boone. Camping at Price Park (M 297.1).

Cone Park is a 3,516-acre tract that commemorates Moses H.
Cone (1857–1908), the North Carolina textile magnate whose love of
horticulture and the mountains are reflected in the beauty of this estate.
Located at the southern end of the Blue Ridge Plateau, Cone Park and
nearby Julian Price Park lie on rolling tableland just back of the escarpment edge, with elevations ranging up to 4,558 feet on Flat Top Mountain.
The diversity of bird life here in large measure reflects the variety of plant
communities in the park, much of that attributable to collaborative work
between Cone and pioneering forester Gifford Pinchot. Pinchot was later
the first director of what is now the U.S. Forest Service and twice governor
of Pennsylvania.

Birds more commonly found at higher elevations often occur in hemlock
and white pine stands; Bass Lake attracts waterfowl much of the year; and
the fields, oak forests, and developed areas harbor species typical of each
habitat. A 25-mile network of old carriage roads meanders through the
park, providing gentle grades for bird-watching hikers and popular routes
for horseback riding and cross-country skiing.

Among the most interesting and attractive bird hikes at Cone Park is the
1-mile loop trail around **Trout Lake** (3,760 ft.), a 16-acre impoundment
nestled in a magnificent hemlock-dominated cove forest, with ancient conifers and a thick rhododendron understory. The plants and summer birds
are similar to those at Sim's Creek in nearby Price Park. Both sites harbor bird species that are also associated with high-elevation spruce-fir and
northern hardwood forests: Yellow-bellied Sapsucker, Red-breasted Nuthatch, Golden-crowned Kinglet, and Blackburnian Warbler, all of which
are usually present during the nesting season. Veery and Rose-breasted
Grosbeak are often noted, and Brown Creeper is a possibility. Other late-
spring and summer birds are Downy and Pileated Woodpeckers, Acadian
Flycatcher, Blue Jay, Carolina Chickadee, Tufted Titmouse, Gray Catbird, Solitary and Red-eyed Vireos, Northern Parula, Chestnut-sided Warbler, Black-throated Blue Warbler, Black-and-white Warbler, Ovenbird,

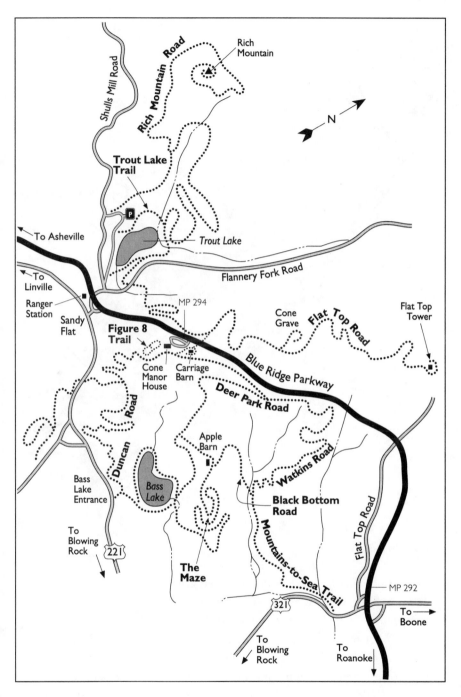

Moses H. Cone Park, N.C.

Yellow-bellied Sapsucker

Common Yellowthroat, Hooded Warbler, Canada Warbler, Rufous-sided Towhee, Song Sparrow, and Dark-eyed Junco.

To reach Trout Lake, turn left at M 294.6 onto the connector toward US 221, but then immediately take the first right toward Shulls Mill and Flannery Fork roads, passing back under the Parkway. Then take the left fork toward Shulls Mill, but just beyond the split take the one-way paved road to the right that runs to Trout Lake parking lot. Proceed down this road to the parking lot and take the trail from there, or park on the grassy shoulder just where the road splits off from Flannery Fork Road and look for the trailhead on the right.

Just below Cone Manor, 22-acre **Bass Lake** (3,560 ft.) often has nesting Wood Ducks in summer and should be checked in spring and fall for migratory loons, grebes, mergansers, geese, ducks, and shorebirds. Anticipate a species list similar to that at Price Lake in nearby Julian Price Park. The carriage road around Bass Lake is more heavily used than the trail at Trout Lake, but some of the same species can be found here in summer, along with Barn Swallow, House Wren, and White-breasted Nuthatch. Check the white pine, hemlock, and spruce for Red-breasted Nuthatch, Golden-crowned Kinglet, and even Brown Creeper. You can walk to the lake from the Manor House or turn left off the Parkway at M 294.6 and then left onto US 221, proceeding 1 mile toward Blowing Rock to the small parking lot on the left. Walk through the metal gate, check the conifers here, and take the carriage path down to the lake.

Another easy hike is the **Figure Eight Trail** (4,000 ft.), a 0.7-mile self-guiding loop that runs through a high, open woods of oak, hickory, maple, and rhododendron. Turn left into the parking lot at M 294.1, park, and locate the trailhead behind the Manor House. Late-spring and summer species include Downy Woodpecker, Tufted Titmouse, Veery, Wood Thrush, Red-eyed Vireo, Chestnut-sided Warbler, Black-throated Blue Warbler, Black-and-white Warbler, Ovenbird, Hooded Warbler, Canada Warbler, Scarlet Tanager, Rose-breasted Grosbeak, Rufous-sided Towhee, and Chipping Sparrow. Be alert for Black-billed Cuckoo and Yellow-bellied Sapsucker, which are occasionally noted.

All the carriage trails provide an excellent way to see the park's bird life, but one of the best routes combines portions of **Watkins Road, Black Bottom Road,** and **Maze Road.** Leave the Parkway at M 291.9 and head south on US 321 toward Blowing Rock. Less than 0.1 miles after getting on US 321, pull off quickly onto the narrow gravel shoulder just before a dirt road that turns right into the woods (3,550 ft.). Park here and head down this road, which is part of the Mountains-to-Sea Trail system. In 0.15 miles the trail turns left and crosses a stream, continuing on for 0.9 miles to the junction with Black Bottom Road on the left. Take Black Bottom Road 0.5 miles to the old Apple Barn and continue on down Maze Road toward the left until the first hairpin switchback (3,730 ft.). Retrace the route to the car at US 321, and be very careful when pulling back into traffic.

This 4-mile round-trip takes you through beautiful hemlock cove forests along Flat Top Branch and Middle Fork, headwater streams of the South Fork New River, and then through a tract of ancient white pine trees on a ridge line. In the late spring and summer, the coves are home to Eastern Wood-Pewee, Acadian Flycatcher, Blue Jay, Golden-crowned Kinglet, Veery, Solitary and Red-eyed Vireos, Northern Parula, Black-throated Blue Warbler, Blackburnian Warbler, Ovenbird, Louisiana Waterthrush, Hooded Warbler, Canada Warbler, and Rufous-sided Towhee. The white pines on Maze Road have Golden-crowned Kinglets and Blackburnian Warblers in their crowns—easy to hear but hard to see.

Another good carriage trail for summer birds is **Flat Top Road**, where Yellow-bellied Sapsuckers are sometimes found, along with many species noted at Trout Lake.

From September through November, **Thunderhill Overlook** (3,776 ft.) at M 290.5 is a good spot to observe the southbound hawk migration. Watch from the car at the overlook or walk across the Parkway, through the cattle guard, and up the hillside. About 100 yards from the fence, turn left and go to the open summit for a wide perspective. The pasture here often has Horned Lark, Song Sparrow, and Dark-eyed Junco in summer.

Julian Price Park

Highlights: Middle- and high-elevation summer residents; Alder Flycatcher.
Season: Spring through fall.
Access: Price Park facilities are located between M 296.5 and M 297.1, a few
   miles south of the junction with US 221 at M 294.6; on US 221 it is 1 mile
   east to Blowing Rock, N.C.
Map: USGS "Boone."
Facilities: Campground (M 297.1) with 134 tent sites and 60 trailer sites; 100
   picnic sites (M 296.5); boat rentals at lake in summer. Gasoline, food, and
   accommodations in Boone, N.C., and Blowing Rock.

Nestled at the foot of Grandfather Mountain, Julian Price Park is a 4,344-acre tract that marks the transition from the Blue Ridge Plateau to the high Blue Ridge province, the latter extending south to the Black Mountains. The summer bird life at Price Park reflects this transition

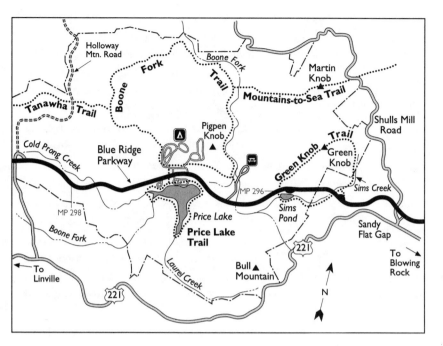

Julian Price Park, N.C.

in the mix of high-elevation and middle-elevation birds, with a number of species not found elsewhere on the plateau section except at adjacent Cone Park. These include Yellow-bellied Sapsucker, Veery, Red-breasted Nuthatch, Golden-crowned Kinglet, and Blackburnian Warbler. The area is heavily timbered with oak forests; but northern hardwoods, beautiful hemlock groves, boggy wetlands, and impounded lakes add diversity to the avifauna. The park's bird life is best sampled along the hiking trails, most of which are fairly easy walks.

A particularly good birding area is along **Sim's Creek,** with its magnificent cove forest of old-growth hemlock, maple, magnolia, birch, beech, and rosebay. There are two ways to see the birds here. Park at Sim's Pond (3,447 ft.) at M 295.9 and take the Green Knob Trail from the base of the dam along the creek into the woodlands. Before leaving the pond, check for Pied-billed Grebe from fall through spring and Spotted Sandpiper and Belted Kingfisher in summer. This easy trail passes under the Parkway at 0.5 miles, where the forest is at its best. The second approach is from the Sim's Creek parking lot (3,608 ft.) on the right at M 295.3, just north of the Parkway bridge. You can often sit in your car here and look out into the canopy to see many of the birds. Others may wish to walk north along the Parkway shoulder or descend the rather steep connector trail that leads down to the Green Knob Trail coming up from Sim's Pond.

Among the species reported along Sim's Creek in late spring and summer are Yellow-bellied Sapsucker, Downy Woodpecker, Hairy Woodpecker, Pileated Woodpecker, Acadian Flycatcher, Eastern Phoebe, Redbreasted Nuthatch, Golden-crowned Kinglet, Veery, Wood Thrush, Gray Catbird, Cedar Waxwing, Solitary and Red-eyed Vireos, Scarlet Tanager, Rose-breasted Grosbeak, and Dark-eyed Junco. Up to ten warbler species are present in some years, including Northern Parula, Chestnutsided, Black-throated Blue, Black-throated Green, Blackburnian, Blackand-white, Ovenbird, Louisiana Waterthrush, Hooded, and Canada. The trail becomes steeper as it continues on to Green Knob (3,930 ft.) and back to the parking lot in a 2.4-mile loop that passes through fields where one may see Eastern Kingbird, Tree Swallow, Barn Swallow, Brown Thrasher, Field Sparrow, Eastern Meadowlark, Common Grackle, Brown-headed Cowbird, and American Goldfinch.

Another popular and easy hike is the 2.5-mile loop around **Price Lake** (3,380 ft.), a 47-acre impoundment of Boone Fork. Turn left at M 297.1 and drive to the parking lot near the boat shed, where the trail begins on the right. Following close by the lake, the trail is sometimes muddy but otherwise an easy walk that passes through an oak forest with laurel and rhododendron understory. A list of typical late-spring and summer birds would include Belted Kingfisher, Eastern Wood-Pewee, Acadian Flycatcher, Eastern Phoebe, Northern Rough-winged Swallow, Barn Swallow, Carolina Chickadee, Tufted Titmouse, White-breasted Nuthatch, Wood Thrush, Gray Catbird, Cedar Waxwing, Solitary and Red-eyed Vireos, Northern Parula, Chestnut-sided Warbler, Black-throated Blue Warbler, Black-andwhite Warbler, Ovenbird, Canada Warbler, Scarlet Tanager, Northern Cardinal, Rose-breasted Grosbeak, Rufous-sided Towhee, Common Grackle, and American Goldfinch. The trail crosses the dam and follows the lake edge back to the parking area.

Although not a hot spot for water birds, the lake occasionally has something interesting, such as Great Blue Heron, Green-backed Heron, Wood Duck, American Black Duck, or Mallard. When the lake is not frozen over, other waterfowl may appear in fall, winter, or spring; possible species include Common Loon, Pied-billed Grebe, Canada Goose, Green-winged

Teal, Blue-winged Teal, Gadwall, Canvasback, Ring-necked Duck, Common Goldeneye, Hooded Merganser, and even Common Merganser. When the lake level is low, spring shorebird migration from mid-April through late May has yielded a considerable list, including Semipalmated Plover, Greater Yellowlegs, Lesser Yellowlegs, Solitary Sandpiper, Spotted Sandpiper, Semipalmated Sandpiper, Least Sandpiper, White-rumped Sandpiper, and Short-billed Dowitcher.

One of the more interesting hikes at Price Park is a segment of the **Boone Fork Trail** near the picnic area. Although the entire 4.9-mile loop provides a good backcountry experience, portions of the trail are strenuous, difficult to follow, and too noisy to hear the birds. Instead of doing the whole thing, try birding the first mile or so from the picnic parking area. Turn right into the picnic grounds at M 296.4 and park on the left just beyond the first set of rest rooms, where a wood sign indicates "Boone Fork Trail." Cross the wooden bridge over Boone Fork, go 40 yards, and take the right branch of the trail, which goes about 100 yards along the stream before entering an ancient lake bed. The lake bed is now the site of the Boone Fork wetlands (3,340 ft.), an extensive sphagnum bog with open sedge flats, willows, shrubs, and a number of rare plants. The trail runs about 300 yards along the edge between the bog and Boone Fork. Two to four pairs of Alder Flycatcher are usually present here in late spring and summer, along with American Robin, Gray Catbird, White-eyed Vireo, Chestnut-sided Warbler, Common Yellowthroat, Rufous-sided Towhee, Indigo Bunting, and Song Sparrow. The aerial courtship display of the American Woodcock can be seen here from mid-March through late April.

The trail continues 300 yards through increasingly thick woodlands to a small bridge, where you should be alert for beavers along the stream. In another 200 yards, the trail passes a large rock outcropping on the left and follows close by Boone Fork, which begins a steep descent down a riverbed of huge boulders reminiscent of western mountain streams. Hiking about a half mile down this portion of the trail will give ample exposure to the bird life; then retrace the route back to the parking lot. In addition to the birds noted previously, expected late-spring and summer species here and along the rest of the trail include Ruffed Grouse, Belted Kingfisher, Downy and Pileated Woodpeckers, Northern Flicker, Carolina Chickadee, Tufted Titmouse, Veery, Wood Thrush, Brown Thrasher, Cedar Waxwing, Solitary and Red-eyed Vireos, Black-throated Blue Warbler, Black-and-white

Warbler, Ovenbird, Canada Warbler, Scarlet Tanager, Northern Cardinal, Rose-breasted Grosbeak, Dark-eyed Junco, Red-winged Blackbird, Common Grackle, and American Goldfinch.

For the physically impaired, many of these species can be seen in the campground (M 296.9), picnic area (M 296.4), and overlooks along the lake edge, including the parking area for the amphitheater (M 297.1), all of which are suitable for wheelchairs or birding from the car. When the weather is dry, the Boone Fork wetland bog may be accessible by wheelchair along the Boone Fork Trail.

One additional spot worth checking is the **Cold Prong wetlands** (3,420 ft.). Pull off on the shoulder near the fence at M 297.7 just north of the Parkway culvert over Cold Prong. Walk along the shoulder or cross the fence into the shrubby area that extends along the stream edge. Willow Flycatchers are reported in some years, and American Bitterns have been seen here, though more likely spring and summer birds include Belted Kingfisher, Eastern Phoebe, Common Yellowthroat, Indigo Bunting, and Song Sparrow.

Grandfather Mountain

Highlights: Middle- and high-elevation woodland species, autumn hawk migration; Hermit Thrush, Magnolia Warbler.

Season: Year-round, but mostly spring through fall.

Access: Grandfather is between BRP M 300 and M 305. On US 221 west of Blowing Rock, N.C., take Holloway Mountain Road north for 1 mile to the BRP junction at M 298.6, or go 3 miles east of Linville, N.C., on US 221 to the BRP junction at M 305.1.

(Note: The easiest route from the BRP to Roan Mountain, an important nearby site, is a 33-mile drive that begins by exiting at BRP M 305.1 onto US 221 toward Linville, N.C., just south of the Linn Cove Visitor Center.)

Maps: USGS "Grandfather Mountain," "Valle Crucis," "Boone"; USFS "Pisgah National Forest—Grandfather, Toecane and French Broad Ranger Districts"; also topographic and trail map available at Grandfather Mountain entrance office; Tanawha Trail map available from Blue Ridge Parkway.

Facilities: Snacks available at the museum and visitor center on Grandfather;

books and information at the Linn Cove Visitor Center on the Parkway
at M 304.5. Parkway camping at Julian Price Park at M 297.1; numerous
backcountry camping sites on Grandfather, all requiring permits for use.
Closest motels and restaurants are at Linville; others at the ski resorts on
NC 184 and in Boone, N.C., and Blowing Rock. For information and hiking
permits, contact Grandfather Mountain, P.O. Box 128, Linville, NC 28646
(704-733-4337 or 800-468-7325).

Grandfather Mountain captured the attention of naturalists as
early as August 1794, when the peripatetic French botanist André Michaux
climbed to the summit and, believing he had found the highest peak in
North America, burst forth with the Marseilles hymn in exuberant celebra-
tion of the event. Those who have explored Grandfather's rugged slopes
can well appreciate Michaux's enthusiasm, for this mountain remains one
of the premier natural sites in the southern Appalachians.

At 5,964 feet, Grandfather is the highest mountain on the Blue Ridge
front, where it rises abruptly some 4,000 feet above the adjacent Piedmont
to dominate the surrounding landscape. Although named for its profile,
Grandfather is in fact one of the most ancient peaks in the world, with esti-
mates that its rugged quartzite rocks are more than 1.1 billion years old.
No other major southern Appalachian mountain is composed of quartzite,
an exceptionally durable rock whose resistance to erosion is well demonstrated in the spectacular scenery. Dramatic cliffs, rocky outcroppings, and
huge boulders are commonplace, while the high crest line is an irregular
jumble of ragged, fractured crags. Streams tumble down the steep slopes,
flowing south into the Catawba River system of the Piedmont and north
into the Watauga, a tributary of the Tennessee.

Diversity is the key word at Grandfather, where visitors encounter a
broad range of scenery, weather, plant life, animals, and activities. The
climate around the summit is notoriously intense. Hundred-mile-per-hour
winds are occasionally reported, and dense fog is not uncommon at any
time of year. Winter months are characterized by heavy ice, deep snow,
and severe windchills in the highest elevations.

The rugged terrain and harsh weather conditions along the main crest
have profoundly affected the summit vegetation, which consists of a mixture of stunted spruce, fir, northern hardwoods, and heath species, often
resembling a subalpine environment in exposed sites. At middle and low
elevations, northern hardwoods and conifers give way to oak forests on

Northern Raven

ridges and slopes and to cove forests in wet ravines and stream borders. Beautiful heath balds are common on steep ridges and open slopes. Many rare and endangered plants are found on the mountain, and sixteen species of salamanders are present.

Eighty-four bird species have been observed during the breeding season, including twenty warblers, giving Grandfather one of the richest avifaunas of any comparably sized area in the southern Blue Ridge. Typical spruce-fir and northern hardwood birds are present in the high and middle elevations; but a few of the northern species reported here, such as Hermit Thrush and Magnolia Warbler, are particularly scarce and localized in the southern mountains. Grandfather is a prime spot for raptors, including some elusive species, such as Northern Saw-whet Owl and Peregrine Falcon. During the fall months, migrating hawks are often seen from the high vantage points.

Most of Grandfather Mountain is privately owned and operated as a recreation area that requires an entrance fee and a hiking permit for use of the trails and other facilities. If you plan to do a lot of exploring, consider a seasonal pass, which may save you some money. The Blue Ridge Parkway skirts along the southeastern slope of the mountain and provides free public access to overlooks and to the park service's delightful Tanawha Trail, which parallels the Parkway through a variety of habitats. Birding opportunities range from areas that are suitable for wheelchairs or roadside birding to some of the most rugged and difficult backcountry trails in the southern mountains.

Several Parkway overlooks and the nearby **Tanawha Trail** offer a good introduction to the summer bird life at Grandfather. The Parkway meanders across the mountain's eastern and southern ridges, gradually climbing above 4,400 feet near **Linn Cove**, site of the viaduct and visitor center. For a good look at middle- to high-elevation forest birds, turn left into the Linn Cove Visitor Center parking lot at M 304.5 (4,315 ft.) and park near the far end of the paved area, where the Tanawha Trail heads north toward the viaduct. The trail is paved and fairly level for about 0.15 miles from the lot, providing an easy hike and an excellent wheelchair-birding route through the dark, cool forest of hemlock, beech, oaks, magnolias, red spruce, and rhododendrons.

In late spring and summer, this segment of the trail and the parking lot are prime spots for Barred Owl, Downy Woodpecker, Blue Jay, Carolina Chickadee, Winter Wren, Golden-crowned Kinglet, Veery, Gray

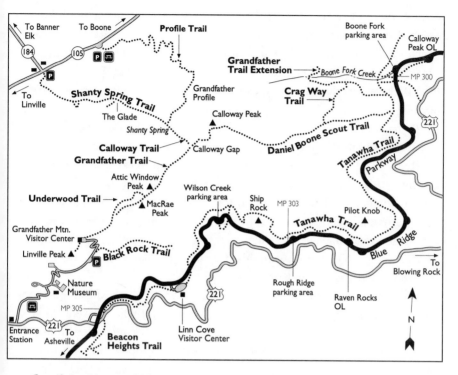

Grandfather Mountain, N.C.

Catbird, Solitary Vireo, Northern Parula, Black-throated Blue Warbler, Black-throated Green Warbler, Black-and-white Warbler, Canada Warbler, Rose-breasted Grosbeak, Indigo Bunting, Rufous-sided Towhee, and Dark-eyed Junco. The visitor center has rest rooms, books, maps, and information about Grandfather and its trails. Another half-dozen overlooks are scattered along the Parkway on Grandfather Mountain, providing additional sites to observe many of the same species or to park your car for access to the Tanawha Trail.

One of the best routes in the southern mountains for scenery, plants, and birds, the **Tanawha Trail** skirts along Grandfather's southeast flank close to the Parkway for 13.5 miles from Price Park campground to Beacon Heights OL. "Tanawha" is said to be Cherokee for "fabulous hawk" or "eagle," reflecting appropriately the trail's excellence for natural history. Completed in 1987 at a cost of $700,000, this moderate-to-easy segment of the Mountains-to-Sea Trail traverses a spectrum of geological features and plant communities. Although the entire trail is good for birding and can be walked in one day, many naturalists prefer to explore selected portions where the birds and vegetation are most interesting. Before hiking any of the Tanawha, get a copy of the trail map from a Parkway visitor center and study the detailed accounts of the route given by Adkins or de Hart in their trail guides. Many access connectors link the Tanawha with the Parkway overlooks, so you can custom design a variety of round-trip or one-way hikes.

Perhaps the most popular area on the Tanawha is the 1.4-mile segment between Rough Ridge parking lot and Wilson Creek parking lot. Arrive early to avoid the often large crowds, especially on weekends. Park in the Rough Ridge lot (4,293 ft.) at M 302.8, take the short connector trail to the Tanawha, and head left (south) for 0.2 miles, passing through northern hardwoods and scattered spruce to the forest edge, where an abrupt transition to an open heath slick occurs as the trail begins its climb across Rough Ridge. Summer birds in this stretch of woodland include the same species noted at the Linn Cove area.

To protect the fragile heath ecosystem that covers Rough Ridge, the first portion of the trail traverses a wooden boardwalk, where several large decks can be used to watch the Broad-winged Hawk migration in September. The trail then ascends to the rugged outcroppings of Ship Rock (4,690 ft.), another good vantage point to catch the autumn hawks. The route wanders through a delightful mix of Catawba rhododendron, mountain laurel, spruce, maples, sand myrtle, blueberry, ferns, wildflowers, and a disjunct population of large-toothed aspen. Expect to find species typical of Appalachian heath balds and woodland margins, such as Cedar Waxwing, Gray Catbird, Chestnut-sided Warbler, Canada Warbler, Rufous-sided Towhee, Song Sparrow, and Dark-eyed Junco. Common Ravens are often seen soaring overhead. On a clear day in early June, the profusion of flowers and abundant bird life combine with views of Grandfather's brooding summit, the Piedmont below, and nearby Linville Gorge to make Rough Ridge a sublime experience.

Beyond Ship Rock toward Wilson Creek, the Tanawha descends quickly into a mature deciduous forest of oak, cherry, birch, beech, maple, spruce, ash, and hemlock, where typical late-spring and summer birds include Great Horned Owl, Barred Owl, Downy Woodpecker, Hairy Woodpecker, Pileated Woodpecker, Blue Jay, American Crow, Carolina Chickadee, White-breasted Nuthatch, Winter Wren, Golden-crowned Kinglet, Veery, Gray Catbird, Solitary Vireo, Chestnut-sided Warbler, Black-throated Blue Warbler, Black-throated Green Warbler, Black-and-white Warbler, Canada

Warbler, Scarlet Tanager, Rose-breasted Grosbeak, Rufous-sided Towhee, and Dark-eyed Junco. From Ship Rock it is 0.9 miles on to the Wilson Creek parking area (4,357 ft.) at M 303.6 or 0.5 miles back to the Rough Ridge parking area.

Although the entire Tanawha Trail provides good birding, other particularly attractive segments include the 0.8-mile portion between the Rough Ridge parking area and Raven Rocks OL (4,335 ft.) at M 302.4 as well as the 3.4-mile trek between Raven Rocks OL and Boone Fork parking lot (3,905 ft.) at M 299.9, both portions passing through northern hardwoods, spruce, and high cove forests.

Two other Parkway trails just south of Grandfather are usually worth a check. The **Beacon Heights Trail** is a moderate 0.7-mile round-trip from the Beacon Heights parking lot (4,220 ft.) at M 305.3 through spruce, hemlock, northern hardwoods, and rosebay and Catawba rhododendrons. Be alert here for Northern Saw-whet Owls calling from April through June. In September and October, the open view at the summit includes not only Grandfather Mountain but also autumn hawks heading south. In late spring and summer, the trail is a good spot for Blue Jay, Common Raven, Carolina Chickadee, Tufted Titmouse, Red-breasted Nuthatch, Winter Wren, Golden-crowned Kinglet, Veery, Wood Thrush, Gray Catbird, Brown Thrasher, Solitary Vireo, Chestnut-sided Warbler, Black-throated Blue Warbler, Black-throated Green Warbler, Black-and-white Warbler, Ovenbird, Canada Warbler, Rufous-sided Towhee, Song Sparrow, and Dark-eyed Junco.

Farther south, the **Flat Rock Trail** is an easy, level 0.7-mile loop that runs from the parking lot (3,987 ft.) at M 308.2 through an open mature oak forest to good views of Grandfather Mountain, Roan Mountain, and the Black Mountains. Many species listed at Beacon Heights are found here also, although Saw-whets and Winter Wrens are not to be expected.

For easy roadside birding and looks at middle-elevation species, exit the Parkway left at M 307.9 (3,940 ft.) onto NC SR 1511, which meanders down the south slopes of Grandfather Mountain and Grandmother Mountain and provides some good birding stops. Many species noted at Beacon Heights and Flat Rock can be found here, in addition to typically lower-elevation summer residents. From the Parkway, state road 1511 descends 4.5 miles before becoming FSR 981, which runs 4.4 miles from the vicinity of Roseborough (2,200 ft.) to Edgemont (1,600 ft.). In the last 2.5 miles before Edgemont, the road follows close by Rockhouse Creek to its junction with Wilson Creek. Look for Least Flycatcher and Warbling Vireo along this lower section.

To get onto the rugged summit peaks of Grandfather, you must use various access routes maintained by the Grandfather Mountain Corporation, which charges a fee for the permits required for hiking or vehicle travel. The easiest and quickest way to the high country is by car on the steep paved road that runs 2.3 miles from the main entrance on US 221 to the Swinging Bridge parking area on Linville Peak. Exit the Parkway at M 305.1 onto US 221 and proceed 1 mile west from the Parkway to the entrance station, where you can obtain permits, refreshments, detailed trail maps, weather reports, and information on backcountry campsites. At 0.6 miles up this road, the picnic area on the right is sometimes worth a quick check for typical middle-elevation woodland birds, mostly the same species found on the Tanawha Trail and at Linn Cove. Proceeding upward, consider a stop at the nature museum and animal habitats at 1.2 miles, where close-up looks at native mammals and raptors may appeal to you and your camera.

Two birding hikes are possible from this road, the first being the **Black Rock Trail**, an easy-to-moderate route that begins in the large parking lot 1.9 miles from the entrance station and runs 1.3 miles through northern hardwood and spruce forests, descending from 5,040 feet down to 4,700 feet. Typical spring and summer birds here include Common Raven, Red-breasted Nuthatch, Winter Wren, Golden-crowned Kinglet, Veery, Gray Catbird, Cedar Waxwing, Solitary Vireo, Chestnut-sided Warbler, Black-throated Blue Warbler, Canada Warbler, Rose-breasted Grosbeak, Rufous-sided Towhee, Song Sparrow, and Dark-eyed Junco. Red Crossbills are always a possibility.

The second hike from the paved summit road involves the **Grandfather Trail**, a rugged and steep route that works its way 3.3 miles along the main crest of Grandfather between the Swinging Bridge parking lot and Calloway Peak (5,964 ft.), the highest point on the mountain. If you plan to do any hiking in the high country, be prepared for severe weather conditions, even in midsummer, and take seriously the warnings that the Grandfather Trail is one of the most physically demanding routes in the southern Appalachians. Fortunately, the first half mile of the trail from the parking lot to the junction with the Underwood Trail is only moderately rigorous and provides an excellent introduction to the bird life found in the stunted spruce-fir forests, northern hardwoods, and heath balds of the high country. For the more resilient and adventuresome, the trail continues on across MacRae Peak (5,939 ft.) and Attic Window Peak (5,949 ft.) to the moderate ridge trek to Calloway Gap, just 0.5 miles from Calloway Peak.

Spring and summer birds typically found along the Grandfather Trail include Ruby-throated Hummingbird, Downy and Hairy Woodpeckers, Common Raven, Red-breasted Nuthatch, Brown Creeper, Winter Wren, Golden-crowned Kinglet, Veery, Gray Catbird, Cedar Waxwing, Solitary Vireo, Chestnut-sided Warbler, Canada Warbler, Common Yellowthroat, Rufous-sided Towhee, Song Sparrow, and Dark-eyed Junco. Other less frequently encountered species are Ruffed Grouse, Sharp-shinned Hawk, Northern Saw-whet Owl, Black-throated Green Warbler, Rose-breasted Grosbeak, Red Crossbill, and Pine Siskin. Be alert for Hermit Thrush and Magnolia Warbler, recently found to be extending their summer ranges southward.

If you prefer longer but less orthopedically demanding hikes into the high country, try the interconnected Shanty Spring Trail and Profile Trail on the northwest slope of Grandfather. Exit the Parkway at M 305.1 and head west 1 mile on US 221 to the main entrance station to obtain a hiking permit. Continue 2 miles west on US 221 into Linville, turn right onto NC 105 toward Boone, and drive 4 miles to the junction with NC 184, where the Shanty Spring Trail parking area is located on the right along NC 105.

The **Shanty Spring Trail** climbs steeply from the parking lot (4,040 ft.) for 1.8 miles to the junction with the Profile Trail at 5,160 feet. From this junction you can take the Calloway Trail for a steep and rocky half mile to the Grandfather Trail along the main crest line, where a fairly easy 0.5-mile walk leads to the highest point on the mountain. The Shanty Spring Trail passes through a cross section of the major plant communities on Grandfather, including rich mixed mesophytic forests, some beautiful stands of old hemlocks with rosebay understory, northern hardwoods, and scattered red spruce. Between 4,600 and 4,900 feet are The Glades, an open grassy forest with oaks, beech, and some hemlock and red spruce. Barred, Northern Saw-whet, and other owl species have been reported at The Glades, and Blackburnian and Black-throated Green Warblers are likely there.

An easier alternative for birding the north slope is the recently completed **Profile Trail,** a 2.6-mile route that begins in the well-marked parking lot (3,880 ft.) along the Watauga River just 0.5 miles beyond the Shanty Spring trailhead on NC 105. This easy to moderately strenuous trail passes through some beautiful mature cove hardwoods, oak forests, and northern hardwood tracts before ending at the junction with the Shanty Spring Trail. If you are in good condition, a popular circuit hike is to go up the Profile Trail, descend the Shanty Spring Trail, and then walk carefully along the shoulder of NC 105 back to the car for a total of 5.1 miles. A side excursion on to the summit via the Calloway and Grandfather trails adds 2 more miles and the satisfaction of having climbed all the way to the top, well worth considering if you are in prime shape.

These hikes on the northwest slope are outstanding in spring migration, when almost anything can turn up. In late spring and summer, one can expect to observe Ruffed Grouse, Downy, Hairy, and Pileated Woodpeckers, Eastern Wood-Pewee, Common Raven, Carolina Chickadee, Tufted Titmouse, Red-breasted Nuthatch, White-breasted Nuthatch, Brown Creeper, Winter Wren, Golden-crowned Kinglet, Veery, Wood Thrush, American Robin, Solitary Vireo, Red-eyed Vireo, Black-throated Blue Warbler, Black-throated Green Warbler, Blackburnian Warbler, Black-and-white Warbler, Ovenbird, Canada Warbler, Scarlet Tanager, Rose-breasted Grosbeak, Rufous-sided Towhee, and Dark-eyed Junco. The side trip to the top may yield the species previously listed for the Grandfather Trail.

On the opposite side of the mountain, **Crag Way Trail** and **Grandfather Extension Trail** provide easy to occasionally steep routes into woodlands and beautiful heath thickets reminiscent of those on the Tanawha Trail around Rough Ridge, but with considerably more privacy than the latter site. Remember to get your hiking permit at the Grandfather entrance station and then park in the Boone Fork parking area at M 299.9. Take the connector to the Tanawha, turn left (south) on the Tanawha, and proceed 0.2 miles to the Grandfather Extension Trail on the right. Head up the trail to the well-marked Crag Way Trail, which begins on the left 0.6 miles from the Tanawha Trail. The Crag Way Trail goes 1 mile from here to its junction with Daniel Boone Scout Trail, which in turn runs up to Calloway Peak.

The main attraction on Crag Way Trail is the possibility of Magnolia Warblers in the Top Crag area, where an open heath thicket and infiltrating spruce trees cloak the rocky outcroppings along the south rim of Boone Fork Bowl, which looks remarkably like a glacial cirque. The late-spring and summer bird life along these two trails is similar to that noted previously for the Tanawha Trail.

Linville Gorge

Highlights: Low-, middle-, and high-elevation woodland species, autumn
   hawk migration; Peregrine Falcon, Red Crossbill.
Season: Spring through fall.
Access: Linville Falls Recreation Area (M 316.4) is north of the junction with
   US 221 at BRP M 317.6; from the BRP on US 221 it is 24 miles south to
   Marion, N.C., which is just north of I-40. The area is south of the junction
   with NC 181 at BRP M 312.2; from the BRP on NC 181 it is 32 miles south
   to Morganton, N.C., which is just north of I-40.
Maps: USGS "Linville Falls" and "Ashford"; USFS "Linville Gorge Wilder-
   ness" is preferred because its shows topography and current trail routes.
Facilities: Gasoline, food, and lodging in Linville Falls, 0.6 miles south of the
   Parkway on US 221. Linville Falls campground (M 316.4) has fifty-five tent
   sites and twenty trailer sites. The visitor center at the falls parking lot has
   books, maps, information, and rest rooms.

The Linville River arises on the slopes of Grandfather Mountain
and carves the deepest gorge in the East as it escapes from the Blue Ridge
to join the Catawba River on the Piedmont below. The surrounding mountains are composed of extremely resistant Precambrian granitic quartzites,
solidified more than a billion years ago from molten rock. Competition
between these durable rocks and the forces of erosion has created distinctive geologic formations, particularly on Jonas Ridge, which forms
the gorge's eastern rim. Bold outcroppings, steep cliffs, and rocky spires
characterize the Jonas Ridge peaks, including Hawksbill, Table Rock, the
Chimneys, and Shortoff. Linville Mountain forms the western rim, with
similar elevations but more subdued topography, except for the high cliffs
at Wiseman's View.

Dropping precipitously some 2,000 feet from rim to valley floor, the
rugged gorge walls made the region unsuitable for extensive logging. Consequently, many areas are cloaked in virgin timber. A botanist's delight,
Linville Gorge is covered largely by oak forests, with cove hardwoods in
sheltered ravines, pitch and Table Mountain pine on dry ridges, and widely
scattered stands of Carolina and Canada hemlock and white pine. Many
rare and endangered plants are included in the rich and diverse flora of
the region. The Linville Falls Recreation Area was preserved through the
generosity of John D. Rockefeller, and 10,975 acres of the gorge have been

incorporated into Linville Gorge Wilderness, a part of the original national wilderness system.

With its diversity of plant communities, unique topography, and wide range of elevations, the Linville area is inhabited by summer birds representing a mix of Piedmont, middle-elevation, and high-mountain species. The gorge is one of the best spots on the Parkway for Peregrine Falcon and Red Crossbill, both of which are known to nest here. Birding opportunities range from easy viewing at overlooks and parking lots to strenuous backcountry wilderness hikes.

To begin a visit, turn left at M 316.4 and proceed to the **Linville Falls parking lot** (3,185 ft.), 1.4 miles from the Parkway. The parking lot and first part of the falls trail across the river are suitable for wheelchairs or casual walking. In the nesting season, check the tall white pines and hemlocks here for Red-breasted Nuthatch, Golden-crowned Kinglet, and Blackburnian Warbler, which are often present. Ruffed Grouse, Least Flycatcher, Cerulean Warbler, and Red Crossbill are always a possibility in the area around the lot, trail, and access road. The more frequently encountered species are Downy and Pileated Woodpeckers, Eastern Phoebe, American Crow, Carolina Chickadee, Tufted Titmouse, White-breasted Nuthatch, Carolina Wren, Wood Thrush, Gray Catbird, Brown Thrasher, Cedar Waxwing, Solitary and Red-eyed Vireos, Scarlet Tanager, Northern Cardinal, Rose-breasted Grosbeak, Rufous-sided Towhee, and Dark-eyed Junco. This is a good spot for summer warblers, including Northern Parula, Chestnut-sided, Black-throated Blue, Black-throated Green, Black-and-white, Ovenbird, Kentucky, and Hooded. Walk onto the bridge behind the visitor center and check the river for Green-backed Heron, Spotted Sandpiper, Belted Kingfisher, Acadian Flycatcher, and Louisiana Waterthrush.

For a short but intermittently steep hike, continue on **Erwin's View Trail** from the bridge toward a group of four overlooks perched above the falls and the head of the gorge. The same species listed for the parking-lot area may be expected along the trail, which passes through a beautiful stand of hemlocks, white pine, and rhododendron. The gravel path is broad and fairly smooth, and the open woods enhance the odds of getting a good look at the birds. Erwin's View (3,360 ft.) is the highest of the four overlooks and also the longest hike from the visitor center (2 miles round-trip), but the view and the bird list are often worth the effort. A less frequently used trail is the **Plunge Basin Overlook Trail**, which runs from the left side

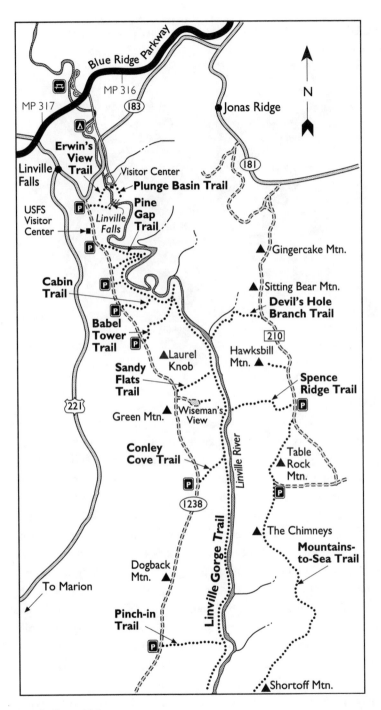

Linville Gorge, N.C.

Red Crossbill

of the visitor center to a spectacular view from the east rim of the gorge in a sometimes steeply descending 1-mile round-trip. A branch of this trail goes down to the riverside, but Plunge Basin OL is usually a better bird spot, in addition to having a fine show of Carolina rhododendron intermixed with the more common Catawba and rosebay. The parking lot and Erwin's View Trail become very crowded on weekends, so arrive early for best birding. Eastern Screech-Owl, Great Horned Owl, and Barred Owl are possibilities for nighttime birding along the trails, parking area, and wooded portions of the access road from the Parkway, as well as at the picnic area, Riverbend OL, and campground.

Other easy birding spots are in the **Linville Falls campground** and **picnic area** and at the **Riverbend Overlook**. All three sites are immediately adjacent to the Linville River (3,200 ft.), flowing placidly here before beginning its 12-mile tumble through the gorge. Many of the same birds noted at Linville Falls parking lot and trails are also found at these sites, along with additional species, most of which are associated with open fields and the river. These include Wood Duck, Broad-winged Hawk, Chimney Swift, Northern Flicker, Eastern Kingbird, Northern Rough-winged Swallow, Barn Swallow, Blue-gray Gnatcatcher, Yellow Warbler, Chipping Sparrow, Field Sparrow, Song Sparrow, and Red-winged Blackbird. Check for Pine Warbler in the pines at the picnic grounds, one of the few spots where this low-country bird summers on the Parkway. From the Parkway on the falls access road (M 316.4), it is 0.3 miles to Riverbend OL and 0.4 miles to the campground. The picnic area runs along the river for 0.4 miles along an access road, which is a right turn off the Parkway at M 316.5. All three sites are flat and suitable for the physically impaired, though the picnic loop road is probably the best spot for wheelchairs.

A trip along the gorge's west rim features several excellent birding spots, spectacular vistas into the chasm, and access trails leading down to the river far below. Exit the Parkway at M 317.6 and proceed 0.6 miles south on US 221 into the town of Linville Falls; turn left onto NC 183 and continue for 0.7 miles; then turn right onto NC SR 1238, a dirt road where a sign indicates "Linville Falls and Linville Gorge Wilderness Area." Parts of this road are bumpy, steep, and sometimes impassable in bad weather, but the family car can usually make it to Wiseman's View when the road is dry. At 0.5 miles after leaving NC 183, the U.S. Forest Service visitor center on the right has books, maps, and information on the gorge and wilderness area.

Beyond the visitor center, a series of seven trails begins on the east (left) side of NC SR 1238 and descends steeply down to join the Linville Gorge Trail, a rugged 11.5-mile route that follows the river's west bank down to the gorge mouth. Noise from the nearby river makes it hard to hear birds along much of this trail, but the seven connector trails from NC SR 1238 are excellent birding routes, despite their often strenuous gradients. The upper portions of several of these trails pass through groves of old hemlock and rhododendron, nestled at the head of moist ravines, where you can get good looks at a mix of high- and middle-elevation summer residents in a beautiful and uncrowded setting only a short distance from the car. Get a copy of the "Linville Gorge Wilderness" topographic and trail map to study the possibilities for in-and-out hikes or combination loops involving part of NC SR 1238. Stay alert all along the road for Red Crossbills, this being one of the best spots in the southern Blue Ridge for these erratic birds.

Stop at 0.9 miles for the **Pine Gap Trail** (3,300 ft.), the first and easiest route to the river. This 1-mile trail passes through a mature forest of oak, hickory, hemlock, rhododendron, and laurel, with good views into the upper end of the gorge. Late-spring and summer birds include Downy and Pileated Woodpeckers, Acadian Flycatcher, Eastern Phoebe, Blue Jay, Carolina Chickadee, Tufted Titmouse, White-breasted Nuthatch, Carolina Wren, Golden-crowned Kinglet, Wood Thrush, American Robin, Cedar Waxwing, Solitary and Red-eyed Vireos, Scarlet Tanager, Rufous-sided Towhee, Indigo Bunting, and Dark-eyed Junco. Expect to see a good variety of warblers, including Northern Parula, Black-throated Blue, Black-throated Green, Black-and-white, Ovenbird, Louisiana Waterthrush, and Hooded.

At 2.7 miles from NC 183 on NC SR 1238, the **Babel Tower Trail** (3,800 ft.) begins its 1.3-mile descent to the river. The first part of the trail is fairly level and passes through an attractive grove of hemlock and rhododendron. The bird list is similar to that at Pine Gap, with the addition of Red-breasted Nuthatch and Canada Warbler. Red Crossbills are often noted along the lower portions of the trail.

At 3.8 miles from NC 183 on state road 1238 is the spur road left to **Wiseman's View** (3,400 ft.), which offers a grand look at the gorge and a good spot for Common Raven and Red Crossbill. The summer bird list here is similar to that for Pine Gap and Babel Tower, except that Red-breasted Nuthatch, Golden-crowned Kinglet, and Canada Warbler are not found at Wiseman's. Great Crested Flycatchers and Worm-eating Warblers are often present here. An Olive-sided Flycatcher was once reported in the vicinity of Wiseman's View, but don't bet on seeing one! The road becomes more difficult beyond 4 miles; however, reaching **Conley Cove Trail** (2,980 ft.) may be worth the extra bumps and jolts. At 5.3 miles from NC 183, the trailhead features an attractive hemlock-rhododendron stand and many of the same birds found at Wiseman's View.

To explore the east rim of the gorge requires another drive on rough backcountry roads. Exit the Parkway at M 312.2 onto NC 181 south, proceed 3 miles to NC SR 1265 (Gingercake Road), and turn right onto state road 1265. At the first fork, turn left and continue through Gingercake Acres onto FSR 210 for 5.5 miles to an intersection, where FSR 210-B to **Table Rock Mountain** turns right and ascends 2.9 miles through a series of switchbacks to a parking area and picnic grounds (3,400 ft.). A moderate-to-strenuous 1-mile hike goes from the north end of the lot to the summit of Table Rock (3,920 ft.), where a sweeping panorama of the gorge, Piedmont, and Blue Ridge provides an excellent spot to view the autumn hawk migration, particularly for Broad-wings in September.

For summer woodland birds, outstanding scenery, and the possibility of Peregrine Falcons, head south from the Table Rock parking lot along the **Mountains-to-Sea Trail** toward **Shortoff** (3,000 ft.), the sentinel peak above the mouth of the gorge. This 4.5-mile one-way trek from Table Rock to Shortoff is a moderately strenuous route along the crest of Jonas Ridge, through oak forests, laurel thickets, and past the Chimneys (3,557 ft.). Watch for Peregrines all along here, particularly between the Chimneys and Shortoff. Late-spring and summer birds include Turkey Vulture, Broad-winged Hawk, Ruffed Grouse, Ruby-throated Hummingbird, Downy and Hairy Woodpeckers, Northern Flicker, Pileated Woodpecker, Eastern Wood-Pewee, Great Crested Flycatcher, Blue Jay, Carolina Chickadee, Tufted Titmouse, White-breasted Nuthatch, Carolina Wren, Wood Thrush, American Robin, Gray Catbird, Cedar Waxwing, Solitary and Red-eyed Vireos, Scarlet Tanager, Rose-breasted Grosbeak, Indigo Bunting, Rufous-sided Towhee, Song Sparrow, Dark-eyed Junco, and American Goldfinch. This is a good hike for seeing warblers, such as Northern Parula, Black-throated Blue, Black-throated Green, Blackburnian, Pine, Black-and-white, Worm-eating, Ovenbird, and Hooded.

An additional birding site back on the Parkway south of Linville Falls is **Chestoa View** (4,090 ft.) at M 320.8, where a flat and easy 0.8-mile loop trail through an open oak forest and stands of Carolina rhododendron leads to views of Linville Gorge and Grandfather Mountain. Late-spring and summer birds along this route include Ruffed Grouse, Downy Woodpecker, Northern Flicker, Eastern Wood-Pewee, Great Crested Flycatcher, Blue Jay, Common Raven, Tufted Titmouse, White-breasted Nuthatch, Wood Thrush, Gray Catbird, Solitary Vireo, Chestnut-sided Warbler, Black-throated Blue Warbler, Black-throated Green Warbler, Black-and-white Warbler, Ovenbird, Hooded Warbler, Canada Warbler, Scarlet Tanager, and Dark-eyed Junco.

South Toe High Country

Highlights: Middle- to high-elevation summer residents; Least Flycatcher,
Swainson's Warbler.

Season: Spring through fall.

Access: The BRP junction with NC 80 is at M 344.1. From the BRP on NC 80
it is 6 miles south to Marion, N.C., just north of I-40, and 14 miles north to
Micaville, N.C.

Maps: USGS "Celo," "Marion," "Montreat."

Facilities: Seventy-one tent sites and twenty-two trailer sites at Crabtree
Meadows campground (M 339.4); additional sites at Black Mountain camp-
ground, Carolina Hemlocks campground, and Curtis Creek campground.
Books, maps, and trail guidebooks at Crabtree Meadows Gift Shop
(M 339.5) and at Neals Creek Information Center near Black Mountain
campground on FSR 472.

Between Bearwallow Gap (M 335.4) and Black Mountain Gap
(M 355.3) the Parkway follows close to the Blue Ridge crest line, which
gradually rises above 5,000 feet as it divides the headwaters of the Catawba
River on the south from those of the Toe River on the north. A tributary
of the Tennessee, the South Fork of the Toe rises in the highlands formed
around the confluence of the Black Mountains and the Blue Ridge at Black
Mountain Gap.

Spruce and northern hardwoods cover the highest peaks and ridge line,
particularly in the few miles north and east of Black Mountain Gap. The
intermediate slopes have mature oak forests, and cove forests occur in sheltered ravines at lower elevations. Hemlocks are common in moist ravines
and along waterways, and heath thickets occupy many exposed sites. The
range of elevations and the varied forest types contribute to the diversity
of bird life in this scenic area, which has some of the best spots along
the Parkway for Least Flycatcher, Blackburnian Warbler, and Swainson's
Warbler.

An excellent place for middle-elevation breeding birds is the **Crabtree
Meadows Recreation Area** (3,500 ft.), a 253-acre site near the Seven-
mile Ridge tableland just back of the Blue Ridge escarpment. Black-billed
Cuckoo, Least Flycatcher, and Great Crested Flycatcher are among the
summer birds sometimes noted here but infrequently encountered elsewhere on the Parkway. Spring migration is often excellent, and summer

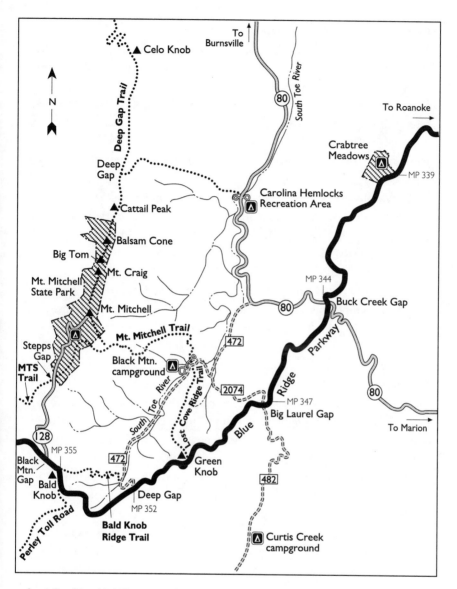

South Toe River High Country, N.C.

species can be observed at the campground and picnic area or along the trails.

Turn right at M 339.4 onto the access road to the campground and proceed to the kiosk and adjacent parking lot, where the trailhead for the **Crabtree Falls Trail** is located. This popular and moderately strenuous loop trail runs 2.5 miles through fairly mature oak woods down to a cove forest with hemlock and rhododendron along the slopes of Big Crabtree Creek. The falls are 0.8 miles from the lot, but the entire loop is worth exploring for Ruffed Grouse, Yellow-billed Cuckoo, Downy and Pileated Woodpeckers, Eastern Wood-Pewee, Acadian Flycatcher, Least Flycatcher, Great Crested Flycatcher, Carolina Chickadee, Tufted Titmouse, White-breasted Nuthatch, Wood Thrush, American Robin, Gray Catbird, Solitary and Red-eyed Vireos, Scarlet Tanager, Rufous-sided Towhee, and Dark-eyed Junco. Black-billed Cuckoos are reported near the trail in some years. Warblers are conspicuous along the trail: watch for Northern Parula, Chestnut-sided, Black-throated Blue, Black-throated Green, Blackburnian, Black-and-white, Ovenbird, Louisiana Waterthrush, and Hooded. Barred Owls are a possibility here at night, and the trail is excellent for spring and summer wildflowers as well.

Many birds noted on the falls trail can also be seen around **Crabtree Meadows campground,** which is situated in a fairly mature open forest of oaks, tuliptrees, maples, and hemlocks, bordered along the south side by a small field. Least Flycatcher, Eastern Phoebe, and Great Crested Flycatcher are present in most years, along with Blue Jay, American Crow, and Common Raven. The adjacent open field and forest edge increase the diversity of summer species found here to include Mourning Dove, Chimney Swift, Ruby-throated Hummingbird, Carolina Wren, Eastern Bluebird, Brown Thrasher, Cedar Waxwing, Common Yellowthroat, Indigo Bunting, Chipping Sparrow, Field Sparrow, Song Sparrow, Eastern Meadowlark, and American Goldfinch. The paved campground loop is a good birding walk in early morning and is suitable for wheelchairs except in spots where the grade is a bit steep. The campground is located at the end of the spur road on the right at M 339.4. A similar but shorter bird list can be expected at nearby **Crabtree Meadows picnic area,** left at M 340.4, which is also good for wheelchairs or casual walking.

South of Crabtree Meadows are a number of interesting side trips down into the Catawba and Toe river valleys. Exit the Parkway at Buck Creek Gap (M 344.1) onto NC 80 and proceed north 5.3 miles to **Carolina Hemlocks Recreation Area** (2,760 ft.), known for its beautiful old hemlock forest along the South Fork Toe River. This is a good spot in late spring and summer for Least Flycatcher, which can usually be heard by walking the paved roads through the campground and picnic area. Check the hemlocks for Golden-crowned Kinglet; this is one of the lowest elevations in the southern mountains where it occurs in the breeding season. The Carolina Hemlock Trail is an easy birding hike that loops through the deciduous woods near the campground. Middle-elevation spring and summer birds here include Belted Kingfisher, Downy and Pileated Woodpeckers, Eastern Wood-Pewee, Acadian Flycatcher, Blue Jay, American Crow, Carolina Chickadee, Tufted Titmouse, White-breasted Nuthatch, Carolina Wren, Blue-gray Gnatcatcher, Wood Thrush, American Robin, Gray Catbird, Cedar Waxwing, Solitary and Red-eyed Vireos, Northern Parula, Black-throated Green Warbler, Black-and-white Warbler, Ovenbird, Louisiana Waterthrush, Hooded Warbler, Northern Cardinal, and American Goldfinch.

For excellent roadside birding, another nearby side trip connects two Forest Service roads in an 8-mile loop from the Parkway down to **Black Mountain Recreation Area and campground** and then back to the Blue Ridge crest. You can do the route in either direction, but the recommended way is to exit the Parkway by turning right at Big Laurel Gap (4,048 ft.) at M 347.6 onto FSR 2074. Beginning immediately after the turn, you should pull over and stop at frequent intervals, get out of the car, and walk along the gravel road for looks at the spring and summer bird life of upper- and middle-elevation forests. Many turnouts are present, and good views of the birds can often be had from your car or by walking along the roadway. The first half mile of the road goes through a mix of spruce, hemlock, birch, oaks, maples, and rhododendron, and by 1 mile from the Parkway, the spruce and northern hardwoods are largely replaced by cove woodlands with hemlock.

Check the conifers all along here for Red-breasted Nuthatch, Golden-crowned Kinglet, and Blackburnian Warbler. Other regular species in late spring and summer include Eastern Screech-Owl, Barred Owl, Downy and Pileated Woodpeckers, Acadian Flycatcher, Blue Jay, Carolina Chickadee, Tufted Titmouse, White-breasted Nuthatch, Winter Wren, Veery, Wood Thrush, American Robin, Solitary and Red-eyed Vireos, Northern Parula, Black-throated Blue Warbler, Black-throated Green Warbler, Black-and-white Warbler, Ovenbird, Louisiana Waterthrush, Canada Warbler, Scarlet Tanager, Rufous-sided Towhee, and Dark-eyed Junco. At 2.4 miles from the Parkway the road breaks out of the woods into open fields near the junction with FSR 472 at Neals Creek Information Center, where books and maps are available.

Turn left onto FSR 472 and proceed 0.7 miles to Black Mountain campground (3,000 ft.), which is located along the South Fork Toe River a few miles upstream from the Carolina Hemlocks area. In addition to many of the birds already noted for spring and summer, the fields and campground area may yield Chimney Swift, Ruby-throated Hummingbird, Northern Flicker, Eastern Phoebe, American Crow, Gray Catbird, Chestnut-sided Warbler, Common Yellowthroat, Hooded Warbler, Northern Cardinal, Indigo Bunting, Chipping Sparrow, Field Sparrow, Song Sparrow, and Brown-headed Cowbird. For those wishing a strenuous wilderness hike, the trailheads for the Green Knob and Mount Mitchell trails are located at the campground, although simply to enjoy the birds, you may prefer to walk down from the high country rather than up from here. From the campground, continue on FSR 472 for 4.9 miles back to the Parkway at Deep Gap at M 351.9.

On the opposite side of the Parkway, **Curtis Creek**, a major tributary of the Catawba River, drains the southeast slopes of the Blue Ridge crest between Big Laurel Gap and Deep Gap. FSR 482 follows close by the creek for much of its course, providing many turnouts and easy stops for strolling along the dirt road. Known as one of the best spots near the Parkway for the elusive Swainson's Warbler, Curtis Creek Road is also an excellent route to study the changes in bird life associated with the transition from middle to low elevations in the southern mountains. Turn left at Big Laurel Gap (M 347.6) onto FSR 482 to begin the 10.5-mile drive down to the junction with US 70 (1,400 ft.) just east of Old Fort, for an elevation change of some 2,500 feet. Note that this road starts on the opposite side of the Parkway from FSR 2074, the latter being the route to Black Mountain campground described above.

For most of the first 3 miles after leaving the Parkway, the road passes through an oak forest, with typical spring and summer birds such as Ruffed Grouse, Downy and Pileated Woodpeckers, Eastern Wood-Pewee, Eastern Phoebe, Blue Jay, Carolina Chickadee, Tufted Titmouse, White-breasted Nuthatch, Veery, Wood Thrush, American Robin, Gray Catbird, Solitary and Red-eyed Vireos, Rufous-sided Towhee, Indigo Bunting, and Dark-eyed Junco. This is a good stretch for warblers, including Chestnut-sided, Black-throated Blue, Black-throated Green, Blackburnian, Cerulean, Black-and-white, Worm-eating, Ovenbird, Hooded, and Canada.

At 3.2 miles from the Parkway, Curtis Creek Road enters an area of beautiful cove forests with hemlock and rhododendron and soon thereafter crosses a number of small streams. From this point on down to Curtis

Creek campground at 5.5 miles you should listen for Swainson's Warbler, as well as Acadian Flycatcher, Northern Parula, and Louisiana Waterthrush. From Curtis Creek campground to US 70 the bird life is typical of the western Piedmont, but the roadside is not as suitable for birding, so you may wish to retrace your route from here.

Another particularly good opportunity for roadside birding is to walk along the **Parkway shoulder** in the high country north of Black Mountain Gap. This stretch from the gap at M 355.3 to around M 353 is reasonably level, with many good views out into the canopy of spruce and deciduous trees downslope from the roadway. The only problem here is that much of the area is backlit in the early morning. Nevertheless, this is one of the best spots in the southern Blue Ridge for Blackburnian Warblers, in addition to many summer residents typical of high-elevation spruce-fir and northern hardwood forests.

A good place to park is at the trailhead for the **Bald Knob Ridge Trail** at MP 355 (5,200 ft.). Walk north from here and watch for Downy and Hairy Woodpeckers, Common Raven, Red-breasted Nuthatch, Brown Creeper, Winter Wren, Golden-crowned Kinglet, Veery, American Robin, Gray Catbird, Cedar Waxwing, Solitary Vireo, Chestnut-sided Warbler, Black-throated Green Warbler, Blackburnian Warbler, Canada Warbler, Rose-breasted Grosbeak, Rufous-sided Towhee, Dark-eyed Junco, and American Goldfinch. Red Crossbills and Pine Siskins are present erratically.

The same species and habitat can be found on the old **Perley Toll Road**, which follows a logging railroad grade from a metal gate on the left at M 354.8 before crossing the continental divide and heading down the Blue Ridge toward the town of Black Mountain. The best birding on this easy jaunt is from the Parkway to a spot about a half mile downslope beyond the high point of the crest. Northern Saw-whet Owls are sometimes reported in the conifers during the calling period of April through June.

For those wishing a good backcountry birding route and a chance to see a black bear, try hiking down the 2.8-mile Bald Knob Ridge Trail from the trailhead here at MP 355 to a parking spot on FSR 471, about 1 mile from the Parkway, for a descent of 1,300 feet. Many of the same species just listed for the shoulder and for the Black Mountain campground circuit drive are found along the trail.

Another good birding trek is the **Lost Cove Ridge Trail**, which passes over the summit of **Green Knob** (4,980 ft.), for a beautiful view of the Black

Mountains, the Toe River valley, Roan Mountain, Grandfather Mountain, Linville Gorge, and the Blue Ridge. The fire tower on Green Knob is an excellent spot to watch the autumn hawk migration, and the 0.6-mile trail from the Parkway to the summit will yield late-spring and summer birds such as Ruffed Grouse, Chimney Swift, Downy Woodpecker, Hairy Woodpecker, Pileated Woodpecker, Eastern Wood-Pewee, Blue Jay, Common Raven, White-breasted Nuthatch, Winter Wren, Veery, American Robin, Cedar Waxwing, Solitary and Red-eyed Vireos, Chestnut-sided Warbler, Black-throated Blue Warbler, Black-throated Green Warbler, Black-and-white Warbler, Canada Warbler, Rufous-sided Towhee, and Dark-eyed Junco. The trailhead is on the right shoulder of the Parkway about 150 yards north of Green Knob OL at M 350.4, and the 0.6-mile section to the summit runs through open hardwoods in a series of switchbacks. The remainder of the 3.3-mile hike runs down to Black Mountain campground for a 2,000-foot elevation change.

Black Mountains and Mount Mitchell

Highlights: Summer birds of spruce-fir and northern hardwoods; American Woodcock aerial display, Northern Saw-whet Owl, Hermit Thrush, Magnolia Warbler.

Season: Spring through fall.

Access: The BRP runs 4.5 miles along the south rim between Black Mountain Gap (M 355.3) and Balsam Gap (MP 360). Mount Mitchell State Park is 2.4 miles from the BRP on NC 128, which begins on the right at M 355.4. This is 27 miles north from the BRP's junction with US 70 at Oteen, N.C. (M 382.6), about 5 miles east of Asheville, N.C. Coming from the north, the NC 128 junction is 11 miles south on the BRP from the junction with NC 80 at Buck Creek Gap (M 344.1), 6 miles north of Marion, N.C., and I-40.

Maps: USGS "Mount Mitchell," "Burnsville," "Celo," "Micaville," "Montreat"; USFS "South Toe River Trail Map."

Facilities: Food at Mount Mitchell Restaurant; nine tent sites at Mount Mitchell campground; nearby camping at Crabtree Meadows, Curtis Creek, Black Mountain campground, and Carolina Hemlocks, described

under South Toe High Country (above). Contact Mount Mitchell State
Park, Rt. 5, Box 700, Burnsville, NC 28714 (704-675-4611).

Encompassing the highest terrain in eastern North America, the
lofty Black Mountains are a U-shaped range composed largely of mica
gneiss, an extremely durable granitic rock whose resistance to erosion is
demonstrated by the presence of seventeen peaks exceeding 6,000 feet in
elevation. The range consists of two parallel, 11-mile long ridges that run
north-south and are connected at their southern ends by a 3-mile ridge
running east-west. This southern transverse portion of the range links the
Blacks with the Great Craggies to the southwest at Balsam Gap and with
the Blue Ridge to the southeast at Black Mountain Gap. The tallest mountains lie along the east rim, culminating at 6,684 feet on Mount Mitchell,
the highest point in the United States east of South Dakota's Black Hills.
The Cane and Toe rivers, tributaries of the Nolichucky and the Tennessee,
drain the region from north and east, while the Swannanoa and small feeders of the French Broad flow from the southern and western portions. The
climate is probably the most severe of any area in the Blue Ridge Province,
with 60 inches of snow annually and an average daily high temperature of
only 51° F at Mount Mitchell.

The Black Mountains were named for the dark forbidding mantle of
conifers that once cloaked their peaks. Logging, wildfires, balsam woolly
adelgids, and airborne pollutants have decimated these once magnificent
forests of Fraser fir and red spruce, leaving comparatively small remnants
amid tracts of dead and dying trees. Rhododendron, hardwood saplings,
and blackberries often become established in openings on high peaks and
ridges. Northern hardwood forests fringe the edges of the spruce-fir belt in
an irregular transition zone. At intermediate and low elevations, the Blacks
are covered with a variety of oak, pine, and cove hardwood forests. The
extensive damage to the spruce-fir zone has been proposed as one of the
possible causes for the extirpation of several birds from the range, including the Olive-sided Flycatcher and Black-capped Chickadee. Nevertheless,
the Blacks remain one of the best areas in the southern mountains for birds
of high-elevation conifer forests.

Some of the earliest accounts of southern Appalachian bird life were
recorded in the Black Mountains, beginning with Moses Ashley Curtis
(1808–72), the eminent botanist who noted Red Crossbills here in 1854.
Johns S. Cairns (1863–95) of nearby Weaverville conducted extensive

studies from 1880 to 1895, and William Brewster (1851–1919) of Harvard included the range in his pioneering 1885 report on the birds of western North Carolina. Portions of the same trails hiked by those men are still used today, although access to the high country is now much easier, thanks to the Parkway and NC 128. Major trails run along the crest line of most of the range, and the Parkway crosses the southern transverse rim between Black Mountain Gap (M 355.3) and Balsam Gap (MP 360). Birding here is largely confined to the period from March through November, but the austere winter beauty of the region can often be sampled by cross-country skiing, hiking, or snowshoeing.

Most birders start with a visit to **Mount Mitchell State Park**, a 1,677-acre tract established in 1916 as North Carolina's first public natural recreation area. The park stretches some five miles along the Black's rugged eastern rim from Stepps Gap to Cattail Peak and includes Mount Mitchell (6,684 ft.), the highest mountain in the eastern United States. To reach the park, turn right off the Parkway at M 355.4 onto NC 128 and proceed 2.4 miles to the park entrance gate. Between the Parkway and entrance are numerous pull offs along NC 128 where you can park and walk along the shoulder for good looks at spring and summer birds in spruce, hardwoods, and rhododendrons. Stop also at the parking area on the left, just inside the entrance gate opposite the park office at **Stepps Gap** (6,100 ft.), and check the area for Common Raven, Red Crossbill, and Pine Siskin, which are always possibilities here and along the summit road. The American Woodcock's aerial courtship display can be seen in the open area just west of the gap at twilight from late March through April.

Proceed on toward the summit parking lot (6,578 ft.), which is 2.3 miles from the gate, stopping at the restaurant area (6,190 ft.) and the campground (6,320 ft.) along the way. The expected spruce-fir birds are present in the vicinity of the restaurant parking lot, which is level, suitable for wheelchairs, and a good place to see Chimney Swift, Common Raven, Red-breasted Nuthatch, Winter Wren, Golden-crowned Kinglet, Veery, American Robin, Gray Catbird, Cedar Waxwing, Rufous-sided Towhee, Song Sparrow, and Dark-eyed Junco. Note that the area around the buildings often has Eastern Phoebe, House Wren, Eastern Bluebird, Indigo Bunting, and Chipping Sparrow, species infrequently encountered at such high elevations. As at Stepps Gap, the parking lot is sometimes the site of Woodcock flight displays in March and April.

The section of **Old Mitchell Trail** south of the restaurant on Mount

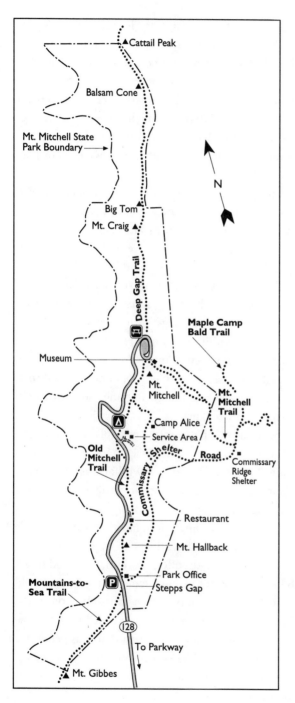

Mount Mitchell State Park, N.C.

Hallback (6,391 ft.) is often worth checking for Hermit Thrush, which extended its summer range south to the Blacks by 1983. Hermit Thrushes are also occasionally heard near the campground and picnic parking lot. The road from the entrance gate all the way to the summit and the parking areas at the restaurant, campground, and picnic area are good sites for Northern Saw-whet Owls from late March through June, but remember that the park entrance is closed after dark. For nighttime birding, leave the car outside the gate, without blocking the entrance, and walk in, or plan to camp overnight in the park.

From the summit parking lot, a short hike runs to the Mount Mitchell observation tower for a panoramic view on clear days and a depressing close-up encounter with the extensive die-off of Fraser fir. Until the late 1970s, when the destruction of conifers became severe, the Summit Trail, Balsam Nature Trail, and parking-lot edges were good places to see Red-breasted Nuthatch, Golden-crowned Kinglet, Black-throated Green Warbler, and Blackburnian Warbler. Now the spring and summer bird life consists mostly of species associated with openings, shrub and heath thickets, and damaged canopy trees. Look for Broad-winged Hawk, Downy Woodpecker, American Crow, Common Raven, Winter Wren, Veery, American Robin, Cedar Waxwing, Chestnut-sided Warbler, Common Yellowthroat, Canada Warbler, Rufous-sided Towhee, Indigo Bunting, Song Sparrow, Dark-eyed Junco, and American Goldfinch.

Stop at the museum about halfway between the parking lot and the top for an interesting interpretative display on the Black Mountains, including a photo of the juvenile Northern Saw-whet Owl that was captured in the park in 1968, the first physical evidence for the bird's nesting in the southern Blue Ridge. During September and October, the parking lot is often used to watch the autumn hawk migration, mostly off the east side looking toward Green Knob and north along the main ridge.

To experience the best the range has to offer, however, you need to get away from the heavily used areas and explore some of the trails or old logging railroad grades into the backcountry. Of the possible choices, the **Commissary Shelter Road** is one of the most pleasant bird walks in the southern Appalachians. This wide, smooth dirt road descends gently for about 2 miles along the east ridge of the Blacks from Stepps Gap (6,100 ft.) to the camping shelter on Commissary Ridge (5,780 ft.). Leave your car in the paved lot on the left just beyond the entrance gate and take the unmarked dirt road that begins on the opposite side of NC 128 in front

Winter Wren

of the park headquarters building. Following an old logging railroad bed, the route is open and easy, providing good looks at bird life as you pass through spruce-fir, northern hardwoods, rhododendron thickets, and open clearings. Wildflowers are abundant, and on clear days there are panoramic views of the Toe River valley and the Blue Ridge. The road is downslope and sheltered from cold prevailing winds, so birds tend to be more active and easier to see than on the high ridge.

This is a good route to get a look at Winter Wrens, elusive little skulkers that are common along the road. Typical high-country spring and summer birds include Golden-crowned Kinglet, Veery, American Robin, Gray Catbird, Cedar Waxwing, Solitary Vireo, Chestnut-sided Warbler, Black-throated Green Warbler, Canada Warbler, Rufous-sided Towhee, Song Sparrow, and Dark-eyed Junco. Other summer residents include Broad-winged Hawk, Ruffed Grouse, Downy Woodpecker, Hairy Woodpecker, Northern Flicker, American Crow, Common Raven, Red-breasted Nuthatch, Common Yellowthroat, and Indigo Bunting. Be alert for Hermit Thrushes in the tops of spruce trees and Alder Flycatchers in shrubby thickets and deciduous second growth. From the area of the shelter, the steep and strenuous Commissary Ridge Trail runs 1.6 miles to the summit of Mount Mitchell, while the trail to Black Mountain campground goes 4 miles down to the valley. The railroad bed continues northward as Maple Camp Bald Trail, but it is overgrown and not very well suited to birding.

Another popular hike is the **Old Mitchell Trail**, which runs along the crest line for 2 miles from Stepps Gap to the top of Mount Mitchell, a climb of about 580 feet. This trail was used by Cairns, Brewster, and many other naturalists and explorers in the 1800s. The trailheads are clearly marked at the park headquarters, restaurant, campground, and junction with the summit trail near the parking lot. Birds found in late spring and summer include most species noted along NC 128 and on Commissary Shelter Road, but this route is more exposed and not quite as good for birding. Furthermore, the trail passes through some of the most severely affected spruce-fir forests in the area, creating a constant risk of injury from down and falling trees.

The other major trek in the park is the **Black Mountain Crest Trail** or **Deep Gap Trail**, a strenuous 12-mile wilderness hike that climbs a dozen peaks exceeding 6,000 feet along the main crest of the Blacks from Mount Mitchell parking lot to NC SR 1109 south of Burnsville. The 3.9-mile section of trail from Mitchell to the camping shelter at Deep Gap passes through badly damaged spruce-fir forests, but north of Deep Gap and beyond the park boundary are some beautiful stands of old-growth spruce and fir. Alder Flycatchers are sometimes present on the north slope of Balsam Cone (6,611 ft.) at 2.0 miles north of Mitchell, and Peregrine Falcons have recently been observed around Deep Gap. Otherwise the spring and summer species are the same as noted elsewhere in the park. If you plan to walk any of these routes, get a copy of de Hart's *North Carolina Hiking Trails* and the USFS map "South Toe River Trail Map," which describe these and other possible hikes in the area.

The southern and western rims of the Black Mountains can be explored by trails that begin at Balsam Gap. Although the Parkway traverses the entire south ridge of the Blacks, no roadside stopping or shoulder walking is permitted within the Asheville watershed. For birding along the south rim, take the **Mountains-to-Sea Trail** for a moderately strenuous hike that combines old-growth spruce-fir forests, rhododendron thickets, spectacular scenery, and excellent views of the high-country birds. The trail runs approximately 5 miles from Balsam Gap parking lot (5,320 ft.)

at M 359.8 across Blackstock Knob (6,325 ft.), Potato Knob (6,440 ft.), and Clingman's Peak to Stepps Gap at the entrance to Mount Mitchell State Park. The trail is still under construction as of 1991, so check with a park ranger before attempting to hike the entire route. Be alert for Northern Saw-whet Owl, Red Crossbill, and Pine Siskin along the trail. More likely spring and summer encounters would include Downy Woodpecker, Common Raven, Red-breasted Nuthatch, Brown Creeper, Winter Wren, Golden-crowned Kinglet, Veery, American Robin, Solitary Vireo, Rufous-sided Towhee, and Dark-eyed Junco. Warblers are conspicuous here, particularly the Chestnut-sided, Black-throated Green, and Canada, as well as an occasional Black-throated Blue or Blackburnian.

Many of these same species can be seen on **Big Butt Trail**, a moderate-to-strenuous route that begins at the south end of Balsam Gap parking lot and runs 6.2 miles through spruce-fir and northern hardwoods along the Black's western ridge to NC 197 at Cane River Gap. Some of the best birding is in the first 3 miles of the trail, which passes over Point Misery (5,715 ft.) at 1.5 miles, Little Butt (5,620 ft.) at 2.4 miles, and around Big Butt (5,920 ft.) at 3 miles. In addition to the birds noted on the Mountains-to-Sea Trail, one may find Gray Catbird, Northern Parula, and Rose-breasted Grosbeak. Juvenile and adult Northern Saw-whet Owls have been observed on this trail in spring and summer along the ridge as far north as Big Butt. Watch for Yellow-bellied Sapsuckers, especially around Little Butt and Big Butt. Be alert for Magnolia Warblers, which are extending their summer range southward, as well as Alder Flycatchers, which have become established just south of Big Butt.

The Balsam Gap area is of some historical interest as well, for in June 1895, John S. Cairns was killed in a hunting accident about 100 yards north of the present-day parking lot. The southern Appalachian race of the Black-throated Blue Warbler was later named in Cairns's honor, but his untimely death at the age of thirty-three resulted in an enormous loss to the scientific community. Cairns was writing a detailed book on the birds of the North Carolina mountains, and the manuscript and most of his unpublished data were lost after his death.

Note that the Mountains-to-Sea Trail also runs south of Balsam Gap parking lot down the main ridge of the Great Craggy Mountains. See the following section on the Craggies for details.

Great Craggy Mountains

Highlights: Spring songbird migration, autumn hawk migration, middle- and
high-elevation breeding birds; Cerulean Warblers.

Season: Spring through fall.

Access: The BRP runs through the Craggies from Balsam Gap at MP 360 to
US 70 at M 382.4 in Oteen, N.C. On US 70 it is 5 miles west to Asheville,
N.C., and 10 miles east to Black Mountain, N.C., with access to I-40 just
east of the BRP.

Maps: USGS "Craggy Pinnacle," "Montreat," "Oteen," "Weaverville."

Facilities: Gasoline, food, and accommodations in Asheville and Oteen; rest
rooms, maps, books, and information at Craggy Gardens Visitor Center at
M 364.6.

The Great Craggies are among the best-known mountains in the
Appalachians because of the extensive Catawba rhododendron balds that
cover large portions of the highest peaks. This beautiful transverse range
extends from Asheville and the Swannanoa River valley for a distance of
some 15 miles to the northeast at Balsam Gap, where the high crest joins
the Black Mountains. Much of the northern ridge line exceeds 5,000 feet
in elevation, with the range's highest point at 6,085 feet on Craggy Dome.
The steep eastern slopes are drained by the North Fork Swannanoa River,
which forms a deep valley enclosed by the Blue Ridge farther east and the
Blacks to the north. Streams on the west side of the Craggies flow into
tributaries of the French Broad River. The Parkway traverses the range
from MP 360 at Balsam Gap down to US 70 at M 382.4 near Oteen.

Regarded by some as the most important botanical area on the Parkway,
the Craggies harbor many nationally endangered and threatened plants,
as well as a complex spectrum of forests, heath balds, and grass balds.
Portions of the high ridge and peaks are covered by a distinctive, open,
orchardlike hardwood forest, composed of stunted mountain ash, beech,
yellow birch, and buckeye. Despite the high elevation, spruce and fir are
absent except in the area immediately adjacent to the Black Mountains
near Balsam Gap. Many of the grass balds are reverting to heath and shrub
balds, and the latter are often progressing to hardwood forests. All this
suggests that much of the current vegetation pattern in the high elevations
may be a result of some prehistoric event, perhaps wildfire, that destroyed
the original forests. In the intermediate and low elevations, the Craggies

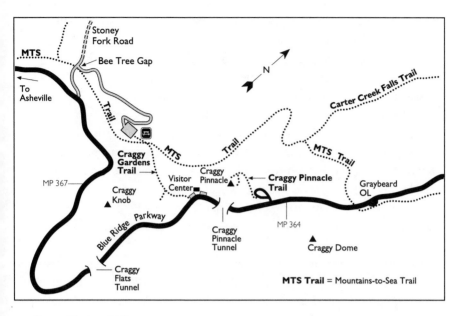

Craggy Gardens, N.C.

are covered by oak and cove hardwood forests, as well as some beautiful groves of hemlock.

The high Craggies were made famous in the annals of Appalachian ornithology during the late 1800s by the field studies of John S. Cairns (1862–95), for whom the southern race of Black-throated Blue Warbler was named. Because of the variety of plant communities, the mountains are home to a diversified avifauna during the spring and summer months, and the high crest often provides an impressive view of autumn hawk migration. Many of the best birding spots in the range are now readily accessible from the Parkway or nearby trails.

The most popular site in the Craggies is **Craggy Gardens Recreation Area,** a 700-acre tract of Catawba rhododendron balds and northern hardwood forest along the main crest of the range between Craggy Dome and Craggy Knob. The often spectacular rhododendron bloom peaks in mid-June, which is also a good time to see the summer birds of these Appalachian heath balds and hardwood "orchards." Stop at Craggy Gardens Visitor Center at M 364.6 in Pinnacle Gap (5,497 ft.), where the large paved parking lot and sidewalk are ideal for viewing into the northern hardwood canopy, especially for wheelchair use. Typical birds in late spring and summer include Downy Woodpecker, Common Raven, Winter Wren,

Veery, American Robin, Gray Catbird, Cedar Waxwing, Solitary Vireo, Chestnut-sided Warbler, Black-throated Blue Warbler, Canada Warbler, Rose-breasted Grosbeak, Rufous-sided Towhee, and Dark-eyed Junco.

The same birds can be seen in the rhododendron bald by taking **Craggy Gardens Self-guiding Trail**, an easy hike that begins at the southern end of the parking lot and runs 0.8 miles to Bearpen Gap (5,220 ft.), site of Craggy Gardens picnic area. Yellow-bellied Sapsuckers are occasionally found along this trail, but Downy and Hairy Woodpeckers are more likely. Before leaving, check the visitor center for books, maps, and interpretative displays. From September through November, you can watch for southbound hawks from the car or lawn chair in the parking lot. The trails and garden area are often excellent for warblers and songbirds in spring migration.

Craggy Pinnacle is another good spot for spring migrants, summer birds, and the autumn hawk migration. Stop at Craggy Dome View parking lot at M 364.1 and take the 1.2-mile round-trip hike through the rhododendron bald to the summit, a climb from 5,640 feet to 5,892 feet at the peak. Also, check the heath-shrub area at the north edge of the parking lot, where Alder Flycatchers are sometimes present in summer. Northern Saw-whet Owls have been heard calling from Craggy Dome, just northeast of the parking lot. The species list is otherwise the same as at Craggy Gardens. The open 360-degree view from the summit makes an excellent spot for autumn hawk migration, but remember that it can be very windy, cold, and exposed here, so dress accordingly.

Segments of the **Mountains-to-Sea Trail** offer some of the best birding in the Craggies, as well as good scenery and botany. Turn at M 367.5 onto the spur road toward Craggy Gardens picnic area, proceed 0.3 miles to **Beetree Gap** (4,900 ft.), and park where a gravel road begins on the left. The gap is the site of an old orchard and successional meadow with invading shrubs and trees. Hike the Mountains-to-Sea Trail both north and south of the gap, where trailheads are well marked. Check near the gap for Yellow-bellied Sapsucker, Golden-winged Warbler, and species listed for Craggy Gardens. The southbound section may be worth walking to Snowball Mountain (5,494 ft.), about an hour's hike from the gap. The northbound route goes back toward Craggy Gardens Visitor Center via the picnic grounds. You can also drive the gravel road left from Beetree down Mineral Creek, stopping at intervals for excellent roadside birding through northern hardwood, oak, and cove forests. Be alert for Black-

Chestnut-sided Warbler

billed Cuckoo, Yellow-bellied Sapsucker, and Brown Creeper, as well as a variety of warblers, vireos, and Scarlet Tanagers.

Another excellent portion of the Mountains-to-Sea Trail runs from Craggy Gardens picnic area across the west shoulder of Craggy Pinnacle and up to Graybeard OL along the Parkway. Continue on the paved spur road beyond Beetree Gap to the parking lot at the picnic grounds, which are 1.1 miles from the Parkway. Take the Craggy Gardens Trail at the far end of the lot near the rest rooms and proceed about 100 yards to the intersection with the Mountains-to-Sea Trail, which drops off to the left, descending into heath thickets and stunted northern hardwoods. At 1.4 miles from the picnic grounds on the MTS Trail, **Carter Creek Falls Trail** begins on the left, for a side trip to **Craggy Scenic Area,** a rather strenuous 3.5-mile one-way hike down about 1,114 feet to a spectacular forest of ancient hemlocks, maple, and birch near Carter Creek Falls. From the junction with Carter Creek Falls Trail, the MTS Trail continues on for about 1 mile to Graybeard Mountain OL at M 363.6 on the Parkway. You can also drive to Craggy Scenic Area by taking NC 197 to Barnardsville, turning onto NC SR 2173, going 5 miles to Dillingham, and taking FSR 74 for 8.7 winding miles to the parking lot and trailhead.

Most birds on this part of the Mountains-to-Sea Trail and on the upper parts of Carter Creek Falls Trail have been listed previously under Craggy Gardens, although Yellow-bellied Sapsuckers and Rose-breasted Gros-beaks are more often noted along these two trails than at the Gardens. The hemlock stand along Carter Creek is a good spot for Red-breasted Nut-hatch and Golden-crowned Kinglet. Other birds expected in late spring and summer at Carter Creek include Eastern Wood-Pewee, Acadian Fly-catcher, Eastern Phoebe, Carolina Chickadee, Tufted Titmouse, Veery, Wood Thrush, Solitary Vireo, Northern Parula, Black-throated Green Warbler, Blackburnian Warbler, Black-and-white Warbler, Worm-eating Warbler, and Canada Warbler.

At the Craggy's northern end, the **Mountains-to-Sea Trail** passes along the main crest and over the high peaks, providing a botanically delight-ful hike with excellent scenery and good birding. The trail parallels the Parkway between Graybeard Mountain OL and Balsam Gap, and clearly marked trailhead signs are present at each intervening overlook. This allows you to explore the range by in-and-out segments from overlooks or to coordinate transportation so that you do not have to retrace your steps. For wildflowers, black bears, and birds of an old-growth spruce forest, park at Balsam Gap (5,320 ft.) at M 359.8 and cross the Parkway to find the obvious trail that heads south over Walker Knob (5,482 ft.). Typical birds in late spring and summer include Ruffed Grouse, Downy Wood-pecker, Red-breasted Nuthatch, Winter Wren, Golden-crowned Kinglet, Veery, American Robin, Solitary Vireo, Northern Parula, Chestnut-sided Warbler, Black-throated Green Warbler, Blackburnian Warbler, Canada Warbler, Rufous-sided Towhee, and Dark-eyed Junco. Be alert for North-ern Saw-whet Owls, which are sometimes noted along the trail, particu-larly in conifers on Walker Knob. The trail comes out at Glassmine Falls View (5,197 ft.) at M 361.1 and continues south across Bullhead Mountain (5,925 ft.) to Graybeard Mountain OL (5,592 ft.) at M 363.6.

Segments of the Mountains-to-Sea Trail around Graybeard OL pass through a good example of a northern hardwood "orchard," where two-hundred-year-old beech, yellow birch, and buckeye grow in a gladelike forest, stunted and twisted by prevailing winds. In addition to many species found on Walker Knob, this section of trail and overlook may yield Common Raven, Gray Catbird, Black-throated Blue Warbler, and Rose-breasted Grosbeak. South from Graybeard OL the MTS Trail goes 1 mile to the junction with Carter Creek Falls Trail and then 1.4 miles back up the west slope of Craggy Pinnacle to join the Craggy Gardens Trail near the picnic area—a prime route for finding Yellow-bellied Sapsucker.

A final spot worth checking in the Craggies is the tract of cove hardwood forests along the Parkway in the headwaters of **Bull Creek**, one of the best spots in the North Carolina mountains for Cerulean Warblers. Park at Bull Creek OL (3,483 ft.) at M 373.8 and walk north along the Parkway shoulder for up to a half mile or south as far as Bull Gap (3,107 ft.) at M 375.3. In addition to the Ceruleans, expected late-spring and summer birds here include Yellow-billed Cuckoo, Ruby-throated Hummingbird, Downy and Pileated Woodpeckers, Eastern Wood-Pewee, Blue Jay, Carolina Chickadee, Carolina Wren, Wood Thrush, Solitary and Red-eyed Vireos, Chestnut-sided Warbler, Black-and-white Warbler, American Redstart, Ovenbird, Kentucky Warbler, Hooded Warbler, Scarlet Tanager, Rufous-sided Towhee, Indigo Bunting, and American Goldfinch. This area is also a good spot to catch the spring songbird migration from mid-April through May.

French Broad River Valley

Highlights: Riparian and low-elevation forest species, water birds, wading
   birds; Brown-headed Nuthatch.

Season: Year-round.

Access: The Parkway traverses the French Broad valley between M 382.4
   at the junction with US 70 in Oteen, N.C., south to the junction with
   NC 191 at M 393.6. Access to much of this portion is from I-40 between
   Oteen and Asheville, N.C., via US 70, US 74, US 25, and NC 191.

(Note: The easiest route from the BRP to Chimney Rock Park, an important
   nearby site, is a 23-mile drive that begins by exiting the BRP at M 384.7
   onto US 74.)

Map: USGS "Skyland."

Facilities: Gasoline, food, and lodging along US 25; boat rental, twenty-three campsites, and eight RV sites at Lake Julian.

Between the Great Craggies and Pisgah Ridge, the Parkway traverses the valleys of the Swannanoa and French Broad rivers, major tributaries of the Tennessee. At elevations of 2,000 to 2,200 feet, the valley's plant and bird life is more typically piedmont than montane, with communities and species not found elsewhere near the Parkway. Two sites are recommended for sampling the avifauna of the region.

The banks of the **French Broad River** (2,000 ft.) are lined by a floodplain tree community more commonly found in the Carolina lowlands. River birch, Catawba tree, sycamore, basswood, Carolina silverbell, box elder, and tuliptree are among the species present where the Parkway crosses the river. Stop at the French Broad River OL (M 393.8), a good perspective for migrating Osprey in the last half of April. The woods adjacent to the overlook are often full of migrating songbirds in April and May. For a closer look at the riparian community, exit the Parkway at M 393.6 onto NC 191 south, and almost immediately turn left into **Bent Creek Recreation Area**.

Check the trees and river edge, starting at the mouth of Bent Creek and walking south underneath the Parkway bridge. Great Blue Heron, Green-backed Heron, Wood Duck, Spotted Sandpiper, and Belted Kingfisher are often present, and the woods are good for spring migration of warblers and orioles in April and May. During summer months, this is one of the best spots along the Parkway for Yellow-throated Warbler and for White-eyed and Yellow-throated Vireos. Other warblers here include Northern Parula, Yellow Warbler, Pine Warbler, Black-and-white Warbler, American Redstart, Louisiana Waterthrush, and Kentucky Warbler. Red-bellied, Downy, and Pileated Woodpeckers are possible, along with Eastern Wood-Pewee, Acadian Flycatcher, Eastern Phoebe, Great Crested Flycatcher, Eastern Kingbird, Blue Jay, American Crow, Carolina Chickadee, Tufted Titmouse, Carolina Wren, House Wren, Blue-gray Gnatcatcher, Wood Thrush, Northern Cardinal, Indigo Bunting, Song Sparrow, and American Goldfinch. In winter months, look for Hermit Thrush, Ruby-crowned Kinglet, White-throated Sparrow, and Purple Finch.

Many of the same birds are found at **Sandy Bottom Recreation Area**, on the left 0.5 miles farther south on NC 191. Check the river edge here from late August through September for post-breeding Great Egrets. These sites are heavily used during the summer months, and noise from the nearby highway can be annoying, so arrive early for best results!

Another interesting spot near the Parkway is **Lake Julian Park** and **Campground** (2,160 ft.). Spring and summer birds here are typical of the French Broad valley and of the southeastern Piedmont; the lake attracts water birds much of the year. Brown-headed Nuthatches are sometimes present in the conifers, particularly the pitch pines in the campground area—probably the only spot near the Parkway where this "low-country" bird can be found. White-breasted Nuthatches are also resident. When Red-breasted Nuthatches show up in winter, all three species can be seen. Pine Warbler and Yellow-throated Warbler, species seldom encountered in the mountains, are also present during the nesting season.

The closest route to Lake Julian is to exit the BRP at M 388.8 onto US 25 south toward Hendersonville, N.C., and continue 2.9 miles to the "Lake Julian Campground" sign on the right, just beyond the railroad overpass. Turn right into the park and explore the full length of the main road; much of the best woodland for birds is in the far end of the campground area. For access to another section of the park, head back on US 25 for 0.4 miles to the stoplight at NC 280, turn left on NC 280, and go 0.7 miles to a stoplight, where you turn left and proceed 0.1 miles to the park entrance.

Lake Julian is used for cooling CP&L's electric generators, so it is often free of ice during winter. Though not a spectacular place for water birds, the lake is often worth scoping from the fishing area, especially from late summer through late spring. Look for Wood Duck, American Black Duck, and Mallard year-round. Post-breeding herons, such as Great Egret and Little Blue, may show up in late August and September. Check here immediately after a hurricane has come ashore in South Carolina or whenever bad weather settles in during migration. Common Loons pass through in late fall and early spring, while Double-crested Cormorants are reported from late summer through fall. Other transients include Pied-billed and Horned Grebes, Canada Geese, Redhead, Ring-necked Duck, Lesser Scaup, Bufflehead, Common and Red-breasted Mergansers, Osprey, and American Coot. Black Terns have been noted in late summer and Forster's Terns in late summer and early spring. Ring-billed, Herring, or Bonaparte's Gulls are a possibility.

Mount Pisgah Area

Highlights: Spring migration, summer forest species from low to high elevations; Peregrine Falcon nesting site.

Season: Spring through fall.

Access: Pisgah Inn and campground are 15 miles south on the BRP from the
junction with NC 191 at the French Broad River (M 393.6) or 3 miles north
on the BRP from Wagon Road Gap (M 411.7). From Wagon Road Gap it is
17 miles south to Brevard, N.C., and 22 miles north to Waynesville, N.C.,
on US 276. The southern end of Pisgah Ridge is accessed at Beech Gap
(M 423.2), which is 17 miles north from Rosman, N.C., on NC 215.

(Note: The easiest route from the BRP to the South Carolina High Country, an important nearby site, is a 34-mile drive that begins by exiting
the BRP at Wagon Road Gap [M 411.7] onto US 276 south. From Beech
Gap [M 423.2], it is 45 miles to the Highlands Plateau and 24 miles to the
Eastatoe area in the Southeastern Blue Ridge Escarpment Gorges.)

Maps: USGS "Cruso," "Dunsmore Mountain," "Pisgah Forest," "Shining
Rock"; USFS "Pisgah National Forest—Pisgah Ranger District"; "Mt.
Pisgah Area Map," Hickory Printing Group, Skyland, N.C.

Facilities: Books, maps, and information at USFS, Pisgah District, 1001 Pisgah Highway (US 276), Pisgah Forest, NC 28768 (704-877-3350). Books,
maps, food, gasoline, and lodging at Pisgah Inn (M 408.7), P.O. Box 749,
Waynesville, NC 28786 (704-235-8228). Trailer and tent camping at Pisgah campground (M 408.8) and USFS Davidson River campground on US
276 between Wagon Road Gap and Brevard. Gas, food, and accommodations in Brevard, 17 miles from Wagon Road Gap via US 276.

With its diversity of topography, plant communities, and bird life,
the Pisgah region is one of the most interesting and popular areas on the
Blue Ridge Parkway. Numerous overlooks, campgrounds, and recreation
areas offer good bird-watching sites, while an extensive network of trails,
ranging from easy to strenuous, provides hiking access to the backcountry.

Many of these trails were developed by George W. Vanderbilt, who acquired the land around Pisgah in the 1880s as part of his vast Biltmore
Estate. Important pioneering work in conservation techniques and forestry
was begun here by Gifford Pinchot in 1891 and by Dr. Carl A. Schenck
in 1895. Both men were hired by Vanderbilt to help manage the forest resources of the estate, where Schenck established the first school of forestry

in the United States. Following Vanderbilt's death, nearly 80,000 acres of his land, including Mount Pisgah and much of Pisgah Ridge, were sold to the government in 1914 as the basis for Pisgah National Forest.

Pisgah Ridge is a high-elevation interior range that runs in a south-westerly direction for twenty-five miles from the vicinity of Asheville to Tanasee Bald, where it joins the Great Balsam Mountains and Tanasee Ridge, two other major transverse ranges of the southern Blue Ridge Province. The ridge separates the French Broad River valley on the east from the headwaters of the Pigeon River on the west. Although Mount Pisgah is the most prominent geographic feature, the highest elevation occurs at Chestnut Bald (6,000 ft.) near the south end of the range, where several high peaks are covered in spruce-fir forests. Elsewhere, the predominant vegetation includes northern hardwoods, oak forests, and heath thickets in the high elevations, with cove hardwoods along waterways and moist slopes. The Parkway meanders thirty miles through the range between the French Broad River (2,000 ft.) at M 393.6 and Beech Gap (5,340 ft.) at M 423.2.

There are three major localities for birding. The Mount Pisgah area at the north end of the range is a prime spot for spring migration and middle- to high-elevation nesting species. The Davidson River and Mills River valleys to the east are good for spring migrants and middle- to low-elevation breeders, and a nesting site for Peregrine Falcon is found at Looking Glass Rock. The Graveyard Fields area, near the southern terminus of the range, hosts a curious mixture of summer birds, due to dramatic alterations in vegetation resulting from logging and wildfires.

Most visitors base their activities at Pisgah Inn, perched on the ridge high above Mills River valley, or at nearby Pisgah campground, nestled snugly at Flat Laurel Gap (4,900 ft.) in a beautiful rhododendron-laurel thicket with scattered hardwoods and spruce. This lovely spot offers excellent spring and summer birding combined with good scenery, comfortable accommodations, and fine cuisine. The 3-mile section of Parkway between Buck Spring Tunnel (M 407) and Fryingpan Gap (M 410) provides access to overlooks and a network of trails that satisfies everyone from roadside birders to those wishing a strenuous hike.

Begin by checking the area at **Pisgah Inn** (M 408.7), where the extensive clearing around the parking lot is favored by American Woodcock for their aerial displays at twilight in March and April. Other late-spring and summer species regularly noted near the Inn include Ruby-throated

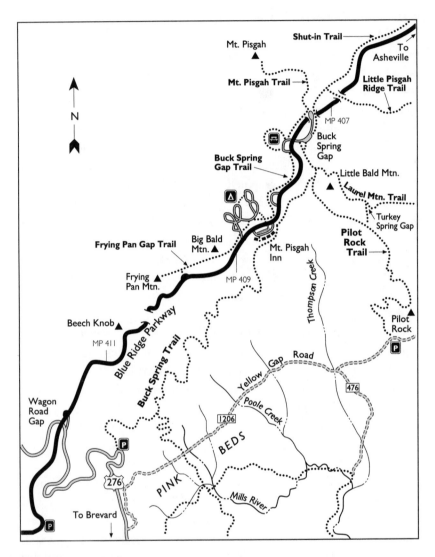

Mount Pisgah Area, N.C.

Hummingbird, Downy Woodpecker, Northern Flicker, Blue Jay, Common Raven, Carolina Chickadee, Tufted Titmouse, White-breasted Nuthatch, House Wren, American Robin, Gray Catbird, Cedar Waxwing, Solitary Vireo, Chestnut-sided Warbler, Black-and-white Warbler, Rufous-sided Towhee, Chipping Sparrow, and Dark-eyed Junco. Check the buildings south of the restaurant and the service buildings in the campground for Eastern Phoebe and Carolina Wren, which are near their highest nesting elevation here, as are Whip-poor-will, Brown Thrasher, and Indigo Bunting. Broad-winged Hawks and Turkey Vultures often soar over the valley, and Barred Owls can be heard downslope at night. Occasionally a Hairy or Pileated Woodpecker or a Great Crested Flycatcher will show up.

Just across the road, **Pisgah campground** (M 408.8) is probably the best campground on the Parkway for bird-watching. The network of paved loop roads penetrates a beautiful heath thicket, admixed with northern hardwoods, red spruce, and grassy openings. Except for a few steep spots near the entrance, the roads are easy to walk, ideal for the handicapped, and generally suitable for wheelchairs, provided you stay alert for cars. Be sure to start early, however, as things get noisy quickly after sunrise in the summer months. The same birds noted at the Inn are also common here, but other high-country species, such as Red-breasted Nuthatch, Golden-crowned Kinglet, Brown Creeper, Veery, Black-throated Blue Warbler, Canada Warbler, and Rose-breasted Grosbeak, are more likely to be encountered in the campground.

Several nearby overlooks are excellent for roadside birding. These flat parking lots and occasional "sidewalks" are suitable for wheelchairs, while the adjacent sloping terrain provides good viewing angles into the forest canopy and thickets. Try the **Pisgah picnic grounds parking lot**, especially along its south end, at M 407.8, where the adjacent mix of northern hardwoods and red spruce often yields the species noted at the Inn and the campground, along with the chance of a Scarlet Tanager or even a flock of Red Crossbills. Common Ravens seem to have a special fondness for this overlook, and Winter Wrens are often singing downslope. The picnic grounds themselves are worth checking, although they are often crowded on summer weekends.

For other opportunities, take the paved spur road left at M 407.6 up to **Buck Spring Gap Overlook** (4,980 ft.) and the **Mount Pisgah parking lot**. These overlooks afford good looks at Mount Pisgah, Shining Rock Ledge, and the French Broad River valley, in addition to many of the birds noted at the Inn and campground.

Those who wish to combine birding with hiking may select from six major trails that offer a broad range of choice for difficulty, distance, and habitats. The easiest and most popular is the multisegmented **Buck Spring Gap Trail**, a 2.8-mile loop route that begins at the large wooden mapboard at the north end of the Pisgah Inn parking lot. The trail ascends around the west slope of Little Bald Mountain, passes the site of Vanderbilt's famed Buck Spring Lodge, and arrives at the Buck Spring Gap OL, described above, at 1.0 mile from Pisgah Inn. Continue 0.3 miles north on the paved spur road to the north edge of Mount Pisgah parking lot and start up the Mount Pisgah Trail. About 100 feet up the trail you will find the junction where a trail comes in sharply from the left; turn onto this route to head back toward the campground and Inn.

After walking 0.5 miles from Mount Pisgah parking lot, you will arrive at the picnic grounds parking lot (M 407.8). Cross the paved area and find the trail about 50 feet south of the lot along the right shoulder of the Parkway. The 0.9-mile route from here to the campground passes through a mixture of red spruce, hemlock, birch, oaks, and rhododendron near Buck Spring—a good spot for Winter Wren, Red-breasted Nuthatch, Golden-crowned Kinglet, Black-throated Blue Warbler, and Canada Warbler. This isolated stand of conifers and its associated birds can also be viewed by walking along the shoulder of the Parkway south from the lot. After arriving at the campground, it is a brief stroll back to the Inn.

The bird life along this route can also be sampled by parking at overlooks and hiking selected in-and-out segments. The birds are the same ones noted at the Inn, the campground, and various overlooks, all typical spring and summer residents of middle- to high-elevation oak and northern hardwood forests, spruce stands, and heath thickets.

Another good birding area for northern hardwood and oak species involves two trails on Little Bald Mountain (5,280 ft.), just northeast of Pisgah Inn. These two routes begin along the Buck Spring Gap Trail, described above, and descend east into the Mills River valley. In addition to many of the birds noted previously, Ruffed Grouse and Black-billed Cuckoos are sometimes heard along the upper portions of **Laurel Mountain Trail**, which skirts the northeast slope of Little Bald Mountain. The trailhead is well marked on the left about 0.3 miles south of Buck Spring Gap OL. You can go the whole 7.1 miles down into the valley to Yellow Gap Road, but most birders stop at Turkey Spring Gap and retrace their route. The **Pilot Rock Trail** begins about 0.4 miles south of the overlook and climbs 0.2 miles to the summit of Little Bald before heading down 2.3 miles to Yellow Gap Road. These two routes are very lightly used and make a nice side excursion from the Buck Spring Gap Trail. If you are alert and a good pathfinder, you can make a loop hike by taking the connector between the two trails at Turkey Spring Gap, which, incidentally, is not a bad spot for Wild Turkey.

Southwest of Pisgah Inn, the **Fryingpan Gap Trail** passes through a beautiful example of northern red oak "orchard" forest on Big Bald Mountain, a good place for Hairy Woodpecker, Downy Woodpecker, Pileated Woodpecker, Rose-breasted Grosbeaks, and many of the other species noted around the campground and the Inn. The trail begins between the gate and the kiosk on the left side of the campground entrance road (4,925 ft.) at M 408.8, heads up across Big Bald Mountain (5,280 ft.), and descends to Fryingpan Gap (4,931 ft.) at 1.3 miles from the campground. You can go an additional 0.3 miles from the gap to the summit tower (5,340 ft.) on Fryingpan Mountain, which is sometimes a good spot for autumn hawk migration. If you don't want to retrace your route, walk 1 mile north along the Parkway shoulder from Fryingpan Gap (M 409.6) back to the campground entrance.

To get a spectacular view of the southern Appalachians, visit the summit of Mount Pisgah by hiking the **Mount Pisgah Trail**, a moderate-to-strenuous 3-mile round-trip through northern red oak forests, stunted beech trees, and heath and shrub balds. Many of the summer birds noted at the campground and Inn are easy to see along the route, which begins at the north end of the Mount Pisgah parking lot, 0.35 miles from the Parkway on the paved spur road left at M 407.6. The first half of the trail is fairly easy, but the last 0.7 miles is a steep haul to the observation platform at the summit (5,721 ft.). Ruffed Grouse, Common Raven, Winter Wren, and many warblers are regularly expected in summer.

For a transition from high-country to middle-elevation birds, try the 6.2-mile segment of the **Buck Spring Trail** south from Pisgah Inn to US 276. This easy-to-moderate hike descends gradually through oak and cove hardwood forests along Pisgah Ledge high above the Pink Beds. The trail starts between the Pisgah Inn office and restaurant, where rock steps lead down to a wide flat grade; turn right and head past the restaurant and into the woods, where the trail soon descends in a series of switchbacks before leveling out. To get to the opposite end of the trail, drive south on the Parkway to Wagon Road Gap at M 411.7, turn on US 276 south toward Brevard, and go 2.3 miles to a small parking lot on the left, where the trailhead is marked. The elevation at this end of the trail is 1,200 feet lower than at Pisgah Inn, resulting in notable differences in the plant and bird life. The first mile of the hike after leaving US 276 passes through a beautiful cove hardwood forest with huge tuliptrees, where typical late-spring and summer birds include Downy and Pileated Woodpeckers, Eastern Wood-

Peregrine Falcon

Pewee, Acadian Flycatcher, Great Crested Flycatcher, Wood Thrush, Red-eyed Vireo, Chestnut-sided Warbler, Black-throated Blue Warbler, Black-throated Green Warbler, Black-and-white Warbler, American Redstart, Worm-eating Warbler, Ovenbird, Hooded Warbler, Canada Warbler, Scarlet Tanager, and Rufous-sided Towhee. Ruffed Grouse and Barred Owls are possible along the entire trail.

The side excursion on US 276 from the Parkway at Wagon Road Gap also leads down to the Davidson and Mills river valleys and the vast Pisgah National Forest Recreation Area. Birding highlights in the valley include a visit to a Peregrine Falcon nesting site and many prime spots for middle-to low-elevation forest birds.

To see the Peregrines, go 4.6 miles south from the Parkway on US 276 toward Brevard to FSR 475-B, also called the **Headwaters Road**, a gravel route that heads off to the right. Proceed on FSR 475-B for 3.4 miles to a sign with a pull off on the left, where a clearing and an observation area provide a good view of the high cliffs at Looking Glass Rock (3,969 ft.). This huge monolithic dome of granitic gneiss looms dramatically some 1,500 feet above the Davidson River valley. Following a reintroduction program near Shining Rock, Peregrine Falcons nested on Looking Glass Rock in 1988, 1989, and 1990. Bring a spotting scope between mid-March and mid-September for a chance to see the Peregrines, which nest in the horizontal crack or gash below an overhang just above the tree line on the exposed cliff face. The birds are most active in March and April and then again after the young have hatched. Check with USFS rangers at the Pisgah National Forest office (704-877-3350) for the status of the nesting site before making the trip. Incidentally, there is good roadside birding in spring and summer all along road 475-B, which passes through some beautiful cove hardwoods and oak forests.

Return to US 276 and continue toward Brevard. The highway soon parallels the Davidson River, a tributary of the French Broad. At 9.9 miles from the Parkway, turn into the **Coontree picnic area**, where hemlocks, sycamores, birch, elms, maples, and rhododendrons line the riverside—a good spot for Belted Kingfisher, Acadian Flycatcher, Northern Parula, and Louisiana Waterthrush.

At 13.1 miles from the Parkway is the Pisgah Ranger District Visitor Center, where you can obtain information and maps detailing the enormous maze of hiking trails, backcountry roads, and campsites in the region.

Watch for Eastern Bluebirds and Yellow-throated and Hooded Warblers around the visitor center.

About 0.2 miles beyond the visitor center is the entrance to **Davidson River campground** (2,150 ft.), an excellent place for easy birding on the paved campground loop roads, which are also suitable for wheelchairs. Despite highway noise, there is good riverside birding along the 0.2-mile gravel road on the right just before the bridge on the entrance road. Several trails begin at the campground, including the **North Slope Loop Trail**, an easy 3.3-mile route for good birding through cove hardwoods and by hemlocks and rhododendrons along the Davidson River.

Species typically found in spring and summer around the campground include Mourning Dove, Ruby-throated Hummingbird, Belted Kingfisher, Downy Woodpecker, Pileated Woodpecker, Eastern Wood-Pewee, Acadian Flycatcher, Eastern Phoebe, Carolina Chickadee, Tufted Titmouse, White-breasted Nuthatch, Carolina Wren, Blue-gray Gnatcatcher, Wood Thrush, American Robin, Gray Catbird, Cedar Waxwing, Northern Parula, Black-throated Blue Warbler, Black-and-white Warbler, American Redstart, Ovenbird, Louisiana Waterthrush, Scarlet Tanager, Northern Cardinal, Indigo Bunting, Rufous-sided Towhee, Chipping Sparrow, and Song Sparrow. A little searching may turn up Solitary, Yellow-throated, and Red-eyed Vireos, as well as Northern Parula, Yellow Warbler, Yellow-throated Warbler, Pine Warbler, Black-and-white Warbler, American Redstart, Louisiana Waterthrush, Common Yellowthroat, Hooded Warbler, and Yellow-breasted Chat. Eastern Screech-Owl, Great Horned Owl, and Barred Owl may be heard at night. The aerial display of American Woodcock can sometimes be observed in the campground around twilight from March through April.

Many of these birds are present also at **Sycamore Flats picnic area**, about 0.7 miles beyond the campground on US 276. Golden-winged Warblers have been noted in the thickets near the roadway, and American Kestrels are found at the adjacent Schenck Job Corps facility. The Davidson River campground and Sycamore Flats picnic area can be excellent for spring songbird migration in April and May. Both are good spots for migrant Northern Orioles.

To explore the Mills River valley and Pink Beds region, take FSR 1206, the **Yellow Gap Road**, which turns left off US 276 at 3.6 miles south from the Parkway toward Brevard. This gravel route runs along the foot of

Pisgah Ridge at the edge of the Pink Beds, a flat valley at 3,200 feet that is heavily forested with second-growth oak, laurel, and rhododendron. Stop often to listen and explore. At 5.1 miles from US 276, the road comes to the first of two trailheads for **Pilot Cove–Slate Rock Creek Loop Trail**, a moderate-to-strenuous 4.3-mile hike that offers good spring and summer birding in beautiful oak and cove hardwood forests downslope from Little Bald Mountain. Park at the trailhead (3,115 ft.) and hike up to the gap on Slate Rock Ridge at 3,840 feet; then descend along Slate Rock Creek back to the second trailhead at 2,800 feet on Yellow Gap Road, 6.7 miles from US 276. The additional 1.6-mile hike back to the starting point on Yellow Gap Road follows close by Bradley Creek, tumbling through a ravine with hemlock cove forest and rosebay rhododendron. This is a good area for warblers, including Northern Parula, Chestnut-sided, Black-throated Blue, Black-throated Green, Black-and-white, Ovenbird, Louisiana Waterthrush, Hooded, and Canada. Other attractions include Ruffed Grouse, Barred Owl, Pileated Woodpecker, Scarlet Tanager, and Rose-breasted Grosbeak.

Yellow Gap Road eventually connects with FSR 479 at the North Mills River campground. Head up FSR 479 through oak forests to a junction with the Parkway at M 400.2 in Bent Creek Gap (3,270 ft.), stopping at regular intervals for roadside birding. Many of the same species on Yellow Gap Road are found along this route, which is also good for Worm-eating Warblers, Ruffed Grouse, owls, and woodpeckers.

For an introduction to the history of conservation and forestry, stop by the **Cradle of Forestry in America** at 3.8 miles from the Parkway on US 276 toward Brevard. In addition to checking the extensive interpretative exhibits, you may want to explore the **Forest Festival Trail**, a 1-mile loop route for easy birding just behind the visitor center. At 3,280 feet, the site has a mix of low- and middle-elevation summer birds.

The high country at the southern end of Pisgah Ridge was once covered by an extensive spruce-fir forest, but logging and a severe wildfire in 1925 created a patchwork mix of grass balds, heath balds, successional thickets, and scattered stands of hardwoods and spruce. Here at the confluence of Pisgah Ridge and Shining Rock Ledge, the Yellowstone Prong of East Fork Pigeon River forms in a hanging valley at an elevation of 5,100 feet— a place called **Graveyard Fields** for the burned-out spruce stumps that once dotted the terrain. Bird life at Graveyard Fields is a curious mix of high-country birds mingled with species more typical of lower elevations.

Park at the overlook at M 418.8, where you can survey the scene, hike south along the Parkway shoulder, or explore the two trails that head toward the river from the parking area. The trail at the north end of the lot is partly paved through a dense rhododendron thicket down to a wooden bridge across Yellowstone Prong; the trail splits immediately on the other side of the river, with the right fork going about 200 yards downstream for a descent to Yellowstone Falls after passing the trailhead for Graveyard Ridge Trail, which runs north to Shining Rock Wilderness. The left fork is the **Graveyard Fields Loop Trail**, which follows the river upstream through an ever-changing array of plant communities to Upper Falls, for an easy round-trip hike of 3.2 miles. The much shorter trail beginning at the south end of the parking lot goes through hardwoods and heath thickets down to the river, which you can sometimes ford to join the longer loop trail. Unfortunately, the Graveyard Fields area is often very crowded on weekends, when there may be more tents than birds!

Spotted Sandpiper and Belted Kingfisher are occasional along Yellowstone Prong—about as high as they occur in the Appalachians. Late-spring and summer birds in the open grassy areas and shrubby margins include Northern Bobwhite, Eastern Phoebe, House Wren, Eastern Bluebird, Brown Thrasher, Common Yellowthroat, Indigo Bunting, Field Sparrow, and Song Sparrow, which are here subsequent to the destruction of forest canopy. Common Snipe may occur during migration in the wet grassy areas, and American Woodcock present their aerial displays around twilight in March and April. From fall through spring, be alert for Golden Eagle and Northern Harrier; even Peregrines and Northern Goshawk have been seen here in autumn.

Other spring and summer birds at Graveyard Fields are Ruffed Grouse, Ruby-throated Hummingbird, Downy and Hairy Woodpeckers, Northern Flicker, Blue Jay, Common Raven, Veery, American Robin, Gray Catbird, Cedar Waxwing, Solitary Vireo, Chestnut-sided Warbler, Black-throated Blue Warbler, Canada Warbler, Rose-breasted Grosbeak, Rufous-sided Towhee, and Dark-eyed Junco. Yellow-bellied Sapsucker and Golden-winged Warbler are rare but always possible.

Shining Rock Ledge and Wilderness

Highlights: Birds of high-elevation spruce-fir and northern hardwood forests, grass balds, heath balds, middle-elevation oak forests, and cove
forests; Northern Harrier, Golden Eagle, Northern Saw-whet Owl, Alder
Flycatcher, Red Crossbill.

Season: Year-round, but mainly spring through fall.

Access: The main access route to Shining Rock is on FSR 816. FSR 816 exits
the BRP at M 420.2, which is 3 miles north of Beech Gap (M 423.2) and
8.5 miles south of Wagon Road Gap (M 411.7). From Beech Gap it is 17
miles south to Rosman, N.C., on NC 215; from Wagon Road Gap it is 17
miles south to Brevard, N.C., and 22 miles north to Waynesville, N.C., on
US 276.

Maps: USGS "Sam Knob," "Shining Rock"; USFS "Shining Rock Wilderness
and Middle Prong Wilderness."

Facilities: Rest rooms at parking lot on FSR 816. Nearest gasoline, food, and
lodging (spring through autumn only) at Pisgah Inn at M 408.7.

Shining Rock Ledge is a lofty, ten-mile-long mountain range that
encompasses some of the most attractive and ecologically diverse terrain in
the southern Blue Ridge Province. At the beginning of the twentieth century, the mile-high plateaulike region at the convergence of Shining Rock
Ledge, Pisgah Ridge, Tanasee Ridge, and the Great Balsams was covered
by the most extensive stand of spruce-fir forest in the southern Appalachian Mountains. In 1858, the roving naturalist Samuel Botsford Buckley
visited the region and reported that the spruce trees at Shining Rock Ledge
were the largest that he had observed in his exploration of the southern
mountains. Some were more than one hundred feet tall and exceeded four
feet in diameter. Between 1913 and 1926, this magnificent forest was destroyed by the Suncrest Lumber Company of Waynesville, which removed
millions of board feet of red spruce from the region, leaving dense piles
of slash and brush. On Thanksgiving Day, 1925, following a prolonged
drought, a wildfire sparked by a logging train burned over 25,000 acres of
virgin spruce-fir forest and destroyed the topsoil in most of the previously
cutover areas.

As a result of this and subsequent wildfires, most of the high elevations
on Shining Rock Ledge are covered by a complex mosaic of heath balds,
grass balds, different stages and types of secondary successional commu-

nities, and scattered remnant stands of deciduous and coniferous forests of varying degrees of maturity. Although similar damage has occurred widely in the southern Appalachians, where over 90 percent of the original spruce-fir forests have been removed, these changes at Shining Rock are among the most severe and extensive alteration of high-elevation habitat in the Blue Ridge. Bird species associated with spruce-fir and northern hardwoods have been reduced in number or extirpated, and species considered to be typical of low elevations and of open or shrubby habitat have increased in number or become established here for the first time.

Named for its beautiful outcrop cliffs of white quartz, Shining Rock Ledge runs in a north-south axis from Black Balsam Knob near the Parkway to Cold Mountain (6,030 ft.) near the confluence of the east and west forks of the Pigeon River. The main crest line of the ledge remains above 5,500 feet through most of its length, with several peaks exceeding 6,000 feet. Much of the range is protected in the Shining Rock Wilderness, an 18,500-acre tract established in 1964. Old logging railroad grades wander through the high country, providing miles of easy hiking, splendid vistas, and good birding. More strenuous trails connect the highest summits with coves and river valleys below.

For quick access to Shining Rock Ledge, take FSR 816, a paved route that leaves the Parkway at M 420.2, ascends gradually across the saddle between Black Balsam Knob and Silvermine Bald, and ends in a parking lot 1.25 miles from the Parkway. The area around **Black Balsam Knob** (6,214 ft.) was severely damaged by wildfires so that grass balds and shrubby fields cover much of the land from the summit to the high plateau southwest of the knob. Stop in the pull off at 0.5 miles from the Parkway; from here to the parking lot is a good area in summer for Alder Flycatchers, which became established locally in the 1970s. Other late-spring and summer birds along the road include Downy Woodpecker, Northern Flicker, Common Raven, Red-breasted Nuthatch, Winter Wren, Golden-crowned Kinglet, Veery, American Robin, Gray Catbird, Cedar Waxwing, Solitary Vireo, Chestnut-sided Warbler, Canada Warbler, Rufous-sided Towhee, and Dark-eyed Junco. Note the House Wrens, Common Yellowthroats, Indigo Buntings, and Song Sparrows that have invaded the area where the forest canopy has been destroyed.

You can hike up Black Balsam Knob by stopping at a widened parking area at 0.7 miles from the Parkway and walking the Art Loeb National Recreation Trail 0.5 miles to the summit, for a spectacular view of the sur-

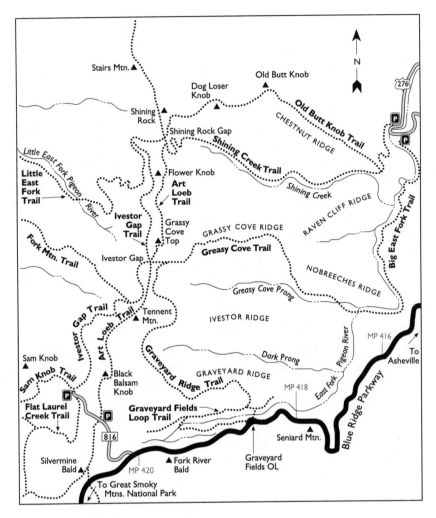

Shining Rock, N.C.

rounding area and lots of Song Sparrows and Dark-eyed Juncos. In March and April, American Woodcock aerial displays can sometimes be seen around dusk in grassy fields on the knob and on the plateau south of the parking lot. From autumn to early spring, scan the open grassy areas on the knob and the plateau for Northern Harriers and rare Golden Eagles.

To explore the area southwest of the parking lot, get a copy of the Forest Service topographic trail map for Shining Rock Wilderness and study the one-way hikes or potential interconnecting loop hikes over the high open plateau and adjacent slopes between Sam Knob, Silvermine Bald, and the West Fork Pigeon River. Parts of the trails follow old logging railroad grades, making for easy walks through a complex array of habitats, including spruce groves, yellow birch stands, northern hardwood forests, rhododendron thickets, and extensive grass balds. The **Flat Laurel Creek Trail, Little Sam Knob Trail, Sam Knob Trail,** and portions of the **Mountains-to-Sea Trail** provide excellent summer birding.

To get into Shining Rock Wilderness, park your car in the lot at the end of FSR 816 and take **Ivestor Gap Trail,** another old logging railroad grade, which begins on the northeast edge of the paved lot and runs north along the west slope of Black Balsam Knob and Shining Rock Ledge toward Ivestor Gap. The trail is flat, broad, and open, with great scenic vistas and easy hiking all the way to Shining Rock. For the first few miles, the route passes through the area heavily logged and damaged by fire, where many of the same birds noted previously at Black Balsam Knob can be found in summer. Watch for Yellow-bellied Sapsuckers, especially in the young hardwoods at the north edge of the parking lot.

Two miles from the parking lot, the trail arrives at Ivestor Gap (5,680 ft.), an interesting spot worth exploring for birds that occur here as a result of the destruction of the original spruce-fir forests. Listen for Northern Bobwhite and Field Sparrows, and check the grassy areas for American Woodcock. Note the abundance of Common Yellowthroats and Song Sparrows, as well as occasional Ruby-throated Hummingbirds and Brown Thrashers. From fall through spring, be alert for Golden Eagle, Northern Harrier, and Common Snipe.

Before going on toward Shining Rock, explore the first 0.5 miles of **Greasy Cove Trail,** which begins at the gap and heads east, eventually descending 6.8 miles to the East Fork Pigeon River. Alder Flycatchers are often present in open shrubby growth on the south slope of Grassy Cove Top, along the left-hand side of the trail just east of the gap. A little farther on the right, near the junction with **Graveyard Ridge Trail,** is a good spot for House Wrens, which are rather unusual at this elevation. Continue on to the east side of Grassy Cove Top. Here a beautiful Catawba rhododendron thicket overlooks a high cove where Black-billed Cuckoos are occasionally heard. Retrace your route back to Ivestor Gap. If you have time, you could explore the Graveyard Ridge Trail toward the south, crossing Ivestor Ridge and Graveyard Ridge, where Golden-winged Warblers are sometimes found in spring and summer.

Resume your hike toward Shining Rock on the Ivestor Gap Trail north into Shining Rock Wilderness. The vegetation soon changes, giving way to increasingly mature spruce and northern hardwood forests as you approach Shining Rock Gap, 2.1 miles north of Ivestor Gap. Along this portion of the route, look for species associated with high-elevation woodlands, such as Yellow-bellied Sapsucker, Black-capped Chickadee, Red-breasted Nuthatch, Brown Creeper, Winter Wren, and even Red Crossbill and Pine Siskin. Other birds include Blue Jay, American Crow, Common Raven, American Robin, Gray Catbird, Rose-breasted Grosbeak, Rufous-sided Towhee, and Dark-eyed Junco. Watch for Downy and Hairy Woodpeckers and Northern Flicker, as well as Veery, Solitary Vireo, Chestnut-sided Warbler, Black-throated Blue Warbler, Black-throated Green Warbler, Canada Warbler, and Common Yellowthroat. Even Northern Goshawk and Peregrine Falcons have been reported, so be alert for raptors.

You can camp at Shining Rock Gap (5,750 ft.) or just climb to the beautiful white quartz cliffs that rise above the spruce trees on the summit of Shining Rock (6,000 ft.), a delightful place to watch the sunset across the Great Balsam Mountains or the sunrise over Pisgah Ridge. Sometimes six or more Barred Owls can be heard barking downslope around dark in the spring and summer months, and Northern Saw-whet Owls are heard from April through June at Shining Rock, Stairs Mountain, and along the Ivestor Gap Trail near Flower Knob.

For a more rigorous hike or to explore other portions of the region, study the Forest Service topographic trail map and read the trail descriptions in hiking guides such as de Hart's. The **Art Loeb National Recreation Trail** parallels the Ivestor Gap Trail as far as Shining Rock Gap but follows the undulating crest line of Shining Rock Ledge rather than the level railroad grade. Most of the other routes are strenuous treks between the Pigeon River valley and the high country.

To see the bird life typical of cove forests along the middle elevations of the Pigeon River, exit the Parkway at Wagon Road Gap (M 411.7) and head north on US 276 toward Waynesville for 2.7 miles to a small parking lot (3,400 ft.) on the left just before the road crosses the East Fork bridge. From here the **Big East Fork Trail** runs 6.8 miles through Shining Rock Wilderness up to Ivestor Gap. The trail ascends 600 feet during the first 3.6 miles, as it follows close by the river through a handsome forest of tuliptrees, buckeyes, maples, birch, hemlocks and rhododendrons. Despite

Red-breasted Nuthatch

the noise of the river, the first few miles of the trail can be a good hike for spring migration and for summer birds of middle-elevation woodlands.

At night, listen for Barred Owls, as well as Eastern Screech-Owls and Great Horned Owls. Belted Kingfishers are regular along the river bank, and Spotted Sandpipers are occasionally seen. Listen for Ruffed Grouse, Black-billed Cuckoo, and Yellow-billed Cuckoo; watch for Downy Woodpecker, Northern Flicker, and Pileated Woodpecker. Expected songbirds during the breeding season include Eastern Wood-Pewee, Acadian Fly-catcher, Eastern Phoebe, Great Crested Flycatcher, Northern Rough-winged Swallow, Blue Jay, Carolina Chickadee, Tufted Titmouse, White-breasted Nuthatch, Carolina Wren, Blue-gray Gnatcatcher, Wood Thrush, American Robin, Solitary Vireo, Red-eyed Vireo, Black-throated Blue Warbler, Black-throated Green Warbler, Black-and-white Warbler, Oven-bird, Louisiana Waterthrush, Common Yellowthroat, Hooded Warbler, Scarlet Tanager, Northern Cardinal, Song Sparrow, and Dark-eyed Junco.

Southern Great Balsam Mountains

Highlights: Spruce-fir residents; Northern Saw-whet Owl, Black-billed Cuckoo, Black-capped Chickadee.

Season: Spring through fall.

Access: The BRP runs along the crest of the Southern Great Balsams from Beech Gap at M 423.2 to Balsam Gap at M 443.1. From Beech Gap, it is 17 miles south to Rosman, N.C., or 23 miles north to Waynesville, N.C., via NC 215. From Balsam Gap it is 8 miles east to Waynesville and 12 miles west to Sylva, N.C., on US 19A and US 23.

(Note: The easiest route to a number of important nearby sites is to exit the Parkway at Balsam Gap [M 443.1]. From here it is 38 miles to Cashiers, N.C., near the Southeastern Blue Ridge Escarpment Gorges, 40 miles to Franklin, N.C., near the Nantahala Mountains, 48 miles to the Highlands Plateau, 76 miles to Murphy, N.C., in the Hiwassee River Basin, and 98 miles to Blairsville, Ga., in the North Georgia Highlands. From Beech Gap [M 423.2], it is 45 miles to the Highlands Plateau and 24 miles to the Eastatoe area in the Southeastern Blue Ridge Escarpment Gorges.)

Maps: USGS "Sam Knob," "Tuckasegee," "Hazelwood," "Waynesville"; USFS "Shining Rock Wilderness and Middle Prong Wilderness."

Facilities: None along the BRP except at Pisgah Inn (M 408.7); closest gasoline, food, and lodging are east of Balsam Gap on US 19A and US 23 toward Waynesville.

Princeton geographer Arnold Guyot, in his pioneering 1863 report on southern Appalachian geography, called the Great Balsam Mountains the "master chain" of the transverse ranges. This lofty mountain mass stretches some forty-five miles northwest from its junction with Pisgah Ridge to its terminus at Tri-corner Knob in the Great Smokies. The crest line remains mostly above 5,000 feet, and many peaks exceed 6,000 feet, culminating at Richland Balsam, the highest point in the range at 6,410 feet. The slopes are drained by the Pigeon, Oconaluftee, and Tuckasegee rivers, tributaries of the Tennessee. Near its midsection, the range is divided into northern and southern halves by the Plott Balsam Mountains.

The Balsams are heavily timbered by medium to mature second-growth oaks and cove hardwoods in low and intermediate elevations. Much of the terrain above 5,000 feet is cloaked with spruce-fir and northern hardwood forests, intermixed with heath balds of Catawba rhododendron and mountain laurel. Distinctive yellow birch stands and oak "orchard" forests cover some high peaks and ridges. Many writers erroneously state that the southernmost extension of the so-called Canadian zone in the eastern United States occurs at Clingman's Dome in the Smokies, but the spruce-fir community is well developed as far south as Tanasee Bald, near M 423.5 in the Great Balsams.

The range has been affected by extensive logging and wildfires, and devastating losses of spruce-fir forests began on the highest peaks during the 1970s, apparently a result of damage from airborne pollutants and balsam woolly adelgids, leaving areas such as Richland Balsam covered with dead and dying trees. The range nevertheless remains an outstanding area for high-mountain bird-watching, especially for those who value solitude and beautiful scenery.

Northern Saw-whet Owls are a major ornithological attraction in the southern Great Balsam range, which is one of the best spots in the eastern United States to hear and see these elusive little raptors. From late March through June, six to eight Saw-whets can often be heard between sunset and dawn along a 14-mile stretch of the Parkway extending from Fork River Bald at M 419 on Pisgah Ridge to the vicinity of Locust Gap at M 433.3. Although the owls have been found at more than a dozen calling areas, several sites produce the most consistent results.

Devil's Courthouse on nearby Pisgah Ridge is probably the best bet for hearing and seeing the owl. Park at Devil's Courthouse OL (5,462 ft.) on the left at M 422.4. Often two or more owls are calling from the ridge area near the summit of Devil's Courthouse or from the right side of the Parkway opposite the overlook. Take a small flashlight and large floodlight up

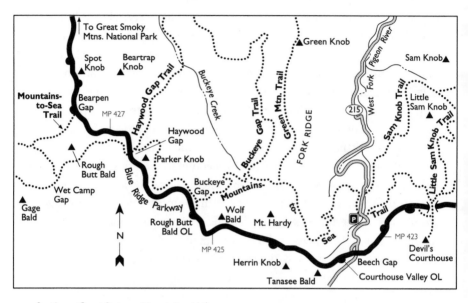

Southern Great Balsam Mountains, N.C.

the moderately strenuous paved trail that runs 0.4 miles from the overlook to the summit. Using the flashlight, continue on the trail into the spruce-fir woods, saving the big floodlight for seeing the bird. Never attempt to walk off the trail in these woods at night.

The owls may be observed anywhere in the forest, but they are most often found where the main trail turns sharply right at a T-shaped inter-section about 0.3 miles from the overlook parking lot. If you are familiar with the trails here, you can also take the left route at the junction and check the ridge line toward Chestnut Bald. If it is very windy or if no birds are calling, you may want to listen for the owls on the opposite side of Devil's Courthouse by parking at Fetterbush OL on the left at M 421.8.

Nearby **Courthouse Valley Overlook** (5,362 ft.) on the left at M 423.5 is a good place to hear the owls calling from adjacent Tanasee Bald, just southwest of the parking lot. Occasionally the owls are active on the oppo-site side of the Parkway in the Middle Prong Wilderness area and can be heard by walking carefully along the Parkway shoulder south toward Mount Hardy. Also try **Cowee Mountain Overlook** on the left at M 430.7, where the owls are sometimes calling on Chestnut Ridge downslope from the Parkway.

Aside from Devil's Courthouse, the best spot for a look at the owls is usually at **Richland Balsam**. The owls are often heard at Richland Balsam OL (6,050 ft.) at M 431.4, but for the chance to see a Saw-whet, park at the Haywood-Jackson OL (6,020 ft.) at MP 431. The Richland Balsam Trail begins at the south end of the parking lot and runs for 1.5 miles to the summit. If the owls are calling between the parking area and summit, you may have a chance to see them along the trail, but be extremely careful hiking here at night. Many dead and downed conifers are strewn across the trail, and others may blow over without warning.

A final spot is around **Lone Bald**, just west of Richland Balsam. Park at the Lone Bald OL (5,635 ft.) at M 432.7 and listen for the owls on Spruce Ridge, above the Parkway just north of the overlook, as well as on the summit of Lone Bald itself. Continue to Roy Taylor OL (5,580 ft.) at Locust Gap, on the opposite side of Lone Bald at M 433.3. The owls are sometimes calling from Lone Bald or from points along the Parkway south of the overlook. If you have plenty of time, try every overlook in the spruce-fir zone of the Parkway, as many of the Saw-whets seem to change calling areas from year to year. Read "Owl Quest" in Section 2 for notes on how to find these intriguing owls.

Unfortunately, most of the other good Saw-whet sites are not close to parking lots or overlooks. Even if you are familiar with the Parkway, it is dangerous to pull off onto the shoulder at night, where you are likely to get stuck, slide down the mountainside, or leave part of your car sticking precariously out into the roadway. Dense fogs are common in spring, making it even more dangerous to park halfway on the shoulder. Remember that you are a long way from civilization up here, and the minimal traffic after dark in April and May provides little chance of emergency assistance.

Daytime birding in the Great Balsams involves overlooks and easy-to-moderate trails through a variety of high-country plant communities. Despite heavy damage, spruce-fir forests dominate much of the fourteen miles along the Balsam crest between Lone Bald and Tanasee Bald and extend to Fork River Bald in nearby Pisgah Ridge. During spring and summer months, the overlooks and trails in this section are worth checking for some uncommon species such as Yellow-bellied Sapsucker, Black-billed Cuckoo, Black-capped Chickadee, Brown Creeper, and Blackburnian Warbler, as well as the erratic Red Crossbill and Pine Siskin. Some overlooks and clearings are good spots to see aerial courtship displays of American Woodcock at twilight in March and April, and Wild Turkeys are possible year-round.

Northern Saw-whet Owl

Typical spring and summer species include Barred and Northern Saw-whet Owls, Chimney Swift, Downy and Hairy Woodpeckers, Northern Flicker, Blue Jay, American Crow, Common Raven, Red-breasted Nuthatch, Winter Wren, Golden-crowned Kinglet, Veery, American Robin, Gray Catbird, Cedar Waxwing, Solitary Vireo, Chestnut-sided Warbler, Black-throated Blue Warbler, Black-throated Green Warbler, Common Yellowthroat, Canada Warbler, Rose-breasted Grosbeak, Rufous-sided Towhee, Dark-eyed Junco, and American Goldfinch.

Although geographically part of Pisgah Ridge, **Devil's Courthouse** is ecologically linked to the Great Balsams, and the overlook and summit trail are excellent for spruce-fir and northern hardwood birds. From the parking lot at M 422.4 (5,462 ft.), you can hike along the Parkway shoulder south to Mount Hardy OL or proceed 0.1 miles on the paved trail running north to the forest edge. Much of the successional vegetation here consists of mountain ash, fire cherry, yellow birch, and beech. This portion of the trail, the overlook parking lot, and the adjacent "sidewalk" may be suitable for the physically impaired, including those using wheelchairs. After entering the mature spruce-fir woods, however, the Devil's Courthouse Trail ascends very steeply for 0.3 miles to the summit (5,720 ft.), which is often a good spot to watch the autumn hawk migration in September and October. American Woodcock, Northern Saw-whet Owl, Common Raven, Black-capped Chickadee, Red-breasted Nuthatch, Brown Creeper, Winter Wren, and Golden-crowned Kinglet are fairly regular here.

Other good overlooks for spruce-fir and northern hardwood birds include **Courthouse Valley Overlook** (5,362 ft.) at M 423.5, where one can find Northern Saw-whet Owls and American Woodcock in early spring or walk along the Parkway shoulder south toward Mount Hardy for other species. The spruce-fir community is near its southernmost limit in the eastern United States on nearby Tanasee Bald, which rises just to the southwest of the parking lot. **Bearpen Gap parking area** (5,560 ft.) at M 427.6 has many spruce-fir birds, including Blackburnian Warbler in some years. Check out **Beartrail Ridge parking lot** (5,865 ft.) at M 430.4, **Lone Bald Overlook** (5,635 ft.) at M 432.7, and even **Richland Balsam Overlook** (5,060 ft.) at M 431.4. For a close-up view of the destruction done by balsam woolly adelgids and pollution, hike the **Richland Balsam Nature Trail**, a moderate-to-strenuous 3.0-mile round-trip from **Haywood-Jackson Overlook** (6,020 ft.) at MP 431 to the summit at 6,410 feet. Despite the death of over 80 percent of the Fraser fir, the parking lot and trail remain a good spot for many spruce-fir birds, including Northern Saw-whet Owl and Black-capped Chickadee, along with some invading species, such as the Common Yellowthroat, which appeared here following destruction of the canopy.

For the physically impaired, the **Roy Taylor Overlook** (5,580 ft.) at M 433.3 in Locust Gap is a good place for birding. The site is dedicated to Roy Taylor, U.S. congressman and chairman of the National Parks and Recreation Committee from 1967 to 1977. A flat paved trail suitable for wheelchairs leads from the parking lot onto a wooden platform perched in the forest canopy. The platform provides close access to spruce-fir birds and a clear view into the valley below.

An easy stroll along the Parkway shoulder south from the Roy Taylor

OL passes through a mix of successional communities, with grass balds, heath thickets, northern hardwoods, and northern red oak "orchards." American Woodcock aerial displays can be seen in the open grassy areas around twilight in late March and April. Watch in late spring and summer for Downy and Hairy Woodpeckers, Blue Jay, Veery, Gray Catbird, Cedar Waxwing, Solitary Vireo, Chestnut-sided Warbler, Black-throated Blue Warbler, Black-and-white Warbler, Canada Warbler, Rose-breasted Grosbeak, Rufous-sided Towhee, and Dark-eyed Junco.

These same birds are associated with several distinctive plant communities, including yellow birch forests and northern red oak "orchards" along the crest from Locust Gap at M 433.5 to Steestachee Bald at M 437. Stop at **Doubletop Mountain Overlook** (5,365 ft.) at M 435.2 and **Licklog Gap Overlook** (5,135 ft.) at M 435.7 for classic open-canopied "oak orchard" stands. At nearby **Glassy Ridge Mine Overlook** (5,260 ft.) at M 436.8, a segment of the Mountains-to-Sea Trail provides excellent birding through a unique forest where yellow birch are growing atop a boulder field on Steestachee Bald. A 30-yard connector trail runs from the south end of the parking lot to the Mountains-to-Sea Trail; turn right onto the trail and bird the area across the northeast slope of Steestachee or turn left onto the trail and work back toward Licklog Gap OL. Be alert for Yellow-bellied Sapsucker and Black-billed Cuckoo, which are occasionally noted around these three overlooks and the interconnecting trail.

Probably the best birding hike in the Southern Great Balsams is the 4.7-mile segment of the **Mountains-to-Sea Trail** between Rough Butt Bald OL and the Bearpen Gap parking area. This easy-to-moderate trek passes through mature spruce-fir forests, northern hardwoods, heath thickets, and grass balds. In addition to the usual species, the route is often a good spot for Black-billed Cuckoo; Wild Turkey and Yellow-bellied Sapsucker are possible; and Brown Creeper and Black-capped Chickadee are regular. You can arrange transportation at either end to avoid retracing your route or hike in-and-out segments between the two parking areas and Haywood Gap, where the trail crosses the Parkway.

The trail begins at the north edge of Bearpen Gap parking area (5,560 ft.) at M 427.6 and runs 0.7 miles through spruce and northern hardwoods to a metal gate near the junction with a dirt road; turn sharply left and proceed uphill at this intersection. At 1.2 miles from the parking area, the trail arrives at Wet Camp Gap, an open grassy area that extends about 300 yards to the south. Wet Camp is a good spot for turkeys, sapsuckers, and cuckoos. After exploring the gap, return to the Mountains-to-Sea Trail, which heads back into the woods at the northeast corner of the clearing. The trail continues around Rough Butt Bald and, at 2.9 miles from the Bearpen Gap lot, crosses the Parkway at M 426.5 in Haywood Gap (5,225 ft.), a good spot for Black-billed Cuckoo and Northern Saw-whet Owl.

From Haywood Gap, the trail runs an additional 1.8 miles to Buckeye Gap, where a 260-yard connector trail on the right takes you to Rough Butt Bald OL parking lot at M 425.4. This connector trail is a good area for Brown Creeper and Black-capped Chickadee, as it passes through a mature spruce-fir tract. You can also hike the route in the opposite direction beginning at Rough Butt Bald OL. The Mountains-to-Sea Trail continues 4.2 miles east beyond Buckeye Gap to NC 215 and beyond there to Shining Rock Ledge.

Although little explored ornithologically, the **Middle Prong Wilderness**, established in 1984, encompasses 7,900 acres of prime birding country on the north slope of the high Balsam crest line between Beech Gap and Richland Balsam. Spring and summer bird species are typical of those noted elsewhere in the Balsams in spruce-fir, northern hardwood, and oak-hickory woodlands. A segment of the Mountains-to-Sea Trail crosses the southern edge of the wilderness just north of the Parkway, while the Green Mountain Trail, Buckeye Gap Trail, and Haywood Gap Trail descend northward into the valley of the West Fork Pigeon River. Be sure to use a detailed map, compass, and trail guides and to check with a USFS ranger for current information.

Plott Balsam Mountains

Highlights: Spruce-fir and northern hardwood species; Northern Saw-whet Owl, Black-capped Chickadee.

Season: Spring and summer.

Access: This section of the BRP lies between M 443.1 at Balsam Gap and M 455.7 at Soco Gap. From Balsam Gap it is 12 miles west to Sylva, N.C., and 8 miles east to Waynesville, N.C., on US 19A and US 23. From Soco Gap it is 8 miles west to Cherokee, N.C., and 13 miles east to Waynesville on US 19.

(Note: The easiest route from the Parkway to a number of important nearby
sites is to exit the BRP at Balsam Gap [M 443.1]. From here it is 38 miles
to Cashiers, N.C., near the Southeastern Blue Ridge Escarpment Gorges,
40 miles to Franklin, N.C., near the Nantahala Mountains, 48 miles to the
Highlands Plateau, 76 miles to Murphy, N.C., in the Hiwassee River Basin,
and 98 miles to Blairsville, Ga., in the North Georgia Highlands in
Section 5.)
Maps: USGS "Dellwood," "Hazelwood," "Sylva North."
Facilities: Rest rooms at Waterrock Knob.

Transecting the Great Balsam Mountains at right angles, the Plott
Balsams are a short but lofty range rising abruptly from the Tuckasegee
and Pigeon river valleys, tributaries of the Tennessee. The high elevations
are covered by spruce-fir and northern hardwood forests, interspersed
with rhododendron balds, while mature oak and cove hardwood forests
are found in the middle and low elevations. The range was named for the
Plott family, descendants of Johannes Plott, who came to America from
Heidelberg in 1750. Ornithological studies began in the range as early as
December 1885, when Charles F. Batchelder (1856–1954) of Massachusetts
discovered Black-capped Chickadees on the high peaks.

A steep 12-mile stretch of the Parkway crosses the range from Balsam
Gap (3,370 ft.) over the shoulder of Waterrock Knob and down to Soco
Gap (4,345 ft.). Spring and summer birds are characteristic of the highest
elevations in the southern Appalachians, and the range is one of the few
spots outside the Great Smokies where Black-capped Chickadees can be
regularly expected. Although the Mountains-to-Sea Trail will eventually
cross the Plotts, most of this rugged mountain range is inaccessible, so
birding is confined to the Parkway overlooks, a short trail to the summit of Waterrock Knob, and a rigorous 3-mile hike to the peak of Mount
Lyn Lowry.

For a view of high-elevation summer birds, the area at **Waterrock Knob**
provides both easy and strenuous alternatives. Turn right at M 451.2 for
a 0.3-mile spur road to the rest rooms and parking lot (5,820 ft.). The
flat paved lot is nestled among the spruce-fir woods and rhododendron
thickets below the peak, with clear views from both sides of the main
crest of the Plotts. The lot is good for wheelchairs, and strolling along the
shoulder of the connector road is easy. At night from April through June,
listen and whistle for Northern Saw-whet Owls from various corners of

the parking area. To get back into the woods, take the steep and strenuous 0.6-mile trail from the far end of the parking lot for a climb of 470 feet to the summit of Waterrock Knob (6,292 ft.), highest point in the Plotts and a great view of the Smokies, Balsams, and surrounding valleys. Species typical of this high spruce-fir community and rhododendron balds in late spring and summer include Common Raven, Black-capped Chickadee, Red-breasted Nuthatch, Brown Creeper, Winter Wren, Golden-crowned Kinglet, Veery, American Robin, Gray Catbird, Cedar Waxwing, Solitary Vireo, Chestnut-sided Warbler, Black-throated Green Warbler, Canada Warbler, Rufous-sided Towhee, Song Sparrow, and Dark-eyed Junco.

Despite the noise of car traffic, the **Parkway overlooks** between Balsam Gap and Soco Gap can be excellent spots to see spring and summer birds of oak, northern hardwood, and spruce-fir forests. Most are flat and level, suitable for wheelchairs or easy walking, with good views into the surrounding canopy. The Woodfin Valley OL at MP 446 (4,120 ft.) and Woodfin Cascade OL at M 446.7 (4,535 ft.) edge onto open oak forests, where possibilities include Black-billed Cuckoo, Tufted Titmouse, Gray Catbird, Solitary Vireo, Chestnut-sided Warbler, Black-throated Blue Warbler, Black-and-white Warbler, Rufous-sided Towhee, and Dark-eyed Junco. Overlooks at higher elevations border northern hardwoods, spruce-fir forests, and heath thickets, where Saw-whet Owl, Black-capped Chickadee, and other species noted at Waterrock Knob may be expected. Recommended sites include Wesner Bald OL (4,914 ft.) at M 447.8, Scott Creek OL (5,050 ft.) at M 448.3, Fork Ridge OL (5,280 ft.) at MP 449, Yellowface OL (5,588 ft.) at M 450.2, and Cranberry Ridge OL (5,475 ft.) at M 452.1.

Until the Mountains-to-Sea Trail is completed, the only practical hiking access to the high Plotts is a 3-mile haul to the summit of **Mount Lyn Lowry** (6,280 ft.). Park at Woodfin Valley OL (4,120 ft.) at MP 446 and walk north on the Parkway about 0.1 miles; turn at right angles to the roadway and head uphill through the woods to the ridge line about 100 yards from the Parkway. A gravel road runs along the ridge; turn left and follow the road for 3 miles to the peak. This rather strenuous hike is good for summer birds of oak, northern hardwood, and spruce-fir forests, despite the die-off of some conifers near the top. Trails lead from the summit to Waterrock Knob and Plott Balsam (6,200 ft.), but you are unlikely to find any species not already encountered in the climb up Mount Lyn Lowry. In late spring and summer, this is a good route for Common Raven, Black-capped Chickadee, Red-breasted Nuthatch, Brown Creeper, Winter Wren,

Golden-crowned Kinglet, Veery, Solitary Vireo, Chestnut-sided Warbler, Black-throated Blue Warbler, Canada Warbler, and Dark-eyed Junco.

To see waterfowl in the valley at the foot of the Plotts, leave the Parkway at Balsam Gap (M 443.1) and head north 9 miles on US 19 to the **Lake Junaluska** exit at NC 209. Go 0.2 miles on NC 209, which runs under a railroad bridge, and make an immediate left turn, proceeding then 0.1 miles to the entrance to Lake Junaluska on the right. Just inside the gate, South Lakeshore Drive turns left and runs 1.6 miles, while North Lakeshore Drive turns right and goes 1.5 miles. Drive slowly around the lake, stop at the occasional pull offs, and scan the area for birds. Pied-billed Grebes are often present year-round and have nested in shallow areas. Green-backed Herons are often present in summer. During migration and occasionally in winter, one may find Common Loon, Canada Goose, Mallard, Hooded Merganser, and American Coot. Red-throated Loon, Horned Grebe, Common and Red-breasted Mergansers, and other waterfowl species have been reported. Even American White Pelicans have been seen here, but don't count on finding one!

Northern Great Balsam Mountains

Highlights: Spruce-fir and northern hardwood summer residents; Northern Saw-whet Owl, Least Flycatcher, Black-capped Chickadee.

Season: Year-round, but mainly spring through summer.

Access: From Soco Gap at M 455.7, it is 8 miles west to Cherokee, N.C., and 13 miles east to Waynesville, N.C., on US 19. From the southern end of the BRP at M 469, it is 2 miles south to Cherokee and 29 miles north to Gatlinburg, Tenn., on US 441.

Maps: USGS "Bunches Bald," "Luftee Knob," "Smokemont."

Facilities: Rest rooms and forty-five campsites at Balsam Mountain campground at 8.4 miles from the BRP; many campgrounds in GSMNP; gasoline, food, and lodging in Cherokee, Maggie Valley, N.C., and Waynesville; maps, books, and information at Oconaluftee Visitor Center in GSMNP, 0.2 miles north of the BRP terminus on US 441.

Longest of the interior transverse ranges, the Great Balsam Mountains reach their northern terminus at Tri-corner Knob in the Great

Smokies. Much of the Northern Balsam range actually lies within Great Smoky Mountains National Park; and the topography, vegetation, and bird life are essentially a continuum of that in the Smokies. Although the Parkway and a spur road traverse part of the Balsams, the area receives only a fraction of the heavy traffic found in the main portions of GSMNP. Ornithologically, therefore, a visit to the northern Great Balsams is much like a trip to the Smokies but without the crowds—a great way to experience the natural history of the high country in a beautiful, remote, and lightly used area.

There are three major birding activities in the northern Great Balsams. A variety of trails provide easy-to-moderate hikes through mature second-growth and virgin spruce-fir, northern hardwood, and oak forests. Balsam Mountain campground and many overlooks are excellent birding sites, especially for the physically impaired. Finally, roadside birding is available on Round Bottom Road as it descends through a variety of mature woodlands from the high country down to the Oconaluftee River valley.

The main attractions are the usual spruce-fir and northern hardwood species, including Northern Saw-whet Owl and possibly Red Crossbill and Pine Siskin. Black-capped Chickadees are often conspicuous along the high crest, and Least Flycatcher is a regular summer resident at several overlooks. Elusive Mourning Warblers are believed to have nested in the range in past years but are not known to have become established at this site, which was their southernmost reported occurrence during the breeding season in the eastern United States.

Many overlooks on the Parkway and the Heintooga Spur Road offer excellent birding. Mature oak forests and cove hardwoods along the Parkway are among the best places in the southern mountains for Eastern Screech-Owl, Great Horned Owl, and Barred Owl, as well as Broad-winged and Sharp-shinned Hawks. **Jonathan Creek Overlook** (4,460 ft.) at M 456.2 is a consistent spot for Scarlet Tanager and Rose-breasted Grosbeak in spring and summer, along with American Robin, Veery, Winter Wren, Solitary Vireo, Black-and-white Warbler, Chestnut-sided Warbler, Black-throated Blue Warbler, Canada Warbler, Rufous-sided Towhee, and Dark-eyed Junco. Most of these species are found at **Plott Balsam View** (5,020 ft.) at M 457.9, where the angle of vision into the downslope forest canopy provides a good perspective for seeing birds. **Jenkins Ridge Overlook** (4,445 ft.) at M 460.8 has similar species but is also worth checking for Yellow-bellied Sapsucker and Least Flycatcher. Jenkins Ridge OL is the site

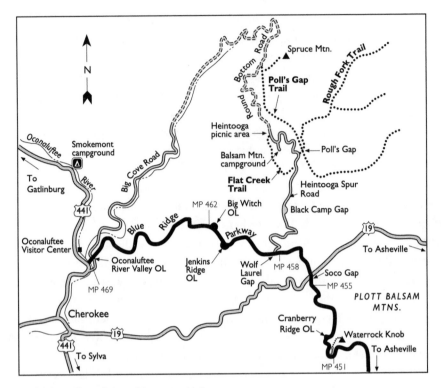

Northern Great Balsam Mountains, N.C.

where Mourning Warblers are believed to have nested from 1983 to 1986. The **Big Witch Overlook** (4,150 ft.) at M 461.9 is located at an outstanding example of cove hardwood forest, home to most species noted at Jonathan Creek, as well as Great Horned and Barred Owls, Pileated and Downy Woodpeckers, Black-billed Cuckoo, White-breasted Nuthatch, Carolina Chickadee, Tufted Titmouse, and Ovenbird.

The best high-country birding in the range is on Heintooga Spur Road, a 9-mile extension that begins at M 458.2 at **Wolf Laurel Gap** (5,100 ft.) and runs along the Balsam's main crest. From Wolf Laurel Gap, the Parkway heads westward, leaving the Balsams and descending into the Oconaluftee River valley. To see the birds at Wolf Laurel Gap, turn onto Heintooga Spur Road and proceed 0.1 miles from the Parkway to the intersection with a gravel road. Park here without blocking traffic. Walk along the highway shoulder and explore the adjacent dirt road, both of which pass through a mixture of spruce, northern hardwoods, rosebay, and Catawba rhododendron. This is often a good spot for Blackburnian Warbler and Red Crossbill. Other late-spring and summer birds include Common Raven, Black-capped Chickadee, Tufted Titmouse, Red-breasted Nuthatch, Brown Creeper, Winter Wren, Golden-crowned Kinglet, Veery, American Robin, Gray Catbird, Cedar Waxwing, Solitary Vireo, Northern Parula, Chestnut-sided Warbler, Black-throated Blue Warbler, Canada Warbler, Rose-breasted Grosbeak, Rufous-sided Towhee, and Dark-eyed Junco.

Proceed on Heintooga Spur Road, stopping along the way at various overlooks, most of which are flat enough for wheelchairs and suitable for the physically impaired. **Mile High Overlook** (5,250 ft.) at 1.3 miles and **Lake Junaluska Overlook** (5,034 ft.) at 2.0 miles have spring and summer birds typical of high-elevation oak forests: Hairy Woodpecker, Eastern Wood-Pewee, Common Raven, White-breasted Nuthatch, Veery, American Robin, Gray Catbird, Solitary Vireo, Red-eyed Vireo, Chestnut-sided Warbler, Black-and-white Warbler, Rufous-sided Towhee, and Dark-eyed Junco. **Maggie Valley Overlook** (5,220 ft.) at 1.4 miles has many of the same birds but is also a good spot for Least Flycatcher. Be alert for Yellow-bellied Sapsuckers at all overlooks.

Black Camp Gap (4,450 ft.) at 3.5 miles is another consistent site for Least Flycatcher, which can usually be heard around the Masonic Monument at the end of a flat, paved walkway that provides wheelchair access from the parking lot. Other spring and summer species at the gap include American Crow, Veery, American Robin, Gray Catbird, Brown Thrasher, Solitary and Red-eyed Vireos, Chestnut-sided Warbler, Blackburnian Warbler, Ovenbird, Indigo Bunting, Rufous-sided Towhee, Chipping Sparrow, Field Sparrow, Song Sparrow, Dark-eyed Junco, Brown-headed Cowbird, and American Goldfinch. The parking lot at **Poll's Gap** (5,130 ft.) at 6.2 miles often has Blackburnian Warbler in spring and summer. For 2.7 miles from the gap on to the campground and picnic area, the spur road traverses the fringes of spruce-fir forests, providing good chances for Saw-whet Owls from April through June.

Another easy birding spot is the **Balsam Mountain campground** (5,310 ft.) at 8.4 miles from the Parkway on Heintooga Spur Road. Nestled in a forest of spruce, northern hardwoods, and rhododendron, the campground and adjacent **Balsam Mountain Nature Trail** are prime sites for Black-capped Chickadee, Red-breasted Nuthatch, Brown Creeper, Winter Wren, Golden-crowned Kinglet, Veery, American Robin, Solitary Vireo,

Brown Creeper

Chestnut-sided Warbler, Blackburnian Warbler, and Dark-eyed Junco. The trail is an easy 0.5-mile route that begins between campsites 44 and 45 and has a self-guiding pamphlet available to interpret the markers.

Similar species can be observed by walking 0.5 miles along the roadway shoulder from the campground to **Heintooga picnic ground**, which is also a good spot when not crowded. The nature trail connects to the spur road about 100 yards south of the picnic ground parking lot, making a convenient 1-mile loop hike. Be alert for Red Crossbill and Pine Siskin along the trail and roadway. Northern Saw-whet Owls are sometimes heard at night from April through June between the campground and picnic area. Although parts of the campground loop road are steep, some portions are suitable for the physically impaired, including the use of wheelchairs.

Where the paved road ends at Heintooga picnic ground, 8.9 miles from the Parkway, the one-way **Round Bottom Road** begins as a gravel route that runs 14 miles to the valley below, providing excellent roadside birding as it descends from 5,323 feet at the picnic grounds to 2,450 feet at Raven Fork. The road passes through spruce-fir, northern hardwoods, oak forests, and cove hardwoods. There are numerous spots to stop, look, and listen from the car or get out and hike along this lightly used road for good looks at the birds. In addition to the late-spring and summer species already mentioned for the Balsams, one may expect Sharp-shinned Hawk, Ruffed Grouse, Yellow-billed Cuckoo, Belted Kingfisher, Acadian Flycatcher, Carolina Wren, Wood Thrush, White-eyed and Red-eyed Vireos, Worm-eating Warbler, and Louisiana Waterthrush. Several trails to the high crest line connect to the road as well. Remember, however, that Round Bottom Road is a one-way route: to return to the campground one must drive to the edge of Cherokee and come back up the Parkway and Heintooga Spur Road, for a trip that exceeds 40 miles.

Most spring and summer birds noted at the campground and picnic area can also be seen on **Poll's Gap Trail**, also known as **Spruce Mountain Trail**, a moderate 4.8-mile trek that wanders through beautiful spruce-fir and northern hardwood forests along the remote main crest line of the Balsams. The trailhead is on Heintooga Spur Road at Poll's, or Paul's, Gap (5,130 ft.), which is 2.2 miles south of the campground and 6.2 miles from the Parkway. Three trails begin at the gap parking lot; check the signs carefully to be certain of taking the proper route.

The trail climbs over Cataloochee Balsam Mountain (5,970 ft.) at 1.8 miles, descends into Horse Creek Gap (5,580 ft.) at 2.5 miles, and crosses over Chiltoes Mountain (5,900 ft.) at 3.1 miles. At 4.0 miles the trail intersects a connector route on the left that descends 0.8 miles to a parking spot (4,800 ft.) located 5.8 miles from the Heintooga picnic ground on the Round Bottom Road. The summit of Spruce Mountain (5,647 ft.) is not easily accessible, because the trail runs into tangled undergrowth just beyond the junction with the connector. The connector route is also a good spot for Black-throated Blue, Black-throated Green, and Canada Warblers. The other trails that begin at Poll's Gap are sometimes worth checking, although they are often muddy from horse travel and seldom have the diversity of birds noted along Spruce Mountain Trail.

The other popular hiking route is **Flat Creek Trail**, a rather easy 2.6-mile ramble from the Heintooga picnic area through spruce, birch, and rhododendrons. The trail begins at the far end of the Heintooga picnic ground parking area, passes a spectacular view of the Smokies at the Heintooga OL (5,340 ft.), and continues on to its junction with the spur road (4,900 ft.) at 3.7 miles from the picnic ground. This allows a 6.3-mile loop by hiking back along the road shoulder or retracing steps for a 5.2-mile hike. The bird life on this route is similar to that noted elsewhere in the Balsams, although Black-throated Blue and Black-throated Green Warblers are more likely here.

Little Tennessee River Valley

Highlights: Spring migration, especially shorebirds and songbirds; summer warblers.

Season: Year-round.

Access: Exit the BRP at its terminus (M 469), turn left onto US 441 south into Cherokee, N.C., and head out of Cherokee on US 19 west for 5 miles to Ela, N.C., just east of Ferguson Fields, N.C. To avoid the traffic at Cherokee, exit the Parkway at Balsam Gap (M 443.1) and proceed 23.8 miles west on US 74 to the exit to Ela. For Fontana Village, N.C., exit at BRP M 443.1 but continue for 7 miles west beyond Bryson City, N.C., on US 74 to the junction with NC 28; turn right on NC 28 and proceed 24 miles to Fontana Village. From Knoxville, Tenn., head south on US 129 for

57 winding miles to the NC 28 junction; turn left and go 8 miles on NC 28
to Fontana Village.

Maps: USGS "Bryson City," "Fontana Dam," "Tapoco," "Tuskeegee."

Facilities: Gasoline, food, and accommodations at Cherokee, Bryson City,
and Fontana Village.

The Little Tennessee River basin encompasses about 1,600 square
miles of mountainous terrain in southwestern North Carolina, where the
Little Tennessee and its major tributaries, the Tuckasegee, Nantahala, and
Cheoah rivers, drain much of the Great Smoky Mountains, Great Balsam Mountains, Tanasee Ridge, Unicoi Mountains, Cowee Mountains, and
Nantahala Mountains. In the low elevations, many areas along the river
and its tributaries provide good spots for observing migratory shorebirds
and waterfowl, as well as migratory and nesting songbirds.

One interesting area is **Ferguson Fields**, or **Governor's Island**, roughly
one-half a square mile of river-bottom land at 1,750 to 1,800 feet in elevation, located along a sweeping bend in the Tuckasegee River just east of
Bryson City, N.C. Prior to the arrival of European civilization, this was
the site of Kituwha, the central village of the Cherokee Indian nation—
a settlement that extended from the confluence of the Oconaluftee and
Tuckasegee rivers almost into present-day Bryson City. The name "Governor's Island" was applied after N.C. governor David Swain met here to
negotiate a boundary dispute with Cherokee chief Yonaguska, or Drown-
ing Bear.

The property is now privately owned, and much of the land is operated as a dairy farm. Under no circumstances should you enter the area
until you have obtained permission from the owner; stop at the large dairy
barns to inquire. While exploring the site, be sure to stay out of any planted
or plowed fields, and do not leave any gates open. Be careful of uneven
terrain, which could result in serious injury; and take great care if walking along the railroad tracks, which are still used. Also beware of electric
fences and aggressive cattle!

If coming south on US 19, the entrance to the dairy barns is on the left at
1.7 miles south from Ela; if coming north from Bryson City on US 19, the
entrance is on the right at 0.5 miles north of the Tuckasegee River bridge.
Access to the fields is from a dirt road at 0.1 miles south of the barns and
from a dirt road at 0.3 miles north of the barns. The former road, which

can be very muddy at times, leads down to the vicinity of an old silo, surrounded by shrubs and small trees; sloughs and wet fields are nearby. Field and edge birds are numerous in this area.

Most birders begin their explorations at the more northerly access. Here the road immediately crosses the railroad tracks, where you can park next to the old airplane hanger. Walk down toward the river or follow the vehicle tracks along the railroad toward the dairy barns. After about 0.2 miles, this dirt "road" swings away from the railroad to parallel a shrub-bordered slough that runs toward the river and connects with other marshy stream margins. The adjacent cultivated field is often flooded and muddy, especially in spring, when large pools of standing water are sometimes present. Check the flooded fields, mud flats, and sloughs in April and early May for migrating shorebirds, waterfowl, and other birds, including American Bittern, Great Blue Heron, Green-backed Heron, Wood Duck, Blue-winged Teal, Lesser Scaup, Osprey, Northern Harrier, Semipalmated Plover, Killdeer, Greater Yellowlegs, Lesser Yellowlegs, Solitary Sandpiper, Spotted Sandpiper, Least Sandpiper, Common Snipe, Ring-billed Gull, Common Nighthawk, and American Pipit. Some rarities may turn up, such as Lesser Golden-Plover.

Soras are to be found skulking in the sloughs, Marsh Wrens have been reported in the cattails, and all five swallow species have been seen in spring over the fields. Large flocks of Bobolinks pass through the fields each spring; and Red-winged Blackbird, Eastern Meadowlark, Rusty Blackbird, Common Grackle, Brown-headed Cowbird, Orchard Oriole, and Northern Oriole may be seen in the fields and woody margins. Carefully walk the railroad right-of-way to the cattle barns and scan the adjacent waste-holding tanks for shorebirds.

Check the fields and shrubby borders in late winter and early spring for sparrows: Chipping, Field, Vesper, Savannah, Grasshopper, Fox, Song Sparrow, White-throated, and White-crowned. Even an elusive Henslow's Sparrow has been observed here in spring. Migrating flycatchers, vireos, warblers, and finches are also found, and occasionally something unexpected, such as a Merlin, makes an appearance.

Year-round species include Wood Duck, Turkey Vulture, Red-tailed Hawk, Red-bellied Woodpecker, Downy Woodpecker, Hairy Woodpecker, Northern Flicker, and Pileated Woodpecker. Although seldom visited in summer, mostly because of the flies and mosquitoes, Ferguson Fields typically has Green-backed Heron, Eastern Wood-Pewee, Great

Crested Flycatcher, Eastern Kingbird, White-eyed Vireo, Red-eyed Vireo, Yellow Warbler, Yellow-throated Warbler, Black-and-white Warbler, Common Yellowthroat, Northern Cardinal, Indigo Bunting, Rufous-sided Towhee, Field Sparrow, Song Sparrow, Brown-headed Cowbird, and American Goldfinch.

Farther west, the Little Tennessee River has been impounded to form Fontana Lake, nestled at the southern foot of the Great Smokies. This area is rich in breeding warblers, with over twenty species found in summer. From Fontana Village (1,800 ft.), head east on NC 28 and stop at intervals in pull offs where mature hardwood forests occur on steep slopes. Listen for Cerulean and Worm-eating Warblers, as well as an occasional Golden-winged.

In the opposite direction, head out of Fontana Village on NC SR 1246 (Welch Road) and go 5.5 miles to NC SR 1247, where you turn right and continue 0.5 miles on state road 1247 to Lake Cheoah (1,276 ft.). Stop frequently along this 6-mile drive and listen for various warblers, including Black-throated Green, Yellow-throated, and Worm-eating. Check for Golden-winged Warblers in deciduous second growth on hillsides, as, for instance, where power lines cross the roadway. Stop at 1.5 miles from Fontana Village and at the intersection of state roads 1246 and 1247; Swainson's Warblers have been reported in the rhododendron thickets at both spots. Finally, drive east from Fontana Village on NC 28 for 2.0 miles to NC SR 1245, turn left onto state road 1245, and proceed out to **Fontana Dam** (1,700 ft.), where Cliff Swallows often nest. Blue-winged Warblers are sometimes reported in scrubby deciduous saplings and field thickets along this route.

Downriver from Fontana and Lake Cheoah, the gorge of the Little Tennessee has been drowned under **Calderwood Lake** (1,086 ft.), a good spot for water birds such as Pied-billed Grebe, Wood Duck, and Belted Kingfisher, as well as Yellow Warblers, which are often present in late spring and summer near the bridge. Park in the lot just south of the US 129 bridge over the lake, some 15 miles north of Robbinsville or 10.2 miles from Fontana Village on NC 28 and US 129 south. The Slickrock Creek Trail begins at the lot and runs 1.6 miles along the south shore of the lake before turning to ascend its namesake creek. Although often crowded during summer, this easy hike provides good spring and summer birding.

Great Smoky Mountains National Park

Highlights: Spring songbird migration, summer residents in heath balds and
in mature and old-growth virgin forests (cove hardwood, oak, northern
hardwood, spruce-fir); Northern Saw-whet Owl, Olive-sided Flycatcher,
Black-capped Chickadee, Red Crossbill, Pine Siskin.

Season: Year-round, but mainly spring through fall.

Access: The main park entrances are on US 441 at Cherokee, N.C., and
Gatlinburg, Tenn. The BRP terminates at M 469, about 1 mile south of the
Oconaluftee Visitor Center entrance on US 441 near Cherokee. To reach
Gatlinburg from Knoxville, Tenn., take exit 407 on I-40, 15 miles east of
Knoxville, for a thirty-minute drive on TN 66 and US 441.

Maps: USGS "Clingman's Dome," "Mt. LeConte," "Gatlinburg"; "Wild-
life Map of the Great Smoky Mountains National Park," by American
Nature Maps; "Great Smoky Mountains Trail Map," by National Park Ser-
vice; "Walks and Hikes in Great Smoky Mountains National Park," by
Great Smoky Mountains Natural History Association; "Hiker's Map of the
Smokies," by Sierra Club Books.

Facilities: Gasoline, food, and lodging at Gatlinburg, Cherokee, and numerous
other local towns. Ten Park Service campgrounds in GSMNP (reservations
needed). LeConte Lodge on the summit of Mount LeConte(reservations
needed). Numerous backcountry campsites, especially along the AT.
Books, maps, and information at Oconaluftee Visitor Center near Cherokee and Sugarlands Visitor Center near Gatlinburg. For information,
contact GSMNP, Gatlinburg, TN 37737 (615-436-1200).

The Great Smoky Mountains have been called "the majestic cli-
max of the Appalachian Highlands"—an appropriate description for this
beautiful range, whose geomorphology and vegetation set it apart from all
other mountains of eastern North America. The massive crest line exceeds
5,000 feet in elevation for thirty-six of its seventy-one miles, sweeping in a
northeast-southwest axis along the border between Tennessee and North
Carolina. Through most of its distance, the main ridge is some fifteen miles
wide, with bulky outliers and subjacent ridges enclosing a maze of ravines
and deep coves, whose streams feed the Tennessee River system.

Encompassing more than 500,000 acres, Great Smoky Mountains National Park was established in 1934 to preserve this last great wilderness
tract of the southeastern United States. Elevations vary from 857 feet on

Abrams Creek to the summit of Clingman's Dome (6,643 ft.). The range harbors a remarkably diversified flora and the world's best examples of temperate deciduous forests. More than 1,500 species of vascular plants are present, including 130 species of trees, many of which reach world-record sizes in the Smokies. The park contains the largest tracts of uncut old-growth forest in the southern Appalachians, estimated at approximately 150,000 acres of virgin woodland, mostly cove hardwood, northern hardwood, and red spruce. With this rich natural heritage, the Smokies have been designated an International Biosphere Reserve area and a World Heritage Site.

The extensive acreage of high-elevation terrain and of major plant communities provides many bird species with their largest contiguous tracts of habitat in the southern Appalachians. Consequently, the park supports sizable populations of certain species that are very localized, rare, or absent elsewhere in the region. The Smokies probably has the largest concentration of Northern Saw-whet Owls in the Southeast, and the majority of Black-capped Chickadees in the southern Blue Ridge Province are confined to the park. That most elusive of all Appalachian nesters, the Olive-sided Flycatcher, is more likely here than at any other spot in the Blue Ridge. Furthermore, the vast expanse of old-growth forest provides naturalists an opportunity to see the region's bird life under conditions that may approximate those prior to the arrival of European civilization.

Wild and rugged, most of the park is accessible only on foot or horseback. Some 900 miles of trails, including a major segment of the Appalachian Trail, wind through the backcountry, providing the greatest variety of hikes anywhere on the East Coast. The only drawbacks to birding in the Smokies are the crowds and the traffic congestion that unfortunately prevail during most of the late spring and throughout the summer. One frustrated wag called US 441 "the world's longest parking lot," a sentiment easily appreciated by anyone who gets stuck behind a 10-mile-per-hour motor home on the way to Newfound Gap. Much of the irritation can be avoided by arriving at your destination by sunrise; but even then little solitude may be found in this heavily visited park. Unless you choose backcountry trails and remote areas, you are likely to be sharing your route with a lot of people before the morning is over.

Beginning in the low country, there are good birding sites around the visitor centers near the two main entrances on opposite sides of the park, where typical low-elevation species are found. On the North Carolina side,

Black-capped Chickadee

the **Oconaluftee River valley** is an excellent spot for the spring migration in late April and early May. Park near the Oconaluftee River bridge (2,000 ft.) at MP 469 on the Blue Ridge Parkway just before its southern terminus at US 441. Walk along the roadway shoulder here as far as the Oconaluftee River Valley OL at 468.4 miles for good views of warblers, vireos, tanagers, flycatchers, and other songbirds milling about in trees bordering the Parkway and the river.

Proceed from the Parkway terminus to the Oconaluftee Visitor Center (2,100 ft.) 0.6 miles north on US 441, the Newfound Gap Road. Explore the woodlands and fields along the river near the adjacent Pioneer Farmstead. Belted Kingfishers are permanent residents on the Ocona-

luftee. During the late spring and summer months, this is a good spot for Yellow-throated Vireo, Yellow Warbler, and Yellow-throated Warbler in woods bordering the river and for White-eyed Vireo and Yellow-breasted Chat in scrubby thickets. Fields and edges may have Turkey Vulture, Broad-winged Hawk, Northern Bobwhite, Mourning Dove, Eastern King-bird, Barn Swallow, American Crow, Eastern Bluebird, European Star-ling, Northern Cardinal, Indigo Bunting, Field Sparrow, Song Sparrow, Eastern Meadowlark, Brown-headed Cowbird, American Goldfinch, and House Sparrow. Forests and hardwood groves are home to Downy Wood-pecker, Northern Flicker, Pileated Woodpecker, Acadian Flycatcher, East-ern Wood-Pewee, Carolina Chickadee, Tufted Titmouse, Carolina Wren,

Blue-gray Gnatcatcher, Wood Thrush, American Robin, Red-eyed Vireo, Northern Parula, Black-and-white Warbler, Hooded Warbler, and Chipping Sparrow.

On the opposite side of the park, the Sugarlands Visitor Center, just south of Gatlinburg on Newfound Gap Road (US 441), is the site of park headquarters and of **Sugarlands Nature Trail** (1,500 ft.). The trail is an easy, flat, partially paved, 1-mile loop route, suitable in parts for wheelchairs, and travels through a mixed hardwood forest for typical lowland birds. Regular spring and summer birds along the trail include Mourning Dove, Yellow-billed Cuckoo, Chimney Swift, Downy Woodpecker, Acadian Flycatcher, Eastern Phoebe, Carolina Chickadee, Tufted Titmouse, Blue-gray Gnatcatcher, Wood Thrush, American Robin, Gray Catbird, Red-eyed Vireo, Northern Parula, Yellow Warbler, Black-throated Green Warbler, Yellow-throated Warbler, Black-and-white Warbler, Worm-eating Warbler, Ovenbird, Louisiana Waterthrush, Kentucky Warbler, Hooded Warbler, Northern Cardinal, Indigo Bunting, Rufous-sided Towhee, and Song Sparrow. Be sure to check the visitor center for maps, books, information, and the latest update on bird observations in the park.

Swainson's Warblers are occasionally present during summer in rhododendron thickets near the Sugarlands Visitor Center. Take the paved walkway from the visitor center to the park headquarters building and on to the maintenance area, where the **Gatlinburg Trail** begins. This easy walk parallels and crosses the West Prong Little Pigeon River, where the Swainson's are sometimes noted. Listen along the trail by the river and along US 441 between the Sugarlands area and the town of Gatlinburg.

Another popular, but often crowded, birding hike is the **Laurel Falls Trail**, an easy paved route that begins at Fighting Creek Gap (2,320 ft.), 3.8 miles west of the Sugarlands Visitor Center on the Little River Road toward Elkmont. The pavement ends at the falls, 1.3 miles from the trailhead, but many birders prefer to continue on toward Cove Mountain, as the trail passes through some beautiful virgin forests of hemlock, tuliptree, and birch. The bird life is similar to that at Sugarlands, but a few montane species also occur. Expect to see Black-throated Blue Warbler and Scarlet Tanager, as well as Ruffed Grouse, Pileated Woodpecker, Blue Jay, and White-breasted Nuthatch.

For roadside birding on the Tennessee side of the park, try the **Cades Cove Loop Road**, an 11-mile route circling through a beautiful rolling valley (1,800–1,900 ft.) that was settled in the early 1800s. Cades Cove is 25 miles west of Sugarlands Visitor Center by way of Little River Road and Cades Cove Road. Get a copy of the interpretative booklet that identifies and discusses the numbered sites along the route, where the park maintains old pioneer cabins, farm buildings, churches, mills, and pastures. Stop at the many pull offs, markers, and trails along the road to see low-elevation birds typical of valleys and fields. Try birding along the shoulder of the loop road, Sparks Lane, and Hyatt Lane.

Cades Cove is noted for Wild Turkeys, which are often seen near woodland edges in early morning or late afternoon. In late spring and summer, check the fields and pastures for Northern Bobwhite, Mourning Dove, Chimney Swift, Ruby-throated Hummingbird, Eastern Kingbird, Barn Swallow, American Crow, Eastern Bluebird, Common Yellowthroat, Northern Cardinal, Indigo Bunting, Blue Grosbeak, Field Sparrow, Song Sparrow, Red-winged Blackbird, Eastern Meadowlark, Common Grackle, Brown-headed Cowbird, and American Goldfinch. Wooded areas are good for Yellow-billed Cuckoo, Downy and Pileated Woodpeckers, Northern Flicker, Eastern Wood-Pewee, Acadian Flycatcher, Great Crested Fly-catcher, Blue Jay, Carolina Chickadee, Tufted Titmouse, White-breasted Nuthatch, Carolina Wren, Blue-gray Gnatcatcher, Wood Thrush, American Robin, Yellow-throated and Red-eyed Vireos, Yellow-throated Warbler, Pine Warbler, Black-and-white Warbler, Ovenbird, Hooded Warbler, Summer Tanager, and Chipping Sparrow. At night, listen for Eastern Screech-Owl, Barred Owl, and Whip-poor-will.

Several spots may be worth checking on Cades Cove Loop Road in spring and summer. The pine woods near the Missionary Baptist Church at marker 7 are good for Yellow-throated and Pine Warblers. The **Abrams Falls Trail** is a moderate 5-mile round-trip hike along Abrams Creek, where many deciduous woodland species noted previously are found, along with Northern Parula, Yellow-throated Warbler, Swainson's Warbler, and Louisiana Waterthrush. The sewage ponds near the east end of the cove are occasionally good for shorebirds during migration. The ponds are west of the horse stables, down an unmarked gravel road that turns left just before the end of the loop road.

Another popular route for roadside birding is the **Roaring Fork Motor Nature Tour,** which provides easy views of many middle-elevation forest birds at the various pull offs. Along the road are access points to several trails toward Mount LeConte, such as the Trillium Gap Trail at the Grotto

Falls parking lot. Passing through an attractive hemlock forest, this trail provides an easy-to-moderate 3-mile round-trip hike up to Grotto Falls. In addition to many of the birds noted at Laurel Falls Trail, you may encounter some high-elevation species such as Red-breasted Nuthatch, Golden-crowned Kinglet, and Dark-eyed Junco. Turn off US 441 at a traffic light in Gatlinburg onto Airport Road toward Cherokee Orchard and follow the signs to this one-way loop that climbs toward the northwest slope of Mount LeConte. The interpretative booklet for this route will enhance your appreciation of the trip.

Despite the crowds, some of the best birding in the Smokies is along the Newfound Gap Road (US 441) between Gatlinburg and Newfound Gap and along the spur road from Newfound Gap to Clingman's Dome. Birding this route takes you from the valley avifauna, typical of the southeastern United States, to the birds of spruce-fir and northern hardwood forests, typical of Canada and northern New England. In a mere 20-mile drive from valley to summit, you have covered an ecologic distance similar to a 1,000-mile drive north to Maine!

Three sites provide good birding between Gatlinburg and Newfound Gap. The **Chimneys picnic area** (2,700 ft.) is 4.4 miles south of Sugarlands Visitor Center or 23.8 miles north of Oconaluftee Visitor Center on US 441. Arrive early to avoid the crowds and check the picnic grounds and the Cove Hardwood Self-guiding Nature Trail, a moderate 0.7-mile route through a beautiful old cove hardwood forest. In late spring and summer, expect to find Ruffed Grouse, Barred Owl, Downy and Pileated Woodpeckers, Eastern Wood-Pewee, Tufted Titmouse, White-breasted Nuthatch, Winter Wren, Wood Thrush, Solitary Vireo, Red-eyed Vireo, Black-throated Green Warbler, Black-throated Blue Warbler, Black-and-white Warbler, Ovenbird, Scarlet Tanager, and Dark-eyed Junco.

Many of the same birds are present at **Chimney Tops parking area** (3,400 ft.) and on Chimney Tops Trail, a steep and strenuous 4-mile round-trip to the summit (4,755 ft.) that offers spectacular views of Sugarlands Valley and Mount LeConte. The parking lot is 6.8 miles south of Sugarlands Visitor Center or 21.3 miles north of the Oconaluftee Visitor Center on the Newfound Gap Road (US 441). In addition to the species noted at the Chimneys picnic area and on the Cove Hardwood Trail, one can expect some birds typical of the high elevations of the park, such as Black-capped Chickadee, Veery, Chestnut-sided Warbler, Canada Warbler, and Rose-breasted Grosbeak.

Perhaps the premier birding hike in the park is **Alum Cave Bluffs Trail,** a spectacularly scenic route that runs 5 miles from Newfound Gap Road (US 441) to the summit of **Mount LeConte** (6,593 ft.), third highest point in the Smokies. This is an excellent route for summer birds of northern hardwood and spruce-fir forests, and it includes the best site in the southern Appalachians for the very rare Olive-sided Flycatcher. Although you may want to do the entire route, the 10-mile round-trip with a 2,800-foot elevation change can be rather daunting unless you are in good condition and want to spend most of the day hiking. Many birders are content to go a mile or so beyond Alum Cave Bluffs and then return. The total elevation change from the parking lot to the bluffs is 1,160 feet. The trail begins at Alum Cave Trail parking lot (3,840 ft.), which is 8.6 miles south of Sugarlands Visitor Center or 19.6 miles north of Oconaluftee Visitor Center on Newfound Gap Road (US 441).

The trail follows close by noisy Alum Cave Creek and Styx Branch through rhododendron thickets, hemlocks stands, and cove hardwood forests for 1.3 miles from the parking lot to Arch Rock (4,200 ft.). Just beyond Arch Rock the trail leaves Styx Branch and passes into northern hardwood and spruce forests, where in late spring and summer you may find Common Raven, Black-capped Chickadee, Red-breasted Nuthatch, Brown Creeper, Winter Wren, Golden-crowned Kinglet, Veery, American Robin, Solitary Vireo, Northern Parula, Black-throated Blue Warbler, Black-throated Green Warbler, Blackburnian Warbler, Canada Warbler, Rose-breasted Grosbeak, and Dark-eyed Junco.

At 2.0 miles from the parking lot, the trail breaks out of the woods into a beautiful open expanse of rhododendron and laurel, a classic heath bald, where you may find Gray Catbird, Chestnut-sided Warbler, and Rufous-sided Towhee. Beginning just before the edge of the spruce woods at 2.0 miles, you should listen carefully for Olive-sided Flycatchers, which have been found in the past from here to the Alum Cave Bluffs at 2.3 miles. Although this is probably the best site in the Blue Ridge for summer records of the Olive-sided, this rare bird is not reported here every year, and its numbers have been declining in the past few decades. If your only goal is to see this species, you may want to contact the park naturalist before hiking the trail.

Be alert for Peregrine Falcons around the bluffs; these birds nested here in the past and have recently been observed in the vicinity following efforts to reestablish the bird in the southern mountains. Common Ravens often nest on the steep knife-edge ridge just across from the bluffs, usually below and to the left of the hole in the ridge. The best angle for viewing the nest site is from the switchback in the open heath thickets about 0.2 miles before arriving at Alum Cave Bluffs.

Beyond the bluffs, the trail passes through spruce-fir and northern hardwoods, where you should continue to watch for Red Crossbills, Pine Siskins, and most species noted previously. If you stay on LeConte overnight between late March and June, listen for Northern Saw-whet Owls.

Most of these same birds can be observed during spring and summer in spruce-fir and northern hardwood forests along the main crest of the Smokies from Newfound Gap southwest to Clingman's Dome or northeast to Mount Guyot. Check both sides of the crest around **Newfound Gap** (5,040 ft.), highest point on US 441, where the parking lot and adjacent paved walkways provide easy views into the adjacent canopy. Much of the gap area, particularly on the North Carolina side, is suitable for wheelchairs and the physically impaired. Arrive early to avoid the mob scene that develops here most mornings. The gap is 12.8 miles south of Sugarlands Visitor Center and 15.2 miles north from Oconaluftee Visitor Center on US 441.

Listen for Red Crossbills and Pine Siskins, which are occasionally noted. Olive-sided Flycatchers once occurred here but have not been reported in recent years. Northern Saw-whet Owls can be heard in season at the gap and from the two overlooks on US 441 just north of the gap. For a brief hike for birding with privacy, try the roadbed of old US 441—an unmarked, grassy, steep grade that begins at the extreme south end of the gap, just beyond the short connector road between the two parking lots. The old roadway heads downslope on the North Carolina side below the new road. This route provides almost instant solitude, because most visitors to the gap are unaware of its existence. This is a good area for Barred Owls, Brown Creepers, and Red-breasted Nuthatches.

From the gap, there is excellent birding along the Appalachian Trail, both north toward Mount Guyot and south to Clingman's Dome. The latter route parallels the Clingman's Dome Road and allows auto pickup or drop-off. There is usually less traffic on the southbound part of the trail, probably because the northbound trailhead is much more conspicuous to the general public. The AT passes mainly through spruce-fir and northern hardwoods along this section, yielding most of the same summer birds noted previously at Alum Cave Bluffs Trail. If you plan more than a casual hike on these routes, study the AT guidebooks and maps before starting out.

You can also sample the spruce-fir birds by stopping at various pull offs along **Clingman's Dome Road**, a 7-mile cruise from Newfound Gap to the parking lot below the summit of Clingman's (6,643 ft.), the highest point in the Smokies. On calm nights from late March through June, as many as eleven Northern Saw-whet Owls have been heard along this route. The road is probably the best area in the Blue Ridge Province for seeing Black-capped Chickadees. For these and other high-country summer residents, park at the Indian Gap OL (5,266 ft.) at 1.2 miles, the Spruce-fir Nature Trail (6,000 ft.) at 2.7 miles, and an unnamed parking lot at 4.7 miles from Newfound Gap. You can access the AT at Indian Gap to get away from the highway noise or to do an early-morning loop hike using the roadway shoulder and AT between here and Newfound Gap. The Spruce-fir Nature Trail is an easy half-mile route that provides a discouraging close-up of damage to the conifers from balsam woolly adelgids and airborne pollutants. Most of the woodland birds noted on the Alum Cave Bluffs Trail and at Newfound Gap can be observed along this road, and the overlooks are much less crowded than the parking lot at the gap.

For more detailed information on the bird life in the Great Smoky Mountains, get a copy of Alsop's *Birds of the Smokies*. Stupka's *Notes on the Birds of Great Smoky Mountains National Park* is very useful but now hard to find. To plan any major hikes, consider getting a copy of *Hiker's Guide to the Smokies*, by Murlless and Stallings, in addition to the Appalachian Trail guides.

MAJOR BIRDING SITES AWAY FROM THE BLUE RIDGE PARKWAY

5

Northern Blue Ridge Mountains

Highlights: Middle-elevation nesting species, spring songbird migration, autumn hawk migration; Black-crowned Night-Heron, Long-eared Owl, Fish Crow, Hermit Thrush, Black-capped Chickadee, Nashville Warbler, Swamp Sparrow.

Season: Spring through fall.

Access: As described below, this area is accessed from I-70 between Hagerstown, Md., and Frederick, Md.; from US 15 between Frederick and Gettysburg, Pa.; and from I-81 east from Chambersburg, Pa., on US 30 toward Gettysburg.

Maps: "Maps 5 & 6 Appalachian Trail Across Maryland including the Catoctin Trail," by Potomac Appalachian Trail Club, 1718 N Street, NW, Washington, DC 20036; "Michaux State Forest Public Use Map," by Bureau of Forestry, 10099 Lincoln Way East, Fayetteville, PA 17222; USGS "Blue Ridge Summit, MD," "Caledonia Park, PA," "Catoctin Furnace, MD," "Dickinson, PA," "Frederick, MD," "Harpers Ferry, W.Va." "Middletown, MD," "Myersville, MD," "Walnut Bottom, PA."

Facilities: Food, gasoline, and accommodations in Harpers Ferry, Frederick, Hagerstown, Gettysburg, and Chambersburg. Campgrounds at Cunningham Falls State Park, Catoctin Mountain Park, and Greenbrier State Park in Maryland, and at Caledonia State Park and Pine Grove Furnace State Park in Pennsylvania; backcountry camping along the Appalachian Trail. For information, contact the Department of Natural Resources, Maryland Forest, Park and Wildlife Service, Tawes State Office Building, Annapolis, MD 21401; Bureau of State Parks, P.O. Box 1467, Harrisburg, PA 17120; Michaux State Forest, District Forester, R.D. 2, Fayetteville, PA 17222;

Catoctin Mountain Park, Thurmont, MD 21788; Harpers Ferry National
Historical Park, Harpers Ferry, W.Va. 25425; C & O Canal National
Historical Park, P.O. Box 4, Sharpsburg, MD 21782.

The northern Blue Ridge Mountains lie barely one to two hours'
drive from Washington, Baltimore, and Philadelphia, yet very few birders
are familiar with this attractive and ornithologically diverse area. For naturalists whose Blue Ridge birding has been confined to the high country of
North Carolina and Tennessee, a visit to Pennsylvania's South Mountain
provides a striking lesson on how latitude affects the elevation limits of
nesting birds. Here at the northern extremity of the province, the summer
bird life is, in fact, an interesting mix of piedmont and montane species.
Birds such as Yellow-bellied Sapsucker, Black-capped Chickadee, Red-
breasted Nuthatch, Brown Creeper, and Hermit Thrush occur at elevations
below 2,000 feet, with some of these birds even found locally at spots
below 700 feet. This is the only spot in the Blue Ridge Province where
Long-eared Owls and Nashville Warblers are known to breed. Fish Crows
are locally common, and Black-crowned Night-Herons roost near Yellow
Breeches Creek, where a marshy pond is home in summer to Swamp Sparrows and an occasional Virginia Rail. Spring songbird migration is often
outstanding, and several lookouts provide excellent views of the autumn
hawk migration.

This rich avifauna inhabits a mountainous region that lacks the topographic diversity so characteristic of the province elsewhere. Compared to
the lofty Blue Ridge peaks in North Carolina and Tennessee, the northern
end of the Blue Ridge Mountain Province is quite subdued—seldom rising
above 2,000 feet in its seventy-mile sweep from the Potomac River gap to
its terminus near Harrisburg, Pa. Through most of this area, the province
consists of two roughly parallel ridge lines, Catoctin Mountain on the east
and South Mountain to the west. Both run approximately from northeast to southwest and are covered with early- to medium-age oak forests,
scrub oak and pine barrens, and local stands of hemlock, white pine, and
rhododendron. The region is drained by tributaries of the Potomac and
Susquehanna rivers.

A good place to begin your exploration is around Harpers Ferry, W.Va.,
where the Potomac River escapes from the Great Valley by carving its way
through the Blue Ridge and flowing eastward onto the Piedmont. This
beautiful area at the confluence of the Potomac and Shenandoah rivers is

rich not only in history but also in bird life. The elevation along the river-banks is a mere 260 feet above sea level, perhaps the lowest point in the Blue Ridge. Several birds found here, such as the Prothonotary Warbler, are seldom encountered elsewhere in the province, and the best birding sites are located on easy trails that are preserved by the National Park Service.

For convenient access, take exit 52 from I-70 in Frederick, Md.; proceed west on US 340 toward Charlestown, W.Va., for 15.5 miles to the Potomac River bridge; and continue on for 2 more miles to the Shenandoah River. Almost immediately after crossing the Shenandoah River bridge, turn sharply right onto the road toward Harpers Ferry, proceed about 100 feet, and turn right into the river access parking lot. Lock your car and walk toward Harpers Ferry by heading down the faint pathway next to the road.

The footpath soon parallels the old **Shenandoah Canal,** passing the ruins of the Shenandoah Pulp Factory at 0.1 miles and coming to a footbridge over the canal at 0.3 miles. The area around the footbridge usually has nesting Prothonotary Warblers in late spring and summer. The adjacent woods on Virginius Island between the canal and the Shenandoah River can be full of migrant songbirds in spring and home to Warbling Vireos and Northern Orioles in the breeding season. A network of trails on Virginius Island provides easy views of the bird life; you might want to get a copy of the trail guide at a bookstore. During the migration and in winter months, you can scan the Shenandoah for waterfowl or walk to downtown Harpers Ferry, only 0.8 miles from the parking lot, and check the Potomac from a high vantage point. Canada Geese and Mallards are resident breeders along both rivers. If you arrive too late in the morning, the parking lot may be full, in which case you will need to go to the main visitor center at Harpers Ferry National Historical Park and take the shuttle bus to the canal area.

Return to your car and head back east on US 340, recrossing the Shenandoah and Potomac rivers. Just after crossing the Potomac bridge into Maryland, take the first exit off US 340 onto Keep Tryst Road, proceed 0.3 miles, and turn right onto Sandyhook Road. Continue on Sandyhook Road as it heads down to the **Chesapeake and Ohio Canal.** Small parking lots are located on the right at 2.1 and 2.2 miles and on the left at 2.5 miles from the junction with Keep Tryst Road. You can cross the canal bed at these points and then hike or bike along the canal towpath, which is wide, smooth, and flat. Running 184.5 miles from Washington, D.C., to Cumberland, Md., the C & O Canal National Historical Park is renowned among local enthusiasts as one of the best birding areas in the region. The National Park Service has labeled most historic structures and placed milepost markers along the towpath, so it is fairly easy to figure out where you are. This is an ideal place for birding from a bicycle, particularly if you want to cover a lot of ground in a brief time. For a detailed description of the entire route, get Hahn's *Towpath Guide to the Chesapeake & Ohio Canal.*

The sycamores and other tall trees along the river and canal are often thick with spring migrants and are home in the breeding season to Warbling Vireos and Northern Orioles. Other birds in late spring and summer include Barred Owl, Whip-poor-will, Belted Kingfisher, Chimney Swift, Red-bellied Woodpecker, Northern Flicker, Pileated Woodpecker, Eastern Wood-Pewee, Acadian Flycatcher, Eastern Phoebe, Blue Jay, American Crow, Fish Crow, Carolina Chickadee, Tufted Titmouse, Carolina Wren, Blue-gray Gnatcatcher, American Robin, Red-eyed Vireo, Northern Parula, Yellow Warbler, Northern Cardinal, Song Sparrow, and Common Grackle. Canada Geese, Wood Ducks, and Mallards are resident breeders along the river. Spotted Sandpipers are occasionally noted on the rocks in the river. During migration and sometimes in winter, the area may have loons, grebes, swans, geese, ducks, mergansers, and gulls. Osprey or a rare Bald Eagle may show up, particularly in migration, and in August and September, post-breeding wanderers, such as Great Egrets, may appear.

The access parking lots mentioned previously are located between mile 61.2 and mile 61.6 of the towpath. Begin by heading downriver (eastward) toward Washington. Just beyond lock 33 at mile 60.7 is the B & O Railroad bridge to Harpers Ferry. The Appalachian Trail uses the bridge's walkway, which provides a good vantage point to scan the river. Then continue eastward along the canal towpath, passing under the US 340 bridge near mile 59.6. From around milepost marker 60 to mile 58.7, the canal is often filled with standing water, in which case you are likely to find several Prothonotary Warblers in late spring and summer. This is perhaps the best spot in the entire Blue Ridge Province for Prothonotaries.

Retrace your route upstream (westward) past lock 34 near mile 61.6; from here to Feeder Dam 3 near mile 62.3, the Potomac is dotted with rocky outcroppings and small islets. Watch along here for Canada Geese, Wood Ducks, Mallards, and Spotted Sandpipers. Above the Feeder Dam, the Potomac is wide, flat, and open; several spots provide good vistas for migrant or wintering waterfowl. From the Feeder Dam to Dargan Bend Recreation Area at mile 64.9, the towpath runs through a beautiful mature woods of tuliptrees, sycamore, and maples. This stretch is rather closed in, but you may pick up Northern Parula, Yellow-throated Warbler, Worm-eating Warbler, Louisiana Waterthrush, and other warblers.

The main spot in the northern Blue Ridge to see autumn hawks is at **Washington Monument State Park,** a 147-acre site just south of I-70 between Hagerstown and Frederick. If coming from the west, leave I-70 at exit 35 (M 34.8) onto MD 66 and proceed south 5.1 miles to US 40-A in Boonsboro, Md.; turn left (east) onto US 40-A and proceed 2.8 miles to Washington Monument Road, a left turn just at the ridge crest. If coming from the east, leave I-70 at exit 49 (M 49.4) onto US 40-A and proceed west 8.9 miles to Washington Monument Road. Turn onto the road and continue 0.8 miles to the entrance gate; park and walk 0.2 miles to the tower. Perched along the ridge of South Mountain near the summit of Monument Knob (1,540 ft.), the tower provides excellent views and some protection from the wind. Organized hawk watches are often conducted here from late August through November.

For spring and summer forest birds, try **Gambrill State Park,** a 1,139-acre wooded tract located off US 40 just west of Frederick. Take exit 53 off I-70 in Frederick onto US 15N/40W and continue on US 40 west for 5.4 miles to Gambrill Road. Alternatively, take exit 42 off I-70 and proceed 1.1 miles north on MD 17; turn right onto US 40 and head east for 5.5 miles to Gambrill Road. Turn onto Gambrill Road and go 1.8 miles to the park office. The main highway, dirt roads, and 15 miles of trails, including a 3-mile segment of the Catoctin Trail, provide easy-to-moderate hikes through oak forests at elevations ranging up to around 1,700 feet. For roadside birding, try the short spur road to the picnic area on High Knob (1,540 ft.), near the park's south end. Get a park trail map from the office to help choose among the six hiking routes, most of which are accessible from the picnic parking lot.

Spring songbird migration is often excellent in April and May. Later in spring and summer, typical birds found at Gambrill include Turkey Vulture, Broad-winged Hawk, Northern Bobwhite, Mourning Dove, Yellow-billed Cuckoo, Barred Owl, Chimney Swift, Ruby-throated Hummingbird, Belted Kingfisher, Red-bellied Woodpecker, Downy Woodpecker, Hairy Woodpecker, Northern Flicker, Pileated Woodpecker, Eastern Wood-

Pewee, Acadian Flycatcher, Eastern Phoebe, Great Crested Flycatcher, Barn Swallow, Blue Jay, American Crow, Fish Crow, Common Raven, Carolina Chickadee, Tufted Titmouse, White-breasted Nuthatch, Carolina Wren, House Wren, Blue-gray Gnatcatcher, Wood Thrush, American Robin, Gray Catbird, Northern Mockingbird, Yellow-throated Vireo, Red-eyed Vireo, Black-and-white Warbler, Worm-eating Warbler, Ovenbird, Louisiana Waterthrush, Kentucky Warbler, Common Yellowthroat, Scarlet Tanager, Northern Cardinal, Indigo Bunting, Rufous-sided Towhee, Chipping Sparrow, Field Sparrow, Song Sparrow, Common Grackle, Brown-headed Cowbird, and American Goldfinch.

Farther north along the eastern ridge line, Catoctin Mountain Park and adjacent Cunningham Falls State Park provide 10,000 acres of wooded mountains with good trails and roadside birding. Take US 15 north from I-70 in Frederick for 17 miles to Thurmont, Md.; turn onto MD 77 and proceed 2.7 miles west to the visitor center for **Catoctin Mountain Park**. Stop here for maps, brochures, information on interpretative hikes, and a copy of "Birds: A Checklist for Catoctin Mountain Park." Established in 1936, the park is heavily forested with second-growth chestnut oak, red oak, white oak, tuliptree, American beech, yellow birch, sugar maple, hemlocks, and various hickories.

Roadside birding is possible along MD 77 for 2 miles east and 2.5 miles west of the visitor center along hemlock-lined Big Hunting Creek at elevations ranging from 750 feet to 1,450 feet. Stop at various pull offs, trailheads, and parking lots along MD 77, but get started early to avoid the noise from the usually heavy traffic. This route yields many spring and summer birds noted previously for Gambrill State Park. The hemlocks along the creek are good for Black-throated Green Warblers, Northern Parulas, and an occasional Blackburnian Warbler. At 1.0 mile west of the visitor center on MD 77, the Cunningham Falls Trail (1,180 ft.) is an easy 0.3-mile hike for these species. The trail is wheelchair accessible, but you may need assistance in a few spots.

Other roadside birding spots involve the Park Central Road, which begins at the visitor center (920 ft.) and climbs to 1,820 feet on the south slope of Catoctin Mountain (1,880 ft.) before descending toward the picnic and camping areas in the park's northwest section. Trailhead parking lots provide spots to park and stroll along the shoulder or hike back into the oak forests. Many spring and summer species listed previously for Gambrill State Park can be expected, in addition to Veery, Cerulean Warbler, and Northern Oriole. Stop at Hog Rock parking lot, 1.3 miles from the visitor center, and take the easy 1.6-mile Hog Rock Nature Trail. This self-interpretative hike leads by **Hog Rock** (1,620 ft.), a Catoctin greenstone outcrop that provides a good view for watching the autumn hawk migration. From the same parking lot you can hike 0.3 miles north to **Blue Ridge Summit Vista** (1,560 ft.), another perspective for autumn raptors and a good route for breeding-season forest birds.

Most trails in Catoctin Park and Cunningham Falls State Park are suitable for birding, but particular favorites include Deerfield Nature Trail, a moderate 1.5-mile hike that begins near campsite 30 in the Owens Creek campground (1,320 ft.), and segments of the Catoctin Trail, which rambles across both parks.

Another recommended route begins at the junction of Park Central Road and Manahan Road, 3.4 miles from the visitor center. Park in the small gravel pull off at the intersection (1,580 ft.), and walk north on the gravel Manahan Road for 0.3 miles to a metal gate on the left, where a wide horse trail heads downslope, while the blue-blazed Catoctin Trail parallels Manahan Road from the same gate. Take the horse trail to Owens Creek picnic area (1,340 ft.), about three-fourths of a mile; walk through the picnic area; and pick up the Brown's Farm Nature Trail. Continue to the midpoint of Brown's Farm Trail and turn off onto the path that heads upslope toward Round Meadow. When the trail hits Park Central Road, turn left and walk carefully along the shoulder uphill for 0.5 miles to the intersection and your car. This moderate, approximately 2.5-mile hike provides good birding throughout the year. Check in winter for Common Raven, both chickadees, White-breasted Nuthatch, Brown Creeper, Winter Wren, Golden-crowned Kinglet, Hermit Thrush, Yellow-rumped Warbler, Purple Finch, and Pine Siskin. In late spring and summer, the route is good for most species noted previously for the park.

Near the northern extremity of the Blue Ridge Province, Pennsylvania's Caledonia State Park, Pine Grove Furnace State Park, and Michaux State Forest offer diverse habitats and birding activities on South Mountain. All three areas can be accessed from PA 233, which crosses US 30 between Gettysburg and Chambersburg. From the intersection with US 15 in downtown Gettysburg, head west on US 30 for 14.0 miles to Michaux State Forest Ranger station, and stop for maps and brochures. Continue for 0.4 miles to the junction with PA 233. If coming from Chambersburg, take exit 6 at M 15.6 on I-81 and head east on US 30 for 8.4 miles to PA 233.

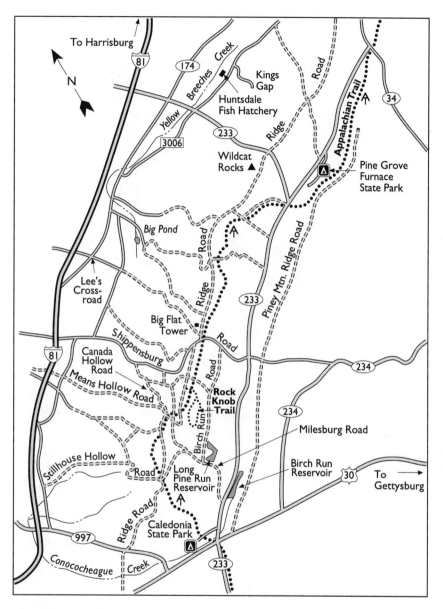

South Mountain, Pa.

Turn north onto PA 233 and proceed 0.1 miles to the entrance of **Caledonia State Park**, a 1,130-acre preserve with elevations ranging from around 900 feet along the East Branch Conococheague Creek to 1,522 feet on Chinquapin Hill. Get maps, trail guides, and brochures at the entrance office; check to see if any naturalist programs are scheduled. Although crowded on summer weekends, the campgrounds and picnic areas can be good for spring migration and for summer residents. The park is covered mostly by oak forests, although there are many beautiful tracts of hemlock, white pine, and rhododendron. In addition to a segment of the Appalachian Trail, the park has seven hiking routes, of which the Whispering Pine Nature Trail (0.4 miles), Ramble Trail (2.2 miles), and Charcoal Hearth Trail (2.7 miles) offer the best variety of birds and vegetation.

Year-round residents at Caledonia include Ruffed Grouse, Wild Turkey, Mourning Dove, Eastern Screech-Owl, Great Horned Owl, Barred Owl, Belted Kingfisher, Red-bellied Woodpecker, Downy Woodpecker, Hairy Woodpecker, Northern Flicker, Pileated Woodpecker, Blue Jay, American Crow, Common Raven, Black-capped Chickadee, Carolina Chickadee, Tufted Titmouse, White-breasted Nuthatch, Brown Creeper, Carolina Wren, Northern Cardinal, Rufous-sided Towhee, Song Sparrow, and American Goldfinch. In late spring and summer, other possible species include Great Blue Heron, Wood Duck, American Black Duck, Mallard, Sharp-shinned Hawk, Broad-winged Hawk, American Woodcock, Yellow-billed Cuckoo, Common Nighthawk, Whip-poor-will, Ruby-throated Hummingbird, Eastern Wood-Pewee, Acadian Flycatcher, Eastern Phoebe, Northern Rough-winged Swallow, Barn Swallow, House Wren, Blue-gray Gnatcatcher, Veery, Hermit Thrush, Wood Thrush, American Robin, Brown Thrasher, Solitary Vireo, Red-eyed Vireo, Chipping Sparrow, Field Sparrow, Swamp Sparrow, and House Finch. Warblers are richly represented, including Blue-winged, Golden-winged, Northern Parula, Yellow, Black-throated Green, Blackburnian, Pine, Black-and-white, American Redstart, Ovenbird, Louisiana Waterthrush, Kentucky Warbler, Common Yellowthroat, and Hooded.

For access to the upper elevations of South Mountain, drive north from Caledonia State Park on PA 233 into **Michaux State Forest**, an 82,261-acre tract named in honor of André Michaux and his son François André Michaux. Before exploring the area, pick up a copy of "Michaux State Forest Public Use Map," available at the nearby Forest Ranger Station on US 30. If coming from I-81, you can get into the northern end of the forest by taking exit 11 at M 36.9 onto PA 233 south and driving 5.6 miles to Ridge Road.

A network of gravel roads and trails, including portions of the Appalachian Trail, wander through the forest, providing easy to strenuous access. To combine birds and hiking, try the AT from Shippensburg Road north to Pine Grove Furnace State Park or south to Caledonia State Park. Another good birding hike is the Rocky Knob Trail, a 4.2-mile loop route that begins along Ridge Road 1.9 miles south of Shippensburg Road.

Many naturalists, however, prefer roadside bird-watching in this area, which allows the most efficient use of one's time. You can profitably spend several days birding by car along the maze of roadways both north and south of US 30, but visitors generally concentrate on Ridge Road, which runs more than 20 miles along the main crest. You might want to get a copy of the "Self-guided Automobile Trail" brochure from Michaux State Forest. The brochure describes the natural history at selected stops along a 19-mile route on Milesburn Road, Stillhouse Hollow Road, Ridge Road, Shippensburg Road, and PA 233. Portions of this tour make an excellent birding route, as described below, but be sure to study the maps carefully to avoid getting lost in this tangle of roads.

From US 30 at Caledonia Park, proceed north on PA 233 for 1.6 miles to Birch Run Reservoir (1,100 ft.); stop at the dam and scan the lake for waterfowl, especially during migration. Backtrack on PA 233 south from the dam for 0.1 miles and turn right onto Milesburn Road. At 1.3 miles from PA 233, Milesburn Road passes **Long Pine Run Reservoir** (1,360 ft.), a 150-acre lake that is usually better than Birch Run for water birds. Turn onto the side road that goes 0.1 miles to the boat access area—a good spot to scope the lake. Look for Wood Duck, American Black Duck, and Mallard in spring and summer, and check during migration for Osprey and waterfowl, such as Common Loon, Pied-billed Grebe, Horned Grebe, and Hooded, Common, and Red-breasted Mergansers. Other transients include Tundra Swan, Canada Goose, Northern Pintail, Canvasback, Redhead, Ring-necked Duck, Lesser Scaup, Common Goldeneye, and Bufflehead. Even an Oldsquaw has shown up here. Ring-billed Gulls and an occasional Herring or Bonaparte's may appear.

Return to Milesburn Road, turn right, and continue to Birch Run Road at 1.9 miles from PA 233; turn right and go 0.1 miles on Birch Run Road to a small pull off near the lake edge, where the Beaver Trail provides a good birding route along the upper reservoir. Again go back to Milesburn Road, turn right, and continue to the intersection with Stillhouse Hollow Road at 2.7 miles from PA 233. Stop frequently along this section to check spring and summer birds in the rosebay thickets, tuliptrees, and hemlocks, which are typical of the cool, shaded, moist hollows and ravines that drain both sides of South Mountain. Many species noted at Caledonia State Park can be expected in these forests.

Turn left onto Stillhouse Hollow Road and proceed 1.8 miles to the junction with **Ridge Road** and the Appalachian Trail. Turn sharply right onto Ridge Road and proceed north. This route ascends to the main crest, passing through areas of poor, sandy soil, where the dominant vegetation includes scrub pine and oak barrens, intermixed with medium-aged stands of oaks and beech along with scattered white pine plantations. Elevations on Ridge Road are generally between 1,400 and 2,000 feet, with a maximum of 2,060 feet at Big Flat Fire Tower. Wildfires swept many areas along Ridge Road in the early 1900s and in 1963, causing destruction of the soil. Now much of the ridge is covered by scrub barrens of chestnut oak, pin oak, scarlet oak, pitch pine, Virginia pine, and white pine, with northern red oak, black oak, and white oak on the lower slopes. Mountain laurel and huckleberry are major understory plants. When undisturbed, the vegetation matures to mixed oak forests over a long period of time.

These barrens should be checked for summering Nashville Warblers— South Mountain being the only place in the Blue Ridge Mountain Province where this species is known to nest. Locate the birds by listening for their songs, particularly in areas where the trees are about seven to fifteen feet tall and so dense that the vegetation appears almost impenetrable. The birds occur at widely scattered spots throughout this habitat all along Ridge Road and in similar vegetation elsewhere on South Mountain. Search carefully on Means Hollow Road, beginning at its junction with Ridge Road; this intersection is 2.7 miles north on Ridge Road from its junction with Stillhouse Hollow Road. Also try the stretch of Ridge Road north of Shippensburg Road beyond Big Flat Fire Tower. Elsewhere on South Mountain, the Big Pond area on the west slope near Lee's Cross Roads may be worth checking. Finally, explore the adjacent high ridge line by leaving PA 233, heading 0.6 miles east on Shippensburg Road, and turning left to head north on Piney Mountain Ridge Road, much of which passes through excellent habitat.

Resuming your route on Ridge Road at its junction with Means Hollow Road, you must make a sharp right turn onto Ridge Road, proceed

Long-eared Owl

0.5 miles, and cross Milesburn Road. Just beyond this intersection, Ridge Road turns sharply northward and runs on for 3.4 more miles to its junction with Shippensburg Road. To continue, turn right and head east on Shippensburg Road for 0.2 miles, where Ridge Road resumes on the left and proceeds 8.0 miles north to its junction with PA 233. Beyond its intersection with PA 233, Ridge Road continues 7.9 miles farther north to join PA 34. From here it is 5.4 miles north to exit 14E at M 46.6 on I-81 near Carlisle.

Stop frequently on Ridge Road, including spots where white pine plantations and stands of hemlock add diversity to the route. Northern Saw-whet Owls roost in these conifers during winter, and considering the records at nearby Kings Gap, it may be worth checking these stands for Long-eared Owls at any time of year. In addition to many species noted previously at Caledonia, be alert in late spring and summer along Milesburn Road, Stillhouse Hollow Road, and Ridge Road for Black and Turkey Vultures, Eastern Screech-Owl, Great Horned Owl, Red-bellied Woodpecker, Great Crested Flycatcher, Black-capped Chickadee, Veery, and Cedar Waxwing. This is a good warbler route, including Blue-winged, Golden-winged, Northern Parula, Chestnut-sided, Black-throated Blue, Black-throated Green, Blackburnian, Pine, Prairie, Black-and-white, Worm-eating, Ovenbird, Louisiana Waterthrush, Common Yellowthroat, and Hooded. Although widely dispersed and generally scarce, other breeding-season possibilities include Yellow-bellied Sapsucker, Common Raven, Red-breasted Nuthatch, Brown Creeper, Hermit Thrush, Solitary Vireo, Scarlet Tanager, and Northern Oriole. Incidentally, those large mounds scattered in the sandy woods are home to Allegheny mound-building ants, red and black little creatures whose castles sometimes reach four feet in height and twenty feet in diameter.

Ridge Road even has a good perch for watching the autumn hawk migration. Take PA 233 south for 5.9 miles from exit 11 on I-81 or north for 2.0 miles from Pine Grove Furnace State Park; turn south onto Ridge Road and proceed 0.5 miles. On the right is a small pull off and a faint trail that runs at right angles from the road 250 feet uphill to the ridge line, where you turn left and follow the blue-blazed trail about 300 feet to the open outcroppings of **Wildcat Rocks** (1,380 ft.). The clear, 360-degree view is excellent, and the topography is optimal for north and northwest winds.

Another popular birding spot is **Pine Grove Furnace State Park**, a 696-acre park with picnic areas, campgrounds, hiking trails, and two lakes. The park visitor center is on PA 233, at 7.9 miles south from exit 11 on I-81 or 13 miles north of US 30. From the visitor center, drive north on Hunters Run Road for 1.8 miles to **Laurel Lake** (780 ft.), where most water-bird species noted previously at Pine Run Reservoir may be expected. Continue on for 0.5 miles to Railroad Road, which turns right and runs back along the south shore of Laurel Lake. Drive to the first parking area on the right, and take the three-fourths-mile Pole Steeple Trail, an occasionally steep climb for a superb view and the possibility of summering Goshawks. Barred Owls are resident around Laurel Lake. Three nature trails and a segment of the AT provide other good bird hikes. Most of the late-spring and summer species at Pine Grove have been previously listed for Caledonia State Park.

Nestled along Yellow Breeches Creek in the valley just west of South Mountain, the **Huntsdale Fish Hatchery** (600 ft.) is worth a visit for birds seldom found elsewhere near the Blue Ridge. If coming from the mountain, turn off Ridge Road onto PA 233 and drive 3.3 miles north to PA SR 3006, where signs for Kings Gap Environmental Education and Training Center point right. Turn right on state road 3006, passing the hatchery offices and visitor center at 0.9 miles, and continue to Sheaffer Road at 1.2 miles from PA 233. Turn left onto Sheaffer Road and go 0.1 miles, where you can park in a small lot on the right. Walk across the bridge and immediately turn right for a 0.8-mile loop stroll along a dirt road that passes by old fish-holding ponds and through woods lining the banks of Yellow Breeches Creek, before finally circling a cattail-margined lake.

Black-crowned Night-Herons roost in the trees here during late spring and summer; Great Blue Herons, Wood Ducks, Belted Kingfishers, and Fish Crows may be present year-round. Great Egrets may appear in August and September. American Bitterns have been reported in the past. Soras and Virginia Rails occur in migration, and Virginia Rails have nested in the marsh. Watch for Swamp Sparrows as well, this being among the few nesting sites for this species anywhere near the Blue Ridge Province. This is a good spot for woodland birds during spring migration and in the nesting season; and grebes, Canada Geese, ducks, and mergansers may overwinter or pass through during migration. It is sometimes possible to drive this loop route for birding from the car, but walking usually gives better results. Return to the parking area and check the fish raceways across the road for Ring-billed Gulls in winter and for shorebirds and Osprey during migration. Even an occasional Bald Eagle may show up here.

Drive back to PA SR 3006, turn left, and continue for 0.7 miles to Enck's

Mill Road; turn left onto Enck's Mill Road and go 0.3 miles to the dirt road that parallels the railroad tracks. Turn right and walk or drive along this route to check for herons and waterfowl in the adjacent lake. Avoid trespassing or blocking the roadway. Watch here and around the hatchery area for migrating swallows, particularly Cliff Swallows.

Return to state road 3006, turn left, and continue 0.3 miles beyond Enck's Mill Road to **Kings Gap Environmental Education and Training Center,** a 1,443-acre preserve nestled at the foot of South Mountain. Open year-round for hiking and nature study, this park contains 15 miles of trails, including routes not only suitable for wheelchair use but also with braille interpretative signs for the visually impaired.

A particularly interesting area is the Pine Plantation (630 ft.), located along the entrance road at 0.2 miles from state road 3006. This is the only site in the Blue Ridge Province where Long-eared Owls have been found nesting. Park in the lot and explore the three easy trails that run through the dense tract of Douglas fir, tamarack, and white pine. The Whispering Pines Nature Trail is a 0.5-mile paved loop route designed for wheelchair use; the Pine Plantation Trail is an outer loop that runs 0.6 miles around the perimeter of the stand, while portions of the Rock Scree Trail run straight through the center. You can also stroll for 0.3 miles along the edge of the pine stand by walking carefully along the shoulder of the entrance road beyond the parking lot. Other late-spring and summer birds include Brown Creeper and Pine Warbler, as well as many species noted elsewhere on South Mountain. If you come here looking for owls, remember that the park is closed between sunset and sunrise, so you should contact the headquarters (717-486-5031) to let the staff know of your plans.

Continue on for 3.7 miles from PA SR 3006 to the visitor center to obtain trail maps, brochures, information, and a schedule of special events, programs, and interpretative activities. Most of the center's trails offer excellent birding year-round. Kings Gap and the fish hatchery are also accessible from I-81; just take exit 11 at M 36.9 onto PA 233 south and go 2.3 miles to the junction with PA SR 3006; turn left onto state road 3006 and proceed as noted previously.

Mount Rogers Area

Highlights: Summer birds of spruce-fir, northern hardwoods, heath balds,
and grass balds; Northern Saw-whet Owl, Empidonax flycatchers, Hermit
Thrush, Swainson's Thrush, Magnolia Warbler, Purple Finch.

Season: Year-round, but mainly spring through summer.

Access: From the BRP, exit at M 229.7 onto US 21 north and proceed 17
miles through Sparta, N.C., to Independence, Va.; turn left in Independence onto US 58 west and go 16 miles to Volney, Va.; from Volney it is
7.5 miles west to Grayson Highlands State Park on US 58 or 6 miles north
on VA 16 to Troutdale, Va., and the VA 603 junction. From I-81, take VA
16 south from exit 16 near Marion, Va., for 16 miles to Troutdale, or take
exit 9 near Abingdon, Va., onto US 58 east for 20 miles through Damascus,
Va., to the Konnarock, Va., area.

Maps: USGS "Konnarock," "Park," "Trout Dale," "Whitetop Mountain";
USFS "Mount Rogers High Country and Wilderness," "Jefferson National
Forest," "Jefferson National Forest Map Mount Rogers National Recre-
ation Area"; "High Country Trails Mount Rogers National Recreation
Area," by Larry Landrum and Susan Woodward.

Facilities: For information and maps, contact Mount Rogers National Recreation Area, Rt. 1, Box 303, Marion, VA 24354 (703-783-5196) and Grayson
Highlands State Park, Rt. 2, Box 141, Mouth of Wilson, VA 24363 (703-
579-7092). Food and gasoline at Konnarock, Troutdale, and Damascus; accommodations along I-81. Campgrounds at Grayson Highlands State Park
and at Beartree, Grindstone, Hurricane, and Raccoon Branch campgrounds
in Jefferson National Forest.

Mount Rogers occupies a unique position in the distribution of
bird life in the southern Appalachian Mountains. Not only is it the highest
point in Virginia, but at 5,729 feet, Mount Rogers is also the loftiest peak
in the eight hundred miles between New Hampshire's White Mountains
and North Carolina's Grandfather Mountain. The avifauna around Mount
Rogers is distinctly northern in composition, but the area has also been a
"sentinel post," where the advance guard of certain northern species first
became established when they expanded their breeding ranges into the
southern Appalachians. Such birds as Hermit Thrush, Magnolia Warbler,
and Purple Finch announced their influx here before pushing into North
Carolina and Tennessee. Swainson's Thrush has recently begun summer-

ing on Rogers, and Yellow-bellied Flycatchers nested here in the 1970s and 1980s.

For all its superlatives, Mount Rogers is rather unassuming in appearance—merely the top of a high, gently undulating ridge line that stretches east-west for about eleven miles, separating the valleys of the New River and the Holston River in southwestern Virginia. Much of the region above 4,500 feet was once covered by spruce-fir forests, but logging and wildfires have destroyed most of that plant community, leaving a complex mosaic of grass balds, heath balds, shrub thickets, northern hardwood tracts, and scattered stands of spruce and fir. The vegetation in some areas, such as Pine Mountain and Wilburn Ridge, is reminiscent of conditions at Shining Rock Ledge along the Parkway south of Asheville, where similar episodes of logging and fires severely damaged the forests. Middle and low elevations are covered by medium to mature second-growth oak and cove hardwood forests, in addition to farms, fields, and settled areas.

This diversity of habitat and the extensive acreage of high-elevation terrain combine to make the area one of the most appealing spots in the southern mountains for bird study. Ornithologists have been drawn to the region since the earliest studies here, in July 1888, by Dr. William C. Rives, Jr. (1850–1938), of Washington, D.C.

The first time you visit the Mount Rogers area, it may remind you of that old story about the city slicker who asked directions from a local mountaineer and was told, "You kaint git thar frum here." Persistence will be rewarded, however. In addition to spots suitable for the handicapped, there are 250 miles of hiking trails, numerous bridle trails, and some of the best cross-country skiing routes in the mountains, all of which can be used to sample the region's bird life. Get a detailed map, such as the USFS "Jefferson National Forest Map Mount Rogers National Recreation Area," in order to minimize your geographic confusion.

Many excellent roadside birding opportunities are available, including **Beartree Recreation Area,** located along Straight Branch on the south slope of Iron Mountain. Explore the area by taking FSR 837, which begins east of Damascus along US 58 at a spot 2.9 miles west of the US 58 junction with VA 603. This paved road follows close by Straight Branch from 2,960 feet in elevation at US 58 up to 3,360 feet at its terminus near the campground. After turning onto FSR 837, watch for signs to the fisherman's parking lot at 0.2 miles and to Beartree Lake picnic area at 0.9 miles. An easy loop trail around the lake can be accessed from both of these parking lots. The

Magnolia Warbler

picnic grounds parking area is paved and suited for roadside or wheelchair birding. The lake trail passes through a mix of hemlocks, hardwoods, and rhododendrons, where in late spring and summer you can expect Acadian Flycatcher, Eastern Phoebe, American Crow, Carolina Chickadee, American Robin, Gray Catbird, Cedar Waxwing, Red-eyed Vireo, Northern Parula, Chestnut-sided Warbler, Black-throated Blue Warbler, Black-and-white Warbler, Ovenbird, Hooded Warbler, Scarlet Tanager, Rufous-sided Towhee, Chipping Sparrow, Song Sparrow, and American Goldfinch.

Continue on FSR 837 to the entrance for the group camping area, on the left at 1.4 miles. The bridge over Straight Branch and the flat paved loop roads are excellent for roadside birding and for birding from wheelchairs, if you watch out for vehicles. Proceed farther up the road to the next campground, on the left at 3.5 miles from US 58. Several campsites here are specifically designed for handicapped use, and the rest rooms are wheelchair accessible. A trail heads to nearby beaver ponds, where one may find Common Yellowthroat and Song Sparrow, as well as beaver.

The third and last campground is on the left at 3.9 miles. The same birds noted at Beartree Lake and picnic area are found all along the road and the string of campgrounds, in addition to Eastern Phoebe and Louisiana Waterthrush. At the upper campgrounds you will also encounter Veery, Canada Warbler, Rose-breasted Grosbeak, and Dark-eyed Junco. Listen carefully at the campgrounds and along Straight Branch for Long-eared Owl, Swainson's Warbler, and Northern Waterthrush, all of which have been reported here.

Another good roadside birding route is along FSR 84 at **Skulls Gap** (3,550 ft.). From Konnarock, drive east on VA 603 for 1.8 miles to the junction with VA 600 on the left; turn onto VA 600 and proceed 2.8 miles to the gap area, where you turn right onto FSR 84. Although this gravel road goes quite a distance, the best birding is usually in the first 1.3 miles, as it passes through an attractive mix of hemlock, pines, northern hardwoods, and rhododendron along the upper reaches of Saint Clair Creek. Stop and listen for Blackburnian Warblers in Skulls Gap picnic area, immediately after turning onto the Forest Service road. Other regular birds in late spring and summer are Downy Woodpecker, Acadian Flycatcher, American Crow, Carolina Chickadee, Veery, Solitary Vireo, Red-eyed Vireo, Chestnut-sided Warbler, Black-throated Blue Warbler, Black-throated Green Warbler, Black-and-white Warbler, Ovenbird, Canada Warbler, Scarlet Tanager, Rose-breasted Grosbeak, Rufous-sided Towhee, and Dark-eyed Junco.

Another segment of FSR 84 is also worth checking. Head north out of Troutdale on VA 16 for 2.3 miles to the junction with VA 650 on the left; turn onto VA 650 and proceed 1.3 miles to FSR 84, a left turn toward the Hurricane campground (2,780 ft.). Drive up FSR 84 and stop to bird along **Hurricane Creek**, as the road climbs 5.3 miles from the campground up to Hurricane Gap (3,780 ft.). Many of the same species noted along Straight Branch at Beartree Recreation Area can be found here also, but be alert for Swainson's Warblers in the rosebay thickets along the first 4 miles of the route. Also stop frequently along VA 650 for possible Swainson's Warblers in the first 3.5 miles beyond the junction with VA 16.

A final easy spot for birding the low-to-middle elevations is around **Grindstone campground** (3,700 ft.) on VA 603 at 6 miles west of the VA 16 junction in Troutdale or 6 miles east of Konnarock. Several paved loop roads in the campground are level enough for wheelchairs, and some of the hundred campsites are handicapped accessible. The campground is nestled in a woodland of hemlock, birch, beech, and cherry near the upper end of

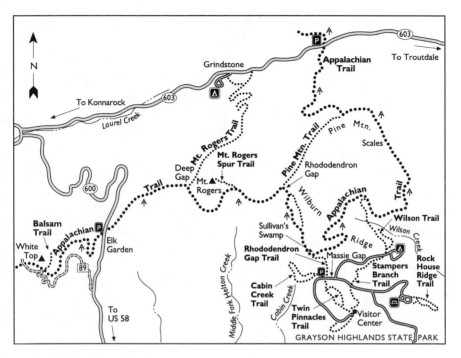

Mount Rogers High Country, Va.

Big Laurel Creek. About 150 feet beyond the entrance kiosk is the trailhead for the climb up the north side of Mount Rogers. Explore the loop roads, the adjacent trails, and portions of the creek along VA 603.

Grindstone campground is known for its Barred Owls and Least Fly-catchers, but other late-spring and summer birds include Ruffed Grouse, Eastern Screech-Owl, Great Horned Owl, Downy and Pileated Wood-peckers, Veery, Wood Thrush, American Robin, Gray Catbird, Cedar Wax-wing, Solitary Vireo, Red-eyed Vireo, Black-throated Blue Warbler, Oven-bird, Canada Warbler, Rose-breasted Grosbeak, Rufous-sided Towhee, and Dark-eyed Junco. Both Louisiana and Northern Waterthrushes are sometimes reported here during the breeding season.

For roadside birding in the high elevations, drive up **Whitetop Mountain** (5,520 ft.), second highest peak in Virginia, where many birds associated with spruce-fir forests can be observed. Access to Whitetop is provided by FSR 89, which turns off from VA 600 at 1.6 miles north of US 58. From the opposite direction, take VA 600 south for 6.4 miles from its junction with VA 603 between Konnarock and Grindstone campground. As you head up FSR 89, stop to explore the spruce and northern hardwoods between

0.6 and 1.0 mile from VA 600. The dirt road, pull offs, and surrounding woods are fairly level here, providing a good spot for birding from the car or wheelchair or for an easy stroll to see Common Raven, Red-breasted Nuthatch, Brown Creeper, Winter Wren, Golden-crowned Kinglet, Veery, Solitary Vireo, Chestnut-sided Warbler, and Dark-eyed Junco. Curiously, this area is often better than Mount Rogers for Black-throated Green and Blackburnian Warblers. Listen for Northern Saw-whet Owls calling from late March through June.

Continuing toward the summit, the road leaves the woods at 1.8 miles and enters an open grassy area, where Golden Eagles are sometimes noted from fall through spring and Horned Larks occasionally nest in summer. In the sharp hairpin turn at 2.5 miles, the old Balsam Trail (5,380 ft.) heads off to the right and runs 0.6 miles around Whitetop's east slope. Park and explore this fairly level but sometimes muddy route through a beautiful old-growth stand of red spruce, where you will find the same species noted at the first stop. The trail becomes hard to follow at 0.2 miles, so you may wish to retrace your route at that point. Return to your car and drive to the end of the road near the summit at 3.0 miles, where you can park and walk the roadway to view the birds in the adjacent spruce trees. Red Crossbills are always a possibility, and Northern Saw-whet Owls have been reported here.

For a bit of hiking on Whitetop, try the 2-mile section of Appalachian Trail that runs from the parking lot at Elk Garden (4,450 ft.) on VA 600 up to FSR 89 at 2.0 miles from VA 600. This route passes through northern hardwood and spruce forests, where most species already listed for Whitetop can be expected. Be alert also for Sharp-shinned and Cooper's Hawks, which are occasionally noted.

Another good area in the high country is **Grayson Highlands State Park** on VA 362, a spur road that turns off US 58 at 24 miles west of Independence or 27 miles east of Damascus. Encompassing 4,934 acres, the park offers year-round birding along bridle paths, cross-country skiing routes, and 11 miles of hiking trails, as well as at roadside facilities. Drive 4.6 miles to the end of the road on the summit of Haw Orchard Mountain, where the park visitor center has maps, books, information, snacks, rest rooms, and interpretive displays. The paved parking lots at the visitor center are good for wheelchairs, providing access to spruce and mixed northern hardwood tracts here and at the adjacent picnic area. Two trails that begin just behind the visitor center are recommended for birding.

The **Twin Pinnacles Trail** is a fairly easy 1.6-mile loop that runs through a forest of yellow birch, hawthorns, and red spruce before breaking into an open area of rocky outcroppings surrounded by cherry, ash, heath thickets, and ferns. This area was formerly covered by spruce forests, which were extensively logged and burned from 1900 to 1912. At 0.3 miles the trail goes over Little Pinnacle (5,094 ft.), where a spectacular 360-degree panorama unfolds. On a clear day you can see Whitetop, Mount Rogers, Pine Mountain, Wilburn Ridge, and south to Grandfather Mountain and the Blue Ridge. Continue on across Big Pinnacle (5,068 ft.) at 0.8 miles and then return to the visitor center, being careful that you do not inadvertently take the Big Pinnacle Trail, which descends sharply to Massie Gap. In late spring and summer, this hike is good for Common Raven, American Robin, Veery, Gray Catbird, Solitary Vireo, Chestnut-sided Warbler, Canada Warbler, Rose-breasted Grosbeak, Rufous-sided Towhee, and Dark-eyed Junco. The major attractions, however, are Black-capped Chickadees and Magnolia Warblers, along with the possibility of Northern Saw-whet Owls. Many of the same birds can be seen along **Stampers Branch Trail**, which runs 1.7 miles from the visitor center down to the park campground, a change of 600 feet in elevation.

Drive back down to **Massie Gap parking area** (4,650 ft.) at 1.2 miles from the visitor center. The stand of spruce trees around the gap is a good spot for Evening Grosbeaks, Red Crossbills, and Pine Siskins during some winters. Walk along the paved spur road toward the stables for a distance of about 300 yards, checking the surrounding deciduous and heath vegetation in late spring and summer for Gray Catbird, Cedar Waxwing, Black-capped Chickadee, Red-eyed Vireo, Chestnut-sided Warbler, Canada Warbler, Rufous-sided Towhee, and Dark-eyed Junco. Beginning near the stables road, **Cabin Creek Trail** is a moderate 1.9-mile loop route that descends to 4,360 feet and passes a handsome waterfall along Cabin Creek. This hike used to be a good spot for the rare Bewick's Wren; but now you are more likely to find Northern Flicker, Blue Jay, Wood Thrush, Gray Catbird, Red-eyed Vireo, Chestnut-sided Warbler, Black-throated Blue Warbler, Ovenbird, Canada Warbler, Scarlet Tanager, Rufous-sided Towhee, and Dark-eyed Junco.

The other interesting hike from Massie Gap parking lot is the **Rhododendron Gap Trail**, which runs 0.5 miles rather steeply up the side of Wilburn Ridge to join the Appalachian Trail, by which you can continue on to Pine Mountain or Mount Rogers. After crossing the split-rail fence, listen for Vesper Sparrows, Field Sparrows, and Song Sparrows as you ascend through the sparsely wooded hillside and grassy pasture. Around the junction with the AT (4,900 ft.) is a good spot for Horned Lark. A stroll along the AT north on Wilburn Ridge will yield Vesper Sparrow, Chipping Sparrow, Field Sparrow, and Song Sparrow, as well as Northern Bobwhite, Northern Flicker, American Robin, Gray Catbird, Rufous-sided Towhee, and Dark-eyed Junco. Watch for Golden Eagle and Northern Harrier in winter.

A few hundred feet due north from the junction of the AT and the Rhododendron Gap Trail is **Sullivan's Swamp** (4,850 ft.), a wet bog of grasses, Catawba rhododendron, mountain laurel, blueberry, ferns, and scattered spruce and northern hardwoods along the head of Quebec Branch. Bewick's Wrens were seen here in the 1970s, and Willow Flycatchers were reported in summer during the 1980s. Alder Flycatchers are fairly regular in June and July, along with American Robin, Gray Catbird, Cedar Waxwing, Chestnut-sided Warbler, Common Yellowthroat, Rufous-sided Towhee, Dark-eyed Junco, Vesper Sparrow, and Song Sparrow.

Other good birding sites include the loops in the park campground and picnic area, located on well-marked side roads between Massie Gap and the park entrance. The Stampers Branch Trail between the campground and the entrance road is fairly easy and a good route for many woodland species noted previously; Wilson Creek Trail and Rock House Ridge Trail yield many of the same birds.

To explore the upper summit of **Mount Rogers**, you must hike one of the moderately strenuous backcountry trails that converge on the upper slopes. The three most commonly used routes are the AT north from Elk Garden (a 5-mile hike with a 1,280-foot elevation gain), the AT south from Grayson Highlands State Park (a 4.5-mile hike with a 1,080-foot elevation gain), and the Mount Rogers Trail from Grindstone campground (a 6.5-mile hike with a 2,040-foot elevation gain).

The most popular hike to Mount Rogers begins in the parking lot at **Elk Garden** (4,450 ft.) on VA 600, at 5.1 miles south of the junction with VA 603 or 2.9 miles north from the US 58 junction. Take the AT north up the open grassy fields of Elk Garden Ridge, where in late spring and summer you may find Horned Larks and Vesper Sparrows, as well as Northern Flicker, Barn Swallow, American Robin, Gray Catbird, Rufous-sided Towhee, Field Sparrow, Song Sparrow, Indigo Bunting, and American Goldfinch. The trail soon enters a northern hardwood forest, a good area for Ruffed Grouse, Black-billed Cuckoo, Downy Woodpecker, Least Flycatcher, Veery, Solitary Vireo, Red-eyed Vireo, Chestnut-sided Warbler, Ovenbird, Canada Warbler, Rose-breasted Grosbeak, Rufous-sided Towhee, and Dark-eyed Junco.

At 2.0 miles from Elk Garden, the AT passes through Deep Gap (4,900 ft.), beyond which the northern hardwoods gradually become mixed with red spruce. In addition to the species already observed along the hike, you may now find birds associated with the high coniferous forest, such as Common Raven, Black-capped Chickadee, Red-breasted Nuthatch, Brown Creeper, Winter Wren, Golden-crowned Kinglet, Black-throated Green Warbler, and Blackburnian Warbler. About 2 miles beyond Deep Gap, the AT breaks out into an open field with blackberry, cherry, hawthorns, grasses, and shrubs. Alder Flycatchers are often present here in late spring and summer, along with Gray Catbird, Chestnut-sided Warbler, Common Yellowthroat, Rufous-sided Towhee, Song Sparrow, and Dark-eyed Junco. Be alert along the trail here for Purple Finches, which are often noted in the spruce trees at the forest edge.

At 4.5 miles from Elk Garden, the 0.5-mile spur trail from the AT to the summit takes off sharply to the left, paralleling and soon entering a dense stand of spruce trees as it climbs to the peak, where, incidentally, the only view is of the trees! Many of the species noted previously on the AT are also present on this summit trail, but the real attractions here are Swainson's Thrush, Hermit Thrush, and Magnolia Warbler. Purple Finches are sometimes noted in the spruce trees bordering the summit trail near its junction with the AT. As of 1991, Mount Rogers is the southernmost point in the Appalachians where Swainson's Thrush and Purple Finch can be expected consistently in summer. Hermit Thrushes and Magnolia Warblers occur south to Grandfather, Roan, and the Black mountains, but the birds are much more conspicuous, and presumably more common, at Mount Rogers. If you are here at night, listen for Northern Saw-whet Owls from late March through June. Yellow-bellied Flycatchers nested on the north side of the summit between 1977 and 1985 but have not been recorded since that time.

After exploring the summit, you can retrace your route to Elk Garden or continue on along the rather flat and easy 1.5-mile segment of the AT from here north to Rhododendron Gap (5,400 ft.). Many of the same birds noted in the open fields and spruce forest on Mount Rogers are also present on this hike. At Rhododendron Gap, two trails descend onto **Pine Moun-**

tain, a fairly level high ridge that sweeps in a 4-mile arc to the northeast. Once covered with spruce and northern hardwoods, this area was logged and burned over, resulting in a complex mixture of beautiful Catawba rhododendron thickets, grass balds, shrubby fields, and infiltrating borders of young hardwoods and conifers.

Despite the mess, the best birding is usually along the horse trail, which is more open than the nearby footpath. The route descends in switchbacks from the gap and continues for 2.5 miles along the main crest at elevations around 5,000 feet before rejoining the AT. In late spring and summer, the Pine Mountain Trail is thick with American Robins, Gray Catbirds, Rufous-sided Towhees, Chestnut-sided Warblers, and Dark-eyed Juncos; and a sizable population of Alder Flycatchers is usually present. The better part of a day can be spent rambling about on Pine Mountain and birding along the various trails, where Yellow-bellied Sapsucker, Hermit Thrush, and Magnolia Warbler are among the other reported species.

If you are coming from Grayson Highlands State Park, leave the car at Massie Gap parking lot; proceed 0.5 miles up Rhododendron Gap Trail to the AT; turn left and head south on the AT for 2.0 miles to Rhododendron Gap; and continue for 1.5 miles on the AT to the spur trail that leads 0.5 miles to the summit of Mount Rogers. The bird life and habitat along this rather open and scenic route resembles that noted previously for Grayson Highlands State Park. The hike from Grindstone campground runs 4 miles up the heavily wooded north side of Mount Rogers to Deep Gap, where it joins the AT and proceeds north just as described for the hike from Elk Garden.

Roan Mountain

Highlights: Residents of spruce-fir and northern hardwood forests, rhododendron balds, grass balds; Northern Saw-whet Owl, Alder Flycatcher, Hermit Thrush, Red Crossbill, Snow Bunting.

Season: Year-round.

Access: Easiest access to Roan Mountain is from Carver's Gap, which is 12.4 miles south on TN 143 from the junction with US 19E in the town of Roan Mountain, Tenn., or 13 miles north of Bakersville, N.C., on NC 261. Quick-

est access from the BRP is to exit at M 305.1 at Beacon Heights onto US
221 south into Linville, N.C. Take NC 181 from Linville to Newland, N.C.;
NC 194 from Newland to Elk Park, N.C.; US 19E from Elk Park to Roan
Mountain; and TN 143 from Roan Mountain to Carver's Gap—a total of 33
miles from the BRP.

Maps: USGS "Carver's Gap," "Bakersville," "Iron Mountain Gap," "White
Rocks Mountain."

Facilities: Gasoline, food, and lodging at Bakersville and the town of Roan
Mountain; food, camping, and lodging at Roan Mountain State Park. For
maps and information, contact the U.S. Forest Service, P.O. Box 128,
Burnsville, NC 28714 (704-682-6146).

The Roan Mountain massif has long been regarded as among the
most scenic and interesting natural history areas in the entire Appalachian
system. Rising to 6,286 feet, the summit of Roan marks the highest point
in the Unaka Mountains. Also knows as the Iron Mountains, this is a short
but lofty range whose eastern peaks are covered by the largest stretch
of grass balds in the world. Other major plant communities in the high
elevations include spruce-fir forests, northern hardwoods, and a variety
of heath and shrub thickets. Best known to the average visitor, however,
is the 600-acre expanse of Catawba rhododendron, the largest natural
rhododendron "garden" in the United States.

Before the Civil War, Professor Elisha Mitchell of the University of
North Carolina described the grass balds in an image of romantic ebul-
lience that can easily be appreciated by the modern hiker. Mitchell noted
that "the top of Roan may be described as a vast meadow . . . without
a tree to obstruct this prospect; where a person may gallop his horse for
a mile or two, with Carolina at his feet on one side, and Tennessee on
the other, with a great ocean of mountains raised into tremendous billows
immediately about him."

Botanists were quick to discover the natural delights of the area. André
Michaux of France and the Scottish plant collector John Fraser explored
the Roan in the 1790s. Harvard botanist Dr. Asa Gray made his first visit
in 1841 and called Roan "without doubt, the most beautiful mountain east
of the Rockies." More than thirty rare or endangered plants are known
to occur in the range, where many are near their southern limit. To help
preserve this rich flora, the U.S. Forest Service acquired some 7,000 acres
on the top of Roan in 1941 for incorporation into Pisgah National For-

est and Cherokee National Forest. The Southern Appalachian Highlands Conservancy has acquired additional acreage from private landholders in recent years and transferred most of the land to the Forest Service.

Serious bird study began here with the work of Samuel Rhoads in the 1890s, but Roan Mountain's fame as a birding site is largely due to the labors of Fred W. Behrend (1896–1976) from Elizabethton, Tenn. Behrend is probably best known for his discovery of Snow Buntings wintering on the high grass balds. Bird-watching at Roan is a year-round activity, however, and naturalists can sample the region from their car, on cross-country skis, by hiking, or even from wheelchairs on specially designed paved trails. The beautiful scenery and diversity of plant and bird life make this one of the most popular and enjoyable birding sites in the southern mountains.

A good place for low- to middle-elevation species during the spring and summer months is at **Roan Mountain State Park**, a 2,156-acre wooded retreat along the Doe River on the north slope of Roan. Elevations range from around 2,800 feet to almost 3,800 feet, with oak and cove hardwood forests the predominant plant communities. Head south on TN 143 from its junction with US 19E in the town of Roan Mountain. Willow Flycatchers are found locally in willow thickets along TN 143 between the town and the park entrance. The park office and the campground are 2.0 miles and 4.4 miles, respectively, from the 143-19E junction. Most of the park's 15 miles of hiking trails are suitable for birding, but a favorite is the **Fred Behrend Nature Trail**, an easy 2.5-mile loop that begins in the campground just beyond the bridge over the Doe River. Another easy route with excellent birding, suitable for wheelchairs, is the paved loop road through the tent campground along the east side of Doe River.

Check the river area for Belted Kingfishers year-round. Summer warblers are conspicuous here, including the Northern Parula, Yellow, Chestnut-sided, Black-throated Blue, Black-throated Green, Black-and-white, Worm-eating, Ovenbird, Louisiana Waterthrush, Kentucky, and Hooded. Elusive Golden-winged Warblers sometimes nest just inside the entrance gate to the campground, particularly around picnic shelter 1. Other summer species include Downy Woodpecker, Hairy Woodpecker, Pileated Woodpecker, Eastern Wood-Pewee, Acadian Flycatcher, Great Crested Flycatcher, Northern Rough-winged Swallow, Blue Jay, American Crow, Carolina Chickadee, Tufted Titmouse, White-breasted Nuthatch, Carolina Wren, House Wren, Wood Thrush, American Robin, Gray Catbird,

Snow Bunting

Brown Thrasher, Cedar Waxwing, Solitary Vireo, Red-eyed Vireo, Scarlet Tanager, Northern Cardinal, Rose-breasted Grosbeak, Indigo Bunting, and American Goldfinch. During invasion winters, the park is sometimes good for Evening Grosbeak, Pine Siskin, and Purple Finch.

Continue south on TN 143 to **Twin Springs Recreation Area** (4,400 ft.)—a picnic ground in the Cherokee National Forest. This is a good spot for middle-elevation birding, where spring and summer birds include a mix of species noted at the state park and higher upslope on Roan. Least Flycatcher, Veery, and Black-throated Blue Warbler are among the summer birds here; and Barred Owls may be heard at night.

To get into the high country at Roan, proceed to **Carver's Gap** (5,512 ft.), which is on the North Carolina–Tennessee state line. The gap parking lot is 12.4 miles south on TN 143 from the US 19E junction in the town of Roan Mountain or 13 miles north of Bakersville, on NC 261. Although often crowded on weekends and during the peak rhododendron bloom, the gap is a good spot for spruce-fir birds, as well as those associated with grass balds and shrub thickets. Check the alder stands in late spring and summer for Alder Flycatchers, which have nested here in the past. Gray Catbirds, Common Yellowthroats, Rufous-sided Towhees, and an occasional Indigo Bunting are present in the tangled thickets and edges. Purple Finches are present erratically, and House Wrens have recently been

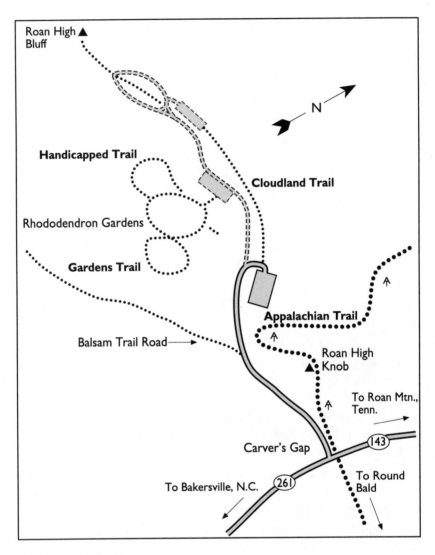

Roan Mountain, N.C.-Tenn.

found nesting at the gap. From late March through June, listen at night for Northern Saw-whet Owls in nearby spruce-fir forests. Around sunset in late March and April, the American Woodcock's aerial display has occasionally been seen in grassy areas around the gap. Red Crossbills are possible year-round, and Pine Siskins are occasionally reported. Evening Grosbeaks may occur during invasion winters, and even White-winged Crossbills have been observed. Spring and fall songbird migration is often dramatic, as large numbers pour across the gap. Dark-eyed Juncos are conspicuous all year.

Many high-country mountain ranges have interesting forest birds, but only the Roan has such an expanse of grass and shrub balds with their associated avifauna. From Carver's Gap, the northbound **Appalachian Trail** runs across this fascinating string of open summits, providing some unique birding experiences. If you are in prime condition, you might want to go all the way to Hump Mountain (5,587 ft.) at 7.8 miles from Carver's Gap, but most birders confine themselves to Round Bald (5,826 ft.) at 0.4 miles, Jane Bald (5,807 ft.) at 1.1 miles, and Grassy Ridge at 1.5 miles. Be sure and get a copy of the *Guide to the Appalachian Trail in Tennessee and North Carolina* if you plan any serious hiking here. In addition, bring topographic trail maps, a compass, and proper hiking equipment. Even in summer, the weather can become severe, and sudden fogs may obscure the trail and disorient the hiker, with disastrous results.

Begin by ascending from the gap to the summit of Round Bald. In late spring and summer, you should find American Robin, Cedar Waxwing, Chestnut-sided Warbler, Common Yellowthroat, Rufous-sided Towhee, and Dark-eyed Junco. Northern Bobwhites are occasionally heard, and be alert for Horned Lark and Vesper Sparrow, which are present in some years. Common Ravens may be noted flying over during any season.

The big attraction at Round Bald, however, is the possibility of seeing Snow Buntings, elusive and rare winter visitors from the far north. The buntings are most likely to be present from November through February, but they are not reported every year. Finding them requires considerable patience, persistence, and good luck. If you feel ambitious, you could also search farther north, as Snow Buntings have been found along the AT at Grassy Ridge Bald and Bradley Gap, 1.5 miles and 6.9 miles from Carver's Gap, respectively. Remember, however, that high-elevation roads may be treacherous or impassable in winter. Check with local authorities before heading up, and don't even think about hiking the AT without proper winter clothing and footgear.

After crossing Round Bald, descend the AT to Engine Gap at 0.7 miles and begin the ascent up Jane Bald. Be alert for Alder Flycatchers, which are present in the alder thickets along the trail from Jane Bald to Grassy Ridge Bald in late spring and summer. Also listen for House Wrens, which are sometimes heard here—a rather high elevation for these birds. At Grassy Ridge Bald, a spur trail leaves the AT and rambles through alder and rhododendron thickets across the bald, where you may find Alder Flycatcher and many of the species noted on Round Bald. Other birds here include Northern Flicker, Winter Wren, Veery, Gray Catbird, Canada Warbler, and Song Sparrow. From Grassy Ridge, you might want to retrace your route to Carver's Gap or explore farther along the AT before returning.

Roan's 850 acres of spruce-fir forests begin at Carver's Gap and extend west along the crest line beyond Roan High Bluff. The bird life in these coniferous woods can be sampled along four trails, of which the Rhododendron Gardens Trail includes segments specifically designed for wheelchair use. A popular hikers' route at the Roan includes the section of **Appalachian Trail** that begins at the gap parking lot and heads west to ascend the north side of **Roan High Knob**. At 1.3 miles from the gap, a spur trail takes off to the left from the AT for 0.1 miles to the top of the knob, an elevation change of about 775 feet from the gap. The camping shelter here is the highest anywhere on the AT. At 1.8 and 1.9 miles the AT comes close to two parking lots along the paved road that runs from the gap to the gardens, so one can arrange transportation or return down the road for a 3.5-mile loop, although walking along the shoulder can be noisy and dangerous, particularly on weekends. This portion of the AT can also be accessed by driving to the first parking lot at 1.6 miles from the gap and then searching for the trail near the site of the old Cloudland Hotel.

This section of AT on Roan High Knob is occasionally a good spot for Hermit Thrush, which was first reported summering here around 1979, as well as for Northern Saw-whet Owls, which are most often heard from late March through June. Other birds likely to be found from spring through summer include Common Raven, Red-breasted Nuthatch, Winter Wren, Golden-crowned Kinglet, Veery, American Robin, Cedar Waxwing, Solitary Vireo, Chestnut-sided Warbler, Canada Warbler, and Dark-eyed Junco. Watch for Brown Creepers anywhere there are dead or dying conifers. Ruffed Grouse may be encountered here and in other wooded areas year-round.

For a much easier stroll through spruce-fir woods, turn at Carver's Gap onto the paved Rhododendron Gardens Road and drive 1.0 mile to the metal-gated **Balsam Trail Road** on the left. There is barely enough room to get your car off the road here, so you may prefer to drive on to the first parking lot, 0.6 miles farther, and then walk carefully back on the roadway shoulder to the trailhead (5,900 ft.). This gravel jeep road descends only 200 feet in 2.5 miles as it swings around the southwest slope of Roan High Bluff. The wide openings provide good views of the birds, which are essentially the same as found on the AT over Roan High Knob. Watch also for Alder Flycatchers near a sharp horseshoe turn. Because most visitors are unaware of this road, it usually offers more solitude than any other hike at Roan.

The easiest, but most crowded, route is the **Rhododendron Gardens Trail**, a complex of three paved loops that wind through the magnificent Catawba rhododendron thickets along the crest between Roan High Knob and Roan High Bluff. Infiltrated by red spruce and mountain ash, the rhododendron gardens are a good spot for both heath bald and forest birds. The rhododendrons are usually at their peak bloom during the last two weeks of June, when the place can be packed with visitors, especially on weekends. The Gardens Trail begins at the second parking lot (6,200 ft.), 1.8 miles from Carver's Gap along the Rhododendron Gardens Road. One section of the trail is specifically designated for wheelchairs, but the other loops are also suitable in part for handicapped use. The trail complex is good in late spring and summer for Chimney Swift, Ruby-throated Hummingbird, Winter Wren, Golden-crowned Kinglet, Veery, American Robin, Gray Catbird, Cedar Waxwing, Solitary Vireo, Chestnut-sided Warbler, Black-throated Blue Warbler, Canada Warbler, Rufous-sided Towhee, and Dark-eyed Junco.

The final route for seeing these birds is the **Cloudland Trail**, an easy 3.0-mile round-trip hike that runs from the first parking lot on the Rhododendron Gardens Road (1.6 miles from Carver's Gap) to the summit of Roan High Bluff (6,267 ft.). The trail passes through spruce-fir forests, rhododendron thickets, and open grassy areas, with connections through parking lots 2 and 3 along the roadway. Most of the spring and summer species noted previously in the spruce-fir can be expected along this route. Watch for Magnolia Warblers, however, which have occasionally been noted around the loop road beyond the third parking lot.

If you arrive early or come on a weekday, you may also enjoy a birding walk along the garden road from parking lot 1 to the farthest point of the loop road, a round-trip distance of 1.5 miles. Before the crowds arrive, the parking lots can be a good spot for birding from wheelchairs, especially the flat paved area at lot 1.

Be alert for unexpected birds any time you visit the Roan. Wintering

Golden Eagles and a Northern Goshawk have been reported. Whimbrels have been seen on Round Bald, and Purple Finches and even a Ruby-crowned Kinglet have been noted irregularly in summer.

During the winter months, the Roan massif is among the most popular areas in the southern Appalachians for cross-country skiing, which is a great way to cover a lot of birding territory. Outfitters and organized expeditions are available locally. The Roan Mountain Naturalists' Rally (the weekend after Labor Day) and the Carter Country Wildflower Tours (first weekend in May) offer organized field trips to see birds, wildflowers, and other natural delights. For details, contact the Carter County Chamber of Commerce, Elizabethton, TN 37643.

Chimney Rock Park

Highlights: Autumn hawk migration, middle- and low-elevation summer
   birds; Peregrine Falcon nesting site.
Season: Spring through fall.
Access: Exit the BRP at M 384.7 onto US 74, near Asheville, N.C., and head
   east 20 miles to the junction with US 64; continue eastward on US 64/74
   for 3 miles to Chimney Rock Park. If coming from I-40, take the exit at
   M 63.8 near Black Mountain, head south on NC 9 for 16.5 miles to the
   junction with US 64 at Bat Cave, and continue on US 64 east for 2.4 miles
   to the park entrance.
Maps: USGS "Bat Cave," "Lake Lure."
Facilities: Contact Chimney Rock Park, P.O. Box 39, Chimney Rock, NC
   28720 (704-625-9611) for information. The park is closed during the winter months. Gasoline, food, camping, and accommodations are present at
   nearby Lake Lure and in the village of Chimney Rock, N.C.

The Blue Ridge crest abruptly changes direction at Black Mountain Gap and runs almost due south for 35 miles to Saluda Gap near the South Carolina–North Carolina line. Located at the midpoint of this east-facing section of the Blue Ridge, Chimney Rock Park is a 1,000-acre scenic and natural preserve where the Rocky Broad River carves its way through Hickory Nut Gorge. The dominant geographic feature is Chimney Rock, a spectacular granite monolith that rises over 300 feet on the south flank of the gorge. Nearby Hickory Nut Falls plunges some 400 feet in a beautiful cascade. With elevations ranging from about 1,100 to 2,800 feet, the park is home in summer to a diversified mixture of low- and middle-elevation birds. One major attraction is the presence of Peregrine Falcons, which began nesting here in 1990 following efforts to reestablish the species as a breeding bird in the southern Blue Ridge.

Principle habitats include floodplain, cove hardwood, and oak forests, often with thick understories of rhododendron, dogwood, and various shrubs. Birding is easy here, with parking lots, overlooks, picnic areas, and three trails providing access to the birds. Get a park map, trail brochures, plant list, and Simon Thompson's "Birds of Chimney Rock Park" at the Nature Center or Sky Lounge before starting your explorations. Remember that an entrance fee is required for admission; consider a season pass if you plan to visit several times in a year.

Begin by checking the area along the **Rocky Broad River** (1,060 ft.) around the bridge near the park entrance gate. Drive 0.1 miles beyond the bridge, park in the office lot on the right, and walk carefully back to the river edge. Belted Kingfisher, Northern Parula, Yellow Warbler, Yellow-throated Warbler, and Louisiana Waterthrush are possible here. Return to your car and drive to **The Meadows** (1,400 ft.), an open picnic and recreation area on the left at 1.4 miles from the park entrance. Explore the pines and mixed forests adjacent to The Meadows in late spring and summer for Pine Warbler, Summer Tanager, and Chipping Sparrow. Good birding is also possible near the picnic tables along the road for about 0.3 miles above and below The Meadows.

Proceed along the road to the parking lot on the left at 2.7 miles from the entrance gate. Park your car and walk back down the road for 0.1 miles to the well-marked trailhead for the **Forest Stroll Self-guided Nature Trail** (1,500 ft.), a particularly interesting bird hike that runs 0.7 miles to the base of Hickory Nut Falls. This easy route climbs about 200 feet as it wanders through a forest of oak, hickory, maple, tuliptrees, basswood, and rhododendrons. Sheltered by the high north-facing cliffs of Chimney Rock Mountain, this trail is perhaps the lowest elevation at which Dark-eyed Juncos occur in the Blue Ridge during the breeding season. Other birds typical of middle to high elevations include Solitary Vireo, Chestnut-sided Warbler, Black-throated Blue Warbler, and Canada Warbler, all of which are occasionally present here in late spring and summer. The trail is also a good route for Swainson's Warblers, which inhabit the rhododendron thickets.

Other birds found during the nesting season include Ruby-throated Hummingbird, Red-bellied Woodpecker, Downy Woodpecker, Hairy Woodpecker, Northern Flicker, Pileated Woodpecker, Eastern Wood-Pewee, Acadian Flycatcher, Eastern Phoebe, Great Crested Flycatcher, Blue Jay, Carolina Chickadee, Tufted Titmouse, White-breasted Nuthatch, Carolina Wren, Blue-gray Gnatcatcher, Wood Thrush, American Robin, Yellow-throated Vireo, Red-eyed Vireo, Black-throated Green Warbler, Cerulean Warbler, Black-and-white Warbler, American Redstart, Worm-eating Warbler, Ovenbird, Louisiana Waterthrush, Scarlet Tanager, Northern Cardinal, Indigo Bunting, and Rufous-sided Towhee.

Some of these species can also be observed along the edges of the parking lots, particularly if you arrive early or come during the week, when the park is less crowded. Cerulean Warblers are usually present in spring and summer and have nested in the tall trees just below the parking lot (1,965 ft.) at the chimney. Chestnut-sided Warblers have been noted here in a stand of scrubby second growth. Common Ravens have a predilection for this area as well—a rather low elevation for this species. Before heading to the top of Chimney Rock, visit the Nature Center next to the parking lot at 2.8 miles from the entrance gate; attractive displays here interpret the natural and human history of the region.

The park's other two trails provide good birding and superb scenery. The **Skyline Trail** and the **Cliff Trail** converge near the top of Hickory Nut Falls, permitting a loop hike of 1.5 miles. Park in the lot at the end of the road, 2.9 miles from the entrance gate, and take the elevator to the Sky Lounge. After checking the view from Chimney Rock, continue up the wooden steps and switchbacks and then along Skyline Trail's high cliffs for a 0.9-mile hike to the falls. From there the Cliff Trail begins its 0.6-mile descent along the steep precipice back to the parking area. With the open vistas, one may see Black Vulture, Turkey Vulture, Broad-winged Hawk, Red-tailed Hawk, Northern Rough-winged Swallow, and Common Raven. Forest species include Eastern Phoebe, Blue Jay, Carolina Chickadee, Tufted Titmouse, Carolina Wren, American Robin, Northern Cardinal, Rufous-sided Towhee, and Dark-eyed Junco. Chestnut-sided and Canada Warblers occur higher up on the mountainside.

Peregrine Falcons have nested above the **Rock Pile**, which is easily visible from a number of observation points. Contact the park naturalist for information about the status of the birds before planning a trip here to see them. This has been the most readily accessible of all Peregrine nesting sites in the southern Blue Ridge, and excellent views are often possible. The birds are most active from late March to mid-May and again from early to mid-summer, when the young have hatched.

In September and October, the summit of **Chimney Rock** (2,280 ft.) and the adjacent overlook area provide an outstanding perspective for watching the autumn hawk migration. Sharp-shinned, Cooper's, Red-shouldered, and Broad-winged Hawks are among the species typically expected. The overlook next to the chimney is wheelchair accessible; just take the elevator to the Sky Lounge and head out along the paved path for good views of the hawks.

Unicoi Mountains

Highlights: Low- to middle-elevation summer birds, old-growth and virgin hardwood forests.

Season: Spring through fall.

Access: If coming from the BRP, exit at Balsam Gap (M 443.1) on US 74 and go west 51 miles, past Sylva, N.C., and Bryson City, N.C., to Topton, N.C., where the junction with US 129 is on the right; turn onto US 129 north and proceed for 10 miles to Robbinsville, N.C. If coming from Tennessee, exit I-40 and I-75 at Knoxville and go south on US 129 for 76 often winding miles to Robbinsville or exit I-75 at TN 68 and head east to Tellico Plains, Tenn., and the Scenic Highway.

Maps: USGS "Big Junction," "Santeetlah Creek," "Tapoco," "Whiteoak Flats"; USFS "Joyce Kilmer–Slickrock Wilderness and Citico Creek Wilderness," "Nantahala National Forest," "Snowbird Area Trail Map."

Facilities: Gasoline, food, and accommodation in Robbinsville; campgrounds in Nantahala and Cherokee national forests.

The Unicoi Mountains are renowned for some of the most beautiful scenery and spectacular forests in the Blue Ridge Province. Although much of the region was heavily logged in the early twentieth century, several outstanding tracts of virgin and old-growth timber escaped the axe and are now protected in wilderness areas. Grass balds are present on some high peaks, but most of the upper slopes are covered with northern hardwoods. Oak forests cloak middle and lower ridges, while cove hardwoods occur in adjacent coves and ravines. With its diversity of elevation and vegetation, the range is home to a variety of birds, which can be seen along the excellent network of roads and hiking trails.

Located southwest of the Great Smokies, the Unicois are the southernmost range of the Unaka chain, which forms the western boundary of the Blue Ridge Province from Virginia to Georgia. The range begins at the Little Tennessee River gorge and runs along the North Carolina state line before meandering into east Tennessee to its terminus near the Hiwassee River—a total span of about 45 miles. A curious topographic feature of the Unicois is that many of the range's tallest peaks are not on the main crest line but are located on numerous ridges that run eastward from the divide. These high ridges enclose a number of streams, such as Santeetlah Creek and Slickrock Creek—all tributaries of the Cheoah River. The western slopes are drained by Citico Creek and other streams in the Tennessee River basin. Elevations vary from around 1,000 feet in the western valleys to 5,580 feet on the summit of Huckleberry Knob, while a half-dozen other named mountains exceed 5,000 feet. The Snowbird Mountains, a minor transverse range, connect with the Unicois near Laurel Top (5,317 ft.), just south of the Tellico Plains–Robbinsville Scenic Highway.

Much of the range is incorporated into Nantahala and Cherokee national forests, and 32,904 acres are protected in Joyce Kilmer–Slickrock Wilderness and Citico Creek Wilderness. Although the area is somewhat remote, the journey is worthwhile for those who like to combine birds, botany, and scenery. Forest Service and state routes provide easy roadside birding, and the backcountry can be sampled along more than 150 miles of trails.

To begin exploring the range, drive north for 1.4 miles on US 129 from its junction with NC 143 in Robbinsville and turn left onto NC SR 1116. Proceed 1.1 miles on state road 1116 to the Cheoah Ranger Station, where you can obtain maps, brochures, and the latest information on the status of trails and roads. Before heading on into the high country, you might want to check some spots along nearby **Santeetlah Lake** (1,940 ft.), an impoundment on the Cheoah River. The boating access just across from the ranger station may have Osprey in April and Spotted Sandpiper in spring and summer. Great Horned Owls have been reported calling here in winter.

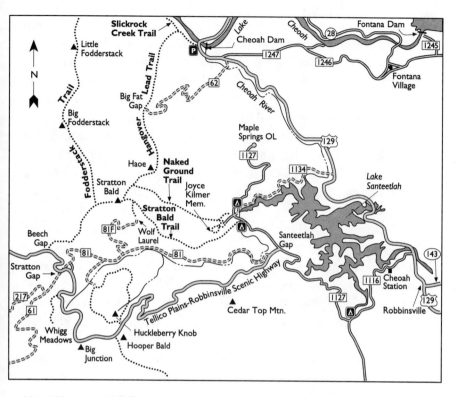

Unicoi Mountains, N.C.-Tenn.

Continue on state road 1116 for 3.5 miles from US 129 to the junction with state road 1127. Turn right onto state road 1127, be careful to take the right fork after 2.0 miles, and go a total of 4.4 miles on state road 1127 to the bridge over West Buffalo Prong of Santeetlah Lake. Park beyond the bridge and walk along state road 1127 an additional 100 to 150 yards, where a shallow cove may have waterfowl and shorebirds during migration. Check the flats for American Pipit in winter and watch for Red Crossbills in the pines. During the breeding season, Green-backed Heron and Prothonotary Warbler have been observed here. Also walk back across the bridge and explore parts of NC SR 1148 along the cove's other side.

For high-country birds, continue on state road 1127 to Santeetlah Gap (2,660 ft.), at 6.9 miles from the junction with state road 1116. Turn left onto the paved road at the gap and proceed a short distance to FSR 81, which drops off to the right before ascending 10.8 miles up the basin of Little Santeetlah Creek to the main crest line of the Unicois at Stratton

Meadows (4,320 ft.). Following close by the creek for much of its journey, FSR 81 passes through cove and oak forests in low and middle elevations and through northern hardwoods along its upper reaches. Hemlock stands are common, and rosebay rhododendron forms a dense understory in many areas. Pull offs and side roads provide opportunities to stop for roadside birding or for a stroll back into the woods.

At Stratton Meadows, FSR 81 connects with Tellico Plains–Robbinsville Scenic Highway. Scheduled for completion in the mid-1990s, this route will eventually run 16.5 miles from Stratton Meadows back down to FSR 81 at Santeetlah Gap. By driving the two roads, birders will have a 27-mile loop that gives easy access to a variety of habitats typical of the Unicoi Mountains. Many excellent trails for backcountry birding begin along this route.

Birds found along FSR 81 in late spring and summer include Ruffed Grouse, Yellow-billed Cuckoo, Eastern Screech-Owl, Barred Owl, Ruby-throated Hummingbird, Downy Woodpecker, Pileated Woodpecker, Eastern Wood-Pewee, Acadian Flycatcher, Great Crested Flycatcher, Blue Jay, Carolina Chickadee, Tufted Titmouse, White-breasted Nuthatch, Winter Wren, Veery, Wood Thrush, American Robin, Solitary Vireo, Red-eyed Vireo, Scarlet Tanager, Northern Cardinal, Rose-breasted Grosbeak, Rufous-sided Towhee, Dark-eyed Junco, and American Goldfinch. Warblers are heavily represented, including Northern Parula, Chestnut-sided Warbler, Black-throated Blue Warbler, Black-throated Green Warbler, Blackburnian Warbler, Black-and-white Warbler, Ovenbird, Louisiana Waterthrush, Hooded Warbler, and Canada Warbler. Brown Creeper and Cerulean Warbler may be found in small numbers. Check the hemlocks at Stratton Meadows for Red-breasted Nuthatches, which are present some years. Beyond Stratton Meadows, the dirt road continues as FSR 217, which may be worth exploring for many of the same birds. Check FSR 61-A and FSR 61, the latter turning off FSR 217 about 1 mile west of Stratton Meadows and providing a potential site for Yellow-bellied Sapsuckers near its junction with FSR 61-A.

From its junction with FSR 81 at Stratton Meadows, the **Tellico Plains–Robbinsville Scenic Highway** runs north for 1.5 miles to Beech Gap before descending westward for 23 miles to Tellico Plains. In the opposite direction, the highway heads south just below the main crest of the Unicois past Whigg Meadow and Haw Knob (5,472 ft.) to Big Junction, where the road turns east along the high ridge to Hooper Bald (5,429 ft.) and Patrick

Meadows (4,760 ft.), before descending back to Santeetlah Gap. This section is reminiscent of the Blue Ridge Parkway, with sweeping curves, wide shoulders, many pull offs, and some grand views. Northern hardwood forests and high oak woodlands cover adjacent ridges and slopes, while grassy balds and meadows are scattered along the crest. The Forest Service plans to build new side paths from some overlooks, and trailheads will be established so the old network of high-country trails can be accessed from the road.

Stop at overlooks on the scenic highway and walk along the shoulder or back into the woods, where you may find Hairy Woodpecker, Northern Flicker, Winter Wren, Veery, American Robin, Catbird, Cedar Waxwing, Solitary Vireo, Chestnut-sided Warbler, Black-throated Blue Warbler, Blackburnian Warbler, Black-and-white Warbler, Canada Warbler, Rose-breasted Grosbeak, Rufous-sided Towhee, and Dark-eyed Junco. Be alert for Yellow-bellied Sapsuckers and Least Flycatchers in open woodlands. In grassy, disturbed, open areas and their adjacent forest edges, watch also for Northern Bobwhite, House Wren, Indigo Bunting, and Song Sparrow—species that have invaded the high elevations following disruption of the forest canopy.

Worthwhile side treks from the scenic highway include a stroll to Whigg Meadow (4,960 ft.), located on the southwest slope of Little Haw Knob south of Stratton Meadows. Least Flycatcher and House Wren are often noted, and Golden Eagles have been observed here on more than one occasion. The trail begins as a jeep road at Mud Gap (4,500 ft.), 1.9 miles from the junction with FSR 81. Birders can get a good look at forest birds along this easy-to-moderate 1.8-mile hike.

Also explore Hooper Bald (5,429 ft.), about 6 miles south of Stratton Meadows, and consider a hike from there north to Huckleberry Knob, highest peak in the Unicoi Mountains, or a hike south on the trail to King Meadows. Many of these routes and spots are currently shown on the USFS "Snowbird Area Trail Map," but check with the Forest Service to determine the location of trailheads and trail conditions once the scenic highway is completed.

After exploring this part of the high country, return to Santeetlah Gap, turn left, and proceed on state road 1127 for 6.8 miles to the road's end at **Maple Springs Observation Area** (3,400 ft.). Beginning at the parking lot, a paved, flat trail crosses a wooden bridge and runs in a 250-yard loop through oak and hemlock woods with a rhododendron understory.

Black-throated Blue Warbler

At the loop's far end, a wooden platform affords a grand view of the Smokies, the Nantahalas, and the Little Tennessee River valley. The entire trail is well suited for wheelchair access. Typical middle-elevation summer birds can be expected here and along the road, including Turkey Vulture, Broad-winged Hawk, Red-tailed Hawk, Downy Woodpecker, Pileated Woodpecker, Eastern Wood-Pewee, Great Crested Flycatcher, Blue Jay, Carolina Chickadee, Tufted Titmouse, White-breasted Nuthatch, Wood Thrush, American Robin, Solitary Vireo, Red-eyed Vireo, Northern Parula, Chestnut-sided Warbler, Black-throated Blue Warbler, Blackburnian Warbler, Black-and-white Warbler, Ovenbird, Hooded Warbler, Scarlet Tanager, Rose-breasted Grosbeak, Indigo Bunting, Song Sparrow, Dark-eyed Junco, and American Goldfinch.

To complete the roadside birding routes of the Unicois, head back south on state road 1127 from Maple Springs for 4.6 miles to the intersection with FSR 416 and NC SR 1134. If you are coming from the opposite direction on state road 1127, this intersection is 2.2 miles from Santeetlah Gap. The magnificent Joyce Kilmer Memorial Forest is accessed on a trail from the parking lot at the end of FSR 416—a hike described later in this chapter. Two nearby campgrounds are often good birding spots for spring migration and low-elevation summer residents. Rattler Ford group campground (2,080 ft.) lies along Santeetlah Creek 0.3 miles south of the intersection on state road 1127, and Horse Cove campground is 0.2 miles from the intersection on state road 1134.

Turn onto NC SR 1134 and proceed 4.6 miles to the spot where a water conduit and power lines cross the road and the nearby Cheoah River. Check the saplings and scrubby growth along the Cheoah for White-eyed Vireo, Common Yellowthroat, and Yellow-breasted Chat. Green-backed Herons are sometimes present along the river edge in summer. Continue on to the junction with US 129, at 5.9 miles from state road 1127. Turn left and proceed north on US 129 for 5.8 miles to FSR 62. Pull offs along the Cheoah provide spots that may be worth checking in migration and during the summer.

Turn left from US 129 onto FSR 62, which runs 7.1 miles to Big Fat Gap (3,060 ft.). Park immediately after the turn and walk carefully along the shoulder of US 129 for 100 yards north to the confluence of Barker Creek and the Cheoah River (1,260 ft.), where Swainson's Warblers are sometimes present in rhododendron thickets. Return to the car and drive 1.4 miles up FSR 62 to another rhododendron tangle, where Swainson's are often found. Stop at promising spots all along FSR 62 for many late-spring and summer birds listed previously for FSR 81 and state road 1127. Several good birding trails begin at Big Fat Gap for access into the high country and to Joyce Kilmer–Slickrock Wilderness.

Perhaps the best bird-watching in the Unicois is along the many hiking paths that wander through the backcountry and the wilderness areas. Trails run along the main crest line, along several of the high ridges, and through many stream basins and valleys. Some thirty-five trails form an interconnected network of easy-to-strenuous routes, whose total distance exceeds 150 miles. Be sure to get a copy of Homan's *Hiking Trails of Joyce Kilmer–Slickrock and Citico Creek Wilderness Areas*, which provides detailed and highly readable descriptions of the trails, including notes on the human and natural history of each route. Also bring along a copy of the USFS topographic trail maps "Joyce Kilmer–Slickrock Wilderness and Citico Creek Wilderness" and "Snowbird Area Trail Map."

On the Tennessee side, **Falls Branch Trail** is an easy-to-moderate 1.3-mile hike through a spectacular forest of old-growth virgin hemlock and hardwoods in Citico Creek Wilderness. The trail begins at Rattlesnake Rock OL (4,000 ft.) on the Tellico Plains–Robbinsville Scenic Highway about 3 miles west of the junction with FSR 81 at Stratton Meadows or 8 miles east of the turnoff to Indian Boundary Recreation Area. Between 0.5 miles and 0.9 miles from the parking lot, the trail passes through the ancient forest, where in late spring and summer one may find Red-breasted Nuthatch, Golden-crowned Kinglet, Blackburnian Warbler, and many species noted along FSR 81. The route is somewhat more difficult in the last 0.4 miles to the waterfall (3,520 ft.).

The easiest and certainly most spectacular recommended hike is the 2.0-mile **Joyce Kilmer National Recreation Trail**, a double loop route through a virgin forest that many consider to be the finest example of its kind in the United States. The trail features giant hemlocks and groves of tuliptrees more than 150 feet tall and approaching 20 feet in circumference. Portions of the route, particularly along Little Santeetlah Creek, have a thick understory of rhododendron, and the spring wildflower display is outstanding. Unfortunately, the extremely high canopy makes it difficult to see many birds, so you may prefer to concentrate on botany here.

The parking lot (2,240 ft.) for the trail is at the end of the 0.5-mile FSR 416, which starts from NC SR 1127 at 2.2 miles north of Santeetlah Gap. The lower loop climbs to 2,520 feet, where the Joyce Kilmer memorial plaque is located, while the upper loop continues up to 2,640 feet, passing through the magnificent cove hardwood forest in Poplar Cove. Winter Wrens have been observed near the Kilmer plaque, a rather low elevation for these retiring little skulkers. Other birds noted in late spring and summer include Downy Woodpecker, Tufted Titmouse, Wood Thrush, Solitary Vireo, Red-eyed Vireo, Northern Parula, Black-throated Blue Warbler, Black-throated Green Warbler, Blackburnian Warbler, Black-and-white Warbler, Worm-eating Warbler, Ovenbird, Louisiana Waterthrush, Hooded Warbler, and Scarlet Tanager. Brown Creepers and Golden-crowned Kinglets may be present but are usually hard to hear and impossible to see in the upper canopy.

A number of moderate-to-strenuous trails provide access to the summit of **Bob Stratton Bald** (5,400 ft.), a popular hiking and birding destination. The routes vary considerably in length, difficulty, and vegetation, so study Homan's hiking guide and the Forest Service maps carefully in planning your hike. Because the trails all converge in the high country, it is easy to design a variety of loop routes that minimize or avoid retracing your steps. All these routes are excellent for bird-watching.

For those who are in good physical condition and willing to spend most of the day walking, a good choice is to combine the Naked Ground Trail, Haoe Lead Trail, and Stratton Bald Trail in a 13.2-mile circuit with a 3,300-foot elevation change. During the nesting season, this hike will provide an opportunity to observe most species listed previously for FSR 81, the Tellico Plains–Robbinsville Scenic Highway, and the Maple Springs Observation Area—a cross section of middle- and high-elevation birds of the Unicois.

Begin by parking at Rattler Ford campground, 1.9 miles north of Santeetlah Gap on NC SR 1127. Walk across the Santeetlah Creek bridge (2,080 ft.) and take the **Stratton Bald Trail**, which runs along Horse Cove Ridge and passes through the upper bowl of Poplar Cove's virgin hardwood tract in Joyce Kilmer forest. The trail runs through a variety of plant communities before arriving on the summit of Bob Stratton Bald at 7.2 miles from Rattler Ford. The bald was established by human activity and is currently maintained by the Forest Service. The trail continues westward and is often worth exploring beyond the bald.

For the return trek, walk back down the trail for 0.8 miles from the peak to Haoe Lead Trail, which comes in on the left; turn onto the trail and descend 0.6 miles to the gap at Naked Ground (4,860 ft.), where the **Naked Ground Trail** comes in from the right. Turn onto Naked Ground Trail, which descends 4.3 miles through Little Santeetlah Creek basin to the parking lot on FSR 416 near its junction with state road 1127. This trail passes through the beautiful virgin woodlands of the Joyce Kilmer Forest, with huge old tuliptrees, hemlocks, oaks, white pine, and maples. From the trailhead parking lot on FSR 416, walk carefully along the shoulder of state road 1127 for 0.3 miles south to Rattler Ford campground and your car.

The easiest access to Stratton Bald is by driving up FSR 81 for 6.8 miles from NC SR 1127 at Santeetlah Gap and turning right onto FSR 81-F, which winds for 4.5 miles to a parking area at Wolf Laurel Basin (4,560 ft.). From here Wolf Laurel Trail runs 0.7 miles to connect with Stratton Bald

Trail (4,880 ft.); turn left onto Stratton Bald Trail, climb 0.6 miles to the junction with Haoe Lead Trail, and continue from there for 0.8 miles to the peak. One final route is by continuing all the way up FSR 81 to Stratton Meadows, heading 1.5 miles north on the Tellico Plains–Robbinsville Scenic Highway to Beech Gap (4,480 ft.), and taking FSR 217-H along the Unicoi's main crest for 1.8 miles to Fodderstack Trailhead. Fodderstack Trail goes 1.1 miles to its junction with the terminus of Stratton Bald Trail; turn right onto the trail and go 0.4 miles to the bald.

The other recommended high-country hike is **Hangover Lead Trail,** which heads south from Big Fat Gap (3,060 ft.) for 2.5 miles to Saddle Tree Gap (5,100 ft.), where a 0.2-mile spur trail runs through Catawba rhododendron thickets to open cliffs at the Hangover (5,180 ft.). The view from the Hangover is exceptional. The main trail continues south for 0.3 miles to the Haoe summit (5,249 ft.). The hike from Big Fat Gap to the Hangover often has Common Raven, in addition to most birds listed previously for high-country hikes to Bob Stratton Bald. For access to the trailhead, drive to Big Fat Gap, at the end of FSR 62, as described previously.

Nantahala Mountains

Highlights: Middle- to high-elevation forest birds; Yellow-bellied Sapsucker, Golden-winged Warbler.

Season: Spring through fall.

Access: From the BRP, exit at Balsam Gap (M 443.1) and go 14 miles south on US 74 to the junction with US 441; turn south on US 441 and continue 24 miles to the junction with US 64 near Franklin, N.C.; turn west onto US 64 toward the Nantahalas. Alternatively, exit at the BRP terminus (M 469) and head south on US 441 through Cherokee, N.C., and continue on to Franklin, a total of 40 miles.

Maps: USGS "Prentiss," "Rainbow Springs," "Shooting Creek," "Topton," "Wayah Bald," "Wesser"; USFS "Southern Nantahala Wilderness and Standing Indian Basin," "Nantahala National Forest," "Appalachian Trail— Nantahala National Forest."

Facilities: Gasoline, food, and accommodations in Franklin. Camping at

Standing Indian campground and information at the USFS Backcountry
Information Center, both on FSR 67.

The Nantahalas are among the most interesting but least-visited
birding areas in the North Carolina mountains. Southernmost of the great
transverse mountain chains, the range extends northward from its Blue
Ridge junction near the North Carolina–Georgia line for twenty-five miles
to its terminus near Fontana Lake. The steep, rugged slopes are drained
by the Little Tennessee River on the east and the Nantahala River on the
west. Numerous peaks along the main crest exceed 5,000 feet, with the
highest elevation at Winespring Bald (5,445 ft.), near the range's midpoint.
At the Nantahala's southern end, the Standing Indian Basin forms a great
horseshoe-shaped valley, surrounded by a rim of high peaks that enclose
the headwaters of the Nantahala River. Some 24,515 acres along this high
south rim have been incorporated into the Southern Nantahala Wilderness,
and the U.S. Forest Service owns a large portion of the remaining land.

A "life zone" map in the 1919 edition of *Birds of North Carolina*, by
T. G. Pearson, H. H. Brimley, and C. S. Brimley, shows so-called Canadian
zone forests covering portions of the Nantahalas, but most botanists doubt
that spruce-fir forests ever existed here during historical times. The high
portions of the range are now cloaked in northern hardwood forests, prin-
cipally of birch, beech, and maples. Grassy openings and heath balds are
present locally. Oak and cove forests occur at middle and low elevations,
and hemlock is a prominent canopy species in ravines and north-facing
slopes. The range has been extensively logged in the past, and much of the
land is presently managed by the Forest Service for commercial timber production. Although certain tree-harvesting practices remain controversial,
the result is often a more diversified bird population, due to the increased
variety of vegetation and successional stages.

Some of the best birding is in the central third of the Nantahalas, particularly the area west and north of Wayah Gap. Head west on US 64 for
3.7 miles from the junction with US 23/441 near Franklin; turn right onto
NC SR 1422; go 0.2 miles to NC SR 1310; turn left onto state road 1310 and
proceed 9.0 miles to Wayah Gap (4,160 ft.). To explore the main crest
line of the high Nantahalas, turn right onto FSR 69 at Wayah Gap and
drive north 4.6 miles to the road's dead end at Wayah Bald (5,342 ft.),
where a tower affords a superb view of the Great Smokies, the Unicois,

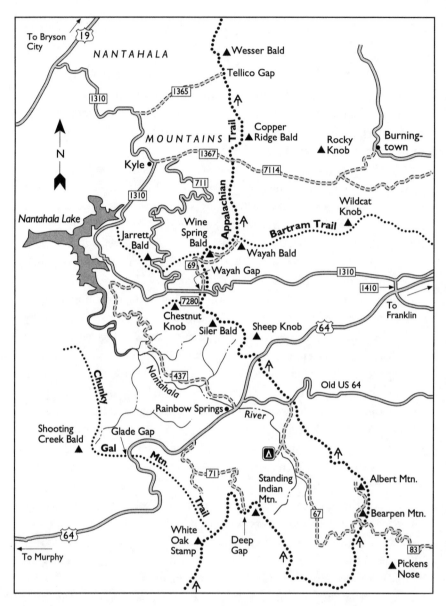

Nantahala Mountains, N.C.

and the valleys of the Nantahala and Little Tennessee rivers. This smooth dirt road passes through northern hardwood forests and azalea stands. You can bird from the car, get out and stroll along the roadway, or hike down the gated side roads that leave FSR 69 at 0.1 and 1.4 miles. Other walking opportunities are on stretches of the AT, which crosses the road at several points, and at Wilson Lick Historical Site. Typical late-spring and summer birds include Ruffed Grouse, Hairy Woodpecker, White-breasted Nuthatch, Winter Wren, Veery, Solitary Vireo, Chestnut-sided Warbler, Black-throated Blue Warbler, Black-and-white Warbler, Ovenbird, Canada Warbler, Scarlet Tanager, Rose-breasted Grosbeak, and Dark-eyed Junco. Be alert for Yellow-bellied Sapsuckers, which have nested along the road in past years.

At 3.4 miles from state road 1310, FSR 69-B leaves FSR 69 and runs 0.6 miles to the summit of Winespring Bald, highest peak in the Nantahalas. The red spruce around the summit appear to have been planted there, but that doesn't seem to bother the Golden-crowned Kinglets and Red-breasted Nuthatches that are present in some years. The section of road from Winespring Bald to Wayah tower is more open than the first 3 miles, with extensive azalea thickets, where likely spring and summer birds are Gray Catbird, Chestnut-sided Warbler, Rufous-sided Towhee, Song Sparrow, and Dark-eyed Junco. The Bartram Trail crosses the range here, providing good birding hikes down the east and west slopes.

Retrace the route to Wayah Gap, turn right onto state road 1310, and immediately turn left into Wayah Crest picnic grounds. Park the car and bird the area on foot, either by walking down the adjacent FSR 7280, which wanders back into the high country, or by taking the nearby Appalachian Trail south. Most of the same species found along FSR 69 will be present here.

Exit the picnic grounds, turn left, and proceed west on NC SR 1310, which winds for 19 miles down to the Nantahala River before ending at US 19. Pull completely off the road at various spots in the first 3.5 miles on state road 1310 west of Wayah Gap, where you can walk the shoulder and check the beautiful northern hardwoods, hemlocks, and rhododendron thickets along Jarrett Creek. In addition to many species noted previously on FSR 69, this area may yield Downy Woodpecker, Wood Thrush, Northern Parula, and Blackburnian Warbler.

At 1.6 miles west of Wayah Gap on state road 1310, you can turn right

Golden-winged Warbler

onto FSR 711, a paved route that rambles along the Nantahala's west flank for 15.1 miles to Kyle (3,216 ft.). This route traverses one of the best areas in the Blue Ridge Mountains for Golden-winged Warblers, as well as a variety of high- and middle-elevation nesting species. Stop frequently, listen, and walk along the shoulder for good views of the bird life. The road receives very little use, so birders often have it all to themselves in the early morning hours.

FSR 711 passes over McDonald Ridge and Rocky Bald Ridge at elevations approaching 5,000 feet. The route runs through areas where logging has produced considerable heterogeneity in the age and species composition of the forest. Most birds found in northern hardwood forests along FSR 69 to Wayah Bald are also present along FSR 711. In addition, Golden-winged Warblers may occur in spots where early- to medium-aged deciduous trees cover the hillsides. Yellow-bellied Sapsuckers are sometimes found in old, open woodlands, especially near the margins of recently cleared areas or where dead trees are present. This route is also excellent for Barred Owl, Eastern Screech-Owl, and Great Horned Owl. At 2.5 miles after leaving state road 1310, the road passes through Sawmill Gap, where the Bartram Trail crosses the road; the Bartram Trail from here back to Wayah Bald is particularly good for birding.

Other late-spring and summer species include Turkey Vulture, Eastern Wood-Pewee, Acadian Flycatcher, Eastern Phoebe, Northern Rough-winged Swallow, Barn Swallow, American Crow, Carolina Wren, Wood Thrush, American Robin, Gray Catbird, Brown Thrasher, Cedar Waxwing, Red-eyed Vireo, Northern Parula, Yellow Warbler, Chestnut-sided Warbler, Black-throated Blue Warbler, Blackburnian Warbler, Black-and-white Warbler, American Redstart, Ovenbird, Louisiana Waterthrush, Hooded Warbler, Canada Warbler, Scarlet Tanager, Northern Cardinal, Indigo Bunting, Rufous-sided Towhee, Field Sparrow, Song Sparrow, Dark-eyed Junco, and American Goldfinch.

From Kyle, you can continue on state road 1310 for 8 miles along the Nantahala River to US 19 for many of these same species, although this area receives very heavy recreational use during the summer. To get into the northern end of the Nantahalas, continue on state road 1310 for 3.0 miles beyond Kyle to NC SR 1365, which runs 4.1 miles to Tellico Gap (3,850 ft.), where you can park and catch the AT north for 1.4 miles to the summit of Wesser Bald (4,627 ft.) or south for 9.8 miles to Wayah Bald.

To explore the southern end of the Nantahalas and the adjacent Blue

Ridge, head west on US 64 for 11.8 miles beyond the US 64 junction with US 23/441 at Franklin; turn left onto old US 64 and proceed 1.8 miles to FSR 67. Turn right onto FSR 67, which runs along the upper portion of the Nantahala River, ascends the south rim of Standing Indian Basin, and ends at Albert Mountain, 11.8 miles from the junction with old US 64. This route is outstanding for roadside birding, with numerous pull offs and trailhead parking lots. The Standing Indian campground (3,400 ft.) is a good birding spot as well, although it can be quite noisy soon after sunrise. Many of the birds listed previously for state road 1310 and FSR 711 are found along this route.

For birders who want to get away into the backcountry, a network of Forest Service trails provides a wide selection of hikes from FSR 67 to the high country of the Southern Nantahala Wilderness. Most of these trails connect with the AT, which skirts the high south rim for 21 miles from Deep Gap to Wallace Gap on US 64. Stop at the Backcountry Information Center, just across from Standing Indian campground on FSR 67, for current trail information from the Forest Service. Read the Appalachian Trail guidebook and de Hart's *North Carolina Hiking Trails* for detailed accounts of these routes, and study the USFS map "Southern Nantahala Wilderness and Standing Indian Basin" for topographic features.

For easy access to the high country, continue on FSR 67 for 9.7 miles from old US 64 to the junction with FSR 83; turn right onto FSR 83 and proceed about 0.5 miles to the crest line at Mooney Gap, where the AT crosses the road. Hike north toward Albert Mountain (5,200 ft.) or south toward Ridgepole Mountain (5,000 ft.) on the AT from Mooney Gap for many of the bird species noted previously along FSR 69 between Wayah Gap and Wayah Bald. Another interesting hike with the same birds is the **Pickens Nose Trail**, which begins along FSR 83 on the right 0.7 miles east of Mooney Gap. This easy 0.7-mile one-way hike heads to a spectacular view from Pickens Nose (5,000 ft.).

Another good route for high-country birding is to take FSR 71, which turns left from US 64 at 2.2 miles west of the junction with old US 64. FSR 71 winds for 6.5 miles to Deep Gap (4,340 ft.), with excellent roadside birding along the route. Park at Deep Gap and hike the AT north for 2.5 miles to the 0.2-mile side spur trail to the summit of Standing Indian (5,499 ft.), the sentinel peak of the southern Blue Ridge. Alternatively, head south from Deep Gap on the AT for 2.9 miles to the junction with Chunky Gal Trail (4,700 ft.), which runs 5.2 miles to US 64 at Glade Gap, located 17.2

miles west of Franklin. Both these routes are excellent for middle-elevation species, including many birds listed for FSR 69 and state road 1310.

Hiwassee River Basin

Highlights: Low-elevation species; Blue-winged Warbler.

Season: Year-round, but mainly spring through summer.

Access: From the BRP, exit at Balsam Gap (M 443.1) and head west on US 74 for 76 miles to Murphy, N.C.

Maps: USGS "Isabella," "Murphy," "Nottely Dam," "Persimmon Creek."

Facilities: Gasoline, food, and accommodations at Murphy, N.C., and Blairs-ville, Ga.; camping at Pottete Creek Recreation Area.

Southernmost of the interior valleys in the Blue Ridge Province, the Hiwassee River basin encompasses about 1,200 square miles in the extreme southwestern corner of North Carolina and portions of adjacent Georgia. Much of the region consists of a broad river valley surrounded by gently undulating hills and ridges, which have been extensively cleared for settlement and cultivation. A mixture of Piedmont and montane birds occurs, but the major attraction has been the Blue-winged Warblers that summer in the area.

To explore the basin on your own, get a copy of the detailed highway map for Cherokee County, N.C., and then drive the many roads that meander through the region, stopping and birding at promising spots. Blue-winged Warblers can usually be located by their distinctive songs, which are heard from May through mid-June. The birds occur in open, early secondary successional woodlands, particularly in thickets or stands of deciduous saplings at six to twelve feet in height. Look on hillsides, in old fields, in overgrown pastures, and along shrub-bordered streamsides and waterways.

In the past, some of the best spots have been south and west of Murphy. From the junction of US 64 with the US 19/129 bypass at Murphy, head out of town on US 64 west and US 19/129 south for 5.5 miles to the stoplight where US 19/129 turns left; continue on US 64 west for 2.5 miles to NC 294. Turn right onto NC 294 and drive 6.1 miles to NC SR 1150, Canedy Mountain Road (1,720 ft.). Turn left onto state road 1150, drive slowly along the 7 miles to the town of Liberty (1,650 ft.), listen from the car for the Blue-winged's song, and stop in spots where the car can be safely pulled out of the roadway. Blue-winged Warblers are also found along NC 294, but the traffic is usually rather heavy and there are few suitable pull offs.

Another good route for Blue-winged Warbler is to proceed as above but turn left at the stoplight 5.5 miles southwest of Murphy and continue on US 19/129 south for 3.0 miles to NC SR 1556, Martin Creek Road. Turn left onto state road 1556 and proceed back toward Murphy; some of the best spots for Blue-wingeds are between 3 and 6 miles from the junction with US 19/129, at elevations of 1,600 to 1,700 feet.

Farther south down US 19/129 is Nottely Lake, which is accessed on GA 325. Either turn right off of US 19/129 onto GA 325 at 2.0 miles below the North Carolina–Georgia border, or, if you are driving north on US 19/129, turn left onto GA 325 8.3 miles north of Blairsville. Proceed 3.5 miles, crossing Nottely Dam, to Pottete Creek Road, which turns left just beyond a white church. Drive 1.0 mile down the road to **Pottete Creek Recreation Area** (1,800 ft.), a Forest Service campground with picnic areas and boat access to Nottely Lake. Easy walking on the loop roads provides a good look at spring and summer birds in a mixed pine-oak woodland. Here and around the recreation area one may find Eastern Screech-Owl, Whip-poor-will, Red-headed Woodpecker, Downy Woodpecker, Eastern Phoebe, Great Crested Flycatcher, Eastern Kingbird, Blue Jay, Carolina Chickadee, Tufted Titmouse, Carolina Wren, White-eyed Vireo, Yellow-throated Vireo, Red-eyed Vireo, Summer Tanager, and Scarlet Tanager. Warblers are well represented, with both Blue-winged and Golden-winged present in some years, along with Yellow, Pine, Prairie, Black-and-white, Ovenbird, Common Yellowthroat, Hooded, and Yellow-breasted Chat.

Highlands Plateau

Highlights: Middle- to high-elevation species; Peregrine Falcon, Least Fly-catcher

Season: Year-round, but mostly spring through summer.

Access: From the BRP, exit at Beech Gap (M 423.2) and go south 16 miles on

NC 215 to Rosman, N.C.; take US 64 west from Rosman for 29 miles to
Highlands, N.C. Another route is to exit the BRP at Balsam Gap (M 443.1)
and go 10 miles to Sylva, N.C., on US 74; then take NC 107 south from
Sylva for 28 miles to Cashiers, N.C., which is 10 miles east of Highlands on
US 64.
Maps: USGS "Highlands"; USFS "Trail Maps—Highlands District N.C."
Facilities: Gasoline, food, and accommodations in Highlands and Cashiers.
USFS Ranger Station, located on US 64 at 4.0 miles east of the US 64
junction with NC 28 in Highlands, has information, maps, brochures, and
books. Camping at the USFS Cliffside Lake Recreation Area and Vanhook
Glade campground, 4 miles west of Highlands on US 64 from the junction
with NC 106.

The Highlands Plateau achieved a lasting place in the history of
Appalachian natural sciences when Harvard ornithologist William Brewster explored the region during his whirlwind tour of the North Carolina
mountains in late May 1885. In old-growth deciduous and hemlock forests
of the plateau, Brewster discovered many birds whose previously known
breeding ranges were far to the north. Prior to his visit at Highlands,
naturalists believed that most of these species reached their southern nesting limits in the mountains between Pennsylvania and the north-central
portion of the Virginias.

Brewster's findings significantly changed the concepts of bird distribution in eastern North America, for here, practically at the Georgia
state line, were a host of "northern" birds, such as Yellow-bellied Sapsucker, Olive-sided Flycatcher, Red-breasted Nuthatch, Brown Creeper,
Veery, Solitary Vireo, Chestnut-sided Warbler, Black-throated Blue Warbler, Blackburnian Warbler, Canada Warbler, Rose-breasted Grosbeak,
and Dark-eyed Junco. In addition, Brewster collected at Highlands speci-
mens that served as the basis for his description of the southern Appalachian subspecies of Solitary Vireo and Dark-eyed Junco. The magnificent
virgin hemlock forests and Olive-sided Flycatchers are no longer to be
seen on the plateau, but other northern species noted by Brewster are still
present, along with some that he missed, such as Least Flycatcher and
Golden-crowned Kinglet.

Lying just north of the Blue Ridge escarpment and west of the Cowee
Mountains, the Highlands Plateau is a knobby tableland of about 12 to
14 square miles, averaging 3,800 to 4,000 feet in elevation. The southern

rim drains into the Savannah River headwaters, while streams north of the divide flow into tributaries of the Little Tennessee. With annual rainfalls often exceeding 85 inches, the plateau's vegetation is both lush and diversified, providing home to a rich avifauna. Although most of the original forests have been removed, there remain some tracts of beautiful old hemlocks and white pines, often densely understoried by rosebay rhododendron. Just to the east, the Cashiers Valley, at 3,400 feet, has many of the same plant and bird species found around Highlands.

Before exploring the region, stop at the U.S. Forest Service Highlands District Office, located on US 64 at 4.0 miles east of the junction with NC 28 in Highlands. Brochures, trail guides, and detailed topographic and trail maps are available to help you explore the Highlands-Cashiers area on your own.

A good spot to begin a visit is at **Highlands Biological Station** (3,840 ft.) at Lake Ravenel, near the eastern edge of town. From the stoplight at the US 64 junction with NC 28 in Highlands, proceed east on Main Street, which soon becomes Horse Cove Road, or NC SR 1603, for a total of 0.3 miles to Sixth Street; turn left on Sixth Street and go 0.15 miles to the sign and entrance road for the station on the right. Check in at the office or visit the museum, which is usually open during the summer months and is well worth the time. Trails around the buildings and around Lake Ravenel provide easy birding and a variety of botanical attractions as well. Check the hemlocks and white pines for Red-breasted Nuthatch, Brown Creeper, and Golden-crowned Kinglet—three species that are perhaps more typically associated with spruce-fir forests. Other birds present here in late spring and summer include Downy Woodpecker, Blue Jay, Wood Thrush, American Robin, Solitary Vireo, Black-throated Blue Warbler, Canada Warbler, Rose-breasted Grosbeak, Dark-eyed Junco, and Song Sparrow. Yellow-bellied Sapsuckers are occasionally noted, and Barred Owls are fairly regular permanent residents around Lake Ravenel.

Most of these same species can be found at **Cliffside Lake Recreation Area**, a U.S. Forest Service campground and picnic area located along the upper end of the Cullasaja River gorge northwest of Highlands. From the junction of NC 106 and US 64 in Highlands, proceed west on US 64 for 4.1 miles to the access road to Cliffside Lake; turn right and continue for 1.5 miles on the paved road to the camping area near the lake, which is at 3,380 feet. Cloaked with white pine, hemlock, rosebay rhododendron, and various hardwoods, the site is located on Skitty Creek, a tributary of the nearby Cullasaja River. Arrive early, especially on weekends, to avoid crowds. There is often good birding from the car or along the road shoulder and around the lake. Six trails provide short hikes back away from the traffic.

Cliffside Lake Loop Trail is an easy three-fourths-mile stroll around the lake, and Clifftop Vista Trail is a moderate 1.5-mile hike to the adjoining ridge line, an ascent of about 500 feet. Clifftop Vista Nature Trail is a moderate 1.1-mile walk through mixed hardwoods, and Potts Memorial Trail is an easy half-mile walk to a stand of white pine. Skitty Creek Trail and Vanhook Trail are both half-mile hikes toward US 64, the former providing access to beautiful Dry Falls and the latter connecting to Vanhook Glade campground. During late spring and summer, watch for the same species listed above for Highlands Biological Station, as well as Carolina Chickadee, Tufted Titmouse, Northern Parula, Chestnut-sided Warbler, Blackburnian Warbler, and Scarlet Tanager.

The Highlands Plateau is also noted for its summer population of Least Flycatchers, which are about as conspicuous here as any place in the Blue Ridge. The birds can often be located by driving slowly along secondary roads, keeping the car windows down and listening for the birds' distinctive calls. One fairly consistent area is the **Highlands Country Club**, located on NC 106 at 1.0 mile south from the junction of US 64 and NC 106. Check for permission before exploring the woodlands around the buildings and along the golf fairways, where the flycatchers are usually heard.

Another interesting spot is **Whiteside Mountain** (4,930 ft.), a towering ridge of granite cliffs rising dramatically above the Cashiers Valley and Chattooga River headwaters at the eastern edge of the Highlands Plateau. Sheer cliffs of 400 to 750 feet are present on both the north and south faces of the mountain, where Peregrine Falcons began nesting in the 1980s following efforts to reintroduce the species in the southern Appalachians. From the junction of US 64 and NC 28 in Highlands, proceed on US 64 east for 5.4 miles to NC SR 1600 at the Wildcat Cliffs Country Club; turn right onto state road 1600 and go 0.9 miles to a gravel parking lot on the left. A moderately strenuous, 2-mile loop trail runs from the lot to the summit. Find the wooden platform at the end of the old dirt road near the top; watch from here for Peregrines and scan the cliff face for the nesting site, which will require at least a 20-power spotting scope for a good view. The best time to see Peregrines is from late March to mid-May and again in early to mid-summer when the young have hatched.

The trail passes through woodlands of oak, birch, maple, rhododendron, mountain laurel, and azaleas. Watch in late spring and summer for Downy Woodpecker, Northern Flicker, Eastern Phoebe, Blue Jay, Carolina Chickadee, Tufted Titmouse, White-breasted Nuthatch, Winter Wren, Veery, Wood Thrush, American Robin, Gray Catbird, Cedar Waxwing, Solitary Vireo, Red-eyed Vireo, Black-throated Blue Warbler, Black-and-white Warbler, Ovenbird, Canada Warbler, Scarlet Tanager, Rose-breasted Grosbeak, Indigo Bunting, Rufous-sided Towhee, Song Sparrow, Dark-eyed Junco, and American Goldfinch.

Not far from Whiteside is a spot often worth checking for water birds. Continue east on US 64 into Cashiers, turn south onto NC 107, and proceed for 0.6 miles from the 64-107 intersection to NC SR 1112. Turn right onto state road 1112, proceed less than 0.1 miles, turn right onto state road 1113, and continue 0.2 miles to the dam at **Cashiers Lake** (3,460 ft.). The lake is locally renowned for migratory and wintering birds, including grebes, geese, ducks, mergansers, and a variety of shorebirds. The only problem here is the lack of public access; be sure to avoid trespassing and don't stop the car where it blocks the roadway.

Before leaving the Highlands area, consider a visit to the gorge of the nearby Chattooga River, where Swainson's Warblers are the prime attraction. See the chapter on the southeastern Blue Ridge escarpment for details.

Southeastern Blue Ridge Escarpment Gorges

Highlights: Middle- to low-elevation species; Swainson's Warbler.

Season: Year-round, but mainly spring through summer.

Access: From the BRP to the Eastatoe Creek area, exit at Beech Gap (BRP M 423.2) and proceed south on NC 215 for 16 miles to Rosman, N.C.; continue south on US 178 from Rosman for about 8 miles to the Eastatoe Creek bridge. From the BRP to the Chattooga River, exit at Balsam Gap (BRP M 443.1) and proceed south 10 miles on US 74 to Sylva, N.C.; then take NC 107 for 28 miles south to Cashiers, N.C. If coming from the south on I-85, take the first South Carolina exit just north of the Georgia line onto SC 11 and proceed north about 18 miles to Walhalla, S.C.

Maps: USFS "Trail Guide—Andrew Pickens Ranger District," "Sumter
National Forest—Andrew Pickens Ranger District," "Chattooga National
Wild and Scenic River," "Trail Maps—Highlands Ranger District N.C.";
"Foothills Trail Guide," by the Foothills Trail Conference; USGS "Cash-
iers," "Eastatoe Gap," "Reid," "Tamassee."

Facilities: USFS Sumter National Forest Ranger Station on SC 28 at 2.0 miles
south of the SC 28–SC 107 junction or 5.6 miles north of Walhalla on
SC 28. For information on the Foothills Trail, contact the Foothills Trail
Conference, P.O. Box 3041, Greenville, SC 39602, or Duke Power Company, Project Recreation, P.O. Box 33189, Charlotte, NC 28242 (704-
373-8032). Gasoline, food, and accommodations available in Cashiers,
Highlands, and Walhalla.

Through most of its course, the Blue Ridge range forms an abrupt
wall of steep mountains rising dramatically from the western Piedmont. In
contrast to this distinct ridge line through Virginia and North Carolina, the
Blue Ridge Mountains become more diffuse and irregular in the western
half of their thirty-mile sweep along the border between North and South
Carolina. From Pennsylvania to South Carolina, the mountains trend from
northeast to southwest, but at the South Carolina line, the range shifts to
an east-west orientation. In this area, the south-facing embayment forms
a barrier to moisture-laden prevailing winds from the Gulf of Mexico and
the Caribbean. These humid air masses cool and become saturated as they
rise in crossing the range, resulting in the highest annual precipitation in
the eastern United States—exceeding 100 inches in some spots.

Heavy rainfall has helped carve deep gorges that extend from the edge
of the Blue Ridge escarpment at about 3,000 feet down to around 900 feet
where the gorges open onto the Piedmont. Forming the Savannah River
headwaters, six major waterways tumble through cascades and beautiful
falls as they descend for three to six miles through rugged gorges. From
east to west, these include Eastatoe Creek and the Toxaway, Horsepasture,
Thompson, Whitewater, and Chattooga rivers. The steepest gradients are
in the five eastern rivers, which plunge downward at about three hundred
feet per mile, whereas the Chattooga descends a lazy fifty feet per mile
over most of its course.

Extensively logged in the past, most of the region is now cloaked in
medium-aged, second-growth mesophytic and oak forests, with an often
dense understory of rosebay rhododendron and mountain laurel. A mix-

ture of Piedmont and mountain bird species are present in summer, but the major attraction is the large population of Swainson's Warbler. The escarpment gorges are the best spots in the Appalachian Mountains, and perhaps in the United States, to see this intriguing warbler.

The area has a particularly rich and storied history in the annals of American natural science. For botanists and zoologists alike, the gorges have been the scene of some of the most famous episodes involving lost and enigmatic species. In December 1788, near the confluence of the Toxaway and Horsepasture rivers, French botanist André Michaux collected a small plant that subsequently lay unnoticed in a Paris museum until 1839, when Asa Gray of Harvard found the specimen. Gray named it *Shortia galacifolia* and initiated what was to become a half-century quest to rediscover the plant and to identify the spot where Michaux took the type specimen. This lovely flower, now called Oconee Bells, has been dubbed the Holy Grail of nineteenth-century American botanists. Michaux also reported *Magnolia cordata* in the gorges, the last time this attractive plant was found in the wild for more than a century.

Meanwhile, near the opposite end of the Savannah River, the gifted artist-naturalist John Abbot (1751–c. 1840) collected and painted a bird he called the "Swamp Worm-eater." Three of Abbot's drawings crafted between 1801 and 1815 obviously illustrate the bird that was later named the Swainson's Warbler. Yet Abbot's work was unrecognized for almost a century, and the traditional view has been that Swainson's Warbler was discovered along the Edisto River in 1832 or 1833 by the Reverend John Bachman (1790–1874) of Charleston, S.C., who conveyed the specimen to John James Audubon. After Audubon described the bird, it remained virtually lost to science for half a century, until Arthur T. Wayne and Harvard ornithologist William Brewster rediscovered the Swainson's near Charleston in the summer of 1884. Excited by his find, Brewster speculated that the southern Appalachians might be the home of other "lost" birds, so in May 1885 he made his pioneering exploration of the mountains of western North Carolina.

Ironically, Brewster climbed Whiteside Mountain and probably gazed down onto the Chattooga River gorge below, but he turned north and missed the chance for a discovery that might have rivaled or surpassed his efforts of the previous summer. Thus another half century was to elapse before scientists recognized that the elusive Swainson's Warbler occurred not only in dense canebrakes of the hot and humid southeastern Coastal Plain but also in cool tangles of rhododendron and laurel in the Appalachian Mountains. Even when the birds were known to inhabit the mountain region, it was not until the 1960s that the large population of Swainson's was discovered in the gorges of the southeastern Blue Ridge escarpment. Because the only data are from years after 1960, the long-term patterns of the bird's density and distribution in the gorges remain unknown.

Despite their tendency to skulk about in the dark understory and shrub layer, Swainson's Warblers are not impossible to find and observe during their nesting season. Furthermore, the escarpment offers a large and diversified population of breeding birds, set in a scenic and botanically interesting area. Access to the gorges and rivers is provided by a network of roads and trails, allowing you to choose roadside birding or a backcountry hike. The central portion of the escarpment from the Toxaway to the Whitewater is inaccessible by car and must be explored by hiking the Foothills Trail. The Chattooga River and the Eastatoe Creek, at the western and eastern ends of the scarp, respectively, can be accessed both by car and by a variety of trails. With good planning and patience, the birds may sometimes be observed from the car, permitting individuals with serious physical handicaps to hear and see Swainson's Warbler. If you plan any hiking, remember that this is one of the wettest areas in North America, so don't forget to bring rain gear and proper footwear.

Probably the easiest bet for Swainson's is along the Chattooga River, which forms much of the state boundary between South Carolina and Georgia in the area just below the North Carolina line. Before visiting the area, get copies of the U.S. Forest Service's two detailed topographic trail maps entitled "Trail Guide—Andrew Pickens Ranger District" and the "Chattooga National Wild and Scenic River."

Upper portions of the river can be explored from along NC 107 south from Cashiers toward Walhalla. One usually reliable area is on NC SR 1100, or **Bull Pen Road**. Proceed south on NC 107 for 6.7 miles from the US 64 junction in Cashiers; turn right onto state road 1100 and proceed down the bumpy gravel road. If coming from South Carolina, go 1.2 miles north on NC 107 from the North Carolina–South Carolina state line and turn left onto state road 1100. At 3.5 miles from NC 107, be sure to bear left to continue on state road 1100, which is also labeled FSR 1178. Between 3.5 and 4.0 miles from NC 107, stop and listen for Swainson's Warblers, which are sometimes present around Scotsman Creek (2,600 ft.). Continue on to Bull Pen Bridge over the Chattooga River (2,400 ft.) at 5.3 miles from

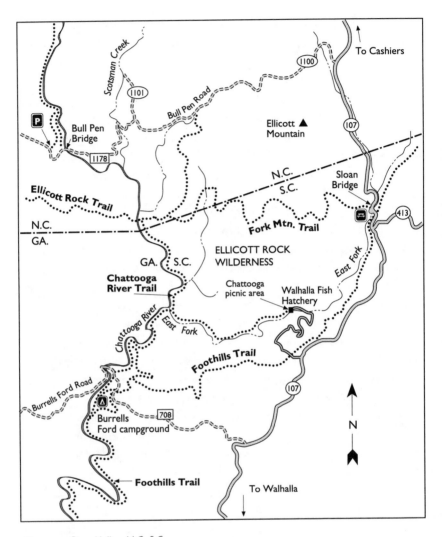

Chattooga River Valley, N.C.-S.C.

NC 107. A very small parking spot is on the right immediately beyond the bridge, where a trail heads upstream along the rhododendron-lined river. Usually you need to proceed another 100 yards to a much larger lot on the left or continue for 0.3 miles beyond the bridge to a sharp right turn into an additional parking area.

The Swainson's can sometimes be heard, and occasionally observed, from the car or by walking along the 0.2-mile section of road on either side of Bull Pen Bridge. The birds are often present along the 3.4-mile segment of trail that runs upstream along the west bank of the Chattooga from the bridge; a side route from this trail loops back up to the parking lot, so you could also do a circuit hike of about 2 miles by using both the road and the trail.

Return to NC 107 and continue south to the **Sloan Bridge picnic area** (2,700 ft.) along the East Fork Chattooga River, located 0.8 miles south of the North Carolina–South Carolina state line. Swainson's Warblers are sometimes in rhododendron thickets behind the picnic tables or along three nearby trails. Try an in-and-out hike for about a mile down the Foothills Trail along the East Fork Chattooga toward Burrell's Ford, or walk eastbound a mile or so on the Foothills Trail toward Whitewater Falls. The trailheads are clearly marked just south of the picnic parking lot. Also consider a stroll on the **Fork Mountain Trail**, which begins on the left of SC 107 about 80 yards north of the parking lot and runs near Slatten Branch toward Ellicott Rock.

Return to the car and continue south for 1 mile along SC 107 to the junction on the left for the paved road out to Whitewater Falls, a 3-mile drive that is worth the trek for a view of this spectacular waterfall. The Foothills Trail heads east from the falls parking area into the remote central gorges of the escarpment, in case you want some strenuous hiking.

Farther south on SC 107 is **Walhalla National Fish Hatchery**, an interesting birding spot at an elevation of 2,500 feet along the East Fork Chattooga River. In addition to being a good site for Swainson's Warbler, the fish hatchery is also known for Common Raven, Red-breasted Nuthatch, Golden-crowned Kinglet, and Dark-eyed Junco—species more typically associated with higher-elevation mountain areas to the north. The paved access road turns off of SC 107 (3,000 ft.) at 3.2 miles south of the North Carolina–South Carolina state line and then runs 1.8 miles down to the hatchery. Winding through oak forests, hemlock groves, and dense rosebay rhododendron thickets, the road is often a good spot for Swainson's, although it is hard to find pull offs wide enough to get the car safely off the pavement. Try spots at 0.1, 1.0, 1.1, 1.5, and 1.6 miles from SC 107; with luck you will be able to see as well as hear the birds from these stops.

Drive to the end of the road and park in the lot adjacent to the fish hatchery. Carefully walk back up the roadside for about 0.3 miles, listening for the Swainson's. Then check the area around the facility buildings and holding tanks, where Common Ravens are occasionally found. Explore the Chattooga picnic grounds beyond the parking lot, where beautiful old-growth hemlock and white pines are sometimes home to Red-breasted Nuthatches and Golden-crowned Kinglets—here probably at or near the southernmost limit of their summer range in the eastern United States.

One of the best places to find Swainson's Warbler is along the hiking trails that run from the fish hatchery through Ellicott Rock Wilderness along the Chattooga River and East Fork Chattooga. At about 200 yards from the hatchery parking lot, the trail leaves the picnic grounds, crosses a wooden footbridge, and descends along the East Fork Chattooga for 2.5 miles to its confluence with the Chattooga (2,080 ft.), where you can turn right and head upstream along the Chattooga for 1.7 miles to Ellicott Rock (2,150 ft.) and then retrace your route. Alternatively, go left and head downstream along the east bank of the Chattooga for 1.5 miles to Burrell's Ford Road (2,050 ft.), where a car can be left 0.4 miles up the road at the campground parking lot, if you don't want to hike back to the hatchery.

These trails go through prime Swainson's Warbler habitat, where several singing males are usually present in the 4-mile walk between the fish hatchery and Burrell's Ford. Other late-spring and summer birds along this trail include Downy Woodpecker, Acadian Flycatcher, Blue Jay, American Crow, Carolina Chickadee, Tufted Titmouse, White-breasted Nuthatch, Carolina Wren, Wood Thrush, Red-eyed Vireo, Northern Parula, Black-throated Blue Warbler, Black-and-white Warbler, American Redstart, Ovenbird, Louisiana Waterthrush, Hooded Warbler, and Rufous-sided Towhee.

To get to **Burrell's Ford** by car, go 1.7 miles south of the fish hatchery road on SC 107 or, if coming from Walhalla, go 10 miles north on SC 107 from its junction with SC 28. Turn onto the gravel Burrell's Ford Road and go 2.2 miles from SC 107 to the parking lot for the campground; from here to the bridge over the Chattooga at 2.7 miles is a good stretch to watch for Swainson's. At 2.6 miles from SC 107, the trail from the Walhalla National Fish Hatchery crosses the road, just 0.1 miles before the river bridge. You can hike up this route, as noted above, for 4.0 miles to the hatchery or for 3.2 miles to Ellicott Rock. Drive on across the bridge and park in the small lot on the left just beyond the river. An easily followed old dirt road now serves as an unmarked trail that runs both upstream and downstream along the west bank of the Chattooga, providing access to prime Swainson's habitat in rhododendron thickets beneath hemlock and white pine. Both routes are easy walking, although they can be slick and muddy at times.

Other trails along the Chattooga are good for Swainson's but involve sections of the river that are more heavily used for recreational activities. From Burrell's Ford, the Chattooga River Trail and portions of the Foothills Trail continue 12.5 miles along the east bank of the Chattooga to Ridley Fields parking lot (1,600 ft.) on SC 28 just east of the river and the Georgia state line. From the Russell Bridge parking lot (1,600 ft.) on GA 28, just west of the river, the Chattooga River Trail and portions of the Bartram Trail continue south along the west side of the river for 20 miles to the parking lot at Chattooga River Information Station on US 76 at the Georgia–South Carolina border. Swainson's may be found all along these routes, but heavy white-water sports use and reduced accessibility make these segments less attractive for birding than the area upstream from Burrell's Ford.

The other area accessible by car is **Eastatoe Creek**, easternmost of the escarpment waterways. US 178 crosses the Eastatoe 2.3 miles south of the North Carolina–South Carolina line or 7.9 miles north of the junction between US 178 and SC 11. Immediately north of Eastatoe bridge (1,640 ft.), a gravel road heads west for 0.3 miles to a parking lot and then continues quite a distance beyond the metal gate at the lot. Listen for Swainson's from the car or walk along the road from its start at US 178 for about 1 mile beyond the metal gate. At the far end of the parking lot, Eastatoe Gorge Spur Trail, another good Swainson's route, begins its easy 2.6-mile descent to Eastatoe Gorge Natural Area. Also try walking carefully along the shoulder of US 178 for about 0.4 miles north of the bridge. Finally, try driving to the pull offs along US 178 at 0.2, 0.4, 0.9, and 1.1 miles south of the junction with Van Clayton Memorial Highway in the community of Rocky Bottom (1,750 ft.), which is 0.9 miles south of the Eastatoe Creek bridge.

As long as you are here, consider driving up the paved Van Clayton Memorial Highway (SC county road 199) for a steep 4.6 miles to the summit of **Sassafras Mountain** (3,548 ft.), the highest point in South Carolina. Swainson's Warblers are sometimes present in the rhododendron tangles along the road at 0.3 to 1.1 and 2.0 to 2.6 miles from US 178. Scrubby second-growth oak forests cover Sassafras, but there are some older trees near the summit. Watch in late spring and summer for species typical of oak woodlands, including Ruffed Grouse, Downy Woodpecker, Eastern Wood-Pewee, Great Crested Flycatcher, Blue Jay, Carolina Chickadee, Tufted Titmouse, Wood Thrush, Solitary Vireo, Red-eyed Vireo, Chestnut-sided

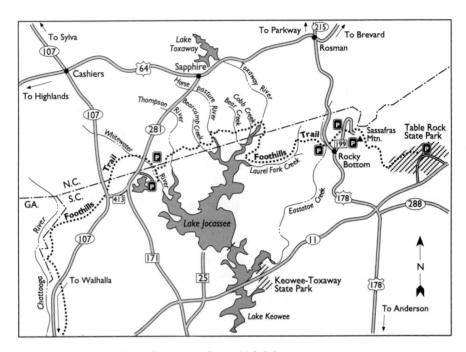

Southeastern Blue Ridge Escarpment Gorges, N.C.-S.C.

Warbler, Black-and-white Warbler, American Redstart, Worm-eating Warbler, Ovenbird, Hooded Warbler, Canada Warbler, Rose-breasted Grosbeak, Rufous-sided Towhee, and Dark-eyed Junco. The Foothills Trail and a 12-mile ridge-line trail to Caesar's Head State Park, accessible from the summit parking lot, provide hiking routes back into the woods.

To explore the middle gorges of the escarpment requires hiking into the backcountry on segments of the **Foothills Trail**. This trail system extends along the southern Blue Ridge Mountains from Table Rock State Park to Oconee State Park. A 4-mile spur trail is planned along the Horsepasture River, a route that will be both scenic and excellent for seeing Swainson's Warblers. The present trail passes through the lower ends of the Toxaway, Horsepasture, Thompson, and Whitewater river gorges. Practical access to the Foothills Trail in this remote and rugged section is by boat across Lake Jocassee. Get a copy of the *Guide to the Foothills Trail*, published by the Foothills Trail Conference, or contact Duke Power Company for detailed route descriptions and topographic trail maps, as well as for information on how to get into the gorges by boat.

Good parts of the trail for Swainson's Warbler are the segments between

Laurel Fork and Cane Brake and those west of Cane Brake toward White-water Falls. Heading east from the Cane Brake boat access on Lake Jocas-see toward Laurel Fork, the trail crosses the Toxaway River at 0.5 miles, just beyond a spot where one may experience the pleasure of listening to Swainson's Warblers near clumps of Oconee Bells, although the plants will probably have finished their annual bloom before the birds arrive. Alter-natively, head west from Cane Brake along the trail for more opportunities to see Swainson's, particularly at 1.3 miles, 3.1 miles near Cobb Creek, 5.3 miles at Bear Creek, and 7.9 miles at the Horsepasture River.

Many other birds are present in the gorges from late spring through summer, with their distribution depending largely on elevation and habi-tat. Watch for Turkey Vulture, Sharp-shinned Hawk, Cooper's Hawk, Broad-winged Hawk, Red-tailed Hawk, Ruffed Grouse, Spotted Sand-piper, Mourning Dove, Yellow-billed Cuckoo, Eastern Screech-Owl, Great Horned Owl, Barred Owl, Whip-poor-will, Chimney Swift, Ruby-throated Hummingbird, Belted Kingfisher, Red-bellied Woodpecker, Downy Wood-pecker, Hairy Woodpecker, Northern Flicker, Pileated Woodpecker, Eastern Wood-Pewee, Acadian Flycatcher, Eastern Phoebe, Great Crested Flycatcher, Northern Rough-winged Swallow, Blue Jay, American Crow, Carolina Chickadee, Tufted Titmouse, White-breasted Nuthatch, Caro-lina Wren, Blue-gray Gnatcatcher, Wood Thrush, American Robin, Gray Catbird, Brown Thrasher, White-eyed Vireo, Solitary Vireo, Yellow-throated Vireo, Red-eyed Vireo, Summer Tanager, Scarlet Tanager, Northern Cardinal, Indigo Bunting, Rufous-sided Towhee, Chipping Spar-row, Field Sparrow, Song Sparrow, and American Goldfinch. Warblers are particularly well represented; watch for Northern Parula, Yellow, Chestnut-sided, Black-throated Blue, Black-throated Green, Blackbur-nian, Yellow-throated, Pine, Prairie, Black-and-white, American Redstart, Worm-eating, Swainson's, Ovenbird, Louisiana Waterthrush, Kentucky, Common Yellowthroat, Hooded, and Yellow-breasted Chat.

South Carolina High Country

Highlights: Spring migration, middle- to low-elevation nesting birds, autumn
   hawk migration.

Season: Year-round, but mainly spring through fall.

Access: Exit the BRP at Wagon Road Gap (M 411.7) and go south on US 276
through Brevard, N.C., and on to Caesar's Head State Park, which is 34
miles from the BRP.

Maps: USGS "Cleveland," "Standingstone Mountain," "Table Rock."

Facilities: Food and information at Caesar's Head State Park; trailside camping in Jones Gap State Park. Gasoline, food, and accommodations at
Brevard. For information, contact Caesar's Head State Park, 8155 Geer
Highway, Cleveland, SC 29635 (803-836-6115) or Jones Gap State Park,
303 Jones Gap Road, Marietta, SC 29661 (803-836-7122).

From the vicinity of Saluda Gap, the Blue Ridge crest runs in a
westerly direction along the North Carolina–South Carolina line toward
the Highlands Plateau. Although the ridge line seldom exceeds 3,000 feet
in elevation, the escarpment is sharply defined along much of the region's
eastern half, with mountains rising dramatically above the Piedmont. Oak
forests cover most of the area, along with cove hardwoods and rhododendron thickets. Summer bird life is a mix of Piedmont and low- to
middle-elevation species, including the elusive Swainson's Warbler. Due
mainly to the absence of any terrain above 3,600 feet, the habitat is suitable for only a small number of strictly montane birds, such as Common
Raven, Chestnut-sided Warbler, Black-throated Blue Warbler, Blackburnian Warbler, and Dark-eyed Junco. Other species, such as Solitary Vireo,
Black-throated Green Warbler, Worm-eating Warbler, and Scarlet Tanager,
are much more common here in the mountains than on the southeastern
Piedmont.

Although a few roads provide access, some of the best birding is along
the hiking trails, many of which are associated with the eleven South Carolina state parks in the region. For backcountry birding and solitude, the
Foothills Trail and its adjoining paths offer more than 80 miles of often
remote and strenuous hiking along the Blue Ridge. To explore portions of
this network, get a copy of *Guide to the Foothills Trail* from the Foothills
Trail Conference. The best introduction to the region's bird life is in the
area encompassed by Mountain Bridge Wilderness and Recreation Area,
which includes Caesar's Head State Park and Jones Gap State Park.

Perched on the escarpment edge, **Caesar's Head State Park** offers easy
bird walks and an impressive view of the Piedmont from high cliffs near
the summit (3,266 ft.). The park office and visitor center are on US 276 at

2.6 miles south of the North Carolina–South Carolina state line, or 7.1 miles north of the junction with SC 11. Park in the lot near the visitor center, and get a copy of "Birds of the Mountain Bridge Wilderness Area," by Irvin Pitts. At the far end of the parking lot, an easy 150-yard trail begins to the right of the tower and runs back into the woods and cliff edge; on the left side of the tower is the more accessible, and thus more crowded, route to the cliffs.

Common Ravens are noted here year-round, and the granite outcroppings at the summit cliffs are an excellent spot to observe the autumn hawk migration in September and October. Red Crossbills have nested in the park, although in the breeding season you are more likely to find Great Crested Flycatcher, Carolina Chickadee, Tufted Titmouse, Wood Thrush, Solitary Vireo, Black-throated Blue Warbler, Black-and-white Warbler, Hooded Warbler, Scarlet Tanager, and Dark-eyed Junco. Inquire in the park office for directions to Oil Camp Road, which runs through oak and cove forests that are often outstanding for spring migration, especially in the first two weeks of May. In some years, as many as thirty species of warblers have been observed along this road during migration.

For backcountry hikes, head north on US 276 to the Raven Cliff parking area, 1.1 miles from the Caesar's Head park office. The lot provides access to trails of the **Mountain Bridge Wilderness and Recreation Area**, a 10,000-acre preserve along the Blue Ridge escarpment. Heading west from the lot, Raven Cliff Falls Trail is a 2.2-mile, moderately strenuous hike through oak forests to a spectacular 420-foot waterfall. This route is heavily used in summer, but you are likely to have the trail to yourself in April and May, when it can be excellent for spring migration. Typical breeding-season species include Ruffed Grouse, Wild Turkey, Downy Woodpecker, Pileated Woodpecker, Eastern Wood-Pewee, Great Crested Flycatcher, Blue Jay, Carolina Chickadee, Tufted Titmouse, Carolina Wren, Wood Thrush, Solitary Vireo, Red-eyed Vireo, Black-and-white Warbler, Worm-eating Warbler, Ovenbird, Hooded Warbler, Scarlet Tanager, Rufous-sided Towhee, and Dark-eyed Junco.

From the east side of the parking lot, the Jones Gap Trail runs on ridge lines and descends along the Middle Saluda River for a total of 5.3 moderately strenuous miles to **Jones Gap State Park**. The trail passes through oak and cove hardwood forests, often with dense rhododendron and laurel thickets. Most species noted on Raven Cliff Falls Trail are also found here, in addition to Acadian Flycatcher, Northern Parula, Black-throated

Blue Warbler, Black-throated Green Warbler, and Louisiana Waterthrush. Although the Middle Saluda River is often rather noisy, it is worth listening for Swainson's Warblers along lower parts of the trail near the park. Two other routes, Cold Spring Branch Trail and Rim of the Gap Trail, can be accessed from the parking area. Jones Gap State Park is located on River Falls Road, 6 miles off US 276 south of Caesar's Head.

North Georgia Highlands

Highlights: Middle- to low-elevation nesting species.

Season: Spring through fall.

Access: From the BRP, exit at Balsam Gap (M 443.1) on US 74 west and continue for 76 miles to Murphy, N.C.; continue south of Murphy on US 19/129 for 22 miles to Blairsville, Ga.

Maps: USGS "Hiwassee," "Jack's Gap," "Mulky Gap"; USFS "Chattahoochee National Forest."

Facilities: Gasoline, food, and accommodations at Blairsville. Camping at numerous USFS campgrounds in the Chattahoochee National Forest.

The Appalachian highlands sweep some two thousand miles from Canada's Gaspe Peninsula to the Blue Ridge Mountains of northeast Georgia, where the province ends in a jumble of rolling hills. Many Georgia peaks exceed 4,000 feet in elevation, but none rise above 5,000 feet. Although the topography is occasionally steep and rugged, the subdued elevations are apparent when compared to North Carolina, which has more than 220 peaks over 5,000 feet. The Georgia mountains are, nevertheless, high enough to provide habitat suitable for many "northern" birds whose breeding distribution is essentially montane. Consequently, a number of birds reach the southern limit of their nesting range in the Georgia mountains. These include Ruffed Grouse, Yellow-bellied Sapsucker, Least Flycatcher, Common Raven, Winter Wren, Veery, Golden-winged Warbler, Chestnut-sided Warbler, Black-throated Blue Warbler, Black-throated Green Warbler, Blackburnian Warbler, Canada Warbler, Rose-breasted Grosbeak, and Dark-eyed Junco. Other birds, such as Cedar Waxwing, Solitary Vireo, Blue-winged Warbler, Worm-eating Warbler, and Scarlet

Tanager, occur farther south but are much more frequently encountered in the mountains.

Much of the region is cloaked in second-growth oak forests, with cove forests in ravines and in valleys at low elevations. Hemlock achieves importance in moist coves and on north-facing slopes, and rhododendrons occur as a dense understory on hillsides and along waterways. Some of the best birding spots are in Chattahoochee National Forest, where numerous trails, recreation areas, and roads provide access to a variety of sites. Other resources include state parks, for easy birding, and the Appalachian Trail, for some rigorous backcountry bird study. For those who wish to combine hiking and bird-watching, the AT guidebook for Georgia and Homan's *The Hiking Trails of North Georgia* are essential. Homan's *Hiking Trails* contains notes on plant communities and provides detailed route descriptions, so the reader can select hikes that sound promising for bird study. Although there are many excellent spots, two areas near Blairsville provide a good introduction to the area's bird life.

At 4,784 feet, **Brasstown Bald** is Georgia's highest mountain, where most of the typically montane breeding birds can be found. Proceed 7.3 miles south of Blairsville on US 19/129 to GA 180; turn left onto GA 180 and proceed 7.2 miles east to Jack's Gap (2,960 ft.), where the GA 180 spur road turns left and goes 2.4 very steep miles to a parking lot (4,320 ft.) just below the peak. A half-mile trail starts behind the concession stand and runs to the summit, which can also be reached by shuttle bus service during the summer. Special arrangements can be made for wheelchair access if necessary. The observation tower provides a grand view of the surrounding mountains, and the trail is an excellent birding hike, provided you get started early enough to avoid the crowds. The parking lot also allows easy birding and views into the woodlands. The mountain is cloaked with maples, hickories, oaks, rhododendrons, and hemlock, but the upper slopes are covered mostly with stunted oak trees.

Check for Common Ravens around the summit and at the picnic area near the parking lot, where the birds often appear late in the afternoon. Birds typically found in late spring and summer include Turkey Vulture, Broad-winged Hawk, Ruffed Grouse, Downy Woodpecker, Northern Flicker, Veery, Wood Thrush, Gray Catbird, Brown Thrasher, Solitary Vireo, Red-eyed Vireo, Rose-breasted Grosbeak, Indigo Bunting, Rufous-sided Towhee, and Dark-eyed Junco. Watch for Chestnut-sided Warbler, Black-throated Blue Warbler, Blackburnian Warbler, Black-and-

white Warbler, Ovenbird, and Canada Warbler. Winter Wrens are sometimes heard, mostly on the north side of the summit.

If the hike between the lot and observation tower is too crowded, con-
sider exploring one of the National Recreation Trails on Brasstown Bald.
Beginning near the rest rooms at the parking lot, the **Arkaquah National
Recreation Trail** is a moderate-to-strenuous 5.4-mile path to Trackrock
Gap (2,280 ft.). Much of the route runs through the 11,789-acre Brasstown
Wilderness area. The first mile of the trail out to Chimney Top Mountain
is not very steep, thus providing a fairly easy walk through heath thickets
and oak forests. Many of the same species noted around the parking lot
and summit of Brasstown Bald can be expected along the trail. At the far
end of the lot, **Jack's Knob National Recreation Trail** begins its 2.3-mile
descent through mixed pine-oak woodlands to Jack's Gap. The first half
mile from the lot is fairly level and suitable for an easy in-and-out bird
walk. From Jack's Gap, the moderately strenuous trail continues south for
2.2 miles to connect with the Appalachian Trail at Chattahoochee Gap
(3,500 ft.).

For low- and middle-elevation birds, an excellent route is FSR 4, which
runs across Duncan Ridge and into the Cooper Creek area. At the junction of U.S. routes 19/76/129 in Blairsville, take US 76 west for only 0.1
miles and turn immediately left onto old US 76; continue for 2.9 miles
to Mulky Gap Road on the left; turn onto **Mulky Gap Road** and go 3.8
miles, where the pavement ends and the road becomes FSR 4. Stop at
promising spots along the way and listen during late spring and summer
for Golden-winged Warbler, Prairie Warbler, Kentucky Warbler, Common Yellowthroat, Hooded Warbler, Yellow-breasted Chat, sparrows, and
other field species. At 4.2 miles from old US 76, FSR 4-C begins on the
right (2,200 ft.); park and walk down the road for many of the same birds,
in addition to possible Swainson's Warblers.

Continue on FSR 4 through oak forests to Mulky Gap (2,800 ft.), at 5.5
miles from old US 76. The Duncan Ridge National Recreation Trail crosses
the gap, and the segments of the trail north and south provide good in-
and-out hikes for birding. Typical species found in late spring and summer
along the road and trail include Ruffed Grouse, Downy Woodpecker, Blue
Jay, Eastern Wood-Pewee, Carolina Chickadee, Tufted Titmouse, White-
breasted Nuthatch, Carolina Wren, Wood Thrush, American Robin, Solitary Vireo, Red-eyed Vireo, Black-throated Blue Warbler, Black-and-white

Warbler, Worm-eating Warbler, Ovenbird, Hooded Warbler, and Scarlet Tanager.

Beyond Mulky Gap, FSR 4 descends into the Cooper Creek basin on the south slope of Duncan Ridge. Following close by Mulky Creek, the road passes through a handsome forest of oaks, maples, and hemlocks, with an often dense understory of rhododendron and laurel. Stop frequently for many of the same species noted previously on the north side of the gap, in addition to Acadian Flycatcher, Northern Parula, Black-throated Green Warbler, Blackburnian Warbler, and Louisiana Waterthrush. At 3.5 miles beyond Mulky Gap, FSR 236 goes left from FSR 4 into Cooper Creek campground (2,160 ft.) and continues southward, crossing Cooper Creek bridge after 0.5 miles. A trail runs upstream along Cooper Creek from the end of the gravel parking lot just beyond the bridge. Explore the campground, the two USFS roads, and the Cooper Creek Trail for many previously noted birds. Be alert for Swainson's Warblers in the rhododendron thickets here, including those along FSR 4 for about 1 mile south from the campground along Cooper Creek.

BIRDS OF THE BLUE RIDGE MOUNTAIN PROVINCE

AN ANNOTATED CHECKLIST

The following checklist delineates the birds that have been documented as occurring in the Blue Ridge Mountain Province. Records from portions of the Ridge and Valley Province have been included for those localities of the Great Valley in Virginia and Tennessee that are immediately contiguous to the western slopes of the Blue Ridge Mountains. The status of each species is defined in terms of seasonal occurrence, relative abundance, habitat preference, and elevation range.

Because the geographic area spans a distance of some five hundred miles, it is often difficult to make valid and meaningful generalizations that describe a bird's status throughout the entire region. Although habitat selection by a particular species is fairly consistent through the area, the arrival and departure dates of nonresident birds and the elevation limits of nesting species often vary considerably in relation to differences in latitude.

Dates of occurrence reflect general or typical patterns based on dividing the month into thirds. Thus "early," "mid-," and "late" refer approximately to ten-day intervals within each month. Extreme dates of occurrence and extreme limits of elevation are often misleading and have therefore been excluded. Bar graph presentation of abundance and occurrence dates has not been attempted, due to the extreme geographic and ecologic range encompassed by this book. The common names and sequence are based on the American Ornithologists' Union's *Check-list of North American Birds*.

For certain rare, local, or particularly interesting species, a list is given in brackets [] to identify those spots described in the site guide where the bird is most likely to be observed. These sites are named in bold print or as main headings in the text, and the relevant page numbers can be located in the index. The sites are listed alphabetically here following each species account.

SEASONAL OCCURRENCE

Permanent resident. Species that occur throughout the entire year, regardless of seasonal fluctuations in relative abundance or dispersal and migratory movements by individuals.

Summer resident. Species absent during the winter season, usually arriving in spring migration, remaining through summer, and departing during fall migration.

Winter resident. Species absent during summer, usually arriving in fall migration, remaining through winter, and departing during spring migration.

Transient. Species present only during part of a season, usually during spring and fall migration.

Post-breeding wanderer. Species that occur as summer or permanent residents and disperse to different elevations or habitats at the conclusion of the nesting cycle, usually in mid- to late summer.

Erratic. Species whose presence and abundance may vary markedly and usually unpredictably over any given period of time.

Accidental. Species whose occurrence is outside their normal range.

RELATIVE ABUNDANCE

Abundant. Very large numbers are observed per unit of available habitat, including marginal and suboptimal habitats.

Very common. Large numbers are observed per unit of available habitat, including marginal and suboptimal habitats.

Common. Moderate numbers are observed per unit of available habitat.

Fairly common. Small to moderate numbers are observed per unit of available habitat.

Uncommon. Small numbers are recorded per unit of available habitat, often with considerable amounts of apparently suitable habitat unoccupied.

Rare. Very small numbers are recorded per unit of available habitat, with extensive fieldwork required for seeing an individual during a given year. *Very rare*. Usually not observed each year.

SPECIES LIST

Red-throated Loon: Rare transient in November and December.

Common Loon: Uncommon transient from early April to mid-May and from mid-October to mid-December; rare winter resident. [Lake Julian Park, Lake Junaluska, Laurel Lake, Long Pine Run Reservoir, Price Lake]

Pied-billed Grebe: Fairly common transient and uncommon winter resident from late August through April; rare summer resident. [Calderwood Lake, Lake Julian Park, Lake Junaluska, Laurel Lake, Price Lake]

Horned Grebe: Uncommon transient and rare winter visitor from mid-October to early May. More frequently observed in fall migration than in spring. [Lake Julian Park, Lake Junaluska, Laurel Lake, Long Pine Run Reservoir]

Red-necked Grebe: Rare transient in November and in March.

Eared Grebe: One record near Stuart's Draft, Va., on 16 August 1980.

White-tailed Tropicbird: Accidental. One at Staunton, Va., on 15 October 1954 during Hurricane Hazel.

American White Pelican: Erratic. Flock of forty on French Broad River, Buncombe County, N.C., in May 1889; three at Clingman's Dome in GSMNP in September 1937; seven on Lake Junaluska, Haywood County, N.C., in May 1953.

Double-crested Cormorant: Rare transient from mid-April to mid-May and from mid-September to mid-December; rare and erratic in summer in the Great Valley of Virginia. [Lake Julian Park]

Anhinga: Accidental. One at Front Royal, Va., on 12 May 1981.

American Bittern: Rare spring and fall transient from April to early May and from mid-August through November; very rare summer resident in wetlands of valleys. [Ferguson Fields, Huntsdale Fish Hatchery]

Least Bittern: Rare and local transient and summer resident in the Great Valley from late April to mid-October; very rare transient in interior valleys of North Carolina.

Great Blue Heron: Uncommon, nonbreeding, year-round resident, mostly below 3,000 feet; most common during migration in April and from July through October. [Abbot Lake Trail, Bent Creek Recreation Area, Canal Locks Trail, Ferguson Fields, Huntsdale Fish Hatchery, Lake Julian Park, Lake Junaluska, Long Pine Run Reservoir, Otter Lake, Price Lake, Roanoke Sewage Treatment Plant, Sherando Lake Recreation Area]

Great Egret: Uncommon summer visitor and fall transient during post-breeding dispersal from mid-July to mid-September; rare spring transient from late March through April. [Bent Creek Recreation Area, Canal Locks Trail, Huntsdale Fish Hatchery, Lake Junaluska, Lake Julian Park, Otter Lake, Sandy Bottom Recreation Area]

Snowy Egret: Rare transient and summer visitor from late April to mid-May and from July through mid-August.

Little Blue Heron: Uncommon to rare post-breeding wanderer from late June through August. [Canal Locks Trail, Lake Junaluska, Lake Julian Park, Otter Lake]

Tricolored Heron: Rare transient in May and late July through August. [Canal Locks Trail, Otter Lake]

Cattle Egret: Rare transient and summer visitor from late March through mid-November.

Green-backed Heron: Fairly common transient and summer resident from early April to early October. [Abbot Lake Trail, Bent Creek Recreation Area, Canal Locks Trail, Chesapeake and Ohio Canal, Ferguson Fields, Huntsdale Fish Hatchery, Lake Julian Park, Lake Junaluska, NC SR 1134, Otter Lake, Price Lake, Roanoke Sewage Treatment Plant, Santeetlah Lake, Sherando Lake Recreation Area]

Black-crowned Night-Heron: Rare transient, post-breeding summer wanderer, and winter visitor; large summer roost along Yellow Breeches Creek near South Mountain, Pa. [Huntsdale Fish Hatchery]

Yellow-crowned Night-Heron: Rare and local transient and summer resident, mainly in the Great Valley of Virginia. [Roanoke Sewage Treatment Plant]

White Ibis: Rare and irregular post-breeding wanderer in summer and fall from mid-June through mid-September. [Canal Locks Trail, Otter Lake]

Glossy Ibis: Rare transient and summer visitor in the Great Valley of Virginia from April through October.

Wood Stork: Very rare summer visitor in the Great Valley of Virginia from July through September; three birds sighted at Asheville, N.C., on 2 December 1977.

Greater Flamingo: Accidental. One at Waynesboro, Va., 10–12 August 1969.

Fulvous Whistling-Duck: Very rare transient and winter visitor in the Great Valley of Virginia from September through June.

Tundra Swan: Rare transient and winter visitor in the Great Valley from November to early April. [Chesapeake and Ohio Canal]

Mute Swan: One record at Luray, Va., on 18 April 1971.

Snow Goose: Rare transient and winter visitor in the Great Valley of Virginia from late September to mid-May.

Brant: Two records from Augusta County, Va., from late November to early December 1979 and 1985.

Canada Goose: Locally fairly common transient and winter visitor from mid-October through mid-April; uncommon, local summer resident south to Augusta County, Va. [Chesapeake and Ohio Canal, Huntsdale Fish Hatchery, Lake Julian Park, Lake Junaluska, Laurel Lake, Long Pine Run Reservoir, Price Lake, Shenandoah Canal]

Wood Duck: Locally common transient and summer resident and rare winter resident. [Bass Lake; Bent Creek Recreation Area; Chesapeake and Ohio Canal; Hare Mill Pond; Ferguson Fields; Huntsdale Fish Hatchery; Lake Julian Park; Lake Junaluska; Linville Falls parking lot, campground, and picnic area; Long Pine Run Reservoir; NC SR 1549; Price Lake; Sandy Bottom Recreation Area; Warbler Road]

Green-winged Teal: Uncommon to rare transient and winter resident from late September through early May. [Price Lake]

American Black Duck: Uncommon to rare transient and winter resident from mid-September through March. [Huntsdale Fish Hatchery, Lake Julian Park, Lake Junaluska, Price Lake]

Mallard: Uncommon transient and winter resident from mid-September through March; rare to uncommon summer resident. [Chesapeake and Ohio Canal, Huntsdale Fish Hatchery, Lake Julian Park, Lake Junaluska, Laurel Lake, Long Pine Run Reservoir, Price Lake]

Northern Pintail: Rare to uncommon transient and winter visitor from September through April. [Huntsdale Fish Hatchery, Long Pine Run Reservoir]

Blue-winged Teal: Uncommon transient from mid-March through April and from late August through October; rare summer and winter visitor. [Ferguson Fields, Huntsdale Fish Hatchery, Price Lake]

Northern Shoveler: Uncommon to rare transient and rare winter visitor from mid-September through April.

Gadwall: Uncommon to rare transient and winter visitor from mid-October to mid-April. [Price Lake]

Eurasian Wigeon: Very rare winter visitor in the Great Valley of Virginia from late October through April.

American Wigeon: Rare to locally fairly common transient and winter resident from mid-September to late April. [Huntsdale Fish Hatchery]

Canvasback: Uncommon transient and rare winter visitor from mid-November to mid-April. [Long Pine Run Reservoir, Price Lake]

Redhead: Rare transient and winter visitor from late October through March. [Lake Julian Park, Long Pine Run Reservoir]

Ring-necked Duck: Fairly common transient and uncommon winter resident from mid-October to mid-April. [Huntsdale Fish Hatchery, Lake Julian Park, Lake Junaluska, Long Pine Run Reservoir, Price Lake]

Greater Scaup: Rare transient and winter visitor from late October to mid-April.

Lesser Scaup: Fairly common transient and uncommon winter resident from mid-October to late April. [Ferguson Fields, Huntsdale Fish Hatchery, Lake Julian Park, Lake Junaluska, Long Pine Run Reservoir]

Harlequin Duck: One record. On the New River near Radford, Va., February through April 1973.

Oldsquaw: Rare transient and winter visitor, mostly in the Great Valley of Virginia, from late October to mid-April.

Surf Scoter: Very rare fall transient and winter visitor in the Great Valley of Virginia from November through mid-January.

White-winged Scoter: Very rare transient and winter visitor in the Great Valley of Virginia from mid-October to early May.

Common Goldeneye: Uncommon transient and winter visitor from late October to mid-April. [Long Pine Run Reservoir, Price Lake]

Barrow's Goldeneye: J. S. Cairns reported collecting a male in Buncombe County, N.C., in May 1893, but the specimen is apparently no longer extant.

Bufflehead: Uncommon transient and winter visitor from November to May. [Lake Julian Park, Lake Junaluska, Long Pine Run Reservoir]

Hooded Merganser: Common to uncommon transient and winter visitor from late October to mid-April; rare and local summer visitor. [Huntsdale Fish Hatchery, Lake Julian Park, Lake Junaluska, Long Pine Run Reservoir, Price Lake, Roanoke Sewage Treatment Plant]

Common Merganser: Rare transient and winter resident from mid-November to early April. [Lake Julian Park, Long Pine Run Reservoir, Price Lake]

Red-breasted Merganser: Uncommon to rare transient and winter visitor from November to early May. [Lake Julian Park, Lake Junaluska, Long Pine Run Reservoir]

Ruddy Duck: Uncommon transient and rare winter visitor from mid-October to late April.

Black Vulture: Uncommon to fairly common permanent resident along the Blue Ridge Plateau and Northern Ridge Province; erratic and rare summer resident in interior valleys of North Carolina section of province from March to October. [Basin Cove OL, Doughton Park, Flat Rock Ridge Trail, Huntsdale Fish Hatchery, Mahogany Rock OL, Ridge Road, Rocky Knob]

Turkey Vulture: Common permanent resident; uncommon to absent above 4,500 feet from early November to early March.

Osprey: Uncommon spring transient, especially along major rivers, from April to mid-May; uncommon fall transient from September through October; rare summer and winter visitor. [Bent Creek Recreation Area, Canal Locks Trail, Harvey's Knob OL, Huntsdale Fish Hatchery, Mahogany Rock OL, NC SR 1549, New River Trail State Park, Rockfish Gap]

American Swallow-tailed Kite: Post-breeding wanderer and fall transient from mid-July to September, with most records from North Carolina; formerly uncommon, now very rare and erratic.

Mississippi Kite: One record on the BRP, Augusta County, Va., on 13 June 1982.

Bald Eagle: Rare transient and winter visitor; peak numbers in September; nested along the French Broad River, N.C., as late as 1880s. [Rockfish Gap]

Northern Harrier: Spring and fall transient and winter resident of open grassy terrain and wetland fields at all elevations; uncommon from mid-August to late December and in April; rare from November through March. [Big Meadows, Black Balsam Knob, Ivestor Gap Trail, Rhododendron Gap Trail, Sams Knob Trail, Whitetop Mountain]

Sharp-shinned Hawk: Uncommon to rare permanent resident in mature deciduous and coniferous forests at all elevations; rare above 5,500 feet, especially from November through March; fairly common during fall migration in September and October. [Cedar Ridge Trail, Flat Rock Ridge Trail, Harvey's Knob OL, Mahogany Rock OL, Rockfish Gap, Round Bottom Road, Sherando Lake Recreation Area]

Cooper's Hawk: Rare permanent resident in mature deciduous and coniferous forests at all elevations; usually absent from spruce-fir forests from November through March; uncommon in September and October. [Cedar Ridge Trail, Flat Rock Ridge Trail, Harvey's Knob OL, Mahogany Rock OL, Rockfish Gap]

Northern Goshawk: Probably a very rare permanent resident, with a handful of summer records, mostly in higher elevations; rare transient and winter visitor, mid-September to late May; has been expanding its range southward since late 1960s. [Pine Grove Furnace State Park, Rockfish Gap]

Red-shouldered Hawk: Uncommon to rare permanent resident in mature forests at low and middle elevations; uncommon transient in October. [Rockfish Gap]

Broad-winged Hawk: Fairly common spring transient and summer resident from mid-April through August; common to abundant fall transient from September to early October. [Harvey's Knob OL, Mahogany Rock OL, Ridge Road, Rockfish Gap]

Red-tailed Hawk: Fairly common permanent resident in medium to mature forests at all elevations; uncommon above 5,000 feet from December through February; common fall transient from mid-October through November. [Harvey's Knob OL, Mahogany Rock OL, Rockfish Gap]

Rough-legged Hawk: Rare and erratic transient and winter visitor, mainly in northern portion of province from late October to mid-April.

Golden Eagle: Formerly a permanent resident; rare transient and winter visitor from mid-October to mid-April, preferring open grassy areas at high elevations; erratic and very rare in summer. [Black Balsam Knob, Harvey's Knob OL, Ivestor Gap Trail, Mount Rogers, Rhododendron Gap Trail, Rockfish Gap, Round Bald]

American Kestrel: Permanent resident in open areas, fields, and farmlands; decreasing numbers in 1980s; uncommon to common transient; uncommon in winter, rare in summer. [Harvey's Knob OL, Mahogany Rock OL, Rockfish Gap]

Merlin: Rare transient and winter visitor from early September through April. [Harvey's Knob OL, Rockfish Gap]

Peregrine Falcon: Formerly a locally common permanent resident; extirpated as a breeding species by 1960s; reintroduced by release programs in 1980s; now a rare resident and uncommon to rare transient from mid-September to early November and from March to early April. Nests on cliffs and high rocky crags. [Alum Cave Bluffs Trail, Chimney Rock Park, FSR 475-B, Grandfather Mountain, Harvey's Knob OL, Hawksbill, Headwaters Road, Rockfish Gap, Shortoff Trail, Whiteside Mountain]

Ring-necked Pheasant: Introduced. Uncommon to rare local permanent resident in northern portion of province; occurs in open country, forest edges, brushy fields, and farmlands.

Ruffed Grouse: Uncommon to locally common permanent resident in deciduous and coniferous forests at all elevations. [Apple Orchard Mountain, Caledonia State Park, FSR 81, Grindstone campground, Gully Creek Trail, Laurel Prong Trail, Linville Gorge area, Mountain Bridge Wilderness, MTS Trail in Great Craggy Mountains, Mount Pisgah area, Pioneer Farm Exhibit]

Wild Turkey: Formerly abundant; greatly reduced by hunting and loss of chestnut trees but now increasing in number, due in part to restocking. Uncommon to locally common permanent resident in deciduous and coniferous forests at all elevations. Often observed near wooded areas and field edges adjacent to the escarpment of the Blue Ridge Plateau. [Basin Cove OL; BRP shoulder at MS 168.5–170.5, 173, 218, 224, and 243–246; Cades Cove Loop Road; Caledonia State Park; Floyd Fields; MTS Trail from Bearpen Gap to Buckeye Gap; Pioneer Farm Exhibit; Rocky Knob Recreation Area]

Northern Bobwhite: Uncommon to common permanent resident in disturbed areas and forest edges up to 6,600 feet; usually abandons elevations above 4,000 feet from September to April. [Cades Cove Loop Road, Canal Locks Trail, Graveyard Fields, Ivestor Gap Trail, Oconaluftee River valley, Rhododendron Gap Trail]

Yellow Rail: Formerly a very rare fall transient from late August to mid-October in the Great Valley of Virginia and French Broad River valley.

Black Rail: Formerly a rare summer resident in wet meadows along the French Broad River in Buncombe County, N.C., and near Franklin, Macon County, N.C.

King Rail: Rare transient and local summer resident in Virginia from mid-May to mid-November.

Virginia Rail: Rare transient; local summer resident in Virginia northward from mid-April to mid-December. [Huntsdale Fish Hatchery]

Sora: Uncommon, irregular transient from mid-April to late May and from late August to late October; rare, local summer resident and winter visitor in Virginia. [Ferguson Fields, Huntsdale Fish Hatchery]

Purple Gallinule: One record. Roanoke, Va., on 30 May 1973.

Common Moorhen: Very rare to rare spring transient from mid-April to early June.

American Coot: Fairly common transient and uncommon to rare local winter resident from early October to mid-May. [Huntsdale Fish Hatchery, Lake Julian Park, Lake Junaluska]

Sandhill Crane: Very rare and irregular transient from late July through November and from April to May.

Black-bellied Plover: Rare transient from late March through May and from mid-July to early November. [Roanoke Sewage Treatment Plant]

Lesser Golden-Plover: Rare transient from early September through October and erratic from late March to early April. [Roanoke Sewage Treatment Plant]

Semipalmated Plover: Uncommon transient in May and from early August through September. [Ferguson Fields, Price Lake, Roanoke Sewage Treatment Plant]

Piping Plover: Three records at Roanoke from August to early September. [Roanoke Sewage Treatment Plant]

Killdeer: Fairly common permanent resident in open grassy areas, meadows, and wet fields, mostly below 5,000 feet; uncommon in winter. [Ferguson Fields, Meadow Fork Creek, Roanoke Sewage Treatment Plant]

American Avocet: Very rare fall transient in the Great Valley in Virginia; four at Lyndhurst, Augusta County, Va., on 7 April 1988. Two North Carolina mountain records: two birds near the BRP at Glendale Springs on 22 September 1968 and one at Cashiers, Jackson County, on 3 July 1985.

Greater Yellowlegs: Uncommon transient from late March through May and from late July through early November; more frequent in spring than in fall; rare in winter. [Ferguson Fields, Price Lake, Roanoke Sewage Treatment Plant]

Lesser Yellowlegs: Uncommon transient from late March through May and from mid-July through October; more common in spring than in fall. [Ferguson Fields, Price Lake, Roanoke Sewage Treatment Plant]

Solitary Sandpiper: Fairly common transient from early April through May and from July through mid-October. [Ferguson Fields, Price Lake, Roanoke Sewage Treatment Plant]

Willet: Rare transient and summer visitor from late April to mid-September.

Spotted Sandpiper: Fairly common transient and uncommon summer resident from mid-April to mid-October along waterways up to 4,000 feet; probably a rare breeder. [Bent Creek Recreation Area; Big East Fork Trail; Chesapeake and Ohio Canal; Ferguson Fields; Graveyard Fields Loop Trail; Linville Falls parking lot, campground, and picnic area; New River Trail State Park; NC SR 1549; Price Lake; Roanoke Sewage Treatment Plant; Santeetlah Lake]

Upland Sandpiper: Rare to uncommon transient from mid-March through mid-May and from mid-July through October. Rare and local summer resident in the Great Valley of Virginia from Pulaski County northward.

Whimbrel: Very rare transient. Records at Roanoke Sewage Treatment Plant on 14 September 1983 and Big Bald on North Carolina–Tennessee line on 30 August 1980.

Hudsonian Godwit: Very rare transient. Eight at Roanoke Airport on 18 August 1985.

Ruddy Turnstone: Rare transient in the Great Valley of Virginia in May and from late July to early September.

Red Knot: Rare transient in the Great Valley of Virginia from late March through May and from July to mid-September.

Sanderling: Rare spring and fall transient in May and from late July through October. [Roanoke Sewage Treatment Plant]

Semipalmated Sandpiper: Uncommon transient from mid-April to early June and from late July through October. [Price Lake, Roanoke Sewage Treatment Plant]

Western Sandpiper: Rare transient from late April to early June and from July through October. [Roanoke Sewage Treatment Plant]

Least Sandpiper: Uncommon transient in May and from late July through September. [Ferguson Fields, Price Lake, Roanoke Sewage Treatment Plant]

White-rumped Sandpiper: Rare transient from early May to early June and from early July to November. [Price Lake, Roanoke Sewage Treatment Plant]

Baird's Sandpiper: Very rare transient from mid-April to late May and from late July to mid-October. [Roanoke Sewage Treatment Plant]

Pectoral Sandpiper: Uncommon transient from late March to late May and from late July through October; more numerous in fall. [Roanoke Sewage Treatment Plant]

Dunlin: Rare transient, mostly in the Great Valley of Virginia from April to early June and from mid-July to early December. [Roanoke Sewage Treatment Plant]

Stilt Sandpiper: Rare fall transient in the Great Valley of Virginia from mid-July through October. [Roanoke Sewage Treatment Plant]

Buff-breasted Sandpiper: Rare fall transient at Roanoke, Va., from late August to early October. [Roanoke Sewage Treatment Plant]

Short-billed Dowitcher: Rare transient from late March to late May and from mid-July to mid-November. [Price Lake, Roanoke Sewage Treatment Plant]

Long-billed Dowitcher: Very rare fall transient in the Great Valley of Virginia, late August to mid-October. [Roanoke Sewage Treatment Plant]

Common Snipe: Rare to fairly common transient and winter resident in grassy fields, meadows, and wet areas from early September to early May; more numerous in spring migration. [Big Meadows, Ferguson Fields, Graveyard Fields, Ivestor Gap Trail, Roanoke Sewage Treatment Plant]

American Woodcock: Fairly common transient and uncommon summer resident from late February to late November; rare winter visitor; open grassy sites with light-to-moderate growth of successional deciduous shrubs contiguous to moist forests and woodlands, particularly disclimax areas along the Parkway, on grass balds, and in burned-over areas at elevations up to 6,200 feet. [Big Meadows, Black Balsam Knob, Boone Fork Trail, Carvers Gap, Courthouse Valley OL, Graveyard Fields, Ivestor Gap Trail, Mount Mitchell Restaurant parking lot, Pioneer Farm Exhibit, Pisgah Inn parking lot, Stepps Gap]

Wilson's Phalarope: Very rare transient from early May through June and from mid-July to early September in the Great Valley of Virginia. [Roanoke Sewage Treatment Plant]

Red-necked Phalarope: Rare transient from early May to early June and from September to mid-October in the Great Valley of Virginia. [Roanoke Sewage Treatment Plant]

Red Phalarope: Very rare transient from late August to mid-December.

Pomarine Jaeger: One record. Claytor Lake, Pulaski County, Va., on 3–9 October 1975.

Laughing Gull: Rare spring transient from late February to late April; very rare fall transient from mid-August to mid-November. [Roanoke Sewage Treatment Plant]

Bonaparte's Gull: Locally uncommon spring transient in April and rare fall transient from late October through mid-December. [Long Pine Run Reservoir]

Ring-billed Gull: Uncommon transient and winter visitor from mid-October through May; increasing numbers in recent years. [Ferguson Fields, Huntsdale Fish Hatchery, Lake Julian Park, Lake Junaluska, Laurel Lake, Long Pine Run Reservoir, Roanoke Sewage Treatment Plant]

Herring Gull: Rare transient and winter visitor from mid-October through mid-April.

Lesser Black-backed Gull: One record. Roanoke Sewage Treatment Plant on 4 April 1984.

Caspian Tern: Rare transient from mid-April to June and from September to mid-October.

Common Tern: Rare transient in the Great Valley of Virginia from late March through May and from late July through mid-November.

Forster's Tern: Rare transient from mid-April to mid-May and from late July through mid-November. [Lake Julian Park]

Least Tern: One record. Waynesboro, Augusta County, Va., on 19 September 1975.

Black Tern: Rare transient from April to mid-June and from July to early October. [Lake Julian Park]

Rock Dove: Introduced. Common permanent resident in settled areas mostly below 2,500 feet.

Band-tailed Pigeon: Provisional list for North Carolina based on single bird at Fetterbush OL near M 422 on the Parkway on 10 June 1980.

Mourning Dove: Common summer resident from March to November, mostly below 3,500 feet; uncommon to fairly common winter resident. Inhabits fields, farmlands, grassy meadows, suburban areas, and disturbed forests.

Passenger Pigeon: Extinct. Formerly an abundant visitor in some winters; known to have bred in the Blue Ridge in Nelson County, Va., in 1874, near present-day Three Ridges OL and The Priest OL on the BRP.

Common Ground-Dove: Two records. One collected in Buncombe County, N.C., by J. S. Cairns on 29 May 1891; one observed in Augusta County, Va., 24 October 1981.

Monk Parakeet: Introduced. Local population at Asheville, Buncombe County, N.C.; disappeared by 1980s. Found around gardens, cultivated fields, and orchards; constructs large bulky stick nest in trees or on telephone poles.

Black-billed Cuckoo: Uncommon to rare transient and summer resident in medium to mature deciduous forests, mostly between 3,000 and 5,500 feet, from late April to mid-October; numbers often fluctuate dramatically from year to year. [Big East Fork Trail, Big Witch OL, Crabtree Falls Trail, Figure Eight Trail, Glassy Ridge Mine OL, Greasy Cove Trail, Laurel Mountain Trail, MTS Trail from Bearpen Gap to Buckeye Gap, Rock Castle Gorge National Recreation Trail, Stillhouse Hollow, Warbler Road]

Yellow-billed Cuckoo: Fairly common summer resident from late April to late October in open, medium to mature deciduous forests, especially along waterways, mostly below 3,500 feet, occasionally up to 4,500 feet. [Big East Fork Trail, Bull Creek, Cades Cove Loop Road, Crabtree Falls Trail, Rock Castle Gorge National Recreation Trail, Sugarlands Nature Trail, Warbler Road]

Barn Owl: Rare, local permanent resident in lowland valleys around farms, abandoned buildings, and forest edges.

Eastern Screech-Owl: Fairly common permanent resident, mostly in medium to mature forests up to 4,000 feet. [Big East Fork Trail, Black Mountain Recreation Area, Cades Cove Loop Road, Caledonia State Park, Davidson River campground, FSR 2074, Grindstone campground, Linville Gorge area, Sherando Lake Recreation Area, Sycamore Flats picnic area]

Great Horned Owl: Uncommon to fairly common permanent resident in mature deciduous forests and field edges, mostly below 4,500 feet. [Big East Fork Trail, Big Witch OL, Brinegar Cabin, Buck Hollow Trail, Davidson River campground, Devil's Garden OL, Grindstone campground, Hazel Mountain Trail, Linville Gorge area, Sherando Lake Recreation Area]

Snowy Owl: Very rare and irregular winter visitor from late November through March, mostly in fields and open areas in northern portion of province.

Barred Owl: Fairly common permanent resident in mature deciduous and coniferous forests up to 6,600 feet; more frequently encountered in middle and low elevations. [Basin Cove OL, Big East Fork Trail, Big Witch OL, Black Mountain campground, Buck Hollow Trail, Cades Cove Loop Road, Chimneys picnic area, Crabtree Falls Trail, Davidson River campground, FSR 1206, FSR 2074, Hazel Mountain Trail, Highlands Biological Station, Ivestor Gap Trail, Laurel Lake, Linville Gorge area, Sherando Lake Recreation Area, Sycamore Flats picnic area, Tanawha Trail, Trail of Trees, Twin Springs Recreation Area]

Long-eared Owl: Status uncertain; probably a very rare and local permanent resident; prefers mixed and coniferous forests, including tracts of white pine, red spruce, and hemlock. Calling records from Beartree Creek near Mount Rogers, from Bluff Mountain, Ashe County, N.C., and from the north slope of Grandfather Mountain. The only breeding records from the Blue Ridge Province are in a pine plantation at Kings Gap, Pa. [Kings Gap Environmental Education and Training Center]

Short-eared Owl: Rare transient and winter resident from November to mid-May in fields and open areas mostly below 2,500 feet.

Northern Saw-whet Owl: Permanent resident. Uncommon to fairly common during calling season of late March to mid-June in spruce-fir and contiguous northern hardwood forests above 4,360 feet at Mount Rogers, Whitetop, Roan Mountain, Long Hope Creek, Grandfather Mountain, Black Mountains, northern Great Craggy Mountains, Pisgah Ridge, Shining Rock Ledge, Great Balsam Mountains, Plott Balsam Mountains, and Great Smoky Mountains. Juveniles reported in Southern Great Balsams, on Pisgah Ridge, and in Black Mountains; nests have been found in Black Mountains. [Balsam Mountain campground, Big Butt Trail, Courthouse Valley OL, Devil's Courthouse, Haywood-Jackson OL, Indian Gap, Ivestor Gap Trail, Lone Bald OL, Mount Mitchell State Park, MTS Trail from Balsam Gap to Stepps Gap and from Balsam Gap to Walker Knob, Newfound Gap, Perley Toll Road, Richland Balsam, Roan High Knob, Waterrock Knob parking lot, Whitetop Mountain]

Common Nighthawk: Locally common to uncommon transient and summer resident, mostly in lowlands and valleys, from late April to late

September; heavy fall migration in last two weeks of August. [Canal Locks Trail]

Chuck-will's-widow: Rare and local summer resident in heavily wooded areas of the Great Valley of Virginia from late April through August.

Whip-poor-will: Fairly common transient and summer resident from early April to October, mostly in wooded areas near fields and forest openings below 3,000 feet, rarely to 5,200 feet. [Cades Cove Loop Road, Caledonia State Park, NC SR 1549, Pottete Creek Recreation Area, Sherando Lake Recreation Area]

Chimney Swift: Fairly common summer resident at all elevations from late March to mid-October; heavy fall migration from late August to mid-September.

Green Violet-ear: Accidental. Sighted October 1987 at Asheville, Buncombe County, N.C.

Ruby-throated Hummingbird: Fairly common transient and summer resident from late April to early October at all elevations in disturbed areas, successional communities, woodland edges, gardens, and the understory of mature deciduous forests.

Rufous Hummingbird: Very rare fall visitor at hummingbird feeders.

Belted Kingfisher: Fairly common permanent resident at lakes and along waterways up to 3,000 feet, rarely up to 5,000 feet; moves to valleys and lowlands from November to early April.

Red-headed Woodpecker: Formerly a fairly common permanent resident; now rare to locally uncommon summer resident in mature, open deciduous forests and wooded parks below 3,500 feet; most often observed in autumn migration from mid-August through October, when individuals may occur at elevations up to 6,300 feet; less frequent in spring migration of April through May; rare and generally absent in winter. [Pottete Creek Recreation Area]

Red-bellied Woodpecker: Permanent resident; fairly common in mature deciduous forests up to 4,200 feet; wanders to 5,500 feet from March to May.

Yellow-bellied Sapsucker: Permanent resident; rare to uncommon, local, and erratic summer resident mainly above 3,500 feet in disturbed or open oak and northern hardwood forests from late April through September; occurs as low as 1,600 feet on South Mountain, Pa. Uncommon to fairly common transient and winter resident in forests at all elevations but mostly below 4,000 feet. [Bee Tree Gap, Big Butt Trail, Craggy Gardens Self-guiding Trail, Figure Eight Trail, Flat Top Trail, FSR 69, FSR 711, Glassy Ridge Mine OL, Ivestor Gap Trail, Jenkins Ridge OL, MTS Trail from Bearpen Gap to Buckeye Gap, MTS Trail from Craggy Gardens to Carter Creek Falls, Pine Mountain, Ridge Road, Sim's Creek, Steestachee Bald, Tellico Plains–Robbinsville Scenic Highway, Trout Lake Trail]

Downy Woodpecker: Permanent resident in medium to mature deciduous and coniferous forests at all elevations; uncommon above 4,000 feet, fairly common below 4,000 feet.

Hairy Woodpecker: Uncommon permanent resident in medium to mature deciduous and coniferous forests at all elevations; often abandons area above 5,000 feet during harsh winters. Less common than Downy Woodpecker, although usually somewhat more numerous than Downy in summer above 4,500 feet.

Red-cockaded Woodpecker: Rare and very local resident in pine forests below 2,200 feet in the extreme southwest corner of the Great Smoky Mountains; reported in Abrams Creek basin and in the Skunk Mountain area.

Northern Flicker: Permanent resident; fairly common up to 5,000 feet; uncommon to 6,600 feet from late March to late October; prefers disturbed, open, mature deciduous forests and medium-age successional communities.

Pileated Woodpecker: Permanent resident in mature deciduous forests at all elevations, uncommon to locally common; often abandons elevations above 4,500 feet from late October to early March.

Olive-sided Flycatcher: Rare spring and fall transient from late April to early June and from August through September; very rare and local summer resident in spruce-fir and hemlock forests: formerly on the Highlands Plateau, at Roan Mountain, in the Great Craggy Mountains, and in the Black Mountains; recent summer records only in the Great Smokies. Often perches in the tops of dead trees or on high, bare limbs. [Alum Cave Bluffs Trail, Newfound Gap]

Eastern Wood-Pewee: Common transient and summer resident from late April to late October in medium to mature deciduous and mixed forests; rare in spruce-fir forests; occurs at all elevations but infrequently above 5,000 feet.

Yellow-bellied Flycatcher: Rare spring and fall transient from late April through May and from mid-August through September; very rare summer resident—breeding at Mount Rogers from 1977 to 1985. Prefers moist spruce-fir forests, particularly areas of dense, stunted growth, with fallen trees and moss-covered mounds, rocks, and tree roots.

Acadian Flycatcher: Uncommon to common summer resident from late April to early October in shrub and understory along streams, ravines, and mature deciduous forests up to 3,500 feet, rarely to 4,000 feet.

Alder Flycatcher: Uncommon to rare spring and fall transient in May and from mid-August to early October; in 1970s spread southward as an uncommon, local summer resident in thickets of alder, deciduous shrubs, and saplings from 2,700 feet to 6,000 feet at Mount Rogers, Roan Mountain, Price Park, the Black Mountains, and Shining Rock Ledge; most numerous above 5,000 feet. [AT at Jane Bald, Balsam Trail Road, Boone Fork Trail, Big Butt Trail, Carver's Gap, FSR 816, Greasy Cove Trail, Ivestor Gap, Mount Rogers, Pine Mountain, Sullivan's Swamp]

Willow Flycatcher: Uncommon to rare spring and fall transient from late April through May and from mid-August to early October; uncommon, local summer resident in wet thickets of willows, alders, and saplings, rarely up to 4,900 feet, mostly in wide valleys and open areas; more widespread than the Alder Flycatcher as a breeder in the Blue Ridge. [Big Meadows, Cold Prong Wetlands, New River Trail State Park, NC SR 1549, Sullivan's Swamp]

Least Flycatcher: Rare to uncommon spring and fall transient from late April to mid-May and from September through early October; uncommon but very local summer resident in open, mature deciduous forests, orchards, and woodland strips bordering streams and fields, mostly from 2,500 feet to 4,500 feet. [AT from Elk Garden to Deep Gap, Big Meadows, Black Camp Gap, Carolina Hemlocks Recreation Area, Crabtree Falls Trail, Crabtree Meadows campground, Grindstone campground, Highlands Country Club, Jenkins Ridge OL, Maggie Valley OL, New River valley, Tellico Plains–Robbinsville Scenic Highway, Twin Springs Recreation Area]

Eastern Phoebe: Fairly common permanent resident up to 3,000 feet in disturbed areas, open forests, field edges, and secondary successional communities, especially along waterways; occurs up to 5,500 feet from April to September. Nests under bridges, in eaves and rafters of buildings, and on ledges of overhanging rock faces.

Great Crested Flycatcher: Uncommon to fairly common summer resident in medium to mature open deciduous forests from late April to early October, generally below 4,000 feet, rarely above 5,000 feet.

Western Kingbird: Very rare fall transient from late August to mid-December.

Eastern Kingbird: Fairly common summer resident from mid-April to mid-September in open fields, clearings, and farmlands generally below 3,000 feet. [Bent Creek Recreation Area, Cades Cove Loop Road, Canal Locks Trail, Ferguson Fields, NC SR 1549, Oconaluftee River valley, Pottete Creek Recreation Area, Sim's Creek]

Scissor-tailed Flycatcher: Very rare transient from late May through July.

Horned Lark: Uncommon permanent resident; prefers farmlands, plowed fields, and close-cropped, open, grassy fields, pastureland, and meadows up to 6,600 feet. [AT at Elk Garden, AT at Round Bald, Big Spy Mountain OL, Black Ridge Trail, Bluff Mountain Trail, Parkway shoulder at M 207.5, Rhododendron Gap Trail, Thunderhill OL]

Purple Martin: Transient at elevations up to 4,500 feet, fairly common from late March to early June and uncommon from late August to mid-September; locally common summer resident, mostly below 2,500 feet, in areas where nesting boxes are provided.

Tree Swallow: Uncommon to common spring and fall transient from late March through May and from mid-August to mid-October, mostly below 4,000 feet; uncommon to rare local summer resident, rapidly extending its range southward into the region since 1977; prefers open areas near water with dead trees and bird boxes as nesting sites, less often nests in fence posts or barns. [Big Meadows, Canal Locks Trail, Meadow Fork Creek, NC SR 1549, Sim's Creek]

Northern Rough-winged Swallow: Fairly common summer resident from late March to early October; occurs at all elevations but uncommon above 4,500 feet and rare above 5,500 feet; solitary nesting around rock cliffs, road cuts, and embankments. [NC SR 1549, Price Lake, Roan Mountain State Park, Roanoke River Trail]

Bank Swallow: Uncommon spring and fall transient from mid-April through May and from late July through September; rare and local summer resident, nesting in colonies in road cuts, gravel pits, steep riverbank cliffs, and vertical embankments, mostly in the Virginia portion of the Blue Ridge. Formerly nested at Tuxedo, Henderson County, N.C.

Cliff Swallow: Uncommon spring and fall transient from mid-April through May and from August to mid-September, mostly below 3,000 feet; locally common summer resident, nesting in colonies at dams and bridges across large bodies of water. [Canal Locks Trail, Fontana Dam]

Barn Swallow: Spring and fall transient at all elevations from early April through May and from late July through September; common at low and middle elevations, less common above 5,000 feet. Locally common summer resident below 4,000 feet around farms, fields, and bridges; nesting in farm buildings, in abandoned structures, in culverts, and under bridges. [Bass Lake, Big Meadows, Cades Cove Loop Road, Canal Locks Trail, NC SR 1549, Oconaluftee River valley, Price Lake, farmland along plateau section of BRP from M 106 to M 297]

Blue Jay: Permanent resident at all elevations, preferring medium to mature deciduous and coniferous forests; common from April through October and fairly common to uncommon from November to March, often abandoning areas above 4,500 feet during harsh winters.

American Crow: Permanent resident at all elevations in a wide variety of habitats, preferring fields, farmlands, clearings, and forest edges; common to abundant up to 4,000 feet, uncommon at higher elevations.

Fish Crow: Uncommon and local permanent resident along waterways in valleys and low mountains, mostly north of the James River in Virginia; more frequent in winter; not yet recorded in North Carolina mountains. [Chesapeake and Ohio Canal, Gambrill State Park, Huntsdale Fish Hatchery]

Common Raven: Permanent resident, mostly above 3,000 feet; locally fairly common in medium to mature coniferous and deciduous forests, particularly around cliffs or rocky crags, which are preferred nesting sites. [Alum Cave Bluffs Trail, Apple Orchard Mountain, Bluff Mountain Trail, Brasstown Bald, Caesar's Head State Park, Cedar Ridge Trail, Clingman's Dome Road, Devil's Courthouse, Grandfather Mountain trails, Hangover Lead Trail, Hawksbill, Mahogany Rock OL, Mount Mitchell State Park, Mount Pisgah Inn and campground, Mount Pisgah Trail, Newfound Gap, Roan Mountain area, Stony Man Nature Trail, Waterrock Knob, Whitetop Mountain]

Black-capped Chickadee: Permanent resident in spruce-fir and adjacent northern hardwood forests above 4,500 feet in the Great Smoky Mountains, Plott Balsam Mountains, Great Balsam Mountains, Pisgah Ridge, Shining Rock Ledge, and Mount Rogers. Recent reports at Grandfather Mountain and Roan Mountain, where status is uncertain. Fairly common in the Great Smokies, where the birds occur in summer down to 4,000 feet; rare to uncommon elsewhere. Found regularly in the Black Mountains prior to logging and fires in early 1900s. Absent prior to the late 1960s in the southern Great Balsam Mountains, at Shining Rock Ledge, and on Pisgah Ridge, but found in increasing numbers in these three ranges during 1970s and 1980s; presumably occurred in the area prior to the logging and wildfires of 1920s. Fairly common resident in mixed forests on South Mountain, Pa., at elevations mostly above 1,200 feet.

Moves to lower elevations in winter, when mixed flocks of Carolina and Black-cappeds are sometimes encountered, especially in the Great Smokies. Cannot be distinguished from Carolina Chickadee on basis of elevation, as Carolinas occasionally range up to 6,000 feet, especially in areas not inhabited by Black-cappeds. Field marks, song, and behavior sometimes inconclusive in separating Black-cappeds from Carolinas, particularly where interbreeding may occur, mostly in populations outside the Great Smokies. [Alum Cave Bluffs Trail, Balsam Mountain campground, Balsam Mountain Nature Trail, Caledonia State Park, Chimney Tops parking area, Clingman's Dome Road, Ivestor Gap Trail, MTS Trail at Buckeye Gap, Mount Rogers, Plott Balsam OLS, Ridge Road, Richland Balsam Nature Trail, Spruce Mountain Trail, Twin Pinnacles Trail, Waterrock Knob, Wolf Laurel Gap]

Carolina Chickadee: Common permanent resident below 4,500 feet in medium to mature deciduous and coniferous forests, woodland edges, and suburban areas; occurs rarely up to 6,000 feet in areas not occupied by Black-cappeds.

Tufted Titmouse: Permanent resident in medium to mature deciduous and coniferous forests, parklands, and suburban areas; common to fairly common up to 5,200 feet, rarely to 6,100 feet; usually abandons areas above 4,500 feet from November to March.

Red-breasted Nuthatch: Permanent resident in spruce-fir forests above 4,500 feet; fairly common from April through October; erratic from November through March, depending on availability of food. Also occurs as a local summer resident in hemlock and white pine forests as low as 3,300 feet, very rarely to 2,500 feet, in southern Blue Ridge; found in summer as low as 630 feet at South Mountain, Pa. Winter resident at all elevations. [In addition to spruce-fir forests, try Babel Tower Trail, Craggy Mountains Scenic Area, Erwin's View Trail, Highlands

Biological Station, Linville Falls parking lot, Ridge Road, Sim's Creek, Trout Lake Trail]

White-breasted Nuthatch: Fairly common permanent resident in mature deciduous forests, particularly oak forests, up to 5,500 feet. Usually abandons areas above 4,500 feet from November to March.

Brown-headed Nuthatch: Rare and local permanent resident in pine forests of French Broad River valley below 2,500 feet. [Lake Julian Park]

Brown Creeper: Permanent resident; local and uncommon in mature spruce-fir forests above 4,400 feet from mid-April to mid-September; rare summer resident in hemlock and white pine forests above 3,100 feet in southern Blue Ridge; occurs down to 630 feet near South Mountain, Pa. Often builds nest between tree trunk and a slab of loose bark, thus preferring areas where dead or dying trees are found. Uncommon to fairly common at all elevations from late October to late March, but often rare or absent above 4,500 feet. [Alum Cave Bluffs Trail, Bald Knob Ridge Trail, Balsam Road, Devil's Courthouse Trail, Grandfather Trail, Highlands Biological Station, Ivestor Gap Trail, MTS Trail from Balsam Gap to Stepps Gap, MTS Trail from Buckeye Gap to Haywood Gap, Mount Rogers, Perley Toll Road, Ridge Road, Spruce Mountain Trail, Trout Lake Trail, Whitetop Mountain, Wolf Laurel Gap]

Carolina Wren: Permanent resident in successional communities, in the shrub layer or understory of deciduous forests, and in wooded areas near settlements; fairly common below 4,000 feet from mid-October through March; common to fairly common up to 5,000 feet from April through mid-July; post-breeding wanderer up to 6,400 feet from mid-July through early October.

Bewick's Wren: Formerly a fairly common to abundant summer resident at all elevations in brushy areas, open woodlands, hedgerows, and shrubby stream borders. Conspicuous decline as early as 1930s continuing through 1980s; now extremely rare transient and summer resident; most recent summer records from Grayson Highlands State Park.

House Wren: Summer resident from mid-April to late October in disturbed brushy areas, successional deciduous communities, and human settlements; fairly common to uncommon up to 5,500 feet, rarely to 6,000 feet. [Bass Lake Carriage Road near Cone Manor, Big Spy OL, Black Balsam Knob, Carver's Gap, Graveyard Fields, Greasy Cove Trail, Roan Mountain State Park]

Winter Wren: Permanent resident; fairly common from mid-March to mid-November above 4,000 feet, rarely down to 3,000 feet, in successional communities, heath balds, and the shrub layer of forests, with a preference for spruce, fir, and hemlocks; uncommon in forests and shrubby tangles at all elevations from early December to late February, although often absent above 4,500 feet. [Alum Cave Bluffs Trail, Balsam Mountain campground, Balsam Trail Road, Brasstown Bald, Clingman's Dome Road, Commissary Shelter Road, Devil's Courthouse, Grandfather Mountain trails, Hemlock Springs OL, Mount Rogers, Rhododendron Gardens Trail, South River Falls Trail, Spruce Mountain Trail, Waterrock Knob, Whitetop Mountain]

Sedge Wren: Uncommon to rare transient in low-elevation marshy areas, wet meadows, and thickets at the edge of fields during May and from mid-August through October.

Marsh Wren: Rare transient in low-elevation marshy fields and wet meadows from mid-April to mid-May and from early August through October.

Golden-crowned Kinglet: Fairly common to common permanent resident in spruce-fir forests above 4,500 feet and fairly common locally in hemlock and white pine forests above 2,500 feet; common in forests at all elevations from late October to early April. [In addition to spruce-fir forests, try Babel Tower Trail, Carolina Hemlocks Recreation Area, Craggy Mountain Scenic Area, Erwin's View Trail, Highlands Biological Station, Linville Falls parking lot, Pine Gap Trail, Sim's Creek, Trout Lake Trail, Watkins Road]

Ruby-crowned Kinglet: Fairly common to uncommon winter resident in coniferous and deciduous forests, woodland margins, brushy thickets, and successional communities; fairly common transient at all elevations from early September through October and again from April to early May; winters mostly at elevations below 5,000 feet from November through March; extremely rare straggler in summer in spruce-fir forests.

Blue-gray Gnatcatcher: Uncommon to fairly common summer resident from late March to mid-October in medium to mature deciduous forests, particularly cove hardwoods, at elevations below 3,500 feet, rarely to 4,000 feet. [Bent Creek Recreation Area, Big East Fork Trail, Cades Cove Loop Road, Canal Locks Trail, Carolina Hemlocks Recreation Area, Chesapeake and Ohio Canal, Oconaluftee River valley, Roanoke River Trail, South River Falls Trail, Sugarlands Nature Trail]

Northern Wheatear: Accidental. One record at Franklin, Macon County, N.C., on 11 October 1981.

Eastern Bluebird: Permanent resident in open woodlands, fields, clearings, and roadsides; fairly common from late February to mid-October at elevations below 5,500 feet, rarely to 6,200 feet; generally abandons elevations above 4,500 feet from November through January. [Cades Cove Loop Road, Kings Gap Environmental Education and Training Center, Meadow Fork, Oconaluftee River valley, Pioneer Farm Exhibit, and along Parkway from M 109 to 297, especially near Roanoke, Va., and Boone, N.C.]

Mountain Bluebird: Accidental. One record near Asheville, Buncombe County, N.C., on 15 June 1985.

Veery: Fairly common to common summer resident from late April to mid-September in medium to mature deciduous and coniferous forests at elevations above 3,000 feet, rarely down to 2,500 feet in southern Blue Ridge; occurs down to 700 feet on South Mountain, Pa. [Apple Orchard Mountain, Balsam Road, Brasstown Bald, Catoctin Mountain Park, Caledonia State Park, Clingman's Dome Road, Craggy Gardens Trail, Flat Top Trail, FSR 69, Grandfather Mountain trails, Mount Mitchell State Park, Mount Pisgah Trail, Mount Rogers area, Ridge Road, Roan Mountain area, Sharp Top Trail, Sim's Creek, South River Falls Trail, Spruce Mountain Trail, Trout Lake Trail, Warbler Road, Waterrock Knob, Watkins Road, Whitetop Mountain]

Gray-cheeked Thrush: Rare to uncommon transient at all elevations in May and from mid-September to mid-October.

Swainson's Thrush: Rare summer resident in spruce-fir forest on Mount Rogers summit since 1966; elsewhere a fairly common to uncommon spring and fall transient at all elevations in May and from mid-September to mid-October. [Mount Rogers]

Hermit Thrush: Fairly common transient and winter resident in forests below 4,500 feet from mid-October to early May; local, uncommon summer resident above 4,800 feet in spruce-fir forests of the southern Blue Ridge, appearing at Mount Rogers in 1966, Roan Mountain in 1979, the Black Mountains in 1983, Grandfather Mountain in 1984, and irregularly in the Great Smoky Mountains. Occurs in summer down at least to 1,600 feet on South Mountain, Pa. [Commissary Shelter Road, Grandfather Trail, Mount Rogers, Old Mitchell Trail, Pine Mountain, Ridge Road, Roan High Knob]

Wood Thrush: Common summer resident from mid-April to mid-October in medium to mature deciduous and mixed forests up to 4,500 feet, occasionally to 5,000 feet.

American Robin: Permanent resident in all habitats and elevations, preferring medium to mature deciduous and coniferous forests, successional communities, and short-grass habitats such as parks and lawns; common to abundant from mid-March to late October; uncommon to rare, especially above 5,000 feet, from November to early March.

Gray Catbird: Common to abundant summer resident from mid-April to mid-October at all elevations in heath and shrub balds, forest shrub layer, dense thickets, and successional communities; rare winter visitor at elevations up to 3,000 feet.

Northern Mockingbird: Common to fairly common permanent resident in fields, thickets, and settled areas, mostly below 3,000 feet.

Brown Thrasher: Summer resident from April to mid-October in shrub layer of deciduous forests, shrubby old fields, hedgerows, woodland edges, and residential areas; fairly common to 4,000 feet, rarely up to 6,200 feet. Rare and erratic winter visitor in valleys below 2,500 feet.

American Pipit: Uncommon and erratic transient in grass balds, fields, and open areas at all elevations from March to May and from October through November; rare winter visitor, mostly below 5,000 feet. [Ferguson Fields, Roanoke Sewage Treatment Plant]

Cedar Waxwing: Erratic uncommon to common permanent resident in open forests and late successional communities; often present at all elevations from May to late October; usually absent from areas above 4,500 feet from November through April.

Northern Shrike: Very rare winter visitor. Two records from Ashe County, N.C., and one from Big Meadows in Shenandoah National Park.

Loggerhead Shrike: Rare permanent resident, more frequent from August through March, mostly in open country and fields at elevations below 3,000 feet; declining in number since 1970s.

European Starling: Introduced. Abundant permanent resident in lowlands around settled areas, mostly below 3,000 feet; wanders to 5,500 feet in April and May.

White-eyed Vireo: Uncommon to locally common transient and summer resident from mid-April to mid-October in dense thickets and shrub understory, especially moist areas near waterways, up to 4,000 feet; uncommon post-breeding wanderer up to 5,800 feet after late July. [Bent Creek Recreation Area, Boone Fork Trail, Ferguson Fields, NC SR 1134, NC SR 1549, Oconaluftee River valley, Pottete Creek Recreation Area, Round Bottom Road, Warbler Road]

Solitary Vireo: Common transient at all elevations from March through April and in October; common summer resident in forests above 2,500 feet, rarely to 1,800 feet in northern portion of province. Rare winter resident, most often in southern half of province.

Yellow-throated Vireo: Uncommon transient and local summer resident in mature forests, usually open hardwoods along waterways below 3,000 feet, rarely to 4,000 feet, from early April to early October. [Bent Creek Recreation Area, Cades Cove Loop Road, Canal Locks Trail, Davidson River campground, New River Trail State Park, NC SR 1549, Oconaluftee River valley, Pioneer Farm Exhibit, Rock Castle Gorge National Recreation Trail, South River Falls Trail, Sycamore Flats picnic area, Warbler Road]

Warbling Vireo: Rare transient from early April to early May and from late August to mid-October; locally fairly common summer resident in mature deciduous trees, especially sycamore and Balm-of-Gilead stands bordering the Shenandoah, James, Roanoke, and New rivers. [Chesapeake and Ohio Canal, New River Trail State Park, NC SR 1549, Shenandoah Canal, Warbler Road]

Philadelphia Vireo: Rare transient from late April to late May and from September to early October; most often observed in fall.

Red-eyed Vireo: Common summer resident from mid-April to mid-October in mature deciduous forests up to 5,000 feet; fairly common post-breeding wanderer and transient at all elevations after mid-August.

Blue-winged Warbler: Uncommon to rare transient from late April to mid-May and from mid-August through September; very rare and local summer resident mostly from 1,500 to 2,500 feet, preferring overgrown old fields, brushy meadows, shrubby streamsides, early to medium second-growth deciduous stands, power line right-of-ways, and disturbed forest openings. [Fontana Dam, NC SR 1150, NC SR 1556, Pottete Creek Recreation Area]

Golden-winged Warbler: Uncommon transient from late April to early May and from late August through September; rare to uncommon local summer resident where young to medium-age trees are present in old fields, power line right-of-ways, and forest openings mostly from 1,800 up to 5,000 feet; occurs as low as 700 feet on South Mountain, Pa. [Bee Tree Gap, FSR 711, Graveyard Fields, Graveyard Ridge Trail, Mulky Gap Road, New River State Park, NC 28, NC SR 1246, NC SR 1247, NC SR 1310, Pottete Creek Recreation Area, Roan Mountain State Park, Warbler Road]

Tennessee Warbler: Uncommon spring transient in low and middle elevations in May; common fall transient at all elevations from late August to late October.

Orange-crowned Warbler: Rare transient in low and middle elevations from early April through early May and from early October through late December.

Nashville Warbler: Uncommon to rare spring transient from late April to mid-May; uncommon fall transient from mid-August to mid-October; uncommon to rare summer resident, mostly between 1,600 feet and 2,000 feet in pine-oak scrub barrens in South Mountain area of Pennsylvania. [Michaux State Forest, Ridge Road]

Northern Parula: Fairly common transient and summer resident from mid-April to mid-October in medium to mature forests up to 5,000 feet; prefers hemlocks with a mixture of hardwoods, particularly near water.

Yellow Warbler: Fairly common to common transient and summer resident from early April through September in deciduous thickets, willow stands, and medium to mature deciduous forests bordering water at elevations below 4,000 feet.

Chestnut-sided Warbler: Fairly common to common transient at all elevations from late April to mid-May and from mid-August to late October. Common to abundant summer resident in disturbed and second-growth deciduous forests, in heath balds, and in woodland edges from 2,500 feet to 6,500 feet, though most common between 3,000 and 5,500 feet; rarely as low as 1,600 feet, as at Chimney Rock, N.C., and at South Mountain, Pa.

Magnolia Warbler: Spring and fall transient at all elevations, uncommon to fairly common from late April to mid-May and fairly common to common from late August through mid-October. Local summer resident in spruce-fir forests, especially in young to middle-aged stands and where conifers are intermixed with heath species; fairly common at Mount Rogers; local at Long Hope Creek; rare at Grandfather Mountain, at Roan Mountain, and in the Black Mountains. [Big Butt

Trail, Crag Way Trail, Grandfather Trail, Grayson Highlands State Park, Mount Rogers, Tanawha Trail, Twin Pinnacles Trail]

Cape May Warbler: Spring and fall transient at all elevations; fairly common from late April to mid-May and from late August to late October.

Black-throated Blue Warbler: Fairly common to common transient at all elevations from mid-April to mid-May and from early September to late October. Common summer resident in understory and shrub layer of deciduous and mixed forests and in heath balds, mostly between 2,500 feet and 5,500 feet; rarely down to 1,600 feet, as at Chimney Rock, N.C.

Yellow-rumped Warbler: Fairly common transient in October and from mid-April to mid-May at elevations up to 5,500 feet; uncommon to fairly common winter resident at elevations below 4,000 feet; inhabits brushy thickets and forest edges; prefers fruit-bearing trees, such as red cedar.

Townsend's Warbler: Hypothetical. Accidental; reported at Nantahala Village, Swain County, N.C., on 23 April 1975.

Black-throated Green Warbler: Fairly common transient at all elevations from mid-April to mid-May and from mid-September to late October; somewhat local in distribution, but generally uncommon to common summer resident in mature coniferous and deciduous forests at all elevations, though mostly above 2,500 feet; numbers vary from year to year.

Blackburnian Warbler: Fairly common spring and fall transient from late April to mid-May and from late August to mid-October. Rare to locally common summer resident, mostly in hemlock, spruce-fir, pine-oak, and white pine forests between 1,600 and 6,600 feet, but mainly from 2,400 to 6,200 feet. Occurs at least down to 800 feet on South Mountain, Pa. Numbers may vary considerably from year to year. [Alum Cave Bluffs Trail; Bald Knob Ridge Trail; Balsam Mountain campground; Big Butt Trail; Black Camp Gap; BRP shoulder at M 353 to 355.3; Brasstown Bald; Caledonia State Park; Catoctin Mountain Park; Cliffside Lake Recreation Area; Flat Creek Trail; Floyd Fields; FSRS 4, 81, 472, and 2074; Hemlock Springs OL; Linville Falls parking lot; Maze Carriage Road; MTS Trail from Balsam Gap to Stepps Gap; MTS Trail from Balsam Gap to Walker Knob; MTS Trail from Table Rock to Shortoff; NC SR 1310; Perley Toll Road; Poll's Gap; Profile Trail; Ridge Road; Shanty

Springs Trail; Sim's Creek; Skulls Gap; South River Falls Trail; Spruce Mountain Trail; Trout Lake Trail; Wolf Laurel Gap]

Yellow-throated Warbler: Uncommon and local summer resident from early April to early October, mostly in pine forests below 2,500 feet and deciduous tracts bordering rivers; rarely to 3,600 feet. [Bent Creek Recreation Area, Cades Cove Loop Road, Canal Locks Trail, Chesapeake and Ohio Canal, Ferguson Fields, Lake Julian Park, NC SR 1246, NC SR 1247, Oconaluftee River valley, Rocky Broad River, Warbler Road]

Pine Warbler: Uncommon to fairly common local summer resident in pine forests, mostly below 3,200 feet, rarely to 3,800 feet, from mid-March to mid-October. Uncommon post-breeding wanderer to all elevations from late July to late September. Rare winter visitor in lowland forests. [Cades Cove Loop Road, Chimney Rock Park, Davidson River campground, Kings Gap Environmental Education and Training Center, Lake Julian Park, Linville Falls picnic area, The Meadows, Otter Creek Trail, Pottete Creek Recreation Area, Ridge Road, VA 610, Warbler Road]

Prairie Warbler: Common transient and locally fairly common summer resident from mid-April to late September, mostly in brushy overgrown fields at elevations below 3,000 feet; rare post-breeding wanderer and fall transient from late July to late September up to 5,000 feet. [Mulky Gap Road, NC SR 1549, NC SR 1730, Pottete Creek Recreation Area, Ridge Road, Warbler Road]

Palm Warbler: Spring and fall transient at all elevations, uncommon from mid-April to mid-May and in September and October; rare winter visitor in forest borders and open brushy areas.

Bay-breasted Warbler: Transient at all elevations; uncommon to rare in May; fairly common to common from late August through mid-October.

Blackpoll Warbler: Fairly common spring transient at all elevations from late April to early June; uncommon to rare fall transient from September to late October.

Cerulean Warbler: Uncommon transient from early April to early May and from late July to mid-September, mostly in low and middle elevations. Rare to locally common summer resident in mature open deciduous forests, particularly where large tuliptrees dominate in cove hardwood forests at elevations from 1,200 to 4,000 feet, rarely above 5,000 feet. Considerably more common and widespread in the Virginia portion of the Blue Ridge than in the Carolinas or Tennessee. [BRP shoulder at M 83.1, Bull Creek OL, Chimney Rock Park, Flat Top Trail parking lot, Humpback Rocks, Lewis Fork OL, NC 28, Rock Castle Gorge National Recreation Trail, Smart View Loop Trail, South River Falls Trail, Stony Fork Valley OL, VA 610, VA 860, Warbler Road]

Black-and-white Warbler: Fairly common summer resident from early April to early October in mature deciduous and mixed forests up to 5,500 feet; post-breeding wanderer at all elevations after mid-July; rare winter visitor in lowlands.

American Redstart: Locally fairly common summer resident from mid-April to mid-October in medium to mature deciduous forests, especially cove hardwoods, up to 3,500 feet; uncommon post-breeding wanderer to all elevations from mid-August to mid-October. [Buck Spring Trail, Bull Creek, Davidson River campground, Flat Top Mountain Trail, Gully Creek Trail, Lewis Fork OL, Rock Castle Gorge National Recreation Trail, Rocky Knob campground, Sherando Lake Recreation Area trails, Smart View Loop Trail, South River Falls Trail, VA 610, VA 860, Warbler Road]

Prothonotary Warbler: Rare to uncommon transient in the Great Valley and along major rivers in Virginia from late April to early May and from mid-August to mid-September; very rare transient in North Carolina mountain valleys. Locally fairly common summer resident in deciduous trees bordering the James River and Shenandoah River. [Canal Locks Trail, Chesapeake and Ohio Canal, Santeetlah Lake, Shenandoah Canal, Warbler Road]

Worm-eating Warbler: Uncommon transient from late April to mid-May and from mid-August to early October at low and medium elevations; uncommon to fairly common summer resident, mainly in oak forests with dense shrub understory on steep hillsides, ridges, and ravines from 1,800 to 4,200 feet. [Cedar Ridge Trail, Chimney Rock Park, Curtis Creek, Flat Rock Ridge Trail, Flat Top Mountain Trail, FSR 479, Mills River Valley Road, MTS Trail to Shortoff, Ridge Road, Roan Mountain State Park, Rock Castle Gorge National Recreation Trail, Sherando Lake Recreation Area trails, Smart View Loop Trail, South River Falls Trail, VA 610, Warbler Road]

Swainson's Warbler: Local and rare to uncommon summer resident from April through September in dense thickets of rhododendron, laurel, and doghobble along waterways, ravines, and steep hillsides mostly below 3,000 feet; highest density apparently in the Savannah River headwaters on the outer escarpment of the Blue Ridge. [Abrams Falls Trail, Bear-tree Recreation Area, Curtis Creek Road, FSR 4, FSR 62, Forest Stroll Self-guided Nature Trail, Gatlinburg Trail, Hurricane Creek, Jones Gap State Park, NC SR 1246, NC SR 1247, Southeastern Blue Ridge Escarpment Gorges, Stone Mountain State Park]

Ovenbird: Fairly common to common summer resident from mid-April to mid-October in shrub understory of forests up to 5,000 feet; post-breeding wanderer to all elevations after early September.

Northern Waterthrush: Uncommon transient near water from late April to late May and from mid-August to early October. Very rare and local summer resident near wooded streams in Virginia portion of Appalachians. [Beartree campground, Grindstone campground]

Louisiana Waterthrush: Fairly common transient and summer resident from late March through early September in rhododendron thickets and the shrub layer of deciduous forests along waterways up to 4,000 feet, rarely to 4,500; rare post-breeding wanderer up to 5,500 feet from mid-July to early September. [Caledonia State Park, Carolina Hemlocks Recreation Area, Crabtree Falls Trail, Curtis Creek, Davidson River campground, FSR 4, Forest Stroll Self-guided Nature Trail, Gully Creek Trail, Linville Gorge area, Little Glade Mill Pond, Roan Mountain State Park, Rock Castle Gorge National Recreation Trail, Rocky Broad River, Sim's Creek, South River Falls Trail, Sugarlands Nature Trail, VA 860, Warbler Road]

Kentucky Warbler: Uncommon to locally fairly common summer resident from late April to mid-September in the dense understory layer of moist deciduous forests, especially cove hardwoods, up to 3,800 feet. [Bull Creek, Elk Run Trail, Linville Falls parking lot, Mulky Gap Road, NC SR 1730, Pioneer Farm Exhibit, Roan Mountain State Park, Rock Castle Gorge National Recreation Trail, Sherando Lake Recreation Area, Smart View Loop Trail, South River Falls Trail, Sugarlands Nature Trail, VA 610, VA 860, Warbler Road]

Connecticut Warbler: Very rare spring transient from late April through May and rare fall transient from mid-September to late October at all elevations.

Mourning Warbler: Very rare spring and fall transient from late April to late May and from late August to early October. Probable breeding in dense, brushy thickets and second growth at Jenkins Ridge OL at M 460.8 on the BRP in mid-1980s.

Common Yellowthroat: Fairly common to common summer resident from mid-April to mid-October in shrubby fields, stream borders, thickets, and woodland openings at all elevations, though uncommon above 6,000 feet. Rare and erratic in lowlands and valleys below 3,000 feet during winter, mostly in southern portion of region. [AT at Round Bald, Beartree Recreation Area, Boone Fork Trail, Cades Cove Loop Road, Canal Locks Trail, Cold Prong Wetlands, Crabtree Meadows campground, Ferguson Fields, FSR 472, FSR 816, Graveyard Fields, Ivestor Gap Trail, Pottete Creek Recreation Area, Sullivan's Swamp, Trout Lake Trail, Warbler Road]

Hooded Warbler: Fairly common summer resident from mid-April to mid-October in shrub layer and dense undergrowth of mature deciduous forests up to 4,000 feet, rarely to 4,500 feet; post-breeding wanderer to all elevations after late July. [Bald Mountain, Bull Creek, Cascades Nature Trail, Flat Top Mountain Trail, FSR 4, Forest Stroll Self-guided Nature Trail, Linville Falls parking lot, Little Glade Mill Pond, MTS Trail to Shortoff, Ridge Road, Rock Castle Gorge National Recreation Trail, Sherando Lake Recreation Area, Sim's Creek, Smart View Loop Trail, South River Falls Trail, Trout Lake Trail, VA 610, VA 860, Warbler Road]

Wilson's Warbler: Uncommon to rare spring and fall transient from late April to mid-May and from mid-August to early October in forests, streamside tangles, and willow thickets up to 4,500 feet.

Canada Warbler: Fairly common transient at all elevations in May and from late August to early October. Fairly common to common summer resident in heath balds, rhododendron tangles, and the dense shrub layer of deciduous forests at elevations mostly above 3,400 feet; rarely as low as 1,600 feet, as at Chimney Rock, N.C. [Alum Cave Bluffs Trail, Apple Orchard Mountain, Babel Tower Trail, Brasstown Bald, Cascades Nature Trail, Cliffside Lake Recreation Area, Craggy Gardens Self-guiding Trail, Doughton Park trails, Flat Top Mountain Trail, Fodder Stack Trail, FSR 69, Forest Stroll Self-guided Nature Trail, Grandfather Mountain trails, Graveyard Fields, Laurel Prong Trail, MTS Trail from Balsam Gap to Stepps Gap, Mount Pisgah Trail, Pisgah campground, Price Lake, Sim's Creek, Skulls Gap, South Toe High Country trails, Trout Lake Trail, Warbler Road, Waterrock Knob, Wolf Laurel Gap]

Yellow-breasted Chat: Fairly common to common summer resident from late April to mid-September, preferring dense thickets and shrubby fields in valleys; uncommon up to 4,000 feet and rarely to 5,000 feet. [Canal

Locks Trail, Davidson River campground, Mulky Gap Road, NC SR 1549, NC SR 1730, Oconaluftee River valley, Pottete Creek Recreation Area, Rockfish Gap]

Summer Tanager: Uncommon and local transient and summer resident from mid-April to mid-October in mature deciduous and mixed forests below 2,000 feet. [Chestnut Ridge Trail, Chimney Rock Park, The Meadows, Pottete Creek Recreation Area, Roanoke Mountain campground]

Scarlet Tanager: Fairly common to common summer resident from late April to mid-October in mature deciduous forests up to 5,000 feet.

Western Tanager: Very rare winter visitor from September through May in lowland valleys, mostly noted at bird feeders.

Northern Cardinal: Common permanent resident, chiefly in woodland margins, shrubby growth, roadside thickets, and deciduous forest understory in lowlands; fairly common up to around 4,000 feet, rare to 5,000 feet in summer.

Rose-breasted Grosbeak: Fairly common transient up to 6,000 feet from mid-April to late May and from late August to mid-October; uncommon to fairly common summer resident in open, medium to mature deciduous forests between 2,500 feet and 5,500 feet; post-breeding wanderer to all elevations after early August. [Alum Cave Bluffs Trail, Apple Orchard Mountain, Bald Knob Ridge Trail, Big Butt Trail, Boone Fork Trail, Brasstown Bald, Craggy Gardens Recreation Area, Figure Eight Trail, Flat Top Mountain Trail, Fodder Stack Trail, FSR 69, Grandfather Mountain trails, Grindstone campground, Highlands Biological Station, Laurel Prong Trail, MTS Trail from Craggy Gardens to Carter Creek Falls, MTS Trail to Shortoff, Mount Pisgah area trails, Price Lake, Roan Mountain State Park, Rock Castle Gorge National Recreation Trail, Skulls Gap, Trout Lake Trail, Wolf Laurel Gap]

Black-headed Grosbeak: Accidental fall transient and winter visitor, mostly noted at bird feeders.

Blue Grosbeak: Uncommon to rare transient and summer resident from late April to mid-October, mostly in brushy fields, woodland edges, and streamside thickets in lowland valleys, rarely up to 4,000 feet. [Big Meadows, Cades Cove Loop Road, NC SR 1549, Warbler Road]

Indigo Bunting: Common to abundant summer resident from late April to mid-October in brushy fields, forest edges, and cleared areas of lowlands, nesting rarely up to around 5,800 feet, with singing males encountered up to 6,500 feet.

Painted Bunting: Accidental in spring and fall in Virginia portion of Blue Ridge.

Dickcissel: Rare and irregular transient and summer resident from late April to mid-September in grassy fields and weedy meadows in the Great Valley of Virginia.

Rufous-sided Towhee: Permanent resident. Fairly common to locally abundant at all elevations from mid-April to late October; uncommon to rare above 5,000 feet from November to March when most birds move to lower elevations. Prefers heath balds, shrubby fields, dense undergrowth, streamside thickets, and the understory of forests.

Bachman's Sparrow: Formerly a locally uncommon to rare transient and summer resident of overgrown fields in lowland valleys from April through August; now apparently absent.

American Tree Sparrow: Fairly common to rare transient and winter resident from late October to April in weedy old fields, marshy meadows, and forest edges in the lowlands; more common in northern than southern portions of region; rare in North Carolina.

Chipping Sparrow: Common transient and summer resident in open mature deciduous forests, in forest edges, and in grassy areas near human habitation; locally up to 5,000 feet, less frequently to 6,000 feet, from mid-March to early November; uncommon to rare winter resident mostly below 3,500 feet.

Clay-colored Sparrow: Rare transient in lowlands from late September through October and from late April to early May; very rare in winter.

Field Sparrow: Common permanent resident in fields and forest edges at elevations below 3,500 feet; uncommon summer resident up to 6,000 feet from late March to mid-October.

Vesper Sparrow: Uncommon to locally common in summer on grass balds, in pastures, and in close-cropped brushy fields at middle to high elevations south to Buncombe County, N.C. Most frequently encountered during summer in areas west of the Blue Ridge Parkway, particularly along the Unaka chain and on adjacent transverse ranges. Uncommon to rare spring and fall transient from March through April and from mid-October to mid-November; rare winter resident. [AT at Elk Garden, AT at Round Bald, Big Meadows, Big Spy Mountain OL, Rhodo-

dendron Gap Trail, Rock Castle Gorge National Recreation Trail, Sullivan's Swamp]

Lark Sparrow: Rare and erratic visitor, most frequent from September to
mid-April, in brushy edges of fields, farmlands, and pastures in valleys.

Lark Bunting: Accidental. One record on 11 February 1932 at Lexing-
ton, Va.

Savannah Sparrow: Fairly common transient from mid-March to mid-
May and from mid-September to early November up to 5,800 feet;
uncommon to rare winter resident in weedy fields and pastures below
3,000 feet from mid-September to mid-May; rare to locally common
summer resident south to Alleghany County, N.C., in fields and pastures
below 3,000 feet.

Grasshopper Sparrow: Locally fairly common summer resident from
mid-April to mid-October in grassy fields and pastures generally below
3,300 feet, rarely to 4,600 feet. Rare winter resident in lowland fields.
Declining numbers in recent years. [Big Spy Mountain OL, Black Ridge
Trail, Bluff Mountain Trail, Pioneer Farm Exhibit]

Henslow's Sparrow: Rare transient in April and October; rare, local summer resident from mid-April through mid-October in low-lying, weedy
fields, in wet meadows, and along the edge of streams below 3,000 feet
in Virginia portion of Blue Ridge; formerly south to Ashe County, N.C.

Le Conte's Sparrow: Very rare transient from mid-September to late
December and again in late April in wet, grassy fields at low elevations.

Sharp-tailed Sparrow: Rare transient from late September to mid-October and from mid- to late May, preferring marshy, wet meadows in
valleys and lowlands, though occasionally up to 3,800 feet, as at Highlands, N.C., on 15 May 1976.

Fox Sparrow: Winter resident in forest undergrowth and thickets, generally below 3,500 feet, from late October through early April; transient
at elevations up to 6,000 feet from late October through November
and from mid-February through March. Numbers and dates vary considerably from year to year, but species is generally uncommon to fairly
common.

Song Sparrow: Fairly common to abundant permanent resident in brushy
fields, residential areas, dense streamside thickets, forest openings, and
woodland borders; all elevations from mid-March through late October; uncommon to rare above 5,000 feet from November through Feb-

ruary. Formerly present only in winter, the species rapidly extended its summer range down the Blue Ridge Mountains in the 1890s.

Lincoln's Sparrow: Elusive and rare winter resident in thickets, brambles, and hedgerows bordering open fields of river valleys from mid-September to mid-May; uncommon transient in October and from late April through mid-May.

Swamp Sparrow: Uncommon spring and fall transient at elevations below 6,000 feet in October and November and from April through mid-May; uncommon winter resident in brushy fields, wet meadows, forest edges, and stream borders below 3,000 feet from October through mid-May. Local summer resident in marshy areas and shrubby pond margins in northern Great Valley. [Huntsdale Fish Hatchery]

White-throated Sparrow: Common to abundant transient at all elevations from early October to late November and from mid-April to mid-May; common winter resident in shrubby fields, forest undergrowth, and settled areas below 4,300 feet from early October through mid-May.

White-crowned Sparrow: Locally fairly common winter resident in brushy fields and open forests of low valleys from early October to mid-May; uncommon transient at all elevations from early October to mid-November and from mid-April to mid-May.

Harris' Sparrow: Very rare and irregular winter visitor from mid-November to early May, preferring open forests and brushy areas.

Dark-eyed Junco: Common to abundant permanent resident, occurring at all elevations from October through late April; mostly above 3,000 feet from May through September, though occasionally down to 1,600 feet, especially in northern portion of province and locally elsewhere, as at Chimney Rock, N.C. Found in a wide variety of habitats, including grass balds, heath balds, all stages of deciduous and coniferous forests, and understory or shrub layer of mature forests.

Lapland Longspur: Very rare to rare and irregular winter visitor in open, plowed fields of river valleys, most often in northern portion of province.

Chestnut-collared Longspur: Accidental. Flock of eight at Roanoke, Va., on 13 April 1958.

Snow Bunting: Rare and erratic winter visitor from November through March, mostly in weedy fields and on high-elevation grass balds along the North Carolina–Tennessee border. [AT at Round Bald, Big Meadows]

Bobolink: Fairly common spring and fall transient in fields and meadows from mid-April through May and from mid-August through mid-October, usually below 3,500 feet. Rare local summer resident in hayfields and weedy meadows of valleys south irregularly to vicinity of Virginia border, very rarely into northwest North Carolina and northeast Tennessee. [Ferguson Fields]

Red-winged Blackbird: Fairly common to common permanent resident in wet fields and shrubby stream margins up to 4,000 feet. Uncommon to rare spring and fall transient from late February to late March and from late October to mid-November at elevations up to 5,500 feet.

Eastern Meadowlark: Fairly common to common permanent resident in fields and pastureland below 3,500 feet; uncommon spring and fall transient from late February to mid-May and from mid-October to late November in open areas at all elevations.

Yellow-headed Blackbird: Very rare winter visitor from September through April; prefers open farmland and grain fields in lowland valleys.

Rusty Blackbird: Uncommon transient and winter visitor from mid-October through April; in fields, farms, and damp forests below 2,500 feet in winter; elevations up to 5,000 feet from mid-October through November and from mid-March through April.

Brewer's Blackbird: Irregular transient and very rare winter visitor in lowland pastures, farms, and fields from late October to mid-April; formerly most often reported in the French Broad River valley around Asheville, Buncombe County, N.C.

Common Grackle: Uncommon to common spring and fall transient at all elevations from March to early April and from October to mid-November; common summer resident and uncommon to abundant winter resident in forest borders and open, cultivated lowlands below 3,000 feet.

Brown-headed Cowbird: Permanent resident in fields, pastures, farmlands, and deciduous forests, mostly below 3,500 feet; uncommon to common from March through November; erratic in winter.

Orchard Oriole: Spring and fall transient at all elevations; summer resident in orchards, shade trees around farms, riverside woods, and open deciduous forests below 2,500 feet. Common to uncommon from mid-April to late August. [Warbler Road]

Northern Oriole: Uncommon spring and fall transient and rare winter visitor through the region. Locally fairly common summer resident from late April to mid-September in orchards, shade trees, and open mature deciduous forests, especially in sycamore and Balm-of-Gilead trees bordering major watercourses north of Asheville, N.C., including the New, Roanoke, James, and Shenandoah rivers. [Chesapeake and Ohio Canal, New River Trail State Park, NC SR 1549, Shenandoah Canal, Warbler Road]

Pine Grosbeak: Very rare and erratic winter visitor from mid-September to mid-May; most frequently reported in northern portion of province.

Purple Finch: Uncommon to fairly common transient and winter resident from late September to early May at all elevations in medium to mature deciduous and coniferous forests. Uncommon summer resident in spruce-fir forests on Mount Rogers; rare and erratic in summer on Roan Mountain, on Grandfather Mountain, and at Pecks Corner in GSMNP. [Grandfather Trail, Mount Rogers]

House Finch: Introduced. Uncommon to common permanent resident, mostly in edge, deciduous forests, and settled areas around buildings below 3,000 feet. Dramatic increase in numbers during 1980s.

Red Crossbill: Erratic, rare to uncommon, local permanent resident, preferring coniferous forests above 3,000 feet. Erratic winter visitor through region from November through May, with flocks rarely exceeding one hundred birds. [Alum Cave Bluffs Trail, Balsam Mountain campground, Balsam Mountain Nature Trail, Clingman's Dome Road, Hemlock Springs OL, Limberlost Trail, Linville Gorge area, Mount Mitchell State Park, MTS Trail from Balsam Gap to Stepps Gap, Mount Rogers area, Newfound Gap, Roan Mountain area, Stony Man Trail]

White-winged Crossbill: Very rare and erratic winter visitor from November through May, preferring coniferous forests at middle to high elevations; most often reported in northern portion of province. [Roan Mountain area]

Common Redpoll: Very rare and erratic winter visitor from late October to early April; most often in northern portion of province and during major winter finch invasion years. Found in brushy and weedy fields, often in flocks with American Goldfinch or Pine Siskin.

Pine Siskin: Erratic resident with widely fluctuating numbers and distribution; may occur at all elevations and in all habitats. Most often encountered during major northern finch invasion winters from mid-October to mid-May, when found in shrubs and fields, usually in flocks with American Goldfinch. Found erratically in summer in middle- to high-elevation coniferous forests. [Alum Cave Bluffs Trail, Balsam Mountain campground, Balsam Mountain Nature Trail, Clingman's Dome Road, Grandfather Trail, Great Balsam Mountains area, Hemlock Springs OL, Limberlost Trail, Mount Mitchell State Park, Mount Rogers area, Newfound Gap, Roan Mountain area, Stony Man Trail]

American Goldfinch: Common to abundant permanent resident in weedy fields, shrubby edges, and open second-growth forests at all elevations; fairly common in all seasons at low to middle elevations; uncommon to rare above 4,000 feet from October to March.

Evening Grosbeak: Erratic winter resident from late October to late April at all elevations; absent in some years; rare to common during invasion years. Prefers coniferous or mixed forests and urban areas with bird feeders.

House Sparrow: Introduced. Common to locally abundant permanent resident around farms and human settlements below 3,000 feet, rarely to 4,500 feet.

RESOURCES

The following contacts and resources should be used to obtain maps, free brochures, publication lists, and current information on the areas covered in this book.

Blue Ridge Parkway

For general information from 8:00 A.M. to 4:30 P.M. on weekdays, contact the Blue Ridge Parkway Headquarters at 704-259-0779 or call the appropriate district offices listed below.

For information on handicapped accessibility, call 704-259-0719.

For emergencies only, call General Dispatch at 1-800-PARKWATCH (1-800-727-5928). In case of emergency, be sure to know your location by milepost number so that the rangers can respond quickly.

PARKWAY DISTRICT INFORMATION NUMBERS

James River District (M 0–69)	Montebello Office (M 29) Big Island Office (M 66.3)	703-377-2377 804-299-5941
Peaks of Otter District (M 69–106)	Peaks of Otter Office (M 85.9)	703-586-4357
Roanoke Valley District (M 106–144)	Vinton Office (M 112)	703-982-6490
Rocky Knob District (M 144–216)	Rocky Knob Office (M 167.1) Fancy Gap Office (M 199.4)	703-745-3451 703-728-4511
Bluffs District (M 216–305)	Bluffs Office (M 245.5) Sandy Flats Office (M 294.4)	919-372-8568 704-295-7591
Gillespie Gap District (M 305–359)	Gillespie Gap Office (M 330.9)	704-765-6082
Asheville District (M 359–469)	Oteen Office (M 382.3) Balsam Office (M 442.8)	704-259-0701 704-456-9530

FOOD, LODGING, AND GASOLINE

These services are provided along the Parkway usually from May through October, except at the Peaks of Otter Lodge and Restaurant, which is open year-around. Reservations are generally advisable.

Peaks of Otter Lodge (M 85.9)
P.O. Box 489
Bedford, VA 24523
703-586-1081

Rocky Knob Cabins (M 174.1)
Meadows of Dan, VA 24120
703-593-3503

Bluffs Lodge (M 241.1)
Rt. 1, Box 266
Laurel Springs, NC 28644-9176
919-372-4499

Pisgah Inn (M 408.6)
P.O. Drawer 749
Waynesville, NC 28786
704-235-8228

Shenandoah National Park

SNP
Luray, VA 22835
703-999-2266 or -2282

Great Smoky Mountains National Park

Great Smoky Mountains National Park
Gatlinburg, TN 37737
615-436-1200

United States Forest Service

SOUTHERN REGION HEADQUARTERS

The Southern Region of the U.S. Forest Service includes Virginia, North Carolina, Tennessee, Georgia, and South Carolina. Maps, booklets, and information on trails, campgrounds, and recreation facilities covering these states may be obtained by contacting the regional headquarters office at the following address:

U.S. Forest Service, Southern Region
Public Affairs Office, Suite 850
1720 Peachtree Rd. N.W.
Atlanta, GA 30367-9102
404-347-2384

Other U.S. Forest Service offices, listed below by state, may provide more detailed local information on areas covered in this book, particularly with regard to the current status of trails, wilderness areas, campgrounds, and Forest Service roads.

VIRGINIA

George Washington National Forest
Pedlar Ranger District
2424 Magnolia Ave.
Buena Vista, VA 24416
703-261-6105

Jefferson National Forest
Glenwood Ranger District
P.O. Box 10
Natural Bridge Station, VA 24579
703-291-2189

Mount Rogers National
Recreation Area
Rt. 1, Box 303
Marion, VA 24354
703-783-5196

Wythe Ranger District
1625 W. Lee St.
Wytheville, VA 24382
703-228-5551

NORTH CAROLINA

Pisgah National Forest
French Broad Ranger District
P.O. Box 128
Hot Springs, NC 28743
704-622-3202

Grandfather Ranger District
P.O. Box 519
Marion, NC 28752
704-652-2144

Pisgah Ranger District
1001 Pisgah Hwy.
Pisgah Forest, NC 28768
704-877-3265

Toecane Ranger District
P.O. Box 128
Burnsville, NC 28714
704-682-6146

Nantahala National Forest
Cheoah Ranger District
Rt. 1, Box 16-A
Robbinsville, NC 28711
704-479-6431

Highlands Ranger District
Rt. 2, Box 385
P.O. Box 749
Highlands, NC 28741
704-526-3765

Tusquitee Ranger District
201 Woodland Dr.
Murphy, NC 28906
704-837-5152

Wayah Ranger District
Rt. 10, Box 210
Franklin, NC 28734
704-524-6441

TENNESSEE

Cherokee National Forest
Hiwassee Ranger District
1401 S. Tennessee Ave.
Etowah, TN 37331
615-236-5486

Nolichucky Ranger District
504 Justis Dr.
Greenville, TN 37743
615-638-4109

Ocoee Ranger District
Rt. 1, Parksville
Benton, TN 37307
615-338-5201

Tellico Ranger District
P.O. Box 339
Tellico Plains, TN 37385
615-253-2520

Unaka Ranger District
Rt. 1, 1205 N. Main St.
Erwin, TN 37650
615-743-4452

Watauga Ranger District
Rt. 9, Box 2235
Elizabethton, TN 37643
615-542-2942

GEORGIA

Chattahoochee National Forest
Brasstown Ranger District
Hwy. 19/129 S.
Box 216
Blairsville, GA 30512
404-745-6928

Chattooga Ranger District
P.O. Box 196
Burton Road
Clarkesville, GA 30523
404-754-6221

Chestatee Ranger District
200 W. Main
P.O. Box 2080
Dahlonega, GA 30533
404-864-6173

Cohutta Ranger District
401 Old Ellijay Rd.
Chatsworth, GA 30705
404-695-6736

Tallulah Ranger District
Chechero/Savannah St.
P.O. Box 438
Clayton, GA 30525
404-782-3320

Toccoa Ranger District
E. Main St.
Box 1839
Blue Ridge, GA 30513
404-632-3031

SOUTH CAROLINA

Sumter National Forest
   Andrew Pickens Ranger District
   Star Route
   Walhalla, SC 29691
   803-638-9568

United States Geological Survey

Obtain copies of the "Catalogue of Topographic and Other Published Maps" and the "Index to Topographic and Other Map Coverage" for each state from which you need maps. Maps can be ordered by mail from any of the following offices:

   United States Geological Survey Map Sales
   Box 25286
   Denver, CO 80225

   United States Geological Survey
   1200 S. Eads St.
   Arlington, VA 22202

   United States Geological Survey
   536 National Center
   12201 Sunrise Valley Dr.
   Reston, VA 22092

Appalachian Trail Conference

This office publishes and sells maps and guidebooks to the Appalachian Trail system from Georgia to Maine. For information write:

   Appalachian Trail Conference
   Box 807
   Harpers Ferry, WV 25425

North Carolina Mountains-to-Sea Trail

Contact the following office for the latest information, maps, and route descriptions on the MTS Trail system:

North Carolina State Parks
P.O. Box 27687
Raleigh, NC 27611
919-733-7701

Foothills Trail Conference

This conference publishes and sells *Guide to the Foothills Trail*, which provides topographic and trail maps as well as a written description of the entire trail. Membership in the conference helps support trail construction and maintenance. For information write:

Foothills Trail Conference
P.O. Box 3041
Greenville, SC 29602

Additional sources for the trail can be obtained from:

Duke Power Company
Lake Management Operations
P.O. Box 33189
Charlotte, NC 28242

Bartram Trail Association

This organization publishes and sells maps and descriptive materials on the Bartram Trail and works to develop and maintain the route. Contact:

Bartram Trail Association
Rt. 3, Box 406
Sylva, NC 28779

Hawk Migration Association of North America

Hawk Migration Association of North America
P.O. Box 3482, Rivermont Station
Lynchburg, VA 24503

Virginia State Parks

Virginia State Parks
203 Governor St., Suite 306
Richmond, VA 23219
804-786-1712

North Carolina State Parks

N.C. Department of Natural Resources
Division of State Parks
P.O. Box 27687
Raleigh, NC 27611
919-733-4181

Tennessee State Parks

Tennessee Tourist Development
P.O. Box 23170
Nashville, TN 37202
615-741-2158

South Carolina State Parks

S.C. Department of Parks, Recreation, and Tourism
1205 Pendleton St.
Columbia, SC 29201
803-734-0153

Georgia State Parks

Georgia State Parks
Floyd Towers East, Suite 1352
205 Butler St. S.E.
Atlanta, GA 30334
404-656-3530

Maryland State Parks

Maryland Forest, Park, and Wildlife Service
Department of Natural Resources
Tawes State Office Bldg.
Annapolis, MD 21401
301-974-3771

Pennsylvania State Parks

Bureau of Pennsylvania State Parks
P.O. Box 1467
Harrisburg, PA 17103
717-787-8800

National Audubon Society

National Audubon Society
950 Third Ave.
New York, NY 14221
212-832-3200

Appalachian Mountain Club

This organization publishes and sells numerous books on the Appalachian Mountains. Contact:

Appalachian Mountain Club
5 Joy St.
Boston, MA 02108
617-523-0636

REFERENCES AND
SUGGESTED READING

General

Adkins, Leonard M. *Walking the Blue Ridge: A Guide to the Trails of the Blue Ridge Parkway*. Chapel Hill: University of North Carolina Press, 1991.

Brooks, Maurice. *The Appalachians*. Boston: Houghton Mifflin Co., 1965.

Catlin, David T. *A Naturalist's Blue Ridge Parkway*. Knoxville: University of Tennessee Press, 1984.

Clark, W. S., and B. K. Wheeler. *A Field Guide to Hawks*. Boston: Houghton Mifflin Co., 1987.

Connor, Jack. *The Complete Birder: A Guide to Better Birding*. Boston: Houghton Mifflin Co., 1988.

Heintzelman, Donald S. *A Guide to Northeastern Hawk Watching*. Privately printed, 1972.

——— . *The Migration of Hawks*. Bloomington: Indiana University Press, 1986.

Johnsgard, Paul A. *North American Owls: Biology and Natural History*. Washington, D.C.: Smithsonian Institution Press, 1988.

Johnson, Randy. *Southern Snow: The Winter Guide to Dixie*. Boston: Appalachian Mountain Club, 1987.

Jolley, Harley E. *The Blue Ridge Parkway*. Knoxville: University of Tennessee Press, 1969.

Lawrence, Susannah, and Barbara Gross. *The Audubon Society Field Guide to the Natural Places of the Mid-Atlantic States: Inland*. New York: Pantheon Books, 1984.

Lord, William G. *Blue Ridge Parkway Guide*. 2 vols. Philadelphia: Eastern Acorn Press, 1990.

Ogburn, Charlton. *The Southern Appalachians: A Wilderness Quest*. New York: William Morrow and Co., 1975.

Pettingill, Olin Sewall, Jr. *A Guide to Bird Finding East of the Mississippi*. New York: Oxford University Press, 1977.

Radford, Albert E., Harry E. Ahles, and C. Ritchie Bell. *Guide to the Vascular Flora of the Carolinas*. Chapel Hill: University of North Carolina, 1964.

——— . *Manual of the Vascular Flora of the Carolinas*. Chapel Hill: University of North Carolina Press, 1968.

Savage, Henry T. *Lost Heritage*. New York: William Morrow and Co., 1970.

The Sierra Club Guides to the National Parks of the East and Middle West. New York: Random House, 1986.

Stupka, Arthur. *Trees, Shrubs, and Woody Vines of Great Smoky Mountains National Park*. Knoxville: University of Tennessee Press, 1964.

Terborgh, John. *Where Have All the Birds Gone?* Princeton, N.J.: Princeton University Press, 1989.

Wofford, B. Eugene. *Guide to the Vascular Plants of the Blue Ridge*. Athens: University of Georgia Press, 1989.

Pennsylvania

Pennsylvania Atlas & Gazetteer. Freeport, Me.: DeLorme Mapping Company, 1990.

Poole, Earl L. *Pennsylvania Birds: An Annotated List*. Narberth, Pa.: Livingston Publishing Company, 1964.

Wood, Merrill. *Birds of Pennsylvania: When and Where to Find Them*. University Park: Pennsylvania State University, Agricultural Experiment Station, 1973.

Maryland

Hahn, Thomas F. *Towpath Guide to the Chesapeake & Ohio Canal*. Shepherdstown, W.Va.: American Canal and Transportation Center, 1985.

Virginia

Beck, Ruth, and Dick Peake. *Virginia Birding Site Guide*. N.p.: Virginia Society of Ornithology, 1985.

Conners, John A. *Shenandoah National Park: An Interpretive Guide*. Blacksburg, Va.: McDonald and Woodward Publishing Co., 1988.

De Hart, Allen. *Hiking the Old Dominion: The Trails of Virginia*. San Francisco: Sierra Club, 1984.

Heatwole, Henry. *Guide to Skyline Drive and Shenandoah National Park*. Luray, Va.: Shenandoah Natural History Association, 1979.

Kain, Teta. *Virginia Birds: An Annotated Checklist*. N.p.: Virginia Society of Ornithology, 1987.

Virginia Atlas and Gazetteer. Freeport, Me.: DeLorme Mapping Company, 1989.

Wilds, Claudia. *Finding Birds in the National Capital Area.* Washington, D.C.: Smithsonian Institution Press, 1983.

North Carolina

Biggs, Walter C., Jr., and James F. Parnell. *State Parks of North Carolina.* Winston-Salem, N.C.: John F. Blair, 1989.

De Hart, Allen. *North Carolina Hiking Trails.* Boston: Appalachian Mountain Club, 1988.

Guide to the Appalachian Trail in Tennessee and North Carolina. Harpers Ferry, W.Va.: Appalachian Trail Conference, 1986.

Homan, Tim. *Hiking Trails of Joyce Kilmer–Slickrock and Citico Creek Wilderness Areas.* Atlanta: Peachtree Publishers, 1990.

Potter, Eloise F., James F. Parnell, and Robert P. Teulings. *Birds of the Carolinas.* Chapel Hill: University of North Carolina Press, 1980.

The Roads of North Carolina. Fredericksburg, Tex.: Shearer Publishing, 1989.

Roe, Charles E. *A Directory to North Carolina's Natural Areas.* Raleigh: North Carolina Natural Heritage Foundation, 1987.

Schwarzkopf, S. Kent. *A History of Mt. Mitchell and the Black Mountains: Exploration, Development, and Preservation.* Raleigh: North Carolina Division of Archives and History, 1985.

Simpson, Marcus B., Jr. "William Brewster's Exploration of the Southern Appalachian Mountains: The Journal of 1885." *North Carolina Historical Review* 52 (1980): 43–77.

Tennessee

Alsop, Fred J., III. *Birds of the Smokies.* Gatlinburg, Tenn.: Great Smoky Mountains Natural History Association, 1991.

Bierly, Michael Lee. *Bird Finding in Tennessee.* Nashville: Michael Lee Bierly, 1980.

Great Smoky Mountains. Washington, D.C.: National Park Service, 1981.

Murlless, Dick, and Constance Stallings. *Hiker's Guide to the Smokies.* San Francisco: Sierra Club, 1973.

Robinson, John C. *An Annotated Checklist of the Birds of Tennessee.* Knoxville: University of Tennessee Press, 1990.

Stupka, Arthur. *Notes on the Birds of Great Smoky Mountains National Park.* Knoxville: University of Tennessee Press, 1963.

Tennessee Atlas & Gazetteer. Freeport, Me.: DeLorme Mapping Company, 1989.

Georgia

Burleigh, Thomas D. *Georgia Birds*. Norman: University of Oklahoma Press, 1958.

Greenberg, Joe, and Carole Anderson. *A Birder's Guide to Georgia*. N.p.: Georgia Ornithological Society, 1984.

Homan, Tim. *The Hiking Trails of North Georgia*. Atlanta: Peachtree Publishers, 1987.

South Carolina

De Hart, Allen. *South Carolina Hiking Trails*. Chester, Conn.: Globe Pequot Press, 1989.

Guide to the Foothills Trail. Greenville, S.C.: Foothills Trail Conference, 1990.

Sprunt, Alexander, Jr., and E. Burnham Chamberlain. *South Carolina Bird Life*. Columbia: University of South Carolina Press, 1970.

Journals

Much of the data on the birds of the Blue Ridge Mountains has been published in the state and regional ornithological literature. Major resources include *Chat* (North Carolina and South Carolina), *Migrant* (Tennessee), *Raven* (Virginia), *Oriole* (Georgia), and *American Birds* and *Wilson Bulletin* (entire region).

INDEX TO BIRD SPECIES

GENERAL INDEX